Few people are better qualified to write a GUIDE TO CHEESES than Pierre Androuet—his father was a cheese merchant and Androuet was involved with cheeses for more than sixty years, making him one of the world's foremost authorities. His restaurant in Paris was famous for its cheeses; and below it Monsieur Androuet had a cheese shop.

The book is in two sections: the first is in the form of a letter to a young person, advising her on how to buy cheese; and the second is a complete table of seasonal cheeses—from France and Europe—with suggestions for serving, and a guide to complimentary wines.

Over 450 cheeses are listed and described in this beautiful and comprehensive book—a bestseller in hardback.

D1339878

GUIDE

TO

CHEESES

REVISED EDITION

Androuet

GUIDE

TO

CHEESES

English Edition

REVISED

with the help of
N. Roche
G. Lambert

Translated from the French
by John Githens and new cheeses by Anthea Bell

AIDAN ELLIS

Cover illustration and inside pictures courtesy of Food &
Wine From France, Piccadilly, London W1V 9AJ

First published in the UK by Aidan Ellis Publishing Ltd,
Cobb House, Nuffield, Henley-on-Thames, Oxon RG9 5RT
under the title *Guide du Fromage*

First published in France under the title *Guide Du Fromage*
by Editions Stock

FIRST EDITION 1973
SECOND EDITION 1977
REVISED EDITION 1983
REPRINTED 1988
FIRST PRINTING THIS EDITION 1993

Jacket and illustrations design: CRAIG DODD

A CIP catalogue record for this book is available from the
British Library

Printed and bound in Great Britain by BPCC Wheatons Ltd,
Exeter EX2 8RP

ISBN: 0 85628 240 5

Contents

A Letter to My Daughter

Nulla fit sine caseo bona digestio.
(School of Salerno, 12th century)

"Listen, My Daughter" is the title of a work by one of France's great poets. I shall cheerfully preface my letter with the same plea, for though I do not pretend to offer you a spiritual message, cheese is a very delicate, sensitive subject . . . the soul, as it were, of the soil.

Soon you will be fifteen years old. Someday you will marry and have a home of your own. People talk a lot about homemakers these days, but are there really so many who merit the title?

I want you to be an accomplished homemaker.

Like the great-aunt in "Gigi" who insists that her niece learn how to pick out good cigars for her future husband, I maintain that no woman can be a perfect homemaker if she lacks the talent —and that is what it is in my eyes, a talent—for picking the right cheeses.

Will you be able to do this? I hope you will, just as I hope that every woman will who finds herself faced with such questions as "How shall I pick a good cheese?" or "How shall I offer a well-balanced selection of cheeses to my guests?" When people ask, "How do you find such wonderful cheese?" I hope you will have the answer.

I think it is safe to assume that you know a bit about cheese. After all, you are the daughter and the granddaughter of cheese-mongers. You have seen how we go about it.

I have often told you the story of your grandfather, Henri Androuët, who came to Paris from Brittany. He tired of his job delivering cheeses for Gervais, and decided to open up his own shop. He was fond of delicate cheeses that were not much on the market in those days. Did you know that cheese was seldom served at 19th-century feasts? Alexander Dumas scarcely mentions cheese in his big dictionary.

And then we come to me, my father's disciple and follower in this business. Today people ask me to send trays of cheese by plane to Washington or Tokyo or almost anywhere else in the world within twenty-four hours. I do not say this to boast; I have simply followed the route they pointed out to me. You will go your own way, perhaps more diffidently—but it would grieve me if the daughter and granddaughter of an Androuët did not live up to the reputation earned by her grandfather and maintained, I make bold to say, by her father. I would hate to see her in a quandary before the cheese counter.

Naturally when our family gets together by ourselves, and even when we have guests, we talk about cheese. There is a lot to say. Perhaps you remember a bit from all those conversations.

At your age, however, one's mind is often a vagabond, and that is why I am writing you this letter. I want to write it in such a way that anyone who reads it will have the feeling that he has had lunch in our home and that his curiosity about cheeses has been satisfied. I don't doubt that such curiosity exists.

I will skip from one subject to another, but I do not intend to leave out anything important. I want to give you the heart of my experience over the past fifty years.

I am not going to begin as they do in school by defining what cheese is. Or tell you how it is made. Or how a certain cheese gets to be what it is rather than something different. All that information is in the glossary at the back of the book.

Imagine that we are seated at our table. The salad has been served, and the cheeses are to be offered. This is the moment when the perfect homemaker in you must come to the fore.

Will you decide with Talleyrand, the great connoisseur, and with Brillat-Savarin, that "cheese is the foremost among deserts"?

Or will you decide that cheese, whether served with salad or not, is just an extension of the meal leading up to what is nowadays called dessert—sweets or fruit?

As you know, most people in France and just about everywhere else consider cheese an extension of the meal rather than a true dessert.

Although the palate is momentarily refreshed by the salad, there can be no thought of serving a lighter wine than the one which was served with the main dish, for the very good reason that Curnonsky has given: "Cheeses for the most part should be eaten with bread, and pastry kills the taste both of bread and of wine." Note this well. You must serve the same wine straight through the cheese course if it goes well with the cheeses, or you must choose stronger wine if your cheeses, or at least some of them, require it.

There are those who prefer red wine with oysters, and others, like the Marquis de Lur-Saluces, serve a mellow Sauterne with a great Roquefort. Each to his own taste. But to me and to the few great gourmets of my acquaintance, this is simply heresy.

Take care then—my first point—to serve a wine with your first cheeses that is at least as strong as the wine that has been served with previous courses. For the last cheeses or just the very last one, choose a wine that is even more full-bodied. A classic Bordeaux will do very well after chicken or veal: a mild cheese would then be in order. On the other hand, after game or some highly flavored dish a strong cheese must be served if one is to observe the sacrosanct rule of the crescendo. Depending upon the number of cheeses that you are serving, this may be followed by a still stronger cheese, a Bleu or some other ripe cheese.

No matter which school you belong to, you must not go from a strong wine to a sweet, syrupy one—unless you consider cheeses to be the same kind of dessert as a cream pie!

At any rate, I hope you will make cheese a regular part of your menu, dropping the salad if you must.

For most people, one or two cheeses usually make up the whole cheese tray. You will set your sights higher, for a country like France offers an extraordinarily broad choice: mild, spicy, strong, soft and tender, semi-hard, hard, etc. The only problem is the embarrassment of riches.

Do me a favor. Distinguish yourself by offering your guests at least four cheeses, no matter what you may have served as a main course. A little further on you will find my suggestions, month by month, for cheese trays appropriate to the seasons and to such preceding dishes as fish, white meats, and red meats.

Why according to the month?

Why is the season important?

Few people know the reason: there are two kinds of cheese, those made from pasteurized milk, which are the same all year, and those made from raw milk, which vary from one season to the next.

Until shortly before World War II—1935, to be exact—there were no pasteurized-milk cheeses. All cheeses were made from raw milk. The only difference was whether the milk came from cows wintered in stalls or fed in open pastures.

Now there was a third element: pasteurization.

The precise definition is given in the glossary. For the time being it will be enough to say that pasteurization "stabilizes" milk, and prevents many of the accidents that can befall so delicate a product as cheese.

Pasteurization began when the rising demand for cheese forced producers to seek new sources of milk outside the traditional cheese-producing areas. Little by little it gained ground as a method of ensuring the longevity of cheeses.

The advantages are obvious. It became feasible to stock cheeses that otherwise would not have kept, an unquestionable advantage to the merchant and to the consumer.

"Yes, but . . ." As it destroys the bacteria which might cause a cheese to spoil, pasteurization also tends to demolish those elements responsible for much of the cheese's flavor—just what in fact makes for highest quality.

All pasteurized-milk cheeses of whatever sort, mild or strong, have one point in common with respect to their flavor: their blandness. The nutritional value does not suffer in the least. Indisputably, the taste does. However, some people mistrust any cheese made from unpasteurized milk. They consider pasteurized cheeses "more hygienic."

Rest assured that you can buy raw-milk cheeses without running the slightest risk to your health. What is more, by doing so you will endear yourself to all true lovers of cheese.

How can you tell if a cheese is made of pasteurized milk? It is seldom possible to tell by its appearance, its smell or its texture. You must taste it. Sometimes this is permitted. It should be. Also, whenever they can, makers indicate on the packaging of their cheeses if these are *fromages fermiers* or farm cheeses.

Remember this: all farm cheeses are made from raw milk. They are true to the soil from which they spring.

Of course, from time to time you will surely have occasion to fall back on the pasteurized-milk cheeses with their milder flavors. During the slack season in the winter when you are unable to obtain good mild raw-milk cheeses, some pasteurized-milk cheeses are welcome substitutes. Let me add that in principle neither goat's-milk nor sheep's-milk cheeses are pasteurized. Both these milks contain fewer bacteria than cow's milk, which is pasteurized only when large-scale production warrants it.

And then there is something else to guide you (besides the label and perhaps the assurance of the man at the counter)—the nature of the cheese and the time of the year when you find it in the shop.

The Nature of the Cheese

Many cow's-milk cheeses of limited distribution are not made from pasteurized milk. Some cheeses are not yet commercially produced and are still made by traditional methods. As far as possible I indicate this in the Dictionary. To cite just a few such cheeses: Maroilles, Bleu cheeses of limited production, semi-soft (monastery) cheeses. On the whole the monks have remained faithful to the old methods and that is all to the good for their cheeses.

The origin of the milk corresponds to the notion of the *cru* or growth in winemaking. It is a subtle business and depends upon the interaction of many natural factors such as the presence of trace minerals in the soil, small variations in the composition of the vegetation, the purity of the water, and the breed of the cattle. Such human elements as respect for tradition and the secrets of local artisans must be taken into account too.

There are "growths" of milk just as there are "growths" of wine. The way the cows are fed, their breed, and weather conditions in the region can make a great difference in the quality of the milk that will be used in the cheese.

The Season

The season of the year is very important to the quality and consequently to the choice of the great cheeses.

You will have much greater luck in finding raw-milk cheeses at certain times of the year—when the cows are in the pastures or in the alpine meadows. Then the mountain chalets, the small dairies in the lowlands, and the farms are in full production. Milk is abundant. "True" cheese comes on the market. You and every reader of this book should try to learn (it isn't hard) two things:

1. The approximate date when the cows are put out to pasture;
2. The length of time it takes to make the cheese.

If you know when the herds begin to graze and how long it takes to cure a certain cow's-milk cheese (see the glossary), you can be fairly sure that you will be able to select a cheese of superior taste.

All this is child's play. Later I shall tell you when the herds are sent to pasture and when they return in the different regions of France, or when the herds are driven to the upland meadows, if I describe a mountain cheese. And the time it takes to make the various cheeses.

Nothing, then, could be simpler.

All the same, I must say again that the only way to be really sure is to taste the cheese. You must find a cheese man who allows you to do this. It is not hard to tell who are the real cheese experts: they do not run just any old store, they do not try to push products on you. There is a fine smell of cheese in the air in their shops and they wait calmly for the real cheese fanciers. You will be one of these.

Promise me that.

It is not just the coffee—I do not remember who it was who said so—that pronounces the final judgment on a good meal. It is also the cheese tray.

A certain "three star" restaurant, one of the best in France, refuses to serve a cheese tray to its patrons when it does not have the best cheeses of the moment. I commend them for this.

But how many private homes can pride themselves on the cheeses they serve? Very few. And that is a pity. My chief reason for writing you this letter is the hope that one day your table will be famous among cheese fanciers.

Of the two sorts of raw-milk cheese that you can buy all year round, one is made with milk from the winter stalls, the other with milk from the pasture.

The latter is by far the better.

That is why I have said that in some cases no one will blame you for including one or two pasteurized-milk cheeses, especially the mild ones, on your tray when meadow-milk cheese is in short supply.

Yes, cheese made with milk from cows at pasture *is* better. Nothing can touch it for quality and sweetness. I am thinking of certain very fresh Tommes, of Vacherin Mont-d'Or and of other cheeses too. We salute the alert housewives who know these cheeses and shop for them.

Only grass can give milk that fresh fragrance and incomparable flavor that is the glory of French cheeses.

Remember, too, that there are three special moments within the pasturing season when the cows give milk that can make the best cheeses truly sublime.

These three moments correspond to:

1. The sprouting of the grass (germination)
2. The prime flowering of the meadows

3. The second growth of grass

Naturally, none of these three moments occurs at the same time throughout France; there is considerable variation according to region and altitude. Study the pages where I indicate these times. This is not difficult—you will memorize them quickly. Simultaneously you will learn about the origins of various cheeses.

Knowing these times will save you time and trouble.

When the cows first crop the fresh young blades of grass after a long winter diet of hay, oil cake and sugar beets, what rich milk they give! And what fine cheeses are made from such milk!

Then three weeks or a month later the meadows bloom. For me this is the high point of the pasturing season. The fragrance of the opening flowers mingles with the fresh perfume of the tender grass.

There is just nothing like it.

The cheeses that are made from milk of flowering meadows are tops. You will be astonished by them.

Finally, there is the later second growth of grass.

Talleyrand, an illustrious cheese fancier, said, "In my opinion Brie made with milk from the second growth is best." Abandoning politics for a moment, the Congress of Vienna concurred. On this point, he and Prince Metternich were in agreement.

But let us not speak only of Brie.

About a month after the hay has been cut, the autumn rains begin and the fields enjoy a final surge of life before winter. Fresh tender shoots sprout again like the grass of early spring, and second-growth milk gives us cheeses that rejuvenate our palates after the parching heat of midsummer.

There you are.

Now you know almost as much about it as I do.

And you will know every bit as much as I do after I explain a few small points about the selection of your cheeses.

Can you trust the label on the box? the name stamped on the rind?

The Dictionary will discuss these questions, because the answer varies from cheese to cheese.

The provenance of a cheese is a matter of no small importance. Did you know that more than 2,000 brands of Camembert are made in France (500 in Normandy and the rest in some eighty French departments)? Did you know that Camembert is imported into France from Germany and even from Russia? Of course, no Camembert is as good as Normandy Camembert, and best of all is the Camembert that comes from the Auge region between Touques and Dive. The letters VCN on the label are your assurance that you have a Camembert with a good pedigree (VCN stands for *Veritable Camembert de Normandie*). If the label states further that the cheese was made in Pays d'Auge, have no hesitation about buying it (provided, of course, that it is ripe). And look around a bit—I know that they are getting rarer—and see if your dealer might not have Camembert *fermier*, that is, farm-produced Camembert. If he does, take it and invite a few well chosen friends to enjoy it with you.

The same is true of Brie.

It is hard to find out if a Brie is made from the good milk of Île-de-France. Just as with Camembert, the producers did not organize soon enough to protect the true product. As a result one often comes across Bries from Champagne or Lorraine.

The grass of Lorraine may possess virtues that the grass of the Seine-et-Marne Department lacks, but it is the grass of Seine-et-Marne that makes Brie, and there is no better Brie than that from Brie. If you are curious take a little outing one day to one of the small outdoor markets of Île-de-France where there are still a few local cheeses for sale. It's an easy trip, and the cheese will be your reward.

Every region has its own special magic which chemistry and technology have thus far been unable to duplicate.

The character, subtlety and perfection of a cheese attest to centuries of refinement in individual cheese-making methods within limited geographical areas sometimes no larger than a few fields.

Vegetation, climate, rainfall, subsoil, and breed all contribute to the production of a cheese which is unique and inimitable.

In the winter the sheep pasture in Camargue. Transport them across the river. What pastures could be more fragrant than those in the Alpilles? Do not imagine that you will find another cheese comparable to the delicious Tomme d'Arles. It is utterly distinctive.

Any cheese gains by being made in the very region where it was produced for the first time.

This is true of Comté.

Do not leave anything to chance. There is a world of difference between lowland Comté and mountain Comté. Comté originated near Verrières-de-Joux, high in the Jura mountains near the Swiss border. Nowadays they call cheeses from the neighboring plains by the same name. The original Comté and the lowland Comté may not differ much in appearance but there are variations in quality (which I give in the Dictionary).

THE HOLES IN GRUYÈRE

The holes in Gruyères disclose their health, whether they have fermented properly, too much or not enough. And a few cracks and a fissure here and there tell us even more.

Some Gruyères come to France from Switzerland, and many are French in origin. The Swiss ones are to be preferred. They have the word "Switzerland" stamped on the rind.

I purposely write "Gruyères" to dispel the common misconception that there is only one Gruyère cheese. There are in fact several. Most large cheeses are called "Gruyère" but one should not confuse the various sorts or accept one in place of the other.

The holes in Swiss Emmental should be spherical and about the size of walnuts. If the holes are oval, the fermentation was abnormal and the cheese will be either sharp or tasteless.

The holes in Comté should be about the size of peas or at most the size of cherries. If they are larger, the cheese is not a real Comté. It will not have the correct taste and you will not have received what you have paid for.

Appenzell should have very small round holes.

The holes in French Emmental should look as much as possible like the holes in its Swiss counterpart. To my taste, it is one of the best Gruyères.

The holes, however, are not the only thing to look for in a Gruyère. There is the rind as well. It should be tough of course, but if it is too thick and has a sort of vague, grayish-yellow subcrust, watch out. Most likely the cheese is old. Not everyone will like it. It will be sharp.

Since you can taste a Gruyère before you buy it, take one that has the full perfume of the mountains in early summer.

To a real fancier of the Ambert region there is just no comparison between a cheese from the big dairy down in the valley and a cheese made in a mountain chalet while the cows are in the high summer pastures.

Apart from these few great cheeses (and a few tricks that I note in the Dictionary) cheeses usually emerge from their proper origins.

I know that some so-called Tommes de Savoie are made with milk from Vendée, but when you come right down to it, is that so important? Many Tommes taste about the same whether they are made from pasteurized milk or from raw milk. Whether the milk is pasteurized in Vendée or the cheese is cured in Savoy does not make much difference, at least to my way of thinking.

As I have told you, any mild or nearly flavorless cheese may be replaced by a cheese made from pasteurized milk.

Buying cheese is an art . . . picking out a Gruyère by its holes or rejecting a Camembert because your knowledgeable thumb tells you that it is too ripe or too soft, like plaster inside or runny. (To think that some people boast of eating only runny Camembert! Don't they know that the runniness is due to a secondary fermentation that alters the true taste of the cheese?)

For one it is the eye; for another, the nose; for still another, a poke of the finger that will tell if a cheese is ripe and perfect. Why must a cheese be ripe or, more accurately, fully cured? Because that is the moment when it begins to exhale, to yield up the maximum of flavor to the nose and tongue. There are Cantals that have been aged for three months and others that have been aged for six, but the real connoisseurs, the good folk of Cantal, like their cheese only when it has acquired its full strength after six months of aging. Sooner than that it may be a good mildish cheese, fit for city palates.

The same is true of Roquefort, a sheep's-milk cheese. It is savored in Rouergue only when it is fully aged, when the mold has fanned out as widely as possible through the buttery mass of the cheese, and the flavor is strong.

Elsewhere, except in the North where people love Roquefort, perhaps because of the beverages they drink with it, and in America where people want a "real" Roquefort, the cheese is consumed too young, with just a hint of blue at the center and far too much white all around it, for the molds have not yet had enough time to fan out. Flavor is of course weaker.

You will not make this mistake. If you want Roquefort, make sure you get it. The real thing. It is just as hard to do this in Paris as it is in the provinces. You must know how to look. Nowadays cheese stores split the Roquefort cylinder in half to facilitate cutting, but even this does not make your job much easier. It is a pity that you cannot taste it in the store, unless a very understanding salesman gives you permission. If he does, remember his name. He is not afraid of a taste test, so he must be sure of his merchandise.

But that is not always true.

Take Camembert for example.

In the area where it comes from and elsewhere as well, people often prefer it on the chalky side—"underdone" as they say. About half-cured, sometimes only a third. Why? I see only one explanation: Normandy is cider-drinking country and the rather mild taste of an underaged cheese goes better with cider than it does with wine. Is that how this preference started? I suppose so.

Cider or white wine. That is why Munster is not much eaten in the region that produces it.

> The celebrated Spanish painter Salvador Dali has, by his eccentric comparisons, made two great cheeses successes in the United States—Roquefort and Camembert.
>
> The first anecdote you may know: To the reporters who questioned him, on his first visit to America, about the impression New York had made on him, Dali answered in his inimitable accent, "New York is a Gothic Roquefort!"
>
> Roquefort? Few Americans had even heard the name. They were curious, and Roquefort was launched.
>
> Several weeks later, Dali was asked what he thought of San Francisco. The surprise effect was by now a little passé, but just the same, a success. This time Dali answered, "A romantic Camembert."

Apart from extremely strong or macerated cheeses which are sometimes accompanied by distilled liquors or Bergues cheese which calls for beer (I indicate in the dictionary where beer is called for), cheese is eaten with red wine, pure and simple.

I shall discuss this in a minute.

Let us finish now with the cheeses. Up to now we have spoken almost entirely of cow's-milk cheeses. But goat's-milk cheeses are legion and sheep's-milk cheeses have many admirers.

What are the rules you must follow?

There is more than one, but do not tear your hair. Once again, I have no intention of giving you a whole course. I will tell you a story. While cows are quite receptive to the bull throughout the year, and take very well to artificial insemination, she-goats, as one might suspect, are very capricious and the he-goat's advances have no chance whatsoever except in the autumn. What is the result?

It is simple. There are so many cows that when one stops giving milk because she is pregnant, another one replaces her.

Goat's-milk cheeses on the other hand go into eclipses.

One day there will be a hundred of them. The next day they will all or almost all have disappeared from the counter.

In this case, leave any that remain to others. They are dried out and will appeal only to eccentric tastes, or else (this is a common occurrence) they are no longer *"purs chèvres"* or pure goat's-milk cheeses, they are mixtures of cow's and goat's milk (the label guaranteeing *"pur chèvre"* is, as you will see, usually missing). This period when you must, according to my way of thinking, deprive yourself of goat's-milk cheese occurs when the goat is pregnant and not giving milk, or during the first few months after she gives birth while she is nursing her kid.

How long is that? It is easy to calculate. By the end of autumn there is no more goat's milk for cheeses. Kids are not weaned until March; this may vary by a few days according to the breed and the region. *In general, however, winter (especially the end of winter) is not the time for goat's-milk cheeses.*

However, as soon as the milk becomes available, as early as the first spring drives to pasture, you will find excellent cheeses.

Second rule: Blue goat's-milk cheeses are preferable.

Let me explain: a thin bloom, either white or blue, covers goat's-milk cheeses. It is white when the cheeses are produced by commercial (I did not say pasteurized) methods used to stabilize production. On the whole, goat's-milk cheeses remain a local and seasonal product and constitute only 3% or 4% of the cheeses sold in France. The manufacturers would like to change all that and have recently introduced the use of milk frozen during the summer to make cheeses during the winter. Their sharp flavor with its hint of carbolic acid makes them quite inedible.

Goat's-milk cheeses come from where they say they come

from. At least they have up till now. If the label in some way shows the origin, there is little cause to doubt. And there is no room at all for doubt if the cheese conforms to the physical description of its type (the typical shapes of goat's-milk cheeses vary greatly according to their place of origin) and if the cheese is blue.

If the cheese is covered with a thin bluish film you know that it has ripened on a wicker tray in the cellar of a farm—that it was made according to traditional methods, which is to say the best way.

And sheep? They are willful too. Some ewes return from summer pasture with their lambs while others give birth later, much later. Near the Mediterranean the lambs arrive in November or December.

In Arles the lambs are born just before Christmas. The lamb of Midnight Mass is a lamb from Camargue. Lambing time is still later, in January, on the limestone plateau of Larzac and in the foothills of the Pyrénées. Naturally the ewe gives no milk during the gestation period, but she will suckle her lamb until it is old enough to fend for itself. This means that from the end of July until midwinter there is very little milk available for sheep's-milk cheeses.

As for the milk that goes into the best Roquefort, the local sheep's milk, this does not reappear until March. That has not kept the makers of these famous cheeses from finding ways to produce Roquefort of acceptable quality in almost all seasons: they bring in sheep's milk from other places where the cycle is somewhat earlier or later.

But you will make it a point of pride to turn down any Roquefort that is not fully aged or made from the milk of the plateau of Larzac. Do the arithmetic and remember it.

It takes three months to cure Roquefort properly. Your calculation is quite simple: March plus three months: June is the month when you begin to have a real chance to find the very finest Roquefort. How long does the season last? The proper milk is no longer available by the end of July or the beginning of August and does not become available again until October. The season is short, so enjoy it while it lasts.

What can be better than Roquefort? Be careful, however. Do not serve it just any old way. Wait until you have prepared some well-seasoned dish and serve the full-bodied wine that it requires.

By the way, let me say something about wines.

No problem here, no reason to cudgel your brains. I have indicated in the Dictionary which wines go best with each cheese. Do not suppose that if you offer a tray with six kinds of cheese you must serve six wines. That would be ridiculous. Even three wines would be too many. Leave such excesses to the nouveaux riches.

Here and there a few brief rules have been set down about which wine goes with which cheese. In general, stick to a few basic principles and all will go smoothly.

If your main dish is fairly bland, serve wines that are also bland in character.

Continue to serve the same wines with the cheeses unless your tray includes one or two selections that are fairly pungent. Obviously they will require a more full-bodied wine.

Just do the best you can. It is a question of experience and that will come in time. And if you serve a rather spicy dish, continue with the same wine. Just be sure you have chosen the right cheeses. Only when you serve very savory cheeses, very strong Bleus for example, will you be obliged to bring out a second bottle, a powerful, commanding, well-knit old Burgundy or some wine of that sort.

In this case, if you are in the mood that day and have invited a few close friends, be subtle in your choice of wines. Perhaps you will want to consult—it is up to you—the small table, beginning on page 139, of corresponding wines and cheeses.

When game is served, it's a festive occasion. Bring out your best wines. Be extravagant! After all, you do not do it every day. The rest of the time be simple; just try to avoid mistakes. That is all I ask. One wine or at the most two.

The cheese-tasting sessions with accompanying wines which I suggest further on are something else again.

Oh yes, I am forgetting something.

Before I began to speak about wines I should have told you something about the importance of how a cheese looks.

It varies.

The appearance of any cheese should correspond to certain norms but cheeses which may look "pretty" to you are not necessarily the best ones.

So it is with Camemberts. Some are covered with fine white down and look as tender as can be. How could you imagine that they are anything but superb cheeses? Nonetheless, as I indicate in the Dictionary, the rind of an excellent Camembert is not necessarily pleasing to the eye. It can be uneven and flecked with red. As a matter of fact, it should be. The same is true of Brie.

You have seen semi-soft cheeses with rinds that have been coated with wax. Fine. But that tells you nothing. The Saint-Nectaire with the unattractive skin is preferable to and no doubt better than the glossy Saint-Paulin next to it on the counter.

In any case you must look deeper. The smell of a cheese presents the same paradox.

You may imagine that cheeses that smell the strongest have the strongest flavor. That is a mistake. Sometimes they do. Sometimes they do not.

Smell a fully ripe Curé Nantais. Ugh! Taste it; it is not the least bit offensive.

A pasteurized Munster, even when it is white inside, often has a rather strong smell. "Great," you say, "I think I have a winner here." Not so fast. If the Munster is a big one, it may have been cut. Take a look at the interior first. If it is not cut, weigh the factors that I have indicated earlier: the season, the pasturing, the length of the curing period.

On the other hand when a cheese that should naturally have a smell does not, pass it by. It is not for your table.

A point about cheeses that retain a large proportion of moisture during their manufacture: learn to inspect labels: "Fat content less than 45%." "Fat content more than 45%." It is all there. If the cheese is in a box, French law requires that the fat content be indicated.

This way you will learn which cheeses are lower in moisture content and consequently richer and more nutritious.

People eat Gruyère quite offhandedly.

But do you know that three or four ounces of Gruyère can replace a steak? Remember that and go easy.

In general, you should prefer cheeses which can be seen to cheeses which are hidden away in cleverly designed packages. I know, the trend is toward more and more camouflage in the packaging of cheese. Some packages even contain toys and prizes for children.

This constitutes an improper enticement to the consumer. An honest cheese, clearly visible and without frills, is, to my way of thinking, the one to buy.

The summer months can be treacherous. Of all succulent foods, good cheeses are among the most fragile. Summer is very hard on them, especially on soft cheeses. The softer they are, the more delicate. I will let you in on a secret: they put a bit more salt in the soft cheeses that are sent to market during the hot weather. The idea is to make them less perishable. But what happens instead? Soft cheeses are loaded on trucks in the heat of summer, overheated and squashed and then perhaps exposed to the sun in the markets. The cheeses sweat and, of course, evaporation increases their salt content.

Can a cheese be good when it is oversalted?

Be careful when you see these cheeses, however good they may be in other seasons or at the moment when they emerge from the cellars where they have been cured.

If by chance you should find one that you like, do not let it spoil at home. Do not put it just anywhere and do not keep it longer than forty-eight hours. It would be a pity to lose it.

Another piece of advice: To balance your cheese tray, offer some harder cheeses or some Bleus along with your soft cheeses. As many as possible. *Soft, semi-soft and Bleu cheeses yield up their aromas on the palate.* For this reason they are tasted by pressing them against the palate with the tongue. *Hard or sharp cheeses* (sharpness is not always a defect) *are tasted with the tip of the tongue:* the papillae at the tip of your tongue will tell you of the virtues of an aged Cantal or a Roquefort.

If you are eager to show your high standards, you will avoid having processed cheeses on your cheese tray. To cheese experts these are cheese foods rather than cheeses and are not to be eaten at mealtime. As with yogurt, you should have one or two processed cheeses on hand, just in case someone should want them. They are no doubt nutritious food, but I am not a dietitian. I never mix them with true cheese.

What of new cheeses? New kinds are always coming out. Double-cream cheeses are blended with Roquefort! Makers do not know what to invent anymore. Are you going to be ruled by advertising copy or by solid French tradition? Aren't there enough cheeses already—the ones that delighted our fathers, the ones that have long graced the best tables—without the benefit of PR agencies?

My job is to tell you what I think, not necessarily what you should do. My letter is merely an invitation.

I think that one should be restrained and traditional in his choice of cheeses and in his choice of the wines that accompany them. Let others try to be novel at any price . . .

Don't be a snob or a blue-stocking.

Don't be ordinary either. No literary allusions. Just because you are serving one or two good cheeses do not drag up that old saw of Brillat-Savarin: "A meal without cheese is like a beautiful woman with one eye."

Know a few facts well and ignore all vague opinions and conjectures.

The great Colette said (I humbly copy her words): "Paris has all the cheeses, the soft, the bitter, the tangy, the strongly fermented, the ones that age in the cellars of France and the ones that come from afar. None lack customers. What is missing are the women, the people who know something about cheese. Women are fond of cheese but they have fallen prey to an obsession with slimness. A woman can do a better job of picking out cheeses than a man can. Poking the rind, testing the elasticity of the cheese, predicting what it will be like is a bit like dowsing. Studying the way in which the rind of a Camembert, a Reblochon or a Maroilles has cracked, gauging whether the runny texture of a Munster means that it will be bitter, pungent instead of mild —all this is a matter of great care and patience and these qualities are disappearing.

"When I go to X's shop where I always examine the cheeses very closely, I am ashamed to see the parade of women who come in and say, 'Do you have a nice runny Camembert? . . . I want your best Pont-l'Évêque.' Not one glance of interest at the cheeses bound in gold leather and jacketed mysteriously in mold. Not one suggestion of personal investigation. They pay their money and leave. Sometimes they muse for a moment in order to seem more knowledgeable. . . .

"If I had a son who was ready to marry, I would tell him: 'Beware of girls who don't like wine, truffles, cheese or music.' "

I hope that you will belie her description of modern women in the cheese shop.

And do not forget that your preference should go to farm cheeses. Often these are the poor relations of the others, naked and unadorned. Love them for it. If that is the way they are it is because: (1) they come from the best place; (2) they are cured right where they are made; (3) the dealer is a good one.

"Why all these lessons?" you will say. "A good cheesemonger that I can trust is enough."

Of course.

That could be the final word: "Find a good cheesemonger." But what could be more pleasant and more rewarding than learning something for yourself, discovering that one cheese is better than another? On this note, dear child, I shall blow out the candle.

PIERRE ANDROUËT

Another Letter to My Daughter

Did you read my letter? And there are still some questions in your mind.

Here, then, are a few clarifications.

First of all, what about the seasons?

As I told you, the best cheeses have seasons when they are at their best.

This does not mean, however, that you will not find them at times other than these seasons. As a matter of fact, with the exception of cheeses that disappear from the market altogether because of an animal's lactation cycle, almost all cheeses are available nowadays in every season of the year.

As far as Camembert and Brie are concerned, new methods of handling pasteurized milk and the curd have made possible slight improvements in the taste of the cheese. Perhaps the day may come when there will be no real difference between farm cheeses and commercial cheeses. We are not at that stage yet, however.

What if you are going on vacation and have decided to pack a lunch for the road?

Do not carry a Camembert. Riding in the trunk of your car will be fatal to the cheese. Instead buy one along the way, especially if you are driving through a region where the cheese is made. It will probably have been stored in a cool place and will not have had time to dry out or sweat. As you know, any drying of a cheese produces a greater concentration of.salt. A cheese that is too salty is not a good cheese.

How should you deal with a cheese merchant?

Do not say "I want a whole-milk cow's-milk cheese with a washed rind, red in color, 5 inches square, with a fat content of 45%, dry weight" if you mean that you want a Puant de Lille.

On the other hand, do not be intimidated by the cheese seller. You know what you want. No one can make you buy anything else.

How can you tell if you are dealing with a good cheesemonger?
A good cheesemonger is one who has a good reputation. Do not put your trust in titles alone. In our profession the title of *maître fromager* or master cheesemonger is not always justified, unfortunately. Do you believe that a member of a wine-tasting society is necessarily a connoisseur?

If all the master cheesemongers were really master cheese-mongers, if they all had cellars for aging, if all the products that they sold were irreproachable . . . then the title would make some sense. A little dairy store with a good stock kept at the right temperature is better than a big pretentious display. Take your cheeses as you find them. What is good one day may be past its prime the next. A cheesemonger worthy of the name will offer only cheeses that may be eaten within the next 48 hours. For no cheese, I repeat, no cheese will benefit from being kept too long at home.

How would you characterize a good cheese store?
The air is fresh but redolent of varied aromas of cheeses. The counters are spotless. Cheeses are never exposed to direct sunlight. They are well separated from one another and carefully labeled. If he is worthy of the title of cheesemonger the shop owner will sniff out a good customer. He will not attempt to put anything over on you. If he recommends a cheese very strongly, follow his advice, but only after you have assessed his choice carefully.

An attractive display is an indication, but no more than an indication, that the shopkeeper enjoys his profession and keeps his eye on the quality of his products. A good shopkeeper is a shopkeeper who can build up his stock and let the cheeses which he has bought from his wholesaler ripen to full flavor and maturity. He has adequate space to store his own cheeses. Find out if he has a cool cellar and a supply in reserve. Not every cheese is sold on the day it comes into the shop (how could it be?). Furthermore, some cheeses need another day or two, or even a week, to ripen to perfection. Consequently, only those shops equipped to store cheeses properly are good shops. To do this, one needs a cellar with the right temperature (46° to 50° Fahrenheit) and the right humidity (85%).

Do all the cheeses in France that sound foreign really come from abroad?

No. In addition to our innumerable domestic cheeses, France also makes imitations of foreign cheeses. Would you like a few examples?

Mimolette, Passe-l'An, Cheddar, Chester, Emmental, and Saint-Gorlon are all more or less savory copies of foreign originals: the Mimolette of Flanders a copy of the Mimolette of Holland, Chester or Cheddar the copy of Cheshire, Saint-Gorlon a copy of Gorgonzola, and Passe-l'An a copy of Parmigiano (Parmesan). Edam and Gouda, which are from the Netherlands, are also made in France. There is also French Fontal.

Some Emmental comes from Germany. On the rind is the stamp *Made in Germany (Bayern).* Emmental is also manufactured in Finland (Suomi).

Flat cheese? Thick cheese?

The thicker the cheese within a given category, the stronger the flavor, provided that the cheese is ripe. But like all rules this one too has its exceptions: Chaource is four or five inches thick and is eaten white. Mold does not penetrate to its center because doing so would take too long and the flavor would become too strong.

What qualities should cheeses have?

That question is much too general. Consult the Dictionary for each cheese. That is what the Dictionary is for. In brief, a cheese should have exactly those qualities which correspond to its type.

Which cheeses keep best?

See "Hints for serving." Let me say right off, however, that the

Bleus are the most delicate. Bleus dry out very quickly. They are the most sensitive to the temperatures at which they are kept. A very low temperature is required. Be careful not to overdo it, however, and never put them in the freezer. That would be an act of murder.

What do you think of supple Gruyère?
Do you mean rubbery Gruyère? Come now, you do not eat plastic! Not yet, at any rate. A "supple" Gruyère is an imperfectly cured Gruyère. It is almost always tasteless.

Is the distribution of the mold the only thing that tells you about the quality of Bleu cheese?
In large measure, yes: wide-spread veins indicate a good cheese and good flavor. But besides that, the cut should look smooth and give the impression that it would feel slippery to your touch. Furthermore, it should have an even color without any sort of ring around the outside.

What if it is not cut?
Have them cut it open.
At very worst a Bleu should be no more than slightly grayish. It may be a little less white than a Roquefort, but in no case should it be gray or brownish.

Why shouldn't a soft cheese like Camembert be eaten runny?
Once more: a Camembert should be supple and creamy, never runny. This is true of all the soft cheeses, for instance Maroilles, Bries, Coulommiers. Runniness is the result of insufficient drying during manufacture. The cheese has retained too much water and excessive lactic fermentation has occurred. If such a cheese is not already sharp on the day you buy it, it will surely be sharp the next day.

Then, too, there is no getting around the fact that a runny Camembert is uneconomical to use. It empties itself.

What do you think of Camemberts from other places besides Normandy?

They are often very good. If you go through Touraine you will be offered a local Camembert. Try it. It may be delicious—a very fine cheese. It is less expensive because it is less well known and milk is cheaper there.

Still there is a world of difference between the Camembert of the Auge region and the Camembert of Touraine. Cheese is above all a flavor, an anticipated flavor, the flavor it should have.

Can a cheese that "runs" just beneath the rind can be a good cheese.

A bad sign. Either the cheese was insufficiently drained or the curing took place at too high a temperature. In any case it will have the consistency of plaster. Do not expect it to improve when you bring it home.

HOW TO CHOOSE A GOOD CAMEMBERT

There are three ways: look it over carefully; smell it if it seems questionable; palpate it correctly.

The first thing you see is the rind. It should be velvety white with reddish or brownish pigmentation. When a Camembert looks like that, experts say that it is *"parti"* or "on the way"; they mean that it is developing properly and has every chance of turning out to be good, if not that day, at least in the next few days. On the other hand, if the rind lacks this pigmentation, you would do well to leave the cheese alone. It is not developing and there is good question whether it ever will.

If the rind of the Camembert shows an abnormal brownish color, especially pronounced around the edges, again do not take it. It has passed the period of fermentation and has deteriorated. It will be sharp.

The smell: the defect to catch is an ammonia smell. If you can detect it, the Camembert is *"passé"* or "gone." It will be sharp.

Palpation: all soft cheeses should be felt gently through-out their mass. Begin at the edges and work toward the center. You see, fermentation begins at the outer edges and moves toward the core. The core of the cheese should be as soft as the rest. Let us note again that a Camembert should not run—no soft cheese should. Runniness comes from improper drying during manufacture.

If it has fermented on the surface and is unevenly supple throughout its mass, do not take it. The fermentation has not reached the interior of the cheese. It is now too late.

Is there any difference between the fermentation of soft cheeses and the fermentation of Bleu cheeses?

The fermentation of soft cheeses starts from the outside. The fermentation of the Bleus starts from the center and works its way toward the edges. Consequently a soft cheese is ripe when the fermentation has spread inward through the cheese and has reached the center. A Bleu cheese is good when the blue internal mold approaches the outer edges. And something else to watch out for: never accept a Bleu if it crumbles and falls apart when cut. For further differences see the Dictionary.

How great a variety of flavors can be found in cheeses?

The nuances in cheese flavor are endless. Their taste ranges from bland or extremely mild to gamy or smoky, and includes cheeses which are fruity, more or less spicy, nutty—even the savory Bleus. There are endless subtleties for the palate. Did you know that a cheese made from milk collected in the morning will taste different from the same kind of cheese made from milk collected in the evening? The former will be lighter. Cheese parallels the milk from which it was made.

The taste of a particular cheese may change with the seasons. Cantal is fruitier in the summer and in the autumn. The grass changes and the quality of the milk changes. In any case, Cantal will never be less fruity than it is in the winter, no matter how good it is in other respects, unless it is an old cheese.

What about flavorings?
Flavorings in no way affect the savor of a cheese. Boursin is an example.

Are there cheeses that you can buy with your eyes shut?
Yes, you could say so. As far as fresh cheeses are concerned, knowing that they are fresh is sufficient. But are they really cheeses for the cheese tray? I do not think so.

Are there cheeses that one should never buy?
Yes, do not buy a cheese unless you can determine in one way or another if it is in perfect condition. As a rule never buy cheeses in hermetically sealed containers. How can you tell what you are getting?

How many cheeses are needed for four, six and eight guests?
At least two more than the number at table. For further details see "How to Serve."

Why do they make large Maroilles?
The large size is for the big families in the North of France (10 or 12 children).

Why are Gruyères so large?
Gruyères keep well, so the large size is easy to stock and store without damage to the cheese.

How long will a goat's-milk cheese stay tender?
About three weeks.

How can you tell if a goat's-milk cheese is made entirely from goat's milk?

As a rule, by the label *"pur chèvre"* (pure goat cheese). The label is not always present, however, and in these cases one must go by the shape of the cheese. It should be neat and have no imperfections. A cheese that has been adulterated with cow's milk is uneven and lacks sharp edges. Study it carefully before you make up your mind. A different label, *"mi-chèvre"* (half goat's-milk cheese), with a yellow band, indicates that the cheese contains at least 25% goat's milk and that the rest is cow's milk. Frankly, there are strong grounds for believing that any goat's-milk cheese sold in the winter is a mixture of goat's and cow's milk unless there is a label plainly stating that it is pure goat's-milk cheese.

What are the defects of goat's-milk cheeses?

Goat's-milk cheeses seldom have any defects when you buy them in season. You must be sure they are not too dried out. When they are, they can be almost as hard as stone. You do not want to send your guests to the dentist. So pick out the tenderest ones. Very hard, stony goat's-milk cheeses have a taste and smell that, believe me, repels most people.

What qualities should a cheese tray have?

It should be neat, well balanced and in season.

How much can you tell about a cheese from the rind, if the rind is good?

The rind is worth about 20 to 30 out of 100 points in rating the cheese's quality.

Appearance is worth 30 to 40 points; palpating it, if you are permitted to, is worth at least 50. How much is the smell worth? That depends. As a rule, not much, for a cheese that smells the way it should smell is not necessarily a good one. A Livarot that smells very good may be tasteless.

The taste, of course, tells the whole story. Every time you can, taste a cheese before you buy it.

Is it true that so-called fermented cheeses are bad for your health?
Not at all. See the paragraph about diets in "How to Serve."

Why are there such differences in price among cheeses coming from the same place, bearing the same name, and containing the same amount of fat—Camembert, for example?
The fame of the brand accounts for many such differences. But that is not all. You tell me that you find Camemberts from places other than Normandy that cost only half the price. Think it over. The price of the milk (which directly affects the quality of the cheese) is not the same everywhere, and Norman milk is the most expensive. It is quite simple. No one is cheating you.

Should you judge fat content by the plasticity of the cheese?
Soft cheeses are not the highest in fat content; they just look that way. They are often no richer than others in fat content.
Feuille de Dreux, a soft cheese, contains 25% to 30% fat. Emmental, a hard cheese, contains 45% to 48%.
Tomme Grise de Savoie, an uncooked pressed cheese of supple consistency, contains 30% to 40% fat.
Beaufort, a hard cheese, contains 53% to 56%.
Only double-cream cheeses with 60% fat and triple-cream cheeses with at least 75% fat are exceptions to the rule.

Are the holes the only thing to go by when you are shopping for Gruyères?
Pay very close attention to their *becs* and *lénures*.
Becs are small slanting cracks beneath the rind; *lenures* are horizontal fissures within the cheese. These are the best signs of high quality. Above all, do not confuse them with the gigantic holes called "caverns" that indicate a serious defect. Such cheeses

have burst open as a result of overly intense fermentation. This flaw is seen only in cheeses that are unfit for consumption. So be careful. And if you see a Comté with small holes damp with salt water, grab it. Such a Gruyère is "weeping" its salt and has been aged to full maturity.

Weeping Gruyères of whatever sort are the very best.

In every case, a Gruyère that is supposed to have holes should have neither too few nor too many, just the right number for the type to which it belongs. Any excess or deficiency of holes indicates that something has gone wrong during manufacture.

Even though Gruyères are not, properly speaking, cheeses for the cheese fancier, still when they exhale the fine perfume of alpine meadows they are truly excellent. When possible it is good to have at least one on your cheese tray. In any group there is always at least one person who prefers Gruyère and it would be a pity to deprive him of it, because very often people who like Gruyère like *only* Gruyère.

Unless you note one of the defects which I have listed in the Dictionary, you can as a rule count on Gruyère that comes from Switzerland (the word *Switzerland* will be stamped on the rind). The Swiss are careful people and the traditional methods of manufacture are still honored there. They do not worry about making the Cheese of the Future. They still make cheeses as they should be made—the way it was done in the good old days.

The mildest of the Gruyères is French Emmental. The fruitiest is a mountain Comté. Of all the Gruyères a well-aged Beaufort is the one that has the most character.

Their color? It falls between straw yellow and chamois yellow. For that you need a practiced eye. Content yourself with judging the holes and the rind. And as a housewife remember that with a 48% to 50% fat content these cheeses have concentrated food value.

Last of all, there is a further way to check Gruyère at home— a good, rich Gruyère "butters" when you roll a small ball of it between your forefinger and your thumb.

Which are my "top three" Gruyères?
In order of preference: Beaufort, mountain Comté, Swiss Emmental.

Why is Beaufort at the head of my top three Gruyères?
Because it is the only high mountain cheese that you can find on the market right up until spring. At that time it is excellent. In the winter when the cows are back in the barn and give very little milk, the cheese is not made. Since it takes six to eight months to ripen fully, you have to wait until winter for it. Beaufort is the king of Gruyères in winter.

How can one steer clear of suspicious semi-soft cheeses?
Since most of them have been stabilized, these cheeses as a rule have almost no defects. Still you should not take semi-soft cheeses like Saint-Paulin and Saint-Nectaire if they have holes, a sign of abnormal fermentation. They will have a bitter taste.

Let the name "Salers" be engraved in your memory. Where white Fourmes are concerned, nothing surpasses the one that comes straight from Salers, especially if it has been fully ripened the way they like it down there, for more than six months.

A Fourme's ivory-yellow or straw-yellow interior should be perfectly homogeneous and supple. Pass over any Fourme that looks grainy, for it has been taken out of the cellars too early or was improperly pressed. Reject Fourmes that ooze fat, for they have been improperly drained. They will be washed out and tasteless, or else they will be sharp. Reject, too, the ones that are bloated or swollen. When these cheeses are good, they are flat.

When Fourmes are three months old, the rind should not be more than 1/10-inch thick. If it is thicker, the cheese is older.

That, in broad outline, is how these rather little-known white Fourmes should look.

Ranging from mellow to nutty when it is young (aged for three months), Salers cheese becomes quite ferocious in taste by the end of six months. Try it once. Some natives go even further. They let the cheese age still longer in their own cellars. It becomes completely hard and the cracked rind teems with cheese mites.

However, there is a limit: when the interior becomes brittle and dry the cheese is consigned to kitchen use as a condiment.

There are other Fourmes seldom mentioned in the big cities: the Fourmes of Laguiole-Aubrac. The cows that produce the milk for these cheeses graze at altitudes of up to 8,000 feet. Pick cheeses that have been cured for at least five months, if not six. You will have the sensation of absolute authenticity. This is also true of the Fourme of Rochefort. If I wax a bit eloquent on the subject of Fourmes, it is because they have not, to my way of thinking, found their rightful place on our city tables.

Do not be too much concerned about the smell of uncooked pressed cheeses. Occasionally a Curé Nantais or a Tête-de-Moine smells fairly strong. Don't faint at your first sniff. It is a perfectly normal phenomenon. The strong odor does not denote a strong taste.

And by all means let me urge you to try a Trappiste de Cîteaux. If it is just ripe and has no defects, you will find its tang incomparable.

What about Tommes?

Consult the Dictionary and choose whichever one you like. Do not forget, however, that Tomme de Romans, a goat's-milk cheese, comes from Dauphiné rather than from Savoy. When it is good, it holds a place of honor among the soft cheeses. The main thing is to find it. Keep looking, even if you have to go to Romans.

In Savoy each valley has its own Tomme and all are more or less equivalent in flavor. The sheep's-milk Tommes form a class apart. When fully ripe Tomme de Brach is more rustic and more savory than a Roquefort. Tomme de Brach is something like a Bleu, but you must try it where it is made. Tomme d'Annot is similar to Esbareich or Laruns, the favorite cheese of the Basques.

Fresh Tomme de Camargue is delicious. It would be a crime to miss it if you are driving through Arles when it is available. To my taste, it is one of the most delicate cheeses in existence.

There is also Grataron d'Arêches and some goat's-milk Tommes in Courchevel. These uncooked, pressed cheeses are curiosities among the goat's-milk cheeses. They are worth a detour, as the Michelin Guide would say.

What should one know about Dutch cheeses?

Some are oily, others are drier. Only Edam is almost a completely dry cheese. Perhaps you will prefer the oily ones like Mimolette, whether waxed or not, although there are excellent drier cheeses such as Edam, Gouda, and the aged, heat-dried Edam cheeses that are so popular in the Bordeaux region.

If you have a chance to get farm-made Present or Leyden cheese flavored with cumin or cloves, by all means do so. My preference in Dutch cheeses goes to these and to nutty Mimolette, the cheese so relished by General de Gaulle.

And Italian cheeses?

Don't lose yourself among them. Some of them are so strong they could fell you with one blow. A few, however, are docile enough for export and, if you are careful in judging their quality, a Gorgonzola, a Provolone, a Fontina, an Asiago that is not too sharp, or a moderately aged Pecorino (Romano, Sardo or Siciliano) will make a welcome addition to your cheese tray.

Pecorino is a sheep's-milk cheese. Choose fresh ones; as a rule they are delicious. When dry, Pecorinos rapidly become sharp. Compare them with the sheep's-milk cheeses of the Pyrénées. There is not much difference. As for Gorgonzola, it is occasionally a good replacement for one of the French Bleus when you find that the latter are not at their best. Anyway, to my taste, Gorgonzola is one of the very best cheeses, provided that its flavor has not yet reached the soapy stage.

I have nothing to say on the score of **Bel Paese**, which is very popular but in no way better than ordinary French Saint-Paulin. Many Italian cheeses are similar to French uncooked pressed cheeses in texture and taste but are made by different methods. Some are scalded (but not cooked); others are cooked and pressed. For you these techniques are merely secondary considerations.

And English cheeses?

It should be noted that Chester and Cheddar cheeses are manufactured in France and in other countries; even in England foreign versions of these cheeses appear on the table. But the Cheshire cheeses are uniquely, authentically English, as are the exquisite Stilton cheeses. Stilton is a peerless cheese.

There is not much difference between the French Chesters or Cheddars and the English ones. If you want to do something imaginative, serve a real Cheshire cheese instead of Cantal. When it is good and ripe and oily, the tip of your tongue will tingle with pleasure.

But now I come to a cheese which should be sampled only on the other side of the Channel: the incomparable Stilton. It is a Bleu cheese. The English soak it for one month in Sherry, or better still in Port or in Madeira. Then they wrap it in a white napkin and slip it into a special wooden or silver container. The Stilton, very strong and aromatic, is scooped from the top with a small spoon. It is a regal cheese, one for real connoisseurs. When you are in England, seize the chance to try a Stilton soaked in wine, and who knows? Perhaps you will bring one back home with you to share with a few special guests.

Why do some cheeses have a rind while others not?

Rinds result from the dissemination of mold (penicillium) and from salting. (See Glossary.)

Does Roquefort always come from Roquefort?

Any cheese bearing the name Roquefort has been cured in the caves of Combalou. It may have been made elsewhere, in Corsica, along the Mediterranean, in Aquitaine, in Quercy, in the Pyrénées, or in lower Provence. One thing, however, is certain: it was aged in Roquefort. Of course, only Roqueforts made with sheep's milk from the limestone plateau of Larzac are truly genuine—these are the best Roqueforts by a wide margin.

In the long run I am sure you will recognize this.

People often mention "Société" Roquefort. Is this the only really authentic Roquefort?

Société is a brand of Roquefort. Other brands also have well-established reputations. Sometimes the makers of one brand are more careful than those of another brand. In any case you cannot depend on brand name alone.

How can one recognize a "real" Brie?

Look closely. Before they are cut, Bries have a little round paper label stuck on the center. If this label indicates that the Brie comes from Brie or from the Department of Seine-et-Marne, no problem.

Bries that come from Meuse are, of course, less expensive than Bries that come from Brie. But are they really the Bries that you are looking for?

Can you still find farm Brie?

They are very rare. One day you will probably find one as you stroll through the markets of Meaux, Coulommiers, Provins or some other town of Seine-et-Marne. Brie de Melun is often sold white.

Do not be surprised if you have to pay more for a farm Brie. It is an uncommon treat, and worth the price. You don't come across these extraordinary cheeses every day.

You cannot tell much about a Brie from its appearance. You

must taste it. Make friends with your cheesemonger. You will not be sorry. What he does not do for others, he will do for you if you show him that you know something about cheeses.

How can you tell if it is a mountain Comté or a lowland Comté?
The holes in a lowland Comté are the size of a cherry or of a walnut and are more rounded than the holes of a mountain Comté. The latter cheese, the real one, has sparse holes that are no bigger than a pea or a hazelnut. You see, it is easy. It is not the milk that makes these differences; it is the temperature of the cellars.

Sometimes you are surprised by the mediocrity of certain cheeses. Well, there are ten to twenty operations between the milking of the cow and the final preparation of the cheese for sale. A little oversight along the way, no matter how small, can change everything and compromise the whole cheese.

The cheesemonger could, of course, help you out and recommend one cheese over another. Sometimes he will. Obviously, though, he cannot do this for everyone if he wants to sell all his cheeses. It's best to rely on your own judgment. You will see, it is a fairly simple science. With practice you will become very good at it and bring home perfect cheeses every time.

A cheese has a good chance of being superb if you buy it in season, and if you know where it comes from and how long it has been aged. But cheese does have its unpredictable side, too. A few hours can spoil everything. Too much traveling changes a cheese. Slight overaging can make a cheese that should have been excellent just barely acceptable. Too much humidity in the cellar, excessive dryness in the storeroom, a draft, is all that is needed to reduce a fine cheese to a mere shadow of itself. When you go to the cheese shop knowing what you know now (about seasons, sources, curing), the laws of probability will naturally orient your choice to certain cheeses.

But you can only be certain when the cheese is right under your nose. In the Dictionary I give you the simplest rules to follow.

Abide by these and you will be able to distinguish between the merely good cheeses and those of unrivaled quality.

If some of your dinner guests are in the habit of eating in so-called modern restaurants, their tastes will probably incline toward mildness. So it is with modern palates—gamy flavors are no longer in season.

Does a farm cheese look different from the same cheese made in a factory?

The farm cheese always looks more rustic in shape or in color.

How do you store cheese at home?

Inasmuch as you should buy cheeses only when they are fully ripe, it is best to eat them the same day or the next—unless, of course, you have a cellar with the right temperature, humidity and ventilation. Alas, not everyone can buy a country house just to store their cheese.

Lest I seem too fussy or pedantic, I will concede that it is possible to store cheeses in the refrigerator, provided that certain conditions are met. See "How to Serve."

Is the choice of the cheeses determined by the dishes that go before it?

Some say a reasonable amount of acidity in seasoning restores the sensitivity of the taste buds and permits them to enjoy very delicate flavors. After a good salad, any cheese may be savored, from the mildest right up to Roquefort. I do not wholly agree. Remember my discussion of wines. In a well planned meal you cannot go back to a wine of lesser character.

A Few Tips

• If you want to make a meal of cheese, autumn is the very best time to do it.

Be on the lookout for new discoveries. Get off the beaten track. Do not be one of those people who buy only Gruyère, Camembert or Pont-l'Évêque. From time to time add some of the wonderful little regional cheeses to your cheese tray when you find them and if they are in good condition. Or else add some of the unsung but admirable cheeses, one of the Trappist cheeses or a Chevrotin.

• Does the problem of wines still disconcert you? Do not despair just because you do not own the wine cellar of the Tour d'Argent. A good inexpensive wine that goes well with your cheeses is better than two great wines that do not.

• If you take a trip, try local cheeses that you do not know. If you drive through Lisieux, Livarot or Vimoutiers, it would be a crime not to pick up a "five star colonel," a big, authentic Livarot cheese. These three towns have the monopoly on it.

• Anticipate all the possible and probable shortcomings of the summer season.

• An increasing number of people want all cheeses to be mild and not too pungent. This is a rampant heresy. A cheese that is by nature zestful *should* be highly flavored, even if this is not to your taste. By the same token mild cheeses should be mild, Bleu cheeses should have the characteristic taste of a Bleu, and goat's-milk cheeses should taste like goat's-milk cheese.

In my opinion, fresh cheeses and processed cheeses don't add much to the cheese tray. They are really cheese foods to be used for dietary purposes or for sandwiches. They are made from pasteurized milk and like all pasteurized-milk cheeses they are available all year round and never vary much in quality, which is uniformly high.

• In the peak season there are hundreds of goat's-milk cheeses in France. They are the least expensive. Take advantage of them.

• Many people have developed a distaste for goat's-milk cheeses simply because the cheeses were badly chosen. That is a pity, because they can be marvelous cheeses. There are fresh ones, semi-fresh ones and even dry ones (but for heaven's sake do not serve flint on your cheese tray!).

• How do you know which goat's-milk cheese is which?
That is easy; you recognize them by their shapes, which vary depending on their origin. You can memorize them if you like. It will be a big help and quite a conversation piece at your table, proving to your guests that you know a thing or two about cheese.

• Women seldom care much for the strong cheeses, perhaps because some of them have an offensive odor. Serve them separately.

• Be eclectic. Do not serve four semi-soft cheeses. Try to serve cheeses of different textures, just as you try to serve cheeses of different flavors. Every man to his taste.

• Fontina and Fontal are supposed to be similar. Choose Fontina over Fontal.

• Because they keep so well, semi-soft cheeses always have their place on the cheese tray, especially if the main dish was not too strong in flavor. Then their mildness is appropriate. Do not limit your choice to the well-known kinds, however. Do not forget Chambarand, so much like Reblochon, and Tamié and tangy Cîteaux. These are cheeses that will keep for a few days without any danger of spoilage.

● Another thing—if you see a Saint-Paulin, a Cantal or a Tomme, or for that matter any cheese of the uncooked pressed type that is not uniform in color, do not buy it. It may be sharp. The fermentation was defective.

● Never buy cheeses with a hard or semi-hard rind that shows signs of swelling or bulging. This is an indication of secondary fermentation that will make the cheese unpleasant, bitter, and even inedible.

● Two cheeses from the same place may look the same, but in terms of taste they may be as different as day and night. Learn to spot the small details that make one preferable to the other.

● When you are buying a full-flavored cheese, do not forget that Époisses is traditionally cured in salt water and marc.
   All washed-rind cheeses may be macerated.

● Some cheeses can be made from several different milks. Banon and Poivre d'Âne can be made from several milks and it is up to you to decide if you want sheep's milk, goat's milk or cow's milk. The seasons are, of course, not the same.

● If the storekeeper offers you a cheese that you had not thought of buying, or if he advertises a certain cheese, have a look at it. Don't be unduly suspicious. Do not automatically jump to the conclusion that he wants to fob off his leftovers on you. On the contrary, such a cheese is probably in abundant supply on the market, with a wide selection available. You may get a cheese at the top of its form.

● Think in terms of equivalents. In your notebook write down that Bleu de Loudes = Bleu de Costaros = Bleu de Velay. Little jottings like that. In the process you will learn something. It is important to know which cheeses will serve as replacements when you do not find the one you are looking for, to know what is just as good.

Another example: Tomme du Mézenc = a rustic version of Fourme d'Ambert. Why not make a list of the principal cheeses according to their flavors? This is not difficult to do. Put in parentheses the months when they are at their best. Another good trick: Have your cheese trays written down in advance.

To make your system perfect add whether a cheese is soft, semi-soft, hard, or a goat's-milk cheese. That is all there is to it.

• "Don't buy anything that isn't signed," Curnonsky used to say. He knew what he was talking about.

• A word about Petit-Suisse: when it is very fresh it fills out its paper wrapper completely.

Conclusion

Winston Churchill said, "A country that produces 325 varieties of cheese cannot be governed." If you offer a nice selection of cheeses to your dinner guests you will prove that your house, at least, is well governed.

Selecting Cheeses by Flavor and Season

The Seven Flavors to Be Found in Cheese

Fresh flavor

1. Very little acidity or very slightly acidulated. Very fatty cheeses (Fontainebleau, fresh Boursin, Petit-Suisse, fresh drained goat's-milk cheeses). Very fresh goat's-milk cheeses (when unmolded). Very fresh sheep's-milk cheeses.

2. Lactic or acidulated. White cheese, green cheese, cottage cheese, Jonchée.

Extra-mild or bland flavor

Numerous cheeses, mainly uncooked pressed cheeses made from pasteurized milk.

All nonaged or very briefly aged cheeses except Bleus and washed-rind cheeses.

Mild flavor

High butter-fat, slightly aged cheeses (Boursault, Boursin, Fin-de-Siècle, Excelsior).

Numerous young or fresh goat's-milk or sheep's-milk cheeses (young Cabécous, young Banon, Tomme de Camargue, Laruns).

Young Dutch cheeses. A few pasteurized-milk cheeses whose mild savor is due to *penicillium glaucum* (Bleu de Bresse is an example) or to the action of fermentations that have not been entirely alkalized (soft cheeses with bloomy rinds, washed rinds, etc.).

Not very pronounced flavor

All types of cheese whose aging is interrupted before full maturity has been reached: Soft cheeses: Camembert, Munster, Maroilles, etc. Semi-soft cheeses: Cantal aged between three and six months. Hard cheeses: Gruyères aged no more than three months. Half-aged thin or flat cheeses (Brie, Coulommiers, Petit Olivet). Uncooked pressed farm cheeses (mountain Saint-Nectaire, Tomme de Savoie). Most monastery cheeses. Aged soft cheeses of special manufacture (Reblochon de Chalet, Vacherin).

Pronounced flavor

Farm cheeses that are soft, aged and not thick (Camembert and various Bries).

Aged, soft, washed-rind cheeses that are not thick (slower fermentation: Pont-l'Évêque, Rollot).

Certain monastery cheeses: Trappe de Laval, Trappe d'Entrammes, Curé Nantais.

Certain rustic Tommes that have been aged for at least three months.

Cheese with internal molds, Bleus at the beginning of the season.

Certain fully aged hard cheeses (Emmental).

Semi-dry goat's-milk cheeses.

Strong flavor

Soft thick, slowly fermented cheeses (Maroilles, Livarot, Époisses, Pavé d'Auge, mountain Munster, Dauphin).

Aged cheeses with internal molds, Bleus at the end of the season.

Thick semi-soft cheeses aged as long as possible: Cantal, Laguiole, Fourme de Rochfort.

Thick hard cheeses aged as long as possible (Beaufort, Comté, Gruyère), very dry goat's-milk cheeses.

Very strong, sharp or high flavor

Macerated cheeses (Tomme au Marc, Niolo).

Some very slowly fermented cheeses (Boulette d'Avesnes).

Worked, crocked cheeses (old goat's-milk cheeses in white wine or marc).

If you know that a cheese has been pasteurized, count the flavor as one degree less. Most such cheeses will not exceed flavor 3, that is, pronounced flavor.

In the SPRING, select from among the following cheeses:

1. MILD FLAVOR

Fresh cheeses

Banon Frais
Caillebotte
Crémet
Demi-sel
Double-Crème
Fontainebleau
Fremgeye

Gournay Frais
Jonchée Niortaise
Jonchée d'Oléron
Pie (Fromage à la Pie)
Suisse
Triple-Crème

Bloomy-rind soft cheeses

Boursault Affiné
Boursin Affiné
Brillat-Savarin
Délice de Saint-Cyr
Excelsior
Explorateur

Fin-de-Siècle
Lucullus
Magnum
Tomme Vaudoise
Tomme Vaudoise au Cumin

Washed-rind soft cheeses—early spring

Vacherin d'Abondance
Vacherin des Beauges
Vacherin Mont-d'Or

Chambarand (Abbaye de)
Colombière
Reblochon

Bleus

Bresse Bleu
Gorgonzola

Sain-Gorlon

Persillés

Tomme de Brach

Uncooked pressed cheeses

Ardi-Gasna
Belval (Abbaye de)
Briquebec (Abbaye de)
Broodkaas or loaf Edam
Campénéac (Abbaye de)
Échourgnac (Abbaye d')
Edam, full-fat
Fontal

Gouda, full-fat
Igny (Abbaye de)
Laruns
Laval (Abbaye de)
La Meillerange (Abbaye de)
Monségur
Murol
Saint-Paulin

Hard cheeses

Emmental
Burrino

Scamorze

Goat's-milk cheeses, half-goat's-milk cheeses

Rigotte
Romans (Tomme de)

Saint-Marcellin

Sheep's-milk cheeses

Banon
Broccio
Brousse du Rove
Brousse de la Vésubie

Cabécous
Poivre-d'Âne
Sableau Trois Cornes

Process cheeses

Crème à Tartiner (sandwich
  spread)

2. SLIGHTLY FRUITY OR SLIGHTLY PRONOUNCED FLAVOR

Fresh cheeses

Aettekees
Bibbelskäse
Boursin aux Herbes
Brie de Melun Frais

Claquebitou Bourguignon
Claqueret Lyonnaise
Double-Crème Aromatisé
Fremgeye

Gérardmer "Lorraine"
Mozzarella
Sainte-Marie
Triple-Crème Aromatisé

Triple-Crème à la Cannelle
Triple-Crème au Cumin
Triple-Crème au Paprika

Bloomy-rind or natural-rind soft cheeses

Bondon de Neufchâtel
Briquette de Neufchâtel
Carré de l'Est
Chaource
Coeur de Bray
Ervy-le-Châtel
Frimault Bleu
Gournay
Monsieur-Fromage (young)

Olivet Bleu
Patan
Petit Bessan
Saint-Benoist
Saint-Gildas-des-Bois
Tarare Crème
Vendôme Bleu
Villebarou

Washed-rind soft cheeses

Chevrotin des Aravis
Pont-l'Évêque

Demi Pont-l'Évêque

Bleus—late spring

Bleu de Gex
Bleu de Sassenage

Bleu de Septmoncel

Persillés—late spring

Persillé des Aravis
Persillé du Grand-Bormand

Persillé de Thônes

Uncooked pressed cheeses

Bel Paese
Cantal-Salers
Cheddar
Chester
Cîteaux (Abbaye de)

Échourgnac (Abbaye de)
Edam Demi-étuvé
Entrammes (Abbaye de)
Fourme de Rochfort
Gouda Demi-étuvé

Laguiole d'Abondance
Laguiole-Aubrac
Leyden with cloves
Leyden with cumin
Mimolette
Mont-des-Cats (Abbaye du)
Present or Boerenkaas
Saint-Paulin
Savaron

Stracchino
Tamié (Abbaye du)
Tomme d'Annot
Tomme des Beauges
Tomme des Belleville
Tomme de Courchevel
Tomme du Revard
Tomme de Valdeblore

Hard cheeses
Burrino, semi-dry
Emmental

Scamorze, semi-dry

Goats-milk cheeses (or so-called goat's-milk cheeses)
Banon
Poivre-d'Âne
Rigotte

Romans
Saint-Marcellin

—with cow's milk—

Real goat's-milk cheeses—late spring
Banon
Brin d'Amour
Cabécou d'Entraygues
Cabécou de Gramat
Cabécou de Rocamadour
Cabrion de Charolles
Cabrion de Mâcon
Chevrotin de Conne

Chevrotin de Moulins
Chevrotin de Souvigny
Vroux
Pouligny
Sainte-Maure
Sancerres: Chavignol, Cré-
zancy, Santranges,
Valençay

Processed cheeses
Fondu au Raisin

Fromage à Tartiner (cheese
spread)

3. FRUITY OR PRONOUNCED FLAVOR

Fresh cheeses

Coulette de Cambrai Tomme d'Aligot
Double-Crème Aromatisé Triple-Crème au Poivre

Bloomy-rind soft cheeses

Brie de Meaux Fougeru
Camembert Monsieur-Fromage
Carré de l'Est Olivet Bleu
Chaource Patay
Chéoy Petit Bessay
Chevru Saint-Benoist
Coulommiers Vendôme Bleu
Ervy-le-Châtel Villebarou

Washed-rind soft cheeses

Chamberat Pavé d'Auge
Chaumont Pierre-Qui-Vire
Coeur d'Arras Pont-l'Évêque
Guerbiny Rollot
Mamirolle Rouy

Bleus

Bleu de Sainte-Foy Bleu du Velay-Loudes
Bleu de Tignes

Persillés

Persillé des Aravis Roquefort

Uncooked pressed cheeses

Asiago Emmental, old
Bethmale Esbareich
Comtal, old Fontina
Edam Étuvé Gouda, dried

Iraty	Oustet
Laguiole, old	Tilsit
Mimolette, old	Tomme au Fenouil
Nantais (Fromage du Curé)	Tomme de Savoie

Hard cheeses

Appenzell	Parmesan
Beaufort, old	Provolone
Caciocavallo	Sbrinz
Comté, old	Scamorze
Emmental, old	

Goat's-milk cheeses—late spring

Cachat du Ventoux	Mâconnais
Chabichou	Mothais
Chabi	Picodon de Valréas
Charolais	Rogeret des Cévennes
Coucé-Vérac	Saint-Maixent
Cressan	

Processed cheese with flavorings

4. VERY FRUITY OR VERY PRONOUNCED FLAVOR

Bloomy-rind or natural-rind soft cheeses

Bondaroy au Foin	Feuille de Dreux
Bouille	Olivet Cendré
Brie de Melun	Pannes Cendré
Brie de Montereaux or	Pithiviers au Foin
Ville de Saint Jacques	Riceys (Cendré des)
Chaource, overripe	Rocroi Cendré
Champenois Barberey	Vendôme Cendré
Champenois Cendré	
Champenois Heiltz-le-Maurupt	

Washed-rind soft cheeses

Baguette Laonnaise	Boulette de la Pierre-Qui-Vire
Chaumont	Limburger
Creusois-Guéret	Livarot
Dauphin	Maroilles
Époisses	Maroilles (mignon or quart)
Gérômé	Mignot
Gérômé anisé	Munster
Hervé	Munster, flavored with cumin
Langres	Romatour or Remoudou
Larron d'Ors	

Bleus

Bleu d'Auvergne	Bleu du Quercy
Bleu des Causses	Stilton
Bleu de Corse	

Persillés

Persillé des Aravis	Roquefort

Uncooked pressed cheeses

Amou, old	Cheshire, old
Anniviers	Conches
Asiago, old	Laguiole, old
Bagnes	Montasio, old
Cantal, old	Tête-de-Moine
Cheddar, old	

Hard cheeses

Caciacavallo	Saanen
Provolone	

Goat's-milk cheeses—late spring

Chabichou	Couhé-Vérac
Chef-Boutonne	Mothais

Mothe-Bougon	Rogeret des Cévennes
Mothe-Saint-Héray	Saint-Maixent
Picodon du Valentinois	

Processed cheeses
Sapsago spread

5. EXTREMELY PRONOUNCED OR SHARP FLAVOR

Washed-rind soft cheeses

Aisy Cendré	Gris de Lille
Boulette d'Avesnes	Puant Macéré
Fromage Fort de Bethune	

Uncooked pressed cheeses
Tomme au Gène de Marc

Goat's-milk cheeses

Arôme de Lyon au Gène de Marc	Fiore Sardo
	Niolo
Arôme de Lyon au Vin Blanc	Pecorino Romano
Broccio, old	Pecorino Siciliano

In the SUMMER, select from among the following:

1. MILD FLAVOR

Fresh cheeses

Caillebotte	Fontainebleu
Chèvre Frais	Fremgeye
Crémet	Gournay Frais
Demi-sel	Jonchée Niortaise
Double-Crème	Jonchée d'Oléron

Pie (Fromage à la Pie)	Tomme d'Aligot
Sarrasson	Triple-Crème

Bloomy-rind soft cheeses

Boursault Affiné	Explorateur
Boursin Affiné	Fin-de-siècle
Brillat-Savarin	Lucullus
Délice de Saint-Cyr	Tomme Vaudoise
Excelsior	Tomme Vaudoise au Cumin

Washed-rind soft cheeses

Colombière	Reblochon

Bleus

Bresse Bleu	Sain-Gorlon
Gorgonzola	

Uncooked pressed cheeses

Ardi-Gasna	Gouda
Beaumont	Igny (Abbaye de)
Belval (Abbaye de)	Laruns
Broodkaas	Laval (Abbaye de)
Campénéac (Abbaye de)	Meilleraye (Abbaye de la)
Chambarand (Abbaye de)	Monségur
Edam	Murol
Fontal	Saint-Paulin

Hard cheeses

Burrino	Scamorze
Emmental	

Goat's-milk cheeses or part goat's-milk cheeses

Cachat	Rigotte de Pelussin
Chèvre Frais	Saint-Marcellin
Rigotte de Condrieu	Tomme de Romans

Processed cheeses

Crème de Gruyère

Crème à Tartiner (cheese spread)

Fondu aux Noix

2. SLIGHTLY FRUITY OR SLIGHTLY PRONOUNCED FLAVOR

Fresh cheeses

Aettekees

Bibbelskäse

Boulette de Cambrai

Boursin aux Herbes

Brie de Melun Frais

Claquebitou Lyonnais

Double-Crème Aromatisé

Gérardmer

Lusignan

Mozzarella

Pierre-Qui-Vire

Sainte-Marie

Triple-Crème Aromatisé

Triple-Crème à la Cannelle

Triple-Crème au Cumin

Triple-Crème au Paprika

Bloomy-rind or natural-rind soft cheeses

Bondon de Neufchâtel

Briquette de Neufchâtel

Carré de l'Est

Chaource

Coeur de Bray

Ervy-le-Châtel

Gournay

Monsieur-Fromage, young

Petit Bessay

Saint-Gildas-des-Bois

Tarare Crème

Washed-rind soft cheeses

Chevrotin des Aravis

Pont-l'Évêque

Pont-l'Évêque (demi-)

Vacherin Fribourgeois

Bleus

Bleu de Bresse

Bleu de Gex

Bleu de Laqueville

Bleu de Sassenage

Bleu de Septmoncel

Persillés
Persillé des Aravis

Persillé du Grand-Bornand

Uncooked pressed cheeses

Amou
Ardi-Gasna
Bel Paese
Bricquebec (Abbaye de)
Cantal-Salers
Cîteaux (Abbaye de)
Échourgnac (Abbaye de)
Edam Demi-étuvé
Entrammes (Abbaye de)
Fourme de Rochefort
Gouda Demi-étuvé
Laguiole-Aubrac
Leyden with clove

Leyden with cumin
Mimolette
Mont-des-Cats (Abbaye du)
Morbier
Present
Savaron
Stracchino
Taleggio
Tamié (Abbaye de)
Tomme d'Abondance
Tomme des Beauges
Tomme des Belleville
Tomme du Revard

Hard cheeses
Burrino, semi-dry
Caciocavallo
Emmental

Provolone
Scamorze, semi-dry

Goat's-milk cheeses
Banon Chèvre
Bressan
Cabécou d'Entraygues
Cabécou de Gramat
Cabécou de Rocamadour
Cabrion de Mâcon
Chevrotin de Charolles
Chevrotin de Conne
Chevrotin de Moulins
Chevrotin de Souvigny

Dornecy
Graçay
Levroux
Lormes
Montrachet
Pouligny-Saint-Pierre
Sableau Trois Cornes
Sainte-Maure
Sancerre-Chavignol
Sancerre-Crézancy

Sancerre-Santranges
Selles-sur-Cher

Tournon-Saint-Martin
Valençay

Processed cheeses
Process Chester
Process Gruyère

Fondu Raisin
Fromage à Tartiner (cheese spread)

3. FRUITY OR PRONOUNCED FLAVOR

Fresh cheeses
Double-Crème Aromatisé

Triple-Crème au Poivre

Bloomy-rind or natural-rind soft cheese
Brie de Meaux
Camembert
Carré de l'Est
Chécy
Coulommiers
Dreux à la Feuille
Fougeru

Monsieur-Fromage
Olivet Bleu
Patay
Saint-Benoist
Vendôme Bleu
Villebarou

Washed-rind soft cheeses
Coeur d'Arras
Demi-baguette Laonnaise
Grataron d'Arêches
Mamirolle
Pavé d'Auge
Pierre-Qui-Vire

Pont-l'Évêque
Rollot
Rouy
Quart Maroilles
Saint-Remy

Bleus
Bleu de Costaros
Bleu de Loudes
Bleu de Montcenis
Bleu de Sainte-Foy
Bleu de Tignes

Bleu de Velay
Fourme d'Ambert
Fourme du Mézenc
Fourme du Montbrison
Fourme de Pierre-sur-Haute

Persillés
Persillé des Aravis   Roquefort
Persillé du Grand-Bornand

Uncooked pressed cheeses
Amou   Laruns
Anniviers   Mimolette, old
Appenzell   Montasio
Ardi-Gasna   Nantais (Fromage du Curé)
Asiago   Orrys
Bagnes   Oustet
Bethmale   Present
Cheddar   Saint-Nectaire
Chester   Taleggio
Conches   Tilsit
Edam Étuvé   Tomme Boudane
Esbareich   Tomme au Fenouil
Fontina   Toupin
Gouda Étuvé   Vachard

Hard cheeses—late summer
Beaufort   Emmental, old
Comté   Gruyère
Caciocavallo   Provolone

Goat's-milk cheeses
Brique du Forez   Fiore Sardo, young
Chabichou   Galette de la Chaise-Dieu
Chabis   Gazimelle de Burzet
Chevret or Tomme de Belley   Gien
Chevrette des Beauges   Lormes
Chevrine de Lenta   Montoire
Chèvreton d'Ambert   Montrachel
Chèvreton de Viverols   Mothais
Couhé-Vérac   Mothe-Bougon
Dornecy   Mothe-Saint-Héray

Pecorino Romano, young
Pecorino Siciliano, young
Pélardon d'Anduze
Pérardon des Cévennes
Pourly

Ramequin de Lagnieu
Ruffec
Saint-Maixent
Tomme de Combevin
Tomme de Crest

Processed cheeses
with flavorings

with sapsago

4. VERY FRUITY OR VERY PRONOUNCED FLAVOR

Bloomy-rind soft cheeses
Barberey Cendré
Bondaroy au Foin
Bouille
Brie de Melun
Brie de Montereau or Ville
   Saint-Jacques
Heiltz-le-Maurupt
Olivet Cendré

Pannes Cendré
Patay Cendré
Pithiviers au Foin
Riceys (Cendré des)
Rocroi Cendré
Vendôme Cendré
Voves Cendré

Washed-rind soft cheeses
Aisy Cendré
Baguette Laonnaise
Boulette de Pierre-Qui-Vire
Creusois-Guéret
Dauphin
Époisses
Gérômé
Gérômé anisé
Hervé
Langres Larron d'Ors
Limburger
Livarot

Maroilles
Mignon Maroilles
Mignot
Munster
Munster au cumin
Remoudou
Romatour
Saint-Florentin
Soumaintrain
Sorbais
Void

Bleus

Bleu d'Auvergne	Fourme d'Ambert
Bleu des Causses	Fourme de Montbrison
Bleu du Quercy	Fourme de Pierre-sur-Haute
Bleu de Thiezac	Stilton

Persillés

Roquefort	Tomme de Brach

Uncooked pressed cheeses

Amou	Esbareich
Anniviers	Iraty
Appenzell	Laruns
Ardi-Gasna	Montasio
Asiago	Orrys
Bagnes	Oustet
Bethmale	Sarteno
Conches	

Hard cheeses

Brindamour	Saanen
Fleur du Maquis	Sbrinz
Parmesan, very old	

Goat's-milk cheeses

Bougon	Picodon de Dieulefit
Mothe-Saint-Héray	Picodon de Saint-Agrève

5. STRONGLY PRONOUNCED OR SHARP FLAVOR

Washed-rind soft cheeses

Aisy Cendré	or Fromage Fort de Bethune
Boulette d'Avesnes	or Puant Macéré
Gris de Lille	

Bleus
possible

Persillés
possible

Hard cheeses
Sapsago

Goat's-milk cheeses
Arôme au Gène à la Lyonnaise   Niolo
Arôme de Lyon au Vin Blanc   Venaco

In the AUTUMN, select from among the following:

1. MILD FLAVOR

Fresh cheeses

Broccio Corse	Fontainebleau
Brousse du Rove	Fremgeye
Brousse de Vesubie	Gournay
Caillebotte	Jonchée
Crémet	Pie (Fromage à la Pie)
Demi-sel	Sarrasson
Double-Crème	Tomme d'Aligot

Bloomy-rind soft cheeses

Boursault Affiné	Explorateur
Boursin Affiné	Fin-de-Siècle
Brillat-Savarin	Lucullus
Caprice des Dieux	Tomme Vaudoise
Délice de Saint-Cyr	Tomme Vaudoise au Cumin
Excelsior	

Washed-rind soft cheeses
Colombière   Reblochon
Chambarand (Abbaye de)

—*late autumn*—

Vacherin d'Abondance   Vacherin Mont-d'Or
Vacherin des Beauges

Bleus
Bresse bleu   Sain-Gorlon
Gorgonzola

Uncooked pressed cheeses
Beaumont   Gouda
Belval (Abbaye de)   Igny (Abbaye de)
Broodkaas   Meilleraye (Abbaye de la)
Campénéac (Abbaye de)   Monségur
Edam   Saint-Paulin
Fontal

Hard cheeses
Burrino   Scamorze
Emmental

Goat's-milk cheeses, part goat's-milk cheeses
Rigotte de Condrieu   Saint-Marcellin
Rigotte de Pelussin   Tomme de Romans

Processed cheeses
Crème à Tartiner (cheese   Fondu aux Noix
  spread)

2. SLIGHTLY FRUITY OR SLIGHTLY PRONOUNCED FLAVOR

Fresh cheeses

Bibbelskäse
Boulette de Cambrai
Boursin aux Herbes
Brie de Melun Frais
Claquebitou
Claqueret
Double-Crème Aromatisé

Mozzarella
Tomme d'Aligot
Triple-Crème Aromatisé
Triple-Crème à la Cannelle
Triple-Crème au Cumin
Triple-Crème au Paprika

Bloomy-rind soft cheeses

Bondon de Neufchâtel
Briquette
Carré de l'Est
Chaource
Coeur de Bray
Ervy-le-Châtel

Gournay
Monsieur-Fromage, young
Olivet Bleu
Saint-Benoist
Saint-Gildas-sur-Bois
Tarare

Bleus

Bleu de Bresse
Gorgonzola

Sain-Gorlon

Uncooked pressed cheeses

Amou
Ardi-Gasna
Bel Paese
Bricquebec (Abbaye de)
Cantal-Salers
Cîteaux (Abbaye de)
Échourgnac (Abbaye de)
Edam Demi-étuvé
Laguiole-Aubrac
Leyden with cloves

Leyden with cumin
Mimolette
Mont-des-Cats (Abbaye de)
Morbier
Present
Savaron
Stracchino
Taleggio
Tamié (Abbaye de)
Tomme d'Abondance

Tomme des Beauges	Tomme des Belleville
	Tomme du Revard

Hard cheeses

Burrino	Provolone
Caciocavallo	Scamorze
Emmental	

Goat's-milk cheeses

Chabis, commercial	Selles-sur-Cher
Graçay	

Processed cheeses

Crème	Fromage à Tartiner (cheese
Fondu au Raisin	spread)

3. FRUITY OR PRONOUNCED FLAVOR

Fresh cheeses

Double-Crème Aromatisé	Triple-Crème au Poivre
Triple-Crème aux Herbes	

Bloomy-rind soft cheeses

Brie de Maux	Monsieur-Fromage
Camembert	Olivet Bleu
Carré de l'Est	Patay
Chécy	Saint-Benoist
Coulommiers	Vendôme Bleu
Dreux à la Feuille	Villebarou
Fougeru	

Washed-rind soft cheeses

Chaumont	Mamirolle
Coeur d'Arras	Pavé d'Auge
Demi-baguette Laonnaise	Pierre-Qui-Vire

Pont-l'Évêque	Rouy
Rollot	Saint-Remy

Bleus

Bleu de Gex	Bleu de Sassenage
Bleu de Laqueville	Bleu de Septmoncel

Persillés—early autumn

Persillé des Aravis	Persillé du Grand-Bornand

Uncooked pressed cheeses

Anniviers	Laguiole-Aubrac
Appenzell	Mimolette, old
Asiago	Montasio
Bagnes	Nantais (Fromage du Curé)
Cantal-Salers	Oustet
Cheddar	Quartirolo
Cheshire	Saint-Nectaire
Conches	Taleggio
Edam Étuvé	Tilsit
Esbareich	Tomme Boudane
Fontina	Tomme au Fenouil
Fourme de Rochefort	Toupin
Gouda Étuvé	Vachard

Hard cheeses

Beaufort	Emmental, old
Caciocavallo	Gruyère
Comté	Provolone

Goat's-milk cheeses

Cabécou d'Entraygues	Chevrette des Beauges
Cabriou de Bresse	Chevrette de Gramat
Cabriou de Mâcon	Chevrette de Rocamadoux
Chevert or Tomme de Belley	Chevrotin de Charolles

Chevrotin de Conne
Chevrotin de Moulins
Chevrotin de Souvigny
Dornécy
Graçay
Lormes
Levroux
Montrachet
Mothe Bougon

Mothe-Saint-Héray
Pouligny-Saint-Pierre
Sainte-Maure
Sancerre-Chavignol
Sancerre-Crézancy
Sancerre-Santranges
Tournon-Saint-Martin
Valençay

4. VERY FRUITY OR VERY PRONOUNCED FLAVOR

Bloomy-rind soft cheeses
Barberey Cendré
Boudard Gris
Boudaroy au Foin
Bouille
Brie de Melun
Brie de Montereau or Ville
Saint-Jacques
Heiltz-le-Maurupt

Olivet Cendré
Pannes Cendré
Patay Cendré
Pithiviers au Foin
Riceys (Cendré des)
Rocroi Cendré
Vendôme Cendré
Voves Cendré

Washed-rind soft cheeses
Aisy cendré
Baguette Laonnaise
Boulette de la Pierre-Qui-Vire
Creusois-Guéret
Dauphin
Époisses
Gérômé
Gérômé Anisé
Hervé
Langres
Larron d'Ors
Limburger

Livarot
Maroilles
Mignon Maroilles
Mignot
Munster
Munster au Cumin
Remoudou
Romadour
Saint-Florentin
Sorbais
Soumaintrain
Void

Bleus

Bleu d'Auvergne
Bleu des Causses
Bleu de Corse
Bleu de Quercy

Bleu de Théziac
Bleu de Tignes
Bleu de Sainte-Foy

Persillés—early autumn

Persillé des Aravis
Persillé du Grand-Bornand

Persillé du Mont-Cenis

Uncooked pressed cheeses

Amou
Ardi-Gasna

Esbareich
Laruns

Hard cheeses

Brisegout
Parmesan, old

Saanen
Sbrinz

Goat's-milk cheeses

Brique du Forez
Chabichou
Chabis, various
Chèvreton d'Ambert
Couhé-Vérac
Fiore Sardo
Galette de la Chaise-Dieu
Gazinelle de Burzet
Mothais
Picodon de Dieulefit
Picodon de Saint-Agrève

Pecorino Romano
Pecorino Siciliano
Pélardon d'Auduze
Pélardon des Cévennes
Ramequin de Lagnieu
Rogeret des Cévennes
Ruffec
Saint-Maixent
Tomme de Combovin
Tomme de Crest

5. STRONGLY PRONOUNCED OR SHARP FLAVOR

Washed-rind soft cheeses

Boulette d'Avesnes

Fromage Fort de Bethune

Gris de Lille

or Puant de Lille

Uncooked pressed cheese

Tomme au Marc

Goat's-milk cheeses

Arôme de Lyon au Gène de
    Marc

Asco

Chèvre, ripened in crocks

Fiore Sardo, old

Niolo

Pecorino Romano, old

Pecorino Siciliano, old

Sarteno

Venaco

In the WINTER, select from among the following

1. MILD FLAVOR

Fresh cheeses

Banon Frais de Brebis

Broccio

Brousse du Rove

Brousse de la Vesuve

Cabécou de Brebis

Caillebotte Cremet

Demi-sel

Double-Crème

Fontainebleau

Fremgeye

Fromage à la Pie

Gournay

Jonchée de Brebis

Suisse

Tomme Arlésienne

Triple-Crème

Bloomy-rind soft cheeses

Boursault Affiné

Boursin Affiné

Brillat-Savarin

Délice de Saint-Cyr

Excelsior

Explorateur

Fin-de-Siècle
Lucullus
Magnum

Tomme Vaudoise
Tomme Vaudoise au Cumin

Washed-rind soft cheeses
Chambarand (Abbaye de)
Colombière
Reblochon

Vacherin d'Abondance
Vacherin des Beauges
Vacherin Mont-d'Or

Bleus
Bleu de Bresse
Gorgonzola

Sain-Gorlon

Persillés
Tomme de Brach

Uncooked pressed cheeses
Beaumont
Belval (Abbaye de)
Bricquebec
Campénéac
Échourgnac
Edam (loaf) or Broodkaas
Edam, young
Fontal

Gouda, young
Igny
Laval
Meilleraye
Monségur
Murol
Saint-Paulin

Hard cheeses
Burrino
Emmental

Scamorze

Goat's-milk cheeses, part goat's-milk cheeses
Rigotte
Saint-Marcellin

Tomme de Romans
Various commercial cheeses

Processed cheeses
Crème à Tartiner

2. SLIGHTLY FRUITY OR SLIGHTLY PRONOUNCED FLAVOR

Fresh cheeses
Aettekees
Bibbelskase
Boursin aux Herbes
Brie de Melun Frais
Claquebitou Bourguignon
Claqueret Lyonnais
Double-Crème Aromatisé
Fremgeye

Gérardmer Lorraine
Mozzarella
Sainte-Marie
Triple-Crème Aromatisé
Triple-Crème à la Cannelle
Triple-Crème au Cumin
Triple-Crème au Paprika

Bloomy-rind soft cheeses
Bourdou de Neufchâtel
Briquette de Neufchâtel
Carré de l'Est
Chaource
Coeur de Braye
Ervy-le-Châtel
Gournay
Monsieur-Fromage Blanc

Olivet Bleu
Patay
Petit Bessay
Saint-Benoist
Saint-Gildas-sur-Bois
Tarare Crème
Vendôme Bleu
Villebarou

Washed-rind soft cheeses
Demi-Pont-l'Évêque

Pont-l'Évêque

Uncooked pressed cheeses
Bel Paese
Bethmale
Cantal-Salers
Cîteaux (Abbaye de)
Échourgnac (Abbaye de)
Edam Demi-étuvé

Entrammes (Abbaye de)
Fontina
Fourme de Rochefort
Gouda Demi-étuvé
Gouda with cumin
Laguiole-Aubrac

Leydin with cloves
Mimolette
Mont-des-Cats (Abbaye de)
Oustet
Present or Boerenkaas
Savaron

Stracchino
Tamié (Abbaye de)
Tomme d'Abondance
Tomme des Beauges
Tomme des Belleville
Tomme du Revard

Hard cheeses
Burrino
Emmental

Scamorze

Processed cheeses
Crème à Tartiner (cheese spreads)

3. FRUITY OR PRONOUNCED FLAVOR

Fresh cheeses
Boulette de Cambrai
Double-Crème Aromatisé

Tomme d'Aligot
Triple-Crème Poivre

Bloomy-rind soft cheeses
Brie de Meaux
Camembert
Carré de l'Est
Chaource
Chécy
Chevru
Coulommiers
Ervy-le-Châtel

Fougeru
Olivet Bleu
Patay
Petit Bessay
Saint-Benoist
Vendôme Bleu
Villebarou

Washed-rind soft cheeses
Chaumont
Coeur d'Arras

Guerbigny
Mamirole

Pavé d'Auge
Pierre-Qui-Vire
Pont-l'Évêque

Quart-Maroilles
Rollot
Rouy

Bleus
Bleu d'Auvergne
Bleu des Causses
Bleu de Gex

Bleu du Quercy
Bleu de Sassenage
Bleu de Septmoncel

Uncooked pressed cheeses
Ardi-Gasna, old
Asiago
Cantal, old
Edam Étuvé
Emmental, old
Esbareich
Fontina
Gouda Étuvé

Iraty, old
Laguiole, old
Mimolette, old
Montasio
Oustet
Tilsit
Tomme de Savoie

Hard cheeses
Appenzell
Beaufort
Caciocavallo
Comté
Emmental

Parmesan
Provolone
Sbrinz
Scamorze

Goat's-milk cheeses
Bouton-de-Culotte
Crottin de Chavignol

a few out of season

Part goat's-milk cheeses
various commercial cheeses

False goat's-milk cheeses

Rigotte   Saint-Marcellin

Processed cheese

Tomme de Romans

4. VERY FRUITY OR VERY PRONOUNCED FLAVOR

Bloomy-rind soft cheeses

Barberey Cendré   Heiltz-le-Maurupt Cendré
Bondaroy au Foin   Olivet Cendré
Bouille   Parmes Cendré
Brie de Melun   Patay Cendré
Brie de Montereau or Ville-   Pithiviers au Foin
   Saint Jacques   Riceys (Cendré des)
Chaource Affiné   Vendôme Cendré
Dreux à la Feuille

Washed-rind soft cheeses

Baguette Laonnaise   Limburger
Boulette de la Pierre-Qui-Vire   Maroilles
Chaumont   Mignon Maroilles
Dauphin   Munster
Époisses   Munster with cumin
Gérômé   Remoudou
Gérômé Anisé   Romalour
Hervé   Saint-Florentin
Langres   Sorbais
Larron d'Ors   Soumaintrain

Bleus

Bleu de Corse

Persillés

Roquefort

Uncooked pressed cheeses

Anniviers
Ardi-Gasna, old
Asiago, old
Bagnes
Bethmale, old
Cantal-Salers, old
Cheddar, old

Chester, old
Conches
Iraty
Laguiole, old
Montasio, old
Tête-de-Moine

Hard cheeses

Beaufort, old
Comté, old

Gruyère, old

Goat's-milk cheeses
a few out of season
Bouton-de-Culotte

Crottin de Chavignol

5. STRONGLY PRONOUNCED OR SHARP FLAVOR

Washed-rind soft cheeses

Boulettes d'Avesnes
Fromage Fort de Bethune

Gris de Lille *or*
Puant de Lille

Uncooked pressed cheeses
Tomme au Marc

Goat's-milk cheeses

Arôme de Lyon au Gène de
  Marc
Asco
Chèvre Confit en Pot
Fiore Sardo
Fromage Fort Malaxé en Pot

Niolo
Pecorino Romano
Pecorino Siciliano
Sarteno
Venaco

Which Cheese Should You Buy Today?

RESUME

The following cheeses may be eaten throughout the year:

Fresh white cheeses
Monastery cheeses
Industrial Bleu cheeses (for example, Bleu de Bresse)
Hard cheeses
Softened crocked cheeses
Processed cheeses

The following cheeses are limited to certain seasons:

Winter and spring
Fresh sheep's-milk cheeses
Vacherins from the low-lying valleys of Jura and Savoy

Spring and summer
Soft goat's-milk cheeses

Summer and autumn
Ash-coated cheeses (cendrés)
Farm Bleu cheeses
Traditionally made Bleu Fourmes (for example, Fourme d'Ambert)
Persillés made from sheep's milk (for example, Roquefort)
White Fourmes from the mountains (for example, Fourme de Cantal)
Mountain Tommes
Other mountain cheeses (for example, Saint-Nectaire)

Autumn, winter and spring
Fermented soft cheeses made from cow's milk (that is, all the great classic cheeses: Brie, Camembert, Livarot . . .)

CHEESE MENUS, MONTH BY MONTH

JANUARY

MAIN COURSES:
veal, chicken, fish

Tray consisting of 4 cheeses
(good for all of France)

To be tasted in ascending order of flavor, 1 to 4
1. Banon de Brebis
2. Échourgnac
3. Chaource
4. Cantal

EQUIVALENT CHEESE FOR:
North: 1. Boursin Herbes, 2. Mont-des-Cats
East, Center-East, Jura: 1. Boursin Herbes, 2. Tomme de Savoie
South, Southeast, Pyrenees: unchanged
Center: 1. Boursin, 2. Saint-Nectaire, 3. Gapron
West, Normandy: 1. Boursin, 2. Bricquebec

POSSIBLE CURIOSITIES:
Jura: Morbier
West: Jonchée d'Oleron from sheep's milk
Center: Gapron

WINES AND LIQUORS:
Beaujolais, Chinon, Loire Valley marc brandy.[1]

Tray consisting of 6 cheeses
(good for all of France)

---

[1]Local brandies usually go best with strong cheeses of the region (for example, quince brandy or black-currant brandy in the southern Pyrenees).

To be tasted in ascending order of flavor, 1 to 6

1. Banon de Brebis
2. Vacherin Mont-d'Or
3. Échourgnac
4. Chaource
5. Cantal
6. Emmental

EQUIVALENT CHEESES FOR:
North: 1. Boursin, 3. Mont-des-Cats
East, Center-east, Jura: 1. Boursin, 3. Cîteaux
South, Southeast, Alps: 1. Boursin, 3. Tomme de Savoie
Southwest, Pyrenees: 1. Boursin, 3. Échourgnac
Center: 3. Saint-Nectaire
West, Normandy: 3. Bricquebec

POSSIBLE CURIOSITIES:
West: Jonchée d'Oleron (sheep's milk)

WINES AND LIQUORS:
Beaujolais, Chinon, Loire Valley marc brandy

MAIN COURSE:
roasts, red meat, dishes of medium flavor

Tray consisting of 4 cheeses
(good for all of France)

To be tasted in ascending order of flavor, 1 to 4.

1. Explorateur
2. Present
3. Pont-l'Évêque
4. Bresse Bleu

EQUIVALENT CHEESES FOR:
North: 3. Rollot.
East, Center-East, Jura: 3. Gérômé
South, Southeast, Alps: 2. Tomme de Savoie

Southwest, Pyrenees: 2. Edam
Center: 2. Cantal
West, Normandy: 2. Bricquebec

POSSIBLE CURIOSITIES:
West: 1. Sableau or Trois Cornes

WINES AND LIQUORS:
Beaujolais-Villages, Bourgeuil, marc brandy from Touraine

Tray consisting of 6 cheeses
(good for all of France)

To be tasted in ascending order of flavor, 1 to 6.
1. Explorateur   4. Comté
2. Vacherin Mont-d'Or   5. Pont-l'Évêque
3. Present   6. Bresse Bleu

EQUIVALENT CHEESES FOR:
North: 3. Mimolette
East, Center-East, Jura: 3. Cîteaux
South, Southeast, Alps: 3. Tomme de Savoie
Southwest, Pyrenees: 3. Edam
Center: 3. Cantal
West, Normandy: 3. Bricquebec

POSSIBLE CURIOSITIES:
West: 1. Sableau or Trois Cornes

WINES AND LIQUORS:
Beaujolais-Villages, Bourgeuil, marc brandy from Touraine

MAIN COURSE
highly flavored dishes, venison

Tray consisting of 4 cheeses
(good for all of France)

To be tasted in ascending order of flavor, 1 to 4

1. Comté
2. Brie de Melun
3. Gérômé anisé
4. Roquefort

EQUIVALENT CHEESES FOR:
North: 1. Mimolette
East, Center-East, Jura: 3. Époisses
South, Southeast, Alps: 4. Niolo
Southwest, Pyrenees: 1. Bethmale
Center: 1. Cantal-Salers
West, Normandy: 3. Livarot

POSSIBLE CURIOSITIES:
Corsica: Niolo

WINES AND LIQUORS:
Côtes-du-Rhône Cornas, Cahors, Calvados

Tray consisting of 6 cheeses
(good for all of France)

To be tasted in ascending order of flavor, 1 to 6

1. Comté
2. Bondard de Neufchâtel
3. Brie de Melun
4. Pont-l'Évêque
5. Gérômé anisé
6. Roquefort

EQUIVALENT CHEESE FOR:
North: 5. Dauphin
East, Center-East, Jura: 2. Chaource

South, Southeast, Alps: 6. Niolo
Southwest, Pyrenees: 1. Bethmale.
Center: 1. Cantal-Salers
West, Normandy: 5. Livarot

POSSIBLE CURIOSITIES:
Tomme de Savoie au Marc Fermenté

WINES AND LIQUORS:
Côtes-du-Rhône Cornas, Cahors, Calvados

FEBRUARY

MAIN COURSE:
veal, chicken, fish

Tray consisting of 4 cheeses
(good for all of France)

To be tasted in ascending order of flavor, 1 to 4
1. Tomme Arlésienne   3. Saint-Marcellin
2. Vacherin Mont-d'Or   4. Beaufort

EQUIVALENT CHEESES FOR:
North: 1. Boulette de Cambrai, 4. Mimolette
East, Center-East, Jura: 1. Sainte-Marie, 4. Emmental
South, Southeast, Alps: 1. Reblochon
Southwest, Pyrenees: 4. Bethmale
Center: 4. Cantal-Salers
West, Normandy: 3. Bondon de Neufchâtel

POSSIBLE CURIOSITIES:
South: Brousse Provençale or Brousse Corse
Pyrenees: Bethmale

WHICH CHEESE TODAY

WINES AND LIQUORS:
Anjou Rosé de Cabernet, Hautes Côtes-de-Beaune Rosé, marc
  brandy from Savoy

Tray consisting of 6 cheeses
(good for all of France)

To be tasted in ascending order of flavor, 1 to 6

1. Tomme Arlésienne
2. Vacherin Mont-d'Or
3. Chambarand
4. Gouda demi-étuvé
5. Laguiole
6. Beaufort

EQUIVALENT CHEESE FOR:
North: 1. Boulette de Cambrai, 3. Mimolette
East, Center-East, Jura: 1. Sainte-Marie, 3. Cîteaux
South, Southeast, Alps: 1. Boursin, 5. Tomme de Savoie
Southwest, Pyrenees: 1. Boursin or Triple-Crème Frais, 4. Saint-
  Nectaire, 6. Emmental
West, Normandy: 1. Boursin Frais or Triple-Crème, 3. Bricque-
  bec, 6. Emmental

POSSIBLE CURIOSITIES:
Brousse Provençale or Brousse Corse

WINES AND LIQUORS:
Anjou Rosé de Cabernet, Hautes Côtes-de-Beaune Rosé, marc
  brandy from Savoy

MAIN COURSE:
roasts, red meats, dishes of medium flavor

Tray consisting of 4 cheeses
(good for all of France)

To be tasted in ascending order of flavor, 1 to 4

1. Coeur de Bray
2. Saint-Marcellin
3. Camembert
4. Sain-Gorlon

EQUIVALENT CHEESES FOR:

North: unchanged
East, Center-East, Jura: 3. Carré de l'Est
South, Southeast, Alps: unchanged
Southwest, Pyrenees: 2. Chabis Laitiers
Center: 1. Tarare
West, Normandy: unchanged

WINES AND LIQUORS:
Beaujolais-Villages, Bourgueil, marc brandy from Savoy

Tray consisting of 6 cheeses
(good for all of France)

To be tasted in ascending order of flavor, 1 to 6

1. Chambarand
2. Coeur de Bray
3. Saint-Marcellin
4. Laguiole
5. Camembert
6. Sain-Gorlon

EQUIVALENT CHEESES FOR:

North: 1. Mont-des-Cats, 4. Mimolette
East, Center-East, Jura: 4. Mimolette, 5. Carré de l'Est
South, Southeast, Alps: 4. Tomme de Savoie
Southwest, Pyrenees: 4. Bethmale
Center: 6. Bleu de Laqueuille
West, Normandy: 1. Bricquebec

WINES AND LIQUORS:
Beaujolais-Villages, Bourgueuil, marc brandy from Savoy

MAIN COURSE:
highly flavored dishes, venison

Tray consisting of 4 cheeses
(good for all of France)

To be tasted in ascending order of flavor, 1 to 4
1. Beaufort
2. Camembert
3. Langres
4. Boulette d'Avesnes

EQUIVALENT CHEESES FOR:
North: 1. Mimolette, 3. Mignon Maroilles
East, Center-East, Jura: 1. Comté, 2. Carré de l'Est, 3. Munster
South, Southeast, Alps: 4. Tomme au Marc
Southwest, Pyrenees: 4. Roquefort
Center: 1. Saint-Nectaire
West, Normandy: 3. Livarot

POSSIBLE CURIOSITIES:
Tomme au Marc

WINES AND LIQUORS:
Hermitage, Madiran, Wambrechies gin

Tray consisting of 6 cheeses
(good for all of France)

To be tasted in ascending order of flavor, 1 to 6
1. Beaufort
2. Coeur de Bray Affiné
3. Camembert
4. Bleu des Causses
5. Langres
6. Boulette d'Avesnes

EQUIVALENT CHEESES FOR:
North: 1. Mimolette, 5. Maroilles
East, Center-East, Jura: 1. Comté, 3. Carré de l'Est, 5. Munster

South, Southeast, Alps: 4. Bleu de Tignes
Southwest, Pyrenees: 6. Roquefort
Center: 1. Saint-Nectaire
West, Normandy: 5. Livarot

POSSIBLE CURIOSITIES:
Bleu de Tignes

WINES AND LIQUORS:
Hermitage, Madiran, Wambrechies gin

MARCH
MAIN COURSE:
veal, chicken, fish

Tray consisting of 4 cheeses
(good for all of France)

To be tasted in ascending order of flavor, 1 to 4
1. Triple-Crème Frais   3. Saint-Paulin
2. Saint-Gildas-des-Bois   4. Emmental

EQUIVALENT CHEESES FOR:
North: 1. Boulette de Cambrai
East, Center-East, Jura: 1. Sainte-Marie
South, Southeast, Alps: 3. Chambarand
Southwest, Pyrenees: 4. Bethmale
Center: 4. Cantal-Salers
West, Normandy: 2. Excelsior

WINES AND LIQUORS:
Bordeaux Clairet Rosé, Touraine-Amboise Rosé, marc brandy
  from Provence

Tray consisting of 6 cheeses
(good for all of France)

To be tasted in ascending order of flavor, 1 to 6
1. Triple-Crème
2. Saint-Gildas-des-Bois
3. Saint-Paulin
4. Edam Demi-étuvé
5. Emmental
6. Coulommiers

EQUIVALENT CHEESES FOR:
North: 1. Boulette de Cambrai
East, Center-East, Jura: 1. Sainte-Marie
South, Southeast, Alps: unchanged
Southwest, Pyrenees: 1. Chèvres frais
Center: 5. Cantal-Salers
West, Normandy: 2. Bondon de Neufchâtel

WINES AND LIQUORS:
Bordeaux Clairet Rosé, Touraine-Amboise Rosé, marc brandy
   from Provence

MAIN COURSE:
roasts, red meat, dishes of medium flavor

Tray consisting of 4 cheeses
(good for all of France)

To be tasted in ascending order of flavor, 1 to 4
1. Edam Demi-étuvé
2. Emmental
3. Coulommiers
4. Vendôme Bleu

EQUIVALENT CHEESES FOR:
North: unchanged
East, Center-East, Jura: 4. Pierre-Qui-Vire
South, Southeast, Alps: 4. Tomme de Romans

Southwest, Pyrenees: 4. Chabis Laitiers
Center: 4. Chèvreton d'Ambert Mi-Chèvre
West, Normandy: 3. Camembert

POSSIBLE CURIOSITIES :
early Chabis

WINES AND LIQUORS:
Bordeaux Haut-Médoc, Côtes-du-Rhône-Villages, marc brandy
from Côtes-du-Rhône

Tray consisting of 6 cheeses
(good for all of France)

To be tasted in ascending order of flavor, 1 to 6
1. Edam Demi-étuvé   4. Vendôme Bleu
2. Emmental   5. Feuille de Dreux
3. Coulommiers   6. Rollot

EQUIVALENT CHEESES FOR:
North: unchanged
East, Center-East, Jura: 4. Pierre-Qui-Vire
South, Southeast, Alps: 4. Tomme de Romans
Southwest, Pyrenees: 4. Chabis
Center: 4. Chèvreton d'Ambert Mi-Chèvre
West, Normandy: 3. Camembert

POSSIBLE CURIOSITIES:
early Chabis

WINES AND LIQUORS:
Bordeaux Haut-Médoc, Côtes-du-Rhône-Villages, marc brandy
from Côtes-du-Rhône

MAIN COURSE:
highly seasoned dishes, venison, etc.

Tray consisting of 4 cheeses
(good for all of France)

To be tasted in ascending order of flavor, 1 to 4
1. Coulommiers   3. Bleu de Septmoncel
2. Rollot   4. Gris de Lille

EQUIVALENT CHEESES FOR:
North: 3. Quart Maroilles
East, Center-East, Jura: 2. Rouy
South, Southeast, Alps: 4. Tomme au Marc
Southwest, Pyrenees: unchanged
Center: Bleu de Laqueuille
West, Normandy: 2. Petit Lisieux

WINES AND LIQUORS:
Côtes-de-Provence Rouge, Patrimonio, Cognac, fine Champagne

Tray consisting of 6 cheeses
(good for all of France)

To be tasted in ascending order of flavor, 1 to 6
1. Coulommiers   4. Chaumont
2. Rollot   5. Gris de Lille
3. Bleu de Septmoncel   6. Boulette d'Avesnes

EQUIVALENT CHEESES FOR:
North: unchanged
East, Center-East, Jura: 2. Rouy
South, Southeast, Alps: 5. Tomme au Marc
Southwest, Pyrenees: unchanged

Center: 3. Bleu de Laqueuille
West, Normandy: 4. Livarot

WINES AND LIQUORS:
Côtes-de-Provence Rouge, Patrimonio, Cognac, fine Champagne

APRIL

MAIN COURSE:
veal, chicken, fish

Tray consisting of 4 cheeses
(good for all of France)

To be tasted in ascending order of flavor, 1 to 4

1. Banon Frais
2. Belval
3. Fourme de Rochefort
4. Sainte-Maure

EQUIVALENT CHEESES FOR:
North: Boulette de Cambrai
East, Center-East, Jura: 2. Cîteaux
South, Southeast, Alps: 2. Tamié
Southwest, Pyrenees: 3. Edam
Center: 4. Chèvreton du Forez
West, Normandy: 4. Bondon de Neufchâtel

WINES AND LIQUORS:
Côtes-du-Rhône Lirac Rosé, Irancy Rosé, marc brandy from
  Champagne

Tray consisting of 6 cheeses
(good for all of France)

To be tasted in ascending order of flavor, 1 to 6

1. Banon
2. Gournay
3. Belval
4. Fourme de Rochefort
5. Tomme de Savoie
6. Sainte-Maure

EQUIVALENT CHEESES FOR:

North: 1. Boulette de Cambrai

East, Center-East, Jura: 3. Morbier, 4. Comté

South, Southeast, Alps: 3. Beaumont, 4. Emmental

Southwest, Pyrenees: 3. Saint-Paulin, 5. Bethmale

Center: 3. Savaron, 6. Chèvreton du Forez

West, Normandy: 1. Triple-Crème, 3. Saint-Paulin

WINES AND LIQUORS:

Côtes-du-Rhône Lirac Rosé, Irancy Rosé, marc brandy from
 Champagne

MAIN COURSE:

roasts, red meat, dishes of medium flavor

Tray consisting of 4 cheeses
(good for all of France)

To be tasted in ascending order of flavor, 1 to 4.

1. Murol
2. Sainte-Maure
3. Camembert
4. Monsieur-Fromage

EQUIVALENT CHEESES FOR:

North: unchanged

East, Center-East, Jura: 2. Chevrotin de Charolles

South, Southeast, Alps: 1. Tamié

Southwest, Pyrenees: 1. Échourgnac

Center: 2. Chèvreton d'Ambert

West, Normandy: unchanged

WINES AND LIQUORS:
Saumur-Champigny, Pomerol, pear brandy

Tray consisting of 6 cheeses
(good for all of France)

To be tasted in ascending order of flavor, 1 to 6.
1. Murol
2. Sainte-Maure
3. Chèvreton de Mâcon
4. Camembert
5. Monsieur-Fromage
6. Pithiviers au Foin

EQUIVALENT CHEESES FOR:
North: unchanged
East, Center-East, Jura: 1. Cîteaux
South, Southeast, Alps: 1. Beaumont
Southwest, Pyrenees: 1. Saint-Paulin
Center: 2. Chevreton d'Ambert
West, Normandy: 1. Saint-Paulin, 2. Bondard de Neufchâtel,
    6. Petit Lisieux

WINES AND LIQUORS:
Saumur-Champigny, Pomerol, brandy from the Rhône Valley

MAIN COURSE:
highly seasoned dishes, venison

Tray consisting of 4 cheeses
(good for all of France)

To be tasted in ascending order of flavor, 1 to 4
1. Camembert
2. Coeur d'Arras
3. Bleu du Quercy
4. Munster au cumin

EQUIVALENT CHEESES FOR:
North: 4. Maroilles
East, Center-East, Jura: 2. Pierre-Qui-Vire, 4. Époisses
South, Southeast, Alps: unchanged
Southwest, Pyrenees: unchanged
Center: unchanged
West, Normandy: 4. Livarot

WINES AND LIQUORS:
Hautes Côtes-de-Beaune, Côtes-Roannaises Ambierle, brandy
   from lower Armagnac

Tray consisting of 6 cheeses
(good for all of France)

To be tasted in ascending order of flavor, 1 to 6
1. Camembert   4. Bleu du Quercy
2. Pithiviers au Foin   5. Munster au Cumin
3. Coeur d'Arras   6. Roquefort

EQUIVALENT CHEESES FOR:
North: 3. Rollot, 5. Dauphin
East, Center-East, Jura: 3. Rouy, 4. Bleu de Septmoncel,
   5. Époisses
South, Southeast, Alps: 4. Bleu de Sassenage
Center: unchanged
West, Normandy: 5. Livarot

WINES AND LIQUORS:
Hautes Côtes-de-Beaune, Côtes-Roannaises Ambierle, brandy
   from lower Armagnac

MAY

MAIN COURSE:
veal, chicken, fish

Tray consisting of 4 cheeses
(good for all of France)

To be tasted in ascending order of flavor, 1 to 4
1. Cachat du Ventoux (fresh   3. Campénéac
   goat's-milk cheese)   4. Emmental
2. Pigouille

EQUIVALENT CHEESES FOR:
North: 1. Boulette de Cambrai, 3. Mont-des-Cats
East, Center-East, Jura: 3. Cîteaux
South, Southeast, Alps: 3. Tamié
Southwest, Pyrenees: 3. Échourgnac, 4. Laruns
Center: 3. Savaron, 4. Cantal-Salers
West, Normandy: 3. Bricquebec

POSSIBLE CURIOSITIES:
Jonchée Niortaise

WINES AND LIQUORS:
Côtes-du-Ventoux Rosé, Coteaux-du-Giénnois Rosé, Kirsch
   from Franche-Comté

Tray consisting of 6 cheeses
(good for all of France)

To be tasted in ascending order of flavor, 1 to 6
1. Cachat du Ventoux (fresh
   goat's-milk cheese)   4. Campénéac
2. Brie de Melun bleu   5. Emmental
3. Pigouille   6. Sainte-Nectaire

EQUIVALENT CHEESES FOR:
North: 1. Boulette de Cambrai
East, Center-East, Jura: 1. Sainte-Marie, 4. Cîteaux
South, Southeast, Alps: 4. Tamié, 6. Tomme de Savoie
Southwest, Pyrenees: 4. Échourgnac, 5. Laruns, 6. Bethmale
Center: 4. Savaron, 5. Cantal-Salers
West, Normandy: 1. Gouvinay frais

POSSIBLE CURIOSITIES:
Jonchée niortaise

WINES AND LIQUORS
Côtes-du-Ventoux Rosé, Coteaux-du-Giénnois Rosé, Kirsch
from Franche-Comté

MAIN COURSE:
roasts, red meat, dishes of medium flavor

Tray consisting of 4 cheeses
(good for all of France)

To be tasted in ascending order of flavor, 1 to 4
1. Emmental   3. Brie de Meaux
2. Bondard de Neufchâtel   4. Chabichou

EQUIVALENT CHEESES FOR:
North: 1. Mimolette
East, Center-East, Jura: 3. Brie de Champagne, 4. Chèvreton de
Mâcon
South, Southeast, Alps: 4. Tomme de Vercors
Southwest, Pyrenees: 1. Laguiole-Aubrac, 4. Cabécou de Gramat
Center: 1. Cantal-Salers, 4. Brique du Forez
West, Normandy: 3. Camembert

WINES AND LIQUORS:

Bordeaux Côtes-de-Canon Fronsac, Rully, marc brandy from Arbois

Tray consisting of 6 cheeses
(good for all of France)

To be tasted in ascending order of flavor, 1 to 6

1. Campénéac
2. Emmental
3. Bondard de Neufchâtel
4. Brie de Meaux
5. Chabichou
6. Bleu des Causses

EQUIVALENT CHEESES FOR:

North: 1. Mont-des-Cats, 2. Mimolette

East, Center-East, Jura: 4. Brie de Champagne, 5. Chèvreton de Mâcon, 6. Bleu de Septmoncel

South, Southeast, Alps: 5. Tomme de Vercors, 6. Bleu de Sassenage

Southwest, Pyrenees: 1. Échourgnac, 2. Laguiole-Aubrac, 5. Cabécou de Gramat

Center: 1. Savaron, 2. Cantal-Salers, 5. Cabécou, 6. Bleu d'Auvergne

West, Normandy: 4. Camembert

WINES AND LIQUORS:

Bordeaux Côtes-de-Canon Fronsac, Rully, marc brandy from Arbois

MAIN COURSE:
highly seasoned dishes, venison

Tray consisting of 4 cheeses
(good for all of France)

To be tasted in ascending order of flavor, 1 to 4

1. Bondard de Neufchâtel   3. Chabichou
2. Brie de Meaux   4. Bleu des Causses

EQUIVALENT CHEESES FOR:
North: unchanged
East, Center-East, Jura: 3. Chèvreton de Mâcon, 4. Bleu de Septmoncel
South, Southeast, Alps: 3. Tomme de Vercors, 4. Bleu de Sassenage
Southwest, Pyrenees: 3. Cabécou de Gramat
Center: 3. Briques du Forez, 4. Bleu d'Auvergne
West, Normandy: 2. Camembert

WINES AND LIQUORS:
Fitou des Corbières du Roussillon, Châteauneuf-du-Pape, bilberry brandy from Velay

Tray consisting of 6 cheeses
(good for all of France)

To be tasted in ascending order of flavor, 1 to 6

1. Bondard de Neufchâtel   4. Bleu des Causses
2. Brie de Meaux   5. Livarot
3. Chabichou   6. Cendré d'Aisy

EQUIVALENT CHEESES FOR:
North: 5. Maroilles
East, Center-East, Jura: 2. Brie de Champagne, 3. Tomme de Belley, 4. Bleu de Septmoncel
South, Southeast, Alps: 3. Tomme du Vercors, 4. Bleu de Sassenage
Southwest, Pyrenees: 3. Cabécou de Gramat

Center: 3. Briques du Forez, 4. Bleu d'Auvergne
West, Normandy: 2. Camembert

WINES AND LIQUORS:
Fitou des Corbières du Roussillon, Châteauneuf-du-Pape, bilberry brandy from Velay

JUNE
MAIN COURSE:
veal, chicken, fish

Tray consisting of 4 cheeses
(good for all of France)

To be tasted in ascending order of flavor, 1 to 4
1. Chèvre Frais   3. Cantal-Salers
2. Colombière or Reblochon   4. Poivre-d'Ane

EQUIVALENT CHEESES FOR:
North: Boulette de Cambrai
East, Center-East, Jura: 1. Gérardmer Frais, 4. Chèvreton de Mâcon
South, Southeast, Alps: 1. Saint-Marcellin Frais, 3. Tomme de Savoie
Southwest, Pyrenees: 3. Laguiole-Aubrac, 4. Cabécou de Gramat
Center: 2. Savaron, 4. Brique du Forez
West, Normandy: 1. Gournay Frais, 2. Pigouille

WINES AND LIQUORS:
Pinot Gris de Sancerre (Rosé), Cassis Rosé, Languedoc wine brandy

Tray consisting of 6 cheeses
(good for all of France)

To be tasted in ascending order of flavor, 1 to 6
1. Chèvre Frais   4. Cantal-Salers
2. Colombière or Reblochon   5. Poivre-d'Âne
3. Ardi-Gasna   6. Sancerre-Chavignol

EQUIVALENT CHEESES FOR:
North: 1. Boulette de Cambrai
East, Center-East, Jura: 1. Gérardmer Frais, 4. Comté,
    5. Chèvreton de Mâcon, 6. Charolles
South, South-East, Alps: 1. Saint-Marcellin Frais, 3. Tomme de
    Courchevel, 4. Beaufort, 5. Pelardon des Cévennes, 6. Picodon
    de Dieulefit
South-West, Pyrenees: 2. Échourgnac, 3. Laguiole-Aubrac,
    5. Pouligny-Saint-Pierre, 6. Cabécou de Gramat
Center: 2. Savaron, 5–6. Brique du Forez
West, Normandy: 1. Gournay Frais, 2. Pigouille

WINES AND LIQUORS:
Pinot Gris de Sancerre (Rosé), Cassis Rosé, Languedoc wine
    brandy

MAIN COURSE:
roasts, red meat, dishes of medium flavor

Tray consisting of 4 cheeses
(good for all of France)

To be tasted in ascending order of flavor, 1 to 4
1. Poivre-d'Âne   3. Brie de Melun
2. Sancerre   4. Bleu de Sassenage

EQUIVALENT CHEESES FOR:

North: 1. Boulette de Cambrai

East, Center-East, Jura: 1. Gérardmer Frais, 2. Chevreton de Mâcon, 4. Bleu de Gex

South, Southeast, Alps: 1. Cachat du Ventoux, 2. Pélardon des Cévennes

Southwest, Pyrenees: 2. Cabécou de Rocamadour, 4. Bleu des Causses

Center: 4. Bleu d'Auvergne

West, Normandy: 1. Gournay Frais

WINES AND LIQUORS:

Bordeaux Graves Martillac, Arbois Rouge de Pupillin, marc brandy from Savoy

Tray consisting of 6 cheeses
(good for all of France)

To be tasted in ascending order of flavor, 1 to 6

1. Poivre-d'Âne
2. Sancerre-Chavignol
3. Pouligny-Saint-Pierre

4. Brie de Melun
5. Bouille
6. Bleu de Sassenage

EQUIVALENT CHEESES FOR:

North: 1. Boulette de Cambrai

East, Center-East, Jura: 1. Gérardmer Frais, 2. Chèvreton de Mâcon, 3. Charolles, 6. Bleu de Gex

South, Southeast, Alps: 1. Cachat du Ventoux, 2. Pélardon des Cévennes, 3. Picodon de Dieulefit

Southwest, Pyrenees: 2–3. Cabécous de Rocamadour, 6. Bleu des Causses

Center: 6. Bleu d'Auvergne

West, Normandy: 1. Gournay Frais

WINES AND LIQUORS:
Bordeaux Graves Martillac, Arbois Rouge de Pupillin, marc
  brandy from Savoy

MAIN COURSE:
highly seasoned dishes, venison

Tray consisting of 4 cheeses
(good for all of France)

To be tasted in ascending order of flavor, 1 to 4
1. Sancerre-Chavignol   3. Saint-Florentin
2. Bouille   4. Roquefort

EQUIVALENT CHEESES FOR:
North: unchanged
East, Center-East, Jura: 1. Chèvreton de Mâcon
South, Southeast, Alps: 1. Tomme de Crest
Southwest, Pyrenees: 1. Cabécou d'Entraygues
Center: unchanged
West, Normandy: 3. Petit Lisieux

WINES AND LIQUORS:
Bandol Rouge, Côtes-du-Rhône Gigondas, Alsatian raspberry
  brandy

Tray consisting of 6 cheeses
(good for all of France)

To be tasted in ascending order of flavor, 1 to 6
1. Sancerre-Chavignol   4. Bouille
2. Pouligny-Saint-Pierre   5. Saint-Florentin
3. Brie de Melun   6. Roquefort

EQUIVALENT CHEESES FOR:

North: 5. Mignon Maroilles

East, Center-East, Jura: 1. Chèvreton de Mâcon, 2. Chevrotin de Charolles

South, Southeast, Alps: 1. Tomme de Crest, 2. Pélardon des Cévennes

Southwest, Pyrenees: 1. Cabécou d'Entraygues

Center: unchanged

West, Normandy: 5. Petit Lisieux

WINES AND LIQUORS:

Bandol Rouge, Côtes-du-Rhône Gigondas, Alsatian raspberry brandy

JULY

MAIN COURSE:
veal, chicken, fish

Tray consisting of 4 cheeses
(good for all of France)

To be tasted in ascending order of flavor, 1 to 4

1. Chèvre Frais
2. Reblochon
3. Edam Gras
4. Nantais (Fromage de Curé)

EQUIVALENT CHEESES FOR:

North: 1. Boulette de Cambrai

East, Center-East, Jura: unchanged

South, Southeast, Alps: unchanged

Southwest, Pyrenees: unchanged

Center: 4. Saint-Nectaire

West, Normandy: 1. Gournay Frais, 2. Pigouille

WINES AND LIQUORS:
Alsace Rosé, Arbois Rosé, marc brandy from the Loire Valley

Tray consisting of 6 cheeses
(good for all of France)

To be tasted in ascending order of flavor, 1 to 6
1. Chèvre Frais
2. Triple-Crème
3. Reblochon
4. Edam Gras
5. Tamié
6. Nantais (Fromage de Curé)

EQUIVALENT CHEESES FOR:
North: 1. Boulette de Cambrai, 6. Mont-des-Cats
East, Center-East, Jura: unchanged
South, Southeast, Alps: 6. Tomme de Savoie
Southwest, Pyrénées: 5. Esbareich, 6. Échourgnac
Center: 4. Cantal-Salers, 6. Saint-Nectaire
West, Normandy: 1. Gournay Frais, 3. Pigouille

WINES AND LIQUORS:
Alsace Rosé, Arbois Rosé, marc brandy from the Loire Valley

MAIN COURSE:
roasts, red meat, dishes of medium flavor

Tray consisting of 4 cheeses
(good for all of France)

To be tasted in ascending order of flavor, 1 to 4
1. Nantais (Fromage de Curé)
2. Camembert
3. Chécy
4. Sainte-Maure

EQUIVALENT CHEESES FOR:
North: 1. Mont-des-Cats
East, Center-East, Jura; 4. Chevrotin de Charolles
South, Southeast, Alps: 4. Pélardon des Cévennes
Southwest, Pyrénées: 4. Mothe-Saint-Héray
Center: 4. Chèvreton d'Ambert
West, Normandy: 3. Feuille de Dreux

WINES AND LIQUORS:
Bordeaux Côtes-de-Bourg, Moulin-à-Vent, apple brandy from
the Risle region

Tray consisting of 6 cheeses
(good for all of France)

To be tasted in ascending order of flavor, 1 to 6
1. Nantais (Fromage de   4. Chécy
   Curé)   5. Sainte-Maure
2. Esbareich   6. Saint-Remy
3. Camembert

EQUIVALENT CHEESES FOR:
North: 1. Mont-des-Cats, 2. Mimolette, 6. Quart Maroilles
East, Center-East, Jura: 5. Chevrotin de Charolles
South, Southeast, Alps: 1. Beaumont, 2. Tomme de Savoie,
   5. Pélardon des Cévennes
Southwest, Pyrénées: 1. Échourgnac, 5. Mothe-Saint-Héray
Center: 1. Saint-Nectaire, 2. Cantal-Salers, 5. Chèvreton d'Am-
   bert
West, Normandy: 3. Feuille de Dreux, 6. Petit Lisieux

WINES AND LIQUORS:
Bordeaux Côtes-de-Bourg, Moulin-à-Vent, apple brandy from
the Risle region

MAIN COURSE:
highly seasoned dishes, venison

Tray consisting of 4 cheeses
(good for all of France)

To be tasted in ascending order of flavor, 1 to 4
1. Camembert
2. Sainte-Maure
3. Saint-Remy
4. Boulette d'Avesnes

EQUIVALENT CHEESES FOR:
North: 3. Quart Maroilles
East, Center-East, Jura: 1. Carré de l'Est, 2. Chevrotin de Cha-
rolles
South, Southeast, Alps: 2. Tomme de Crest
Southwest, Pyrenees: 2. Mothe-Saint-Héray
Center: 2. Chèvreton d'Ambert
West, Normandy: 3. Petit Lisieux

WINES AND LIQUORS:
Cotes-du-Rhône Saint-Joseph, Côtes-de-Duras, plum brandy
from Quercy

Tray consisting of 6 cheeses
(good for all of France)

To be tasted in ascending order of flavor, 1 to 6
1. Camembert
2. Chécy
3. Sainte-Maure
4. Mothais
5. Saint-Remy
6. Boulette d'Avesnes

EQUIVALENT CHEESES FOR:
North: 5. Quart Maroilles
East, Center-East, Jura: 1. Carré de l'Est, 3. Chevrotin de Cha-
rolles

South, Southeast, Alps: 3. Tomme de Crest, 5. Grataron d'Arêches, 6. Tomme au Marc

Southwest, Pyrenees: 3. Mothe-Saint-Héray

Center: Chèvreton d'Ambert

West, Normandy: 2. Feuille de Dreux, 5. Petit Lisieux

WINES AND LIQUORS:

Côtes-du-Rhône Saint-Joseph, Côtes-de-Duras, plum brandy from Quercy

AUGUST

MAIN COURSE:

veal, chicken, fish

Tray consisting of 4 cheeses
(good for all of France)

To be tasted in ascending order of flavor, 1 to 4

1. Boulette de Cambrai	3. Chambarand
2. Saint-Gildas-des-Bois	4. Emmental

EQUIVALENT CHEESES FOR:

North: 3. Mont-des-Cats, 4. Mimolette

East, Center-East, Jura: 1. Sainte-Marie, 3. Cîteaux

South, Southeast, Alps: 1. Cachat du Ventoux

Southwest, Pyrenees: 1. Chabis Frais, 3. Échourgnac

Center: 1. Chèvre Frais, 4. Cantal-Salers

West, Normandy: 1. Caillebotte, 3. Bricquebec

WINES AND LIQUORS:

Hautes Côtes-de-Beaune Rosé, Bouzy Rouge, Burgundy brandy

Tray consisting of 6 cheeses
(good for all of France)

To be tasted in ascending order of flavor, 1 to 6

1. Boulette de Cambrai
2. Saint-Gildas-des-Bois
3. Chambarand
4. Emmental
5. Charolles
6. Sancerre-Crézancy

EQUIVALENT CHEESES FOR:

North: 3. Mont-des-Cats

East, Center-East, Jura: 1. Sainte-Marie, 3. Cîteaux, 5. Chèvreton de Mâcon

South, Southeast, Alps: 1. Cachat du Ventoux, 5. Pélardon des Cévennes, 6. Picodon de Valréas

Southwest, Pyrenees: 1. Chabichou Frais, 3. Échourgnac, 5. Esbareich

Center: 1. Chèvre Frais, 3. Savaron, 5. Brique du Forez, 6. Galette de la Chaise-Dieu

West, Normandy: 1. Caillebotte, 3. Bricquebec

WINES AND LIQUORS:
Hautes Côtes-de-Beaune Rosé, Bouzy Rouge, Burgundy brandy

MAIN COURSE
roasts, red meats, dishes of medium flavor

Tray consisting of 4 cheeses
(good for all of France)

To be tasted in ascending order of flavor, 1 to 4

1. Emmental
2. Coulommiers
3. Charolles (Chevrotin de)
4. Monsieur-Fromage

EQUIVALENT CHEESES FOR:

North: unchanged

East, Center-East, Jura: unchanged

South, Southeast, Alps: 4. Pélardon des Cévennes

Southwest, Pyrenees: 4. Chabichou

Center: 2. Cantal-Salers, 4. Brique du Forez
West, Normandy: 3. Camembert

WINES AND LIQUORS:
Bourdeaux-Pouillac, Beaujolais Côte-de-Brouilly, Quetsch brandy from Alsace

Tray consisting of 6 cheeses
(good for all of France)

To be tasted in ascending order of flavor, 1 to 6

1. Emmental
2. Coulommiers
3. Chaource
4. Charolles
5. Sancerre-Crézancy
6. Monsieur-Fromage

EQUIVALENT CHEESES FOR:
North: unchanged
East, Center-East, Jura: 5. Chèvreton de Mâcon
South, Southeast, Alps: 5. Pélardon des Cévennes
Southwest, Pyrenees: 1. Laruns, 4. Chabichou, 5. Ruffec
Center: 1. Saint-Nectaire, 5. Brique du Forez
West, Normandy: 2. Camembert, 3. Feuille de Dreux

WINES AND LIQUORS:
Bordeaux-Pouillac, Beaujolais Côte-de-Brouilly, Quetsch brandy from Alsace

MAIN COURSE:
highly seasoned dishes, venison

Tray consisting of 4 cheeses
(good for all of France)

To be tasted in ascending order of flavor
1. Coulommiers 3. Levroux
2. Pont-l'Évêque 4. Dauphin

EQUIVALENT CHEESES FOR:
North: unchanged
East, Center-East, Jura: 3. Tomme de Belley, 4. Munster au Cumin
South, Southeast, Alps: 3. Picodon de Saint-Agrève, 4. Tomme au Marc
Southwest, Pyrenees: 3. Ruffec
Center: 3. Brique du Forez
West, Normandy: 1. Camembert, 4. Livarot

WINES AND LIQUORS:
Mondeuse d'Arbin, Côtes-de-Provence Saint-Tropez Rouge, marc brandy from Bugey

Tray consisting of 6 cheeses
(good for all of France)

To be tasted in ascending order of flavor, 1 to 6
1. Coulommiers 4. Sancerre-Crézancy
2. Pont-l'Évêque 5. Persillé des Aravis
3. Monsieur-Fromage 6. Dauphin

EQUIVALENT CHEESES FOR:
North: unchanged
East, Center-East, Jura: 4. Tomme de Belley, 5. Bleu de Gex, 6. Munster au Cumin
South, Southeast, Alps: 4. Picodon de Saint-Agrève, 6. Tomme au Marc
Southwest, Pyrenees: 4. Ruffec, 5. Bleu du Quercy
Center: 4. Chèvreton de Viverols, 5. Bleu d'Auvergne
West, Normandy: 1. Camembert, 6. Livarot

WINES AND LIQUORS:
Mondeuse d'Arbin, Côtes-de-Provence Saint-Tropez Rouge, marc brandy from Bugey

SEPTEMBER

MAIN COURSE:
veal, chicken, fish

Tray consisting of 4 cheeses
(good for all of France)

To be tasted in ascending order of flavor, 1 to 4
1. Boursault
2. Tomme Vaudoise
3. Campénéac
4. Carré de l'Est

EQUIVALENT CHEESES FOR:
North: 1. Boulette de Cambrai, 3. Mont-des-Cats
East, Center-East, Jura: 1. Sainte-Marie, 3. Cîteaux
South, Southeast, Alps: 2. Saint-Marcellin, 3. Tamié
Southwest, Pyrenees: 2. Cabécou Frais, 3. Échourgnac
Center: 2. Sarrasson, 3. Saint-Nectaire
West, Normandy: 2. Pigouille, 4. Camembert

POSSIBLE CURIOSITIES:
Mont-d'Or de Lyon

WINES AND LIQUORS:
Rosé de Marsannay, Rosé des Riceys, marc brandy from Burgundy

Tray consisting of 6 cheeses
(good for all of France)

To be tasted in ascending order of taste, 1 to 6
1. Boursault
4. Carré de l'Est

2. Tomme Vaudoise
3. Campénéac

5. Érvy-le-Châtel
6. Comté

EQUIVALENT CHEESES FOR:
North: 1. Boulette de Cambrai, 3. Mont-des-Cats, 6. Mimolette
East, Center-East, Jura: 1. Sainte-Marie, 3. Cîteaux
South, Southeast, Alps: 2. Saint-Marcellin, 3. Tamié, 6. Emmental
Southwest, Pyrenees: 2. Cabécou Frais, 3. Échourgnac, 6. Laruns
Center: 2. Sarrasson, 3. Saint-Nectaire
West, Normandy: 2. Pigouille, 4. Camembert, 5. Bondard Affiné

WINES AND LIQUORS:
Rosé de Marsannay, Rosé des Riceys, marc brandy from Burgundy

MAIN COURSE:
roasts, red meat, dishes of medium flavor

Tray consisting of 4 cheeses
(good for all of France)

To be tasted in ascending order of flavor, 1 to 4
1. Campénéac
2. Camembert

3. Comté du Haut Jura
4. Picodon de Saint-Agrève

EQUIVALENT CHEESES FOR:
North: 1. Mont-des-Cats
East, Center-East, Jura: 4. Chevrotin de Charolles
South, Southeast, Alps: 1. Tamié, 3. Emmental
Southwest, Pyrenees: 3. Laruns, 4. Chabichou
Center: 3. Cantal-Salers, 4. Brique du Forez
West, Normandy: unchanged

WINES AND LIQUORS:
Bordeaux Puisseguin-Saint-Émilion, choice wines from Côte de
Nuits, marc brandy from Savoy

Tray consisting of 6 cheeses
(good for all of France)

To be tasted in ascending order of flavor, 1 to 6
1. Campénéac
2. Camembert
3. Comté
4. Picodon de Saint-Agrève
5. Chèvreton d'Ambert
6. Saint-Florentin

EQUIVALENT CHEESES FOR:
North: 1. Mont-des-Cats, 6. Mignon Maroilles
East, Center-East, Jura: 1. Cîteaux, 4. Chevrotin de Mâcon,
5. Tomme de Belley
South, Southeast, Alps: 1. Tamié, 3. Emmental, 4–5. Cabécous de
Rocamadour
Southwest, Pyrenees: 3. Laruns, 4. Chabichou
Center: 1. Savaron, 3. Cantal-Salers
West, Normandy: unchanged

WINES AND LIQUORS:
Bordeaux Puisseguin-Saint-Émilion, choice wines from Côte de
Nuits, marc brandy from Savoy

MAIN DISH
Highly seasoned dishes, venison

Tray consisting of 4 cheeses
(good for all of France)

To be tasted in ascending order of flavor, 1 to 4

1. Camembert
2. Picodon de Saint-Agrève
3. Bouille
4. Bleu de Laqueuille

EQUIVALENT CHEESES FOR:

North: unchanged
East, Center-East, Jura: 2. Chevrotin de Charolles, 4. Bleu de Septmoncel
South, Southeast, Alps: 2. Tomme de Crest, 4. Bleu de Sassenage
Southwest, Pyrenees: 2. Chabichou, 4. Bleu du Quercy
Center: 2. Briques du Forez, 4. Bleu de Quercy
West, Normandy: unchanged

WINES AND LIQUORS:

Hermitage, Côtes-de-Fronton, marc brandy from Alsace

Tray consisting of 6 cheeses
(good for all of France)

To be tasted in ascending order of flavor, 1 to 6

1. Camembert
2. Feuille de Dreux
3. Comté du Haut Jura
4. Picodon de Saint-Agrève
5. Bouille
6. Bleu de Laqueuille

EQUIVALENT CHEESES FOR:

North: unchanged
East, Center-East, Jura: 4. Chevrotin de Charolles, 6. Bleu de Septmoncel
South, Southeast, Alps: 4. Tomme de Crest, 6. Bleu de Sassenage
Southwest, Pyrenees: 4. Chabichou, 6. Bleu du Quercy
Center: 4. Briques du Forez
West, Normandy: unchanged

WINES AND LIQUORS:

Hermitage, Côtes-de-Fronton, marc brandy from Alsace

OCTOBER

MAIN COURSE:
veal, chicken, fish

Tray consisting of 4 cheeses
(good for all of France)

To be tasted in ascending order of flavor, 1 to 4
1. Délice de Saint-Cyr
2. Reblochon
3. Gruyère
4. Camembert

EQUIVALENT CHEESES FOR:
North: 3. Mimolette
East, Center-East, Jura: unchanged
South, Southeast, Alps: unchanged
Southwest, Pyrenees: 3. Esbareich
Center: 3. Cantal-Salers
West, Normandy: unchanged

WINES AND LIQUORS:
Muscadet Coteaux-de-la-Loire, Pécharmant, gentian brandy
from Franche-Comté

Tray consisting of 6 cheeses
(good for all of France)

To be tasted in ascending order of flavor, 1 to 6
1. Délice de Saint-Cyr
2. Ducs de Bourgogne
3. Reblochon
4. Tomme des Belleville
5. Gruyère
6. Camembert

EQUIVALENT CHEESES FOR:
North: 4. Edam

East, Center-East, Jura: 4. Morbier, 5. Comté
South, Southeast, Alps: 5. Emmental
Southwest, Pyrenees: 5. Esbareich
Center: 5. Cantal-Salers
West, Normandy: unchanged

WINES AND LIQUORS:
Muscadet Coteaux-de-la-Loire, Pécharmant, gentian brandy
  from Franche-Comté

MAIN COURSE:
roasts, red meat, dishes of medium flavor

Tray consisting of 4 cheeses
(good for all of France)

To be tasted in ascending order of flavor, 1 to 4

1. Gruyère   3. Camembert
2. Selles-sur-Cher   4. Feuille de Dreux

EQUIVALENT CHEESES FOR:
North: 1. Mimolette
East, Center-East, Jura: 1. Comté, 2. Chèvreton de Mâcon,
  3. Carré de l'Est
South, Southeast, Alps: 1. Emmental, 2. Pélardon des Cévennes
Southwest, Pyrenees: 1. Esbareich, 2. Cabécou de Gramat
Center: 1. Cantal-Salers, 2. Brique du Forez
West, Normandy: unchanged

WINES AND LIQUORS:
Beaujolais-Villages, Côte-Rôtie, marc brandy from Frontignan

Tray consisting of 6 cheeses
(good for all of France)

To be tasted in ascending order of flavor, 1 to 6

1. Gruyère
2. Selles-sur-Cher
3. Camembert
4. Feuille de Dreux
5. Vendôme Cendré
6. Fourme de Montbrison

EQUIVALENT CHEESES FOR:

North: 1. Mimolette

East, Center-East, Jura: 1. Comté, 2. Chèvreton de Mâcon, 3. Carré de l'Est, 5. Cendré des Riceys, 6. Bleu de Gex

South, Southeast, Alps: 1. Emmental, 2. Pélardon des Cévennes, 6. Bleu de Sassenage

Southwest, Pyrenees: 1. Esbareich, 2. Cabécou, 6. Bleu des Causses

Center: 1. Cantal-Salers, 2. Brique du Forez, 6. Bleu d'Auvergne

West, Normandy: unchanged

WINES AND LIQUORS:
Beaujolais-Villages, Côte-Rôtie, marc brandy from Frontignan

MAIN COURSE:
highly seasoned dishes, venison

Tray consisting of 4 cheeses
(good for all of France)

To be tasted in ascending order of flavor, 1 to 4

1. Camembert
2. Cabrions de Mâcon
3. Fourme de Montbrison
4. Munster au Cumin

EQUIVALENT CHEESES FOR:
North: 4. Dauphin
East, Center-East, Jura: 3. Bleu de Gex
South, Southeast, Alps: 2. Pélardon des Cévennes, 3. Bleu de Sassenage
Southwest, Pyrenees: 2. Mothe-Saint-Héray, 3. Bleu des Causses
Center: 2. Brique du Forez, 3. Bleu d'Auvergne
West, Normandy: 4. Livarot

WINES AND LIQUORS:
Cahors, Madiran, Mirabelle brandy from Lorraine

Tray consisting of 6 cheeses
(good for all of France)

To be tasted in ascending order of flavor, 1 to 6
1. Camembert
2. Ville-Saint-Jacques
3. Cabrions de Mâcon
4. Vendôme Cendré
5. Fourme de Montbrison
6. Munster au Cumin

EQUIVALENT CHEESES FOR:
North: 6. Dauphin
East, Center-East, Jura: 4. Riceys Cendré, 5. Bleu de Gex
South, Southeast, Alps: 3. Picodon de Dieulefit, 5. Bleu de Sassenage
Southwest, Pyrenees: 3. Mothe-Saint-Héray, 5. Bleu des Causses
Center: 2. Brique du Forez, 5. Bleu d'Auvergne
West, Normandy: 6. Livarot

WINES AND LIQUORS:
Cahors, Madiran, Mirabelle brandy from Lorraine

NOVEMBER

MAIN COURSE:
veal, chicken, fish

Tray consisting of 4 cheeses
(good for all of France)

To be tasted in ascending order of flavor, 1 to 4
1. Brousse de Provence
2. Caprice des Dieux
3. Vacherin Mont-d'Or
4. Tomme de Savoie

EQUIVALENT CHEESES FOR:
North: 1. Boulette de Cambrai, 3. Mont-des-Cats
East, Center-East, Jura: 3. Vacherin des Beauges
South, Southeast, Alps: unchanged
Southwest, Pyrenees: 4. Bethmale
Center: 4. Saint-Nectaire
West, Normandy: 2. Excelsior

WINES AND LIQUORS:
Chignin-Bergeron, Gamay de Chantagne, marc brandy from Auvergne

Tray consisting of 6 cheeses
(good for all of France)

To be tasted in ascending order of flavor, 1 to 6
1. Brousse de Provence
2. Boursin
3. Caprice des Dieux
4. Vacherin Mont-d'Or
5. Igny
6. Tomme de Savoie

EQUIVALENT CHEESES FOR:
North: 1. Boulette de Cambrai, 5–6. Mont-des-Cats
East, Center-East, Jura: 5. Cîteaux, 6. Morbier

South, Southeast, Alps: 4. Vacherin des Beauges, 5. Tamié
Southwest, Pyrenees: 5. Échourgnac, 6. Bethmale
Center: 6. Saint-Nectaire
West, Normandy: 3. Excelsior, 5. Campénéac

WINES AND LIQUORS:
Chignin-Bergeron, Gamay de Chantagne, marc brandy from Auvergne

MAIN COURSE:
roasts, red meat, dishes of medium flavor

Tray consisting of 4 cheeses
(good for all of France)

To be tasted in ascending order of flavor, 1 to 4
1. Beaufort
2. Brie de Meaux
3. Olivet Bleu
4. Montrachet

EQUIVALENT CHEESES FOR:
North: unchanged.
East, Center-East, Jura: 1. Comté, 2. Brie de Meuse
South, Southeast, Alps: 4. Pélardon des Cévennes
Southwest, Pyrenees: 4. Chabichou
Center: 4. Sancerre
West, Normandy: 2. Camembert

WINES AND LIQUORS:
Médoc Moulis, Savigny-lès-Beaune, elderberry brandy from Alsace

Tray consisting of 6 cheeses
(good for all of France)

To be tasted in ascending order of flavor, 1 to 6
1. Beaufort
2. Brie de Meaux
3. Olivet Bleu
4. Bondard
5. Montrachet
6. Mothe-Saint-Héray

EQUIVALENT CHEESES FOR:
North: unchanged.
East, Center-East, Jura: 1. Comté, 2. Brie de Meuse
South, Southeast, Alps: 5. Pélardon des Cévennes, 6. Picodon de Dieulefit
Southwest, Pyrenees: 1. Esbareich, 5. Chabichou
Center: 1. Cantal-Salers, 6. Brique du Forez
West, Normandy: 2. Camembert

WINES AND LIQUORS:
Medoc Moulis, Savigny-lès-Beaune, elderberry brandy from Alsace

MAIN COURSE:
highly seasoned dishes, venison

Tray consisting of 4 cheeses
(good for all of France)

To be tasted in ascending order of flavor, 1 to 4
1. Brie de Meaux
2. Mothe-Saint-Héray
3. Époisses
4. Roquefort

EQUIVALENT CHEESES FOR:
North: 3. Sorbais
East, Center-East, Jura: 1. Brie de Meuse (laitier), Chevrotin de Charolles

South, Southeast, Alps: 2. Pélardon des Cévennes, 4. Bleu de Corse

Southwest, Pyrenees: unchanged

Center: 4. Tomme de Brach

West, Normandy: 1. Camembert, 3. Livarot

WINES AND LIQUORS:
Côtes-du-Rhône-Vacqueyras, Roussillon-des-Aspres, Gewürztraminer marc brandy from Alsace

Tray consisting of 6 cheeses
(good for all of France)

To be tasted in ascending order of flavor, 1 to 6

1. Brie de Meaux
2. Bondard
3. Olivet Bleu
4. Mothe-Saint-Héray
5. Époisses
6. Roquefort

EQUIVALENT CHEESES FOR:

North: 3. Sorbais

East, Center-East, Jura: 1. Brie de Meuse (laitier), Chevrotin de Charolles

South, Southeast, Alps: 2. Pélardon des Cévennes, 4. Bleu de Corse

Southwest, Pyrenees: unchanged

Center: 4. Cabrio du Forez, 6. Tomme de Brach

West, Normandy: 1. Camembert, 3. Livarot

WINES AND LIQUORS:
Côte-du-Rhône Vacqueyras, Roussillon-des-Aspres, Gewürztraminer marc from Alsace

DECEMBER

MAIN COURSE:
veal, chicken, fish

Tray consisting of 4 cheeses
(good for all of France)

To be tasted in ascending order of flavor, 1 to 4
1. Broccio Corse
2. Magnum
3. Échourgnac
4. Beaufort

EQUIVALENT CHEESES FOR:
North: 1. Boulette de Cambrai, 3. Mont-des-Cats, 4. Mimolette
East, Center-East, Jura: 3. Cîteaux, 4. Comté
South, Southeast, Alps: 3. Tamié
Southwest, Pyrenees: 1. Jonchée d'Oléron
Center: 3. Saint-Nectaire, 4. Cantal-Salers
West, Normandy: unchanged

WINES AND LIQUORS:
Coteaux-d'Auvergne-Chanturgue, Coteaux-de-Marigny-Brizay,
   Kirsch from Blanc

Tray consisting of 6 cheeses
(good for all of France)

To be tasted in ascending order of flavor, 1 to 6
1. Broccio Corse
2. Magnum
3. Vacherin des Beauges
4. Échourgnac
5. Laguiole-Aubrac
6. Beaufort

EQUIVALENT CHEESES FOR:
North: 1. Boulette de Cambrai, 4. Mont-des-Cats, 5. Mimolette
East, Center-East, Jura: 4. Cîteaux, 6. Comté
South, Southeast, Alps: 4. Tamié
Southwest, Pyrenees: 1. Jonchée d'Oléron, 5. Esbareich
Center: 4. Saint-Nectaire
West, Normandy: unchanged

WINES AND LIQUORS:
Coteaux-d'Auvergne-Chanturgue, Coteaux-de-Marigny-Brizay,
   Kirsch from Blanc

MAIN COURSE:
roasts, red meat, dishes of medium flavor

Tray consisting of 4 cheeses
(good for all of France)

To be tasted in order of ascending flavor, 1 to 4
1. Échourgnac   3. Tomme de Romans
2. Beaufort   4. Camembert

EQUIVALENT CHEESES FOR:
North: 1. Mont-des-Cats, 2. Mimolette
East, Center-East, Jura: 1. Cîteaux, 2. Comté
South, Southeast, Alps: 1. Tamié
Southwest, Pyrenees: 2. Esbareich
Center: 2. Cantal-Salers
West, Normandy: unchanged

WINES AND LIQUORS:
Bordeaux Haut-Médoc Saint-Estèphe, Bourgogne Saint-Aubin,
    sorb brandy from Alsace

Tray consisting of 6 cheeses
(good for all of France)

To be tasted in ascending order of flavor, 1 to 6
1. Échourgnac
2. Beaufort
3. Tomme de Romans
4. Camembert
5. Brie de Melun
6. Bresse Bleu

EQUIVALENT CHEESES FOR:
North: 1. Mont-des-Cats, 2. Mimolette
East, Center-East, Jura: 1. Cîteaux, 2 Comté, 5. Saint-Florentin
South, Southeast, Alps: 1. Tamié
Southwest, Pyrenees: 2. Esbareich, 6. Bleu du Quercy
Center: 6. Bleu de Laqueuille
West, Normandy: 5. Bondard Gris

WINES AND LIQUORS:
Bordeaux Haut-Médoc Saint-Estèphe, Bourgogne Saint-Aubin,
    sorb brandy from Alsace

MAIN COURSE:
highly seasoned dishes, venison

Tray consisting of 4 cheeses
(good for all of France)

To be tasted in ascending order of flavor, 1 to 4
1. Camembert
2. Fourme d'Ambert
3. Rollot
4. Munster

EQUIVALENT CHEESES FOR:
North: 4. Maroilles
East, Center-East, Jura: 2. Bleu de Septmoncel, 3. Soumaintrain
South, Southeast, Alps: 2. Bleu de Sassenage
Southwest, Pyrenees: 2. Bleu du Quercy
Center: unchanged
West, Normandy: unchanged

WINES AND LIQUORS:
Costières du Gard, Côtes-de-Villaudric, white West Indian rum

Tray consisting of 6 cheeses
(good for all of France)

To be tasted in ascending order of flavor, 1 to 6
1. Camembert
2. Brie de Melun
3. Fourme d'Ambert
4. Rollot
5. Munster
6. Roquefort

EQUIVALENT CHEESES FOR:
North: 5. Dauphin.
East, Center-East, Jura: 3. Bleu de Septmoncel, 4. Soumaintrain
South, Southeast, Alps: 3. Bleu de Sassenage
Southwest, Pyrenees: 3. Bleu du Quercy
Center: unchanged
West, Normandy: 2. Bondard Gris

WINES AND LIQUORS:
Costières du Gard, Côtes-de-Villaudric, white rum from West
  Indies

Month-by-Month Cheese Selection

JANUARY

As cheeses for the month of January I suggest (listed in the order in which they are to be tasted):

CHEESES	WINES
Banon de Brebis Frais	
Excelsior	Beaujolais
Explorateur	or Chinon
Vacherin Mont-d'Or	
Échourgnac (Abbaye de)	
Present	Beaujolais-Villages
Cantal	or Bourgeuil
Comté	or Saint-Émilion
Bondard de Neufchâtel	
Chasource	
Brie de Melun	Cahors
Pont-l'Évêque	Côtes-du-Rhône Cornas
Bresse Bleu	Côtes-du-Rhône
Gérômé Anisé	Vin-Sobres
Dauphin	
Roquefort	
Niolo	

The wines of the first group may be replaced by white wines:
Bordeaux Graves Blancs (Leognan)
Coteaux-d'Ancenis

Loire Valley marc brandy
Calvados apple brandy

FEBRUARY

As cheeses for the month of February I suggest (listed in the order in which they are to be tasted):

CHEESES	WINES
Brousse de la Vesubie	
Tomme Arlésienne	
Vacherin Mont-d'Or	Anjou Rosé de Cabernet
Chambarand (Abbaye de)	Hautes Côtes-de-Beaune Rosé
Gouda Demi-étuvé	
Saint-Marcellin	
Coeur de Bray	
Laguiole	Mondeuse d'Arbin
Beaufort	Bourgogne Passe-tout-grain
Camembert	
Olivet Bleu	
Brie de Montereau	
Pierre-Qui-Vire	
Bleu des Causses	
Langres	Hermitage
Maroilles	Madiran
Chèvre Macéré en pot	
Boulette d'Avesnes	

The wines of the first group may be replaced by white wines:
Anjou Coteaux-de-la-Loire
Pouilly-sur-Loire (Chasselas)

Marc brandy from Savoy
Wambrechies gin

MARCH

As cheeses for the month of March I suggest (listed in the order in which they are to be tasted):

CHEESES	WINES
Triple-Crème Frais	
Fin-de-Siècle	
Saint-Gildas-des-Bois	Bordeaux Clairet Rosé
Saint-Paulin (Bonbel)	Touraine-Amboise Rosé
Cîteaux (Abbaye de)	
Edam Demi-étuvé	
Emmental	
Montasio	
Coulommiers	
Vendôme Bleu	Bordeaux Haut-Médoc
Feuille de Dreux	Côte-Rôtie
Rollot	
Bleu de Septmoncel	
Baguette Laonnaise	
Chaumont	Côtes-de-Provence Rouge
Gris Puant de Lille	Patrimonio
Roquefort	
Boulette d'Avesnes	

The wines of the first group may be replaced by white wines:
Muscadet Sèvre-et-Maine
Bourgogne Mâcon-Lugny or Mâcon-Vire

Marc brandy from Provence
Marc brandy from Côtes du Rhône
Fine champagne brandy

APRIL

As cheeses for the month of April I suggest (listed in the order in which they are to be tasted):

CHEESES	WINES
Banon Frais	
Gournay Frais	Lirac rosé
Tomme Vaudoise	Irancy rosé
Belval (Abbaye de)	
Murol	
Fourme de Rochefort	
Tomme de Savoie	
Sainte-Maure	
Chèvreton de Mâcon	Saumur Champigny
Camembert	Pomerol
Monsieur-Fromage	
Gapron	
Chécy	Côtes-Roannaises
Pithiviers au Foin	(Ambierle, Renaison)
Coeur d'Arras	Hautes Côtes-de-Beaune
Bleu du Quercy	(Dezize, Cheilly and
Munster au Cumin	Sampigny-lès-Maranges)
Roquefort	

The wines of the first group may be replaced by white wines:
Roussette de Seyssel
Pinot d'Alsace

Marc brandy from Champagne
Pear brandy
Bas armagnac

MAY

As cheeses for the month of May I suggest (listed in the order in which they are to be tasted):

CHEESES	WINES
Chèvre Frais (Cachat du Ventoux)	
Brie de Melun Bleu	Côtes-du-Ventoux Rosé
Tarare	Coteaux-du-Giénnois Rosé
Explorateur	
Pigouille	
Laruns	
Emmental	
Saint-Nectaire	Bordeaux Côtes-de-Canon
Rigotte de Condrieu	Fronsac
Bondard de Neufchâtel	Rully (Bourgogne)
Chaource	
Brie de Meaux	
Selles-sur-Cher	
Chabichou	Fitou des Corbières
Bleu des Causses	Châteauneuf-du-Pape
Livarot	
Cendré d'Aisy	

Kirsch from Franche-Comté
Marc brandy from Arbois
Bilberry brandy from Velay

JUNE

As cheeses for the month of June I suggest (listed in the order in which they are to be tasted):

CHEESES	WINES
Chèvre Frais	
Gérardmer Frais	
Colombière	Pinot Gris de Sancerre
Ardi-Gasna	Cassis Rosé
Tomme de Courchevel	
Cantal-Salers	
Poivre-d'Âne Affiné	
Sancerre-Chavignol	
Pouligny-Saint-Pierre	Bordeaux Graves Martillac
Brie de Melun	Arbois Rouge Pupillin
Bouille	
Bleu de Sassenage	
Persillé des Aravis	
Saint-Florentin	
Riceys Cendré	Provence Bandol Rouge
Munster	Côtes-du-Rhône Gigondas
Roquefort	Rouge
Niolo	

The wines of the first group and of the second group as far as Pouligny-Saint-Pierre may be replaced by white wines:

Bordeaux Entre-Deux-Mers Sec
Jurançon Sec

Languedoc brandy
Marc brandy from Savoy
Raspberry brandy from Alsace (framboise)

JULY

As cheeses for the month of July I suggest (listed in the order
in which they are to be tasted):

CHEESES	WINES
Chèvre Frais	
Triple-Crème Boursin	
Tomme Vaudoise	Alsace Rosé
Reblochon	Arbois Rosé
Edam Gras	
Tamié (Abbaye de)	
Nantais (Fromage du Curé)	
Esbareich	
Camembert	
Chécy	Bordeaux Côtes-de-Bourg
Sainte-Maure	Moulin-à-Vent
Mothais	
Rogeret des Cévennes	
Saint-Remy	
Mignon Maroilles	Côtes-du-Rhône Saint-Joseph
Bleu du Velay	Côtes-de-Duras
Boulette d'Avesnes	

The wines of the first group may be replaced by white wines:

Abymes de Myans
Bourgogne Aligoté

Marc brandy from the Loire Valley
Apple brandy from the Risle region
Plum brandy from Quercy

AUGUST

As cheeses for the month of August I suggest (listed in the order in which they are to be tasted):

CHEESES	*WINES*
Boulette de Cambrai	
Saint-Gildas-des-Bois	
Lucullus	
Saint-Paulin (Port-Salut)	Hautes Côtes-de-Beaune Rosé
Chambarand (Abbaye de)	Bouzy Rouge
Emmental	Mondeuse d'Arbin
Mimolette	
Pont-l'Évêque	
Tomme des Beauges	
Coulommiers	
Chaource	
Monsieur-Fromage	Bordeaux Pauillac
Charolles	Beaujolais Côte-de-Brouilly
Sancerre-Crézancy	Côtes-de-Provence Saint-Tro-
Leuroux	pez Rouge
Persillé des Aravis	
Langres	
Dauphin	

The wines of the first group may be replaced by white wines:

Côtes-du-Jura or Arbois Blanc
Saint-Péray (still)

Fine Bourgogne brandy
Quetsch brandy from Alsace
Marc brandy from Bugey

SEPTEMBER

As cheeses for the month of September I suggest (listed in the order in which they are to be tasted):

CHEESES	WINES
Double-Crème	
Boursault Affiné	
Tomme Vaudoise	
Beaumont	
Campénéac (Abbaye de)	Rosé de Marsannay
Camembert	Rosé des Riceys
Ervy-le-Châtel	
Feuille de Dreux	
Comté Haut-Jura	
Picodon de Saint-Agrève	
Saint-Maixent	choice wines of Côte-de-Nuit
Chèvreton d'Ambert	
Chevrotin des Aravis	
Bouille	
Bleu de Laqueuille	Hermitage
Saint-Florentin	Côtes-de-Fronton
Voves Cendré	
Boulette d'Avesnes	

The wines of the first group may be replaced by white wines:

Still Champagne wines
Sylvaner from Alsace

Burgundy marc brandy
Marc brandy from Savoy or Alsace

OCTOBER

As cheeses for the month of October I suggest (listed in the order in which they are to be tasted):

CHEESES	WINES
Chèvre Frais	
Délice de Saint-Cyr	
Ducs de Bourgogne	Muscadet Coteaux-de-la-Loire
Reblochon	Chablis Premier Cru
Tomme des Belleville	
Gruyère	
Camembert	
Saint-Benoist	
Feuille de Dreux	Beaujolais-Villages
Ville-Saint-Jacques	Côte-Rôtie
Cabécou de Gramat	Pécharmant
Cabrions de Mâcon	
Selles-sur-Cher	
Vendôme cendré	
Fourme de Montbrison	Cahors
Langres	Madiran
Munster au Cumin	Patrimonio
Niolo	

gentian brandy from Franche-Comté
marc brandy from Frontignan
Mirabelle from Lorraine

NOVEMBER

As cheeses for the month of November I suggest (listed in the order in which they are to be tasted):

CHEESES	*WINES*
Demi-sel or Brousse Boursin	Chignin-Bergeron
Caprice-des-Dieux	Gamay de Chautagne
Vacherin Mont-d'Or	(in Switzerland: Neufchâtel
Igny (Abbaye de)	Perlant, Dorin Vaudois)
Tomme de Savoie	Fendant du Valais
Cantal-Salers	
Beaufort	
Brie de Meaux	Haut-Médoc Moulis
Olivet Bleu	Savigny-lès-Beaune
Bondard	
Montrachet	
Charolles	
Mothe-Saint-Héray	Côtes-du-Rhône Vacqueyras
Époisses	red wines from Roussillon-des-
Bleu de Tignes	Aspres with the Roquefort
Roquefort	and afterwards a good port
Venaco	is recommended

marc from Auvergne
elderberry brandy from Alsace (sureau)
Gewürztraminer marc from Alsace

DECEMBER

As cheeses for the month of December I suggest (listed in the order in which they are to be tasted):

CHEESES	WINES
Broccio Corse	
Magnum	
Vacherin des Beauges	Coteaux-d'Auvergne
Échourgnac (Abbaye de)	Chanturgue Rosés
Laguiole-Aubrac	Coteaux-de-Marigny-Brizay
Beaufort	Rosé
Tomme de Romans	
Sancerre-Chavignol	
Mothe-Bougon	
Camembert	
Brie de Melun	Costières-du-Gard
Bresse Bleu	Côtes-de-Villaudric
Fourme d'Ambert	
Rollot	If available, a Barolo is
Chaumont	recommended.
Munster	
Roquefort	
Tomme au Marc (fermenté)	

Other white wines:

Sauvignon de Marigny-Brizay (Vienne)
Sauvignon de Saint-Bris (Yonne)

Kirsch from Blanc
Sorb apple brandy from Alsace
White rum

What to Know about Climate and Pasturage

EARLIEST GRASS GROWTH
IN THE DIFFERENT REGIONS OF FRANCE

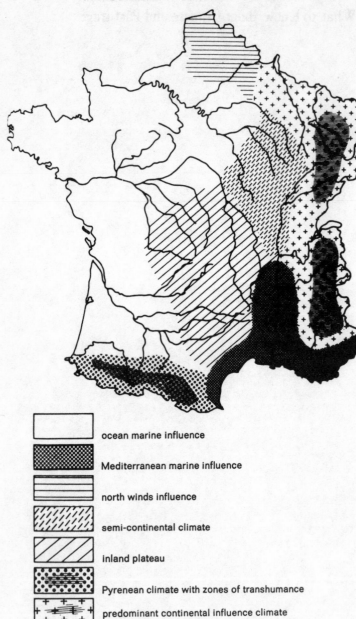

ocean marine influence

Mediterranean marine influence

north winds influence

semi-continental climate

inland plateau

Pyrenean climate with zones of transhumance

predominant continental influence climate
with zones of transhumance

Appearance of the first cheeses from the pastures at various times of the year

From Christmas to Feb. 15	First fresh sheep's-milk cheeses from the South of France (Brousse, Tomme de Camargue).
From Feb. 15 to March 31	Peak season for sheep's-milk cheeses. First fresh goat's-milk cheeses. First Tommes from the lower mountains.
From April 1 to May 15	First cheeses with bloomy rinds (Camembert, Brie, Coulommiers, Neufchâtel). All half-drained pure goat's-milk cheeses. End of fresh sheep's-milk cheeses.
From May 15 to July 1	First washed-rind cheeses (Rollot, Petit Munster, Petit Maroilles). Peak season for lowland goat's-milk cheeses (Levroux, Valencay, Selles-sur-Cher). First uncooked pressed cheeses from the high mountains. The first of the young Roqueforts (aged for three months).
Beginning of July to Aug. 15	Ash-coated cheeses (cendrés) prepared for the harvesting. First uncooked pressed cow's-milk cheeses from lower mountain regions (Saint-Nectaire, Esbareich, etc.). First sheep's-milk cheeses from the

lower mountain regions (Bethmale, Laruns).

First washed-rind cow's-milk cheeses (Maroilles, Livarot, Munster, Époisses).

First appearance of goat's-milk Tommes from the mountains (Grataron d'Arêches, Chevrotins).

First of the Bleus from the midmountain regions (Gex, Septmoncel).

End of summer, Aug. 15 to the end of September	Peak season for internal mold cheeses from the midmountain regions (Bleu de Gex, Bleu de Septmoncel, Fourme d'Ambert, etc.). All goat's-milk cheeses. First large cheeses from the high mountains. Peak season for Bleus from lower mountain regions (Causses, Auvergne, Quercy). Peak season for all washed-rind cheeses.
Beginning of autumn, Sept. 30 to Nov. 15	Hard cheeses from the midmountain regions (Comté, Emmental). Peak season for internal-mold cheeses from lower mountain regions. Continued availability of washed-rind soft cheeses. Return of bloomy-rind soft cheeses. End of the pure goat's-milk cheeses.

End of autumn, beginning of winter, Nov. 15 to the end of December	Mountain cheeses of large size (various Gruyères, Comté, Beaufort, Emmental).
	New peak season for bloomy-rind and washed-rind soft cheeses.
	Soft cheeses from the midmountain regions, return from summer pastures (Vacherin).
	Crocked macerated goat's-milk cheeses.
	Fromage fort (Mont Ventous, Lyonnais).
	End of uncooked pressed sheep's-milk cheeses from the mountains.

Grass does not appear at the same time throughout France. In one place spring comes early; in another, late.

In lowland areas where there is a moderating influence on the climate from the sea, the grass begins to grow as soon as the worst part of the winter is over.

Farther inland in the regions open to winds from the east and north, the ground remains frozen for some time.

In the mountains the herds and flocks follow the retreat of the snows, reaching the high pastures no earlier than the month of May.

From this we can arrive at a rough understanding of the geography of the first cheeses made with milk from the pastures, first the ones from the West, Île-de-France, the South; then those from Burgundy, Franche-Comté, Flanders, etc.

Next comes the flowering of the meadows, slowly where the spring has come early, impatiently and explosively where it has been late in coming. In Ploermel the buttercups open at Easter and in June the bluebells open in Valloires.

Here is a timetable for the pasture lands of France (the timetable may sometimes be off by a few days because of fluctuations in the average temperatures of the season).

Dates for the first appearance of grass in the various regions of France

Regions	Sprouting	Flowering of the meadows	Second growth
FLANDERS	beginning of May	end of May	end of September beginning of October
ARTOIS	beginning of May	end of May	end of September beginning of October
PICARDY	beginning of May	end of May	end of September beginning of October
ILE-DE-FRANCE	beginning of April	end of April	mid-September
ORLEANAIS	beginning of April	end of April	mid-September
NORMANDY	beginning of April	end of April	beginning of September
MAINE	beginning of April	end of April	mid-September
ANJOU	end of March	mid-April	mid-September
TOURAINE	end of March	mid-April	mid-September
BRITTANY	beginning of April	end of April	beginning of September
AUNIS	end of March	end of April	mid-September
SAINTONGE	end of March	end of April	mid-September
ANGOUMOIS	end of March	end of April	mid-September
POITOU	end of March	end of April	mid-September
BERRI	mid-April	mid-May	mid-September
NIVERNAIS	end of April	end of May	mid-September
AUVERGNE	beginning of June	end of June	beginning of September
BOURBONNAIS	mid-April	mid-May	mid-September
LIMOUSIN	mid-April	mid-May	mid-September
MARCHE	mid-April	mid-May	mid-September
GUYENNE	beginning of April	beginning of May	beginning of November
GASCONY	beginning of April	beginning of May	mid-September
PAYS BASQUE (mountains)	end of May	end of June	beginning of September

BEARN	mid-May	mid-June	beginning of September
COMTE DE FOIX	beginning of June	mid-June	end of August
ROUSSILLON	end of March	end of April	beginning of September
LANGUEDOC	end of March	end of April	beginning of September
CEVENNES	beginning of June	end of June	beginning of September
HAUTE PROVENCE	end of March	end of April	beginning of September
BASSE PROVENCE	mid-March	mid-April	beginning of September
CORSICA (lowlands)	mid-March	mid-April	end of September
DAUPHINE (valleys)	mid-May	mid-June	beginning of September
DAUPHINE (mountains)	beginning of June	end of June	beginning of September
SAVOY (valleys)	mid-May	mid-June	beginning of September
SAVOY (mountains)	beginning of June	mid-June	beginning of September
FRANCHE-COMTE (lowlands)	end of May	end of June	beginning of September
FRANCHE-COMTE (mountains)	beginning of June	mid-June	beginning of September
BURGUNDY	end of April	end of May	mid-September
CHAMPAGNE HUMIDE	beginning of May	end of May	mid-September
CHAMPAGNE POUILLEUSE	mid-May	mid-June	mid-September
ALSACE	beginning of June	end of June	end of September
LORRAINE	beginning of June	end of June	end of September
VOSGES (eastern slope)	mid-June	end of June	end of August
VOSGES (western slope)	mid-May	mid-June	beginning of September

Dictionary of Cheeses

There has been cheese since the earth was new.

The first drop of milk that formed in the breast of the first female mammal was the progenitor of Camemberts, Roqueforts and other Gorgonzolas.

All that was necessary was the passage of time.

All cheese is a matter of patience. But also of imagination and skillful knowledge.

Attila and his Mongol horsemen, driven by their need of space, were nourished by cheese made from the milk of their mares.

The ancient Greeks believed cheese to be an antidote for poison. Empedocles was the first known to mention the curdling of milk.

But the Romans, who lingered long over their repasts, were already smoking cheeses brought to Rome from all parts of the empire.

Italians of high Adige pastures produced the first sheep's-milk cheese; the Greeks, the first goat's-milk cheese.

In Gaul, as men hunted across the countryside of Arvernes, they undoubtedly found hard mountain cheeses, forgotten by shepherds, as well as Cabécous de Rocamadour and, almost certainly, Roquefort.

Pliny knew Roquefort in the first century of the Christian era.

Charlemagne, however, was unfamiliar with it until, on his way home from Spain, he was invited by the Bishop of Vabres to share a frugal meal. It was Lent, and the bishop had only some Roquefort and bread to offer.

The Emperor sat down at the table and tried conscientiously to pick the mold from a cheese he undoubtedly thought to be overripe at best. The bishop assured him that the mold was the better part of the cheese.

Charlemagne tasted the cheese, mold and all; liked it, and left for Aix-la-Chapelle that evening with a chest full of Roquefort cheeses.

A Chartist document dated 1000, the year of a great plague, attests the reputation then of Roquefort.

Later, when the Popes resided in Avignon, they received annual tributes of Roquefort brought on mule-back.

But it was not until August 1, 1666, that the Parliament of Toulouse decreed that only cheeses cured in the caves of Roquefort could be called Roquefort.

Rabelais praised the cheese in a letter to the Cardinal of Bellay. Brantôme mentions Roquefort frequently in his writings.

Louis XV was unreserved in his praise, and his table was never without Roquefort during its best season, which he considered to be October.

Casanova expressed his fervent appreciation in his *Mémoires:* "Oh! but Chambertin and Roquefort are excellent foods to revive love and bring to a quick consummation a newborn love."

The Carolingians of the dark Middle Ages left no records of cheese.

Francis I was painted seated at a table heaped with foods, but I have never been able to identify any cheeses.

Charles of Orléans is known to have made a custom of giving his favorite ladies strong cheeses as New Year's gifts.

Louis XIV had cheeses on his table. To gain the favors of the Sun King, la Montespan, it is said, devised and prepared cheese sauces for him.

It is apparently in this period that the first standardized manufacture and commercial marketing of cheese was developed, especially in the areas around Paris.

Until then, cheese had been more of a basic food than a dessert, which it became with Brillat-Savarin.

Without doubt, Brie was the first cheese to be accorded royalty.

Gradually the use of cheese spread to towns and cities everywhere. Nevertheless, the custom of serving it at table was not truly prevalent until the nineteenth century. Even before that, however, cheeses had been advertised for sale; witness this Normandy sales pitch of the eighteenth century (unfortunately, the rhyme is lost in the translation):

> Ah, madame, there is a good cheese;
> There is a good cheese made from milk.
> It comes from the district of the one who made it.

which seems to be concerned with the authenticity of the product.

The various fads, the undesirable and the desirable ways of eating cheese, and the somewhat odd usage of always eating pears before cheese date back to this period.

When did cheese definitely become a part of the art of gastronomy? It is impossible to determine a precise date.

Millions of cheeses are eaten annually in France. And innumerable authors seek to inform the public about cheese.

To my mind, the first to have written learnedly after Brillat-Savarin was the Bishop of Autun, Charles Maurice de Talleyrand-Périgord, before he became Prince de Bénévent. Then, if one excepts Maurice des Ombiaux and the renowned Curnonsky, it is necessary to wait, for her poetic style, for the great Colette.

Today there is abundant literature of varying degrees of accuracy and quality. Good commentaries on cheese are available by the hundreds. I will cite only a few of the best authorities.

Without wishing to slight the others, I think of Gault and Millau, the foremost modern propagandists of the art of eating well; of Arnaboldi; of Roland Tremblay (or Tournebroche); of Edmond Longue; of Courtine, alias La Reynière, alias Savarin; of Amunatéguy; of Clos Jouve; of Christian Guy; of Philippe Couderc; of Bertin Rouleau; of Jacques Cru; of Pierre Luxin; of Jean Valby; and, of course, of women such as Odette Kahn and Ninette Lyon. Someone is sure to point out that there are many others. I can only answer: I have chosen the best.

That said, it seems to me who sees close-up the average French eater of cheese, there is still a great need to inform and educate the public.

Therefore, it is not superfluous, in my opinion, to put into your hands this unpretentious guide that complements the well-known and valued works of Lindon and of Plume.

What, then, is the scope of this book? All the world believes it knows—but in fact, I fear, it ignores or little observes—the best ways of choosing cheeses and of using them. I have tried to present as clearly and as precisely as possible the art of cheese-tasting so that those who take the time to glance through this book will no longer be timid about cheese (as are so many I see) but, on the contrary, have a well-founded confidence.

The reader of this book will learn why and when cheeses are at their best, how to choose them, how to serve them and how to keep them.

Finally I have touched upon cheese customs and history.

Intensity of flavor is numerically graded: (1) very mild, bland; (2) mild; (3) slightly pronounced; (4) pronounced; (5) strong, tangy; (6) very strong, very tangy; (7) high or saponified.

ABONDANCE

Also known as: TOMME D'ABONDANCE
Province: SAVOIE (FAUCIGNY)
Source: The Abondance Valley; additional sources: other valleys of the
 Dranses
Made in or by: mountain chalets
Best seasons: summer, fall; milk from herds grazing in the mountains;
 end of the curing period
Milk: cow's milk, partly skimmed
Fat content: 40%
Type: pressed, uncooked
Rind: natural, brushed
Curing: damp, cool cellars, 2 to 3 months, depending on thickness
Form: small wheel
Dimensions: 14 to 18 in. in diameter; 3 to 4 in. thick
Weight: 11 lb. to 33 lb.
Packaging: unwrapped
Selection:
 Appearance: grayish rind, finely grained, fairly smooth
 Feel: firm, somewhat supple texture
 Smell: slight musty smell
 Taste: from light to full flavored (2–3)
What to watch out for: swelling, heat spoilage, bitterness, excessive dry-
 ness
Uses: end of meals, snacks; additional uses: cheese crusts and toppings
Appropriate wines: local white wines: Crépy, Roussette, Abymes, or the
 reds of Mondeuse and the light Gamays of Chautagne
Origin of name: the producing region surrounding the valley of the same
 and the town in which the main market is held
A good buy locally
Other related cheeses: Tommes de Montagne from other regions: Beth-
 male (Pyrénées), Conches, Bagnes (Valais)
 Differences: origin, size, fineness of texture

AETTEKEES

Country: BELGIUM
Province: BRABANT

> An old Brussels cheese which is not made in Brussels, but is very much at home there. It is a rindless fermented cheese, sharp, strong-smelling, wrapped in parchment paper.
>
> In bygone days it was sold in a wrapping of cabbage leaves at the Saint-Clary market.
>
> Gaston Clement: *Le Folklore de chez nous*

AISY CENDRE

Province: BURGUNDY (AUXOIS)
(*See* CENDRE D'AISY)

ALIGOT

Also known as: TOMME D'ALIGOT or TOMME FRAICHE
Province: AQUITAINE (ROUERGUE)
Source: the mountains of Aubrac; additional sources: the Cantal-Salers producing region
Made in or by: small mountain dairies called *burons*
Best seasons: late spring, summer; higher quality milk from cows grazing in mountain pastures
Milk: cow's milk, Aubrac breed
Fat content: minimum 45%
Type: fresh, pressed, uncooked, the base of Cantal and Laguiole
Rind: none
Curing: none; keeps for a maximum of 48 hours
Packaging: not molded, without wrapping

Selection:

    Appearance: ivory color

    Feel: supple, elastic constistency

    Smell: light sour-milk smell

    Taste: slightly sour, slightly nutty flavor (1–2)

What to watch out for: overage, excessive hardness

Uses: in cooking, in the preparation of a *l'Aligot* soup; additional uses: gratins, croquettes, salted pastries

Appropriate wines: fruity reds from the hillsides of Auvergne, Marcillac and Le Fel, etc.

Origin of name: probably from a verb in the local dialect, *alicoter*, meaning to cut; in cooking, the cheese tends to form strings, which must be cut at table

Brief history: linked with the history of Laguiole, one of the most ancient of cheeses of Gaul

A good buy in the producing region

Related cheeses: Italian Mozzarella

ALTIER

Provinces: LANGUEDOC, AQUITAINE

(*See* PELARDON D'ALTIER)

AMOU

Province: GASCONY

Source: border between Landes and Le Gers

Made in or by: farms

Best seasons: spring, summer part of fall; because of availability of sheep's milk, length of curing period

Milk: sheep's milk

Fat content: minimum 45%

Type: pressed, not cooked

Rind: natural, brushed, washed, oiled

Curing: in humid cellars, 2 to 6 months, according to use

Form: thick disk, convex on one side

Dimensions: 14 in. in diameter, 3 in. thick

Weight: 9 lb. to 11 lb.
Packaging: unwrapped
Selection:
  Appearance: thin, golden rind
  Feel: texture ranging from firm and resilient to hard and crumbly
      (depending upon age)
  Smell: slight rancidity
  Taste: flavor ranging from mild to sharp (3–5)
What to watch out for: lack of homogeneity in texture, graininess, overaging, excessive sharpness
Uses: snacks, dessert; additional uses: dried and grated in local dishes
Appropriate wines: the whites or rosés of Béarn, the wines of Landes, and
      in general, all dry wines with some body
Origin of name: market town closest to the center of production
Related cheeses: Ardi-Gasna, Laruns, cheeses from the Pyrénées
  Differences: origin, fineness of grain, flavor

ANDUZE

Province: LANGUEDOC (*See* PELARDON D'ANDUZE)

ANGELOT

Province: NORMANDY
  Obsolete name for old farm cheeses of the Auge region

ANNIVIERS

  A grating cheese from the Alps near Valais

ANNOT or TOMME D'ANNOT

Province: COMTE DE NICE
Source: valley of upper Var, neighboring plateaus

Made in or by: mountain farms
Best seasons: summer, beginning of autumn; availability of sheep's and
    goat's milk, summer pasturing, end of curing period for last batches
Milk: sheep's or goat's milk
Fat content: 45%
Type: pressed, not cooked
Rind: natural, brushed
Curing: in humid cellars, 2 months
Form: thick disk
Dimensions: 6½ to 8½ in. in diameter, 2 in. thick
Weight: 1 lb. 7 oz. to 2 lb. 10 oz.
Packaging: unwrapped
Selection:
    Appearance: smooth, light rind
    Feel: supple texture
    Smell: slight sheep smell
    Taste: mild flavor, slightly nutty (2–3)
What to watch out for: desiccation, excessive sharpness, overaging
Uses: snacks, dessert
Appropriate wines: all local rosés and whites: Bellet, Saint-Jeannet, Vil-
    lars-sur-Var; light and fruity red wines (the older the cheese, the
    more full-bodied the wine)
Origin of name: an invented name for a mountain cheese that is widely
    produced in the upper Var region
Brief history: linked with that of all shepherd's cheeses made during
    summer pasturing
Related cheeses: Tomme da Chévre or Tommes de Brebis from the alpine
    valleys of Allues, Beaufort
    Differences: size, texture, origin, flavor

APPENZELL

Also known as: BLODERKÄSE
Country: SWITZERLAND
Canton: APPENZELL
Source: mountain meadows of Appenzell; additional sources: a few vil-
    lages in Canton of Saint-Gall
Made in or by: mountain chalets

Best seasons: summer (summer pasturing in the mountains), autumn, winter; end of curing

Milk: cow's milk

Fat content: 45%

Type: pressed, cooked (hard)

Rind: brushed

Curing: humid, in cool cellars, 3 months

Form: small wheel with convex sides

Dimensions: 14 in. in diameter, 2½ to 3 in. thick

Weight: 11 lb. to 15½ lb.

Packaging: unwrapped

Selection:

  Appearance: regular, fairly smooth rind

  Feel: very firm

  Smell: little smell

  Taste: somewhat fruity to very fruity flavor (3–4)

What to watch out for: cracks in the rind; hard, crumbly texture; sharpness (last two characteristics may be desirable for use in cooking)

Uses: end of meals, snacks; additional uses: in cooking, for making *chäs happech* and other dishes

Appropriate wines: fruity wines from eastern Switzerland, from Argovia and Zurich

Origin of name: canton in which cheese is made

A good buy locally

Related cheeses: Tilsit, Anniviers, Bagnes, Conches, cheeses from the valleys of Valais

  Differences: origin, consistency and fineness of grain, flavor, size

ARDI-GASNA

Province: PAYS BASQUE (HAUT NAVARRE)

Source: upper valley of Nive, Arnéguy-Esterençuby; additional sources: Aldudes Valley

Made in or by: mountain farms

Best seasons: end of spring, summer (milk from summer pasturing), autumn; end of the normal curing period for the last batches

Milk: sheep's milk

Fat content: minimum 45%

Type: pressed, not cooked

Curing: humid, in cold cellars, average of 3 months; local people keep them 6 months and longer for winter use

Form: round wheel with a convex protrusion

Dimensions: 12 to 14 in. in diameter, 2½ to 3 in. thick

Weight: 9 lb. to 11 lb.

Packaging: unwrapped

Selection:

    Appearance: straw-yellow to light grayish-yellow rind

    Feel: firm with some give

    Smell: slight smell of the cowshed

    Taste: nutty flavor with a touch of sharpness that increases with age (3–5)

What to watch out for: rind too thick; hard, crumbly texture; patches of mold inside (all these characteristics are desirable qualities to local lovers of this cheese and are sought after for cheese used in cooking)

Uses: snacks, dessert; additional uses: grated, in the local cuisine

Appropriate wines: solids reds of Irouléguy when the flavor of the cheese is well developed; when it is younger, the wines of Beaujolais and all fruity reds

Origin of name: Basque word for "local cheese"

Related cheeses: Laruns, Esbareich

ARECHES

Also known as: GRATARON D'ARECHES

Province: SAVOIE (BEAUFORTIN)

Milk: goat's milk

Fat content: 45%

Type: pressed, not cooked

Rind: natural, brushed, washed

(*See* GRATARON D'ARECHES)

AROMES AU GENE DE MARC

Province: LYONNAIS

These cheeses are not the result of any particular cheese-making process, they are based on Rigottes, Saint-Marcellins, Pélardons, and Picodons. The physical characteristics of these cheeses are listed under their own listings definition of each.

Made in or by: a curing rather than a manufacturing process

Best seasons: autumn, winter; curing begins 2 to 3 months after pressing of grapes for wines

Curing: dry, in vats, in fermenting marc

Packaging: coated with fermented marc

Selection:

Appearance: no surface apoilage

Feel: homogeneous texture, sticky rind

Smell: strong smell of fermenting marc

Taste: sharp flavor (5–7)

What to watch out for: excessive fermentation (a quality desired by local consumers)

Uses: end of meals; additional uses: in *fromage fort*

Appropriate wines: all lively, full-bodied wines; Beaujolais-Villages, Côtes-du-Rhône-Villages

Origin of name: from cheese preparation, and region in which cheeses are cured and consumed

Related cheeses: Tomme de Savoie au Marc

Differences: the thicker, pressed tomme ferments longer, takes on a stronger aroma from the wine ferments

AROMES DE LYON

Province: LYONNAIS

Same ingredients as AROMES AU GENE DE MARC but cured in crocks of white wine

Best seasons: spring, summer, autumn for cheese cured in new white wine

Curing: soaked in wine for 1 month, dry curing for 1 month more

Packaging: unwrapped, or wrapped in chestnut, plane-tree or grape leaves

Flavor: sharp to very sharp (5–6)

Related cheeses: all goat's milk cheeses soaked in crocks

Differences: origin, form, size, fineness of texture, flavor

ASCO

Province: CORSICA
(*See* NIOLO)

ASIAGO

Country: ITALY
Province: VICENZA
Source: Province of Vicenza; additional sources: Padua, Verona, Trento
Made in or by: farms
Best seasons: all year
Milk: cow's milk
Fat content: 30%
Type: pressed, uncooked
Rind: brushed
Curing: dry, damp brushings, in dry cellars for a minimum of 6 months; longer for grating versions
Form: small wheel flat on both sides with a slightly convex rim
Dimensions: 13 to 18 in. in diameter, 3½ to 4¾ in. thick
Weight: 17½ lb. to 26½ lb., sometimes a bit more
Packaging: unwrapped
Selection:
  Appearance: glossy rind, granular texture
  Feel: springy
  Smell: little smell
  Taste: somewhat sharp flavor (3–4)
What to watch out for: too crumbly, smoky (local consumers prefer it this way for use as a condiment)
Uses: end of meals; additional uses: grated for seasoning certain dishes
Appropriate wines: lively wines that are fruity or full-bodied according to age (Piedmont wines)
Origin of name: plateau of Asiago, where the cheese originated

Note: Asiagos with a 45% fat content are still manufactured in the mountain region of Vezzana. The cows are in summer pasture from June to September and the ripe cheeses are eaten from October to March. Such cheese is called Asiago da Allievo.

A good buy locally
Related cheeses: Tomme de Montagne Migrasse, Montasio
   Differences: origin, size, fat content, flavor

AULUS

Province: COMTE DE FOIX
(*See* BETHMALE and OUSTET)

AUTUN

Province: BURGUNDY
Milk: more than half or all goat's milk
Fat content: 40% to 45%
(*See* CHAROLAIS)

BAGNES

Also known as: FROMAGE A RACLETTE
Country: SWITZERLAND
Canton: VALAIS
Source: Bagnes Valley; additional sources: cheeses from other regions
   bear their own names
Made in or by: farms
Best seasons: summer (summer pasturing in mountains), autumn, winter;
   end of curing period
Milk: cow's milk
Fat content: 45%
Type: pressed, cooked (hard)
Rind: brushed
Curing: humid, in cool cellars, 3 months
Form: small cylindrical wheel
Dimensions: 14 to 16 in. in diameter, 2¾ to 3½ in. thick
Weight: 15½ lb. to 20 lb.; sometimes 22 lb.
Packaging: unwrapped

Selection:
  Appearance: regularity of rind, which should be slightly rough and
      without cracks
  Feel: firm consistency with some elasticity
  Smell: fairly pronounced smell
  Taste: fruity, aromatic flavor (3–4)
What to watch out for: flaws in the rind, sandy texture, sharpness
Uses: in the preparation of *raclette*; additional uses: a table cheese served
      at the end of meals
Appropriate wines: Fendant du Valais or Dôle (red)
Origin of name: valley in which cheese is produced
A fairly good buy
Related cheeses: Conches, Anniviers, Saint-Niklaas, etc.
  Differences: none, except that the flavor and texture may vary in
      quality and the name stamped on the sides will be different

BAGUETTE LAONNAISE

Provinces: ILE-DE-FRANCE, CHAMPAGNE
Source: Laon region
Made in or by: commercial plants
Best seasons: summer, autumn, winter; milk is best; end of the curing
      period of the last batches
Milk: cow's milk
Fat content: 45%
Type: soft
Rind: washed
Curing: in humid cellars, with washings of brine, 3 to 4 months
Form: oblong loaf with square ends
Dimensions: 6 in. by 2 in. by 2 in. thick
Weight: 1 lb. 1 3/5 oz.
Packaging: box
Selection:
  Appearance: glossy brown rind
  Feel: soft texture, but not excessivly so
  Smell: strong smelling, sometimes smelling of ammonia
  Taste: highly pronounced flavor (4–5)

What to watch out for: insufficient curing, desiccation (crackled rind), runniness, bitterness, ammonia smell released when the package is opened does not last

Uses: end of meals; additional uses: in dishes incorporating drained cottage cheese and Maroilles

Appropriate wines: all very full-bodied reds of substance and character: Cahors, Madiran, Fitou, Patrimonio, etc.

Origin of name: shape of cheese and name of the most important town in producing region

Brief history: relatively recent cheese developed after World War II

A fairly good buy

> *Note:* There is also a DEMI-BAGUETTE (*see* listing under this name)

Related cheeses: Maroilles of all sizes, Hervé, fatty Limburger
  Differences: origin, shape and size

BANON

Province: PROVENCE
Source: Isère, Drôme, Vaucluse
Made in or by: sheep's and goat's-milk varieties on farms; cow's-milk variety, dairies
Best seasons: sheep's milk: spring, summer; goat's milk: late spring, summer, early autumn; cow's milk: all year (milk is available according to the reproductive cycles of the different species of animal)
Milk: sheep's or goat's or cow's milk
Fat content: 45%
Type: soft
Rind: natural
Curing: dry, from 2 weeks to 2 months
Form: small disk
Dimensions: 3 in. in diameter, 1 in. thick
Weight: 3½ oz. to 4½ oz.
Packaging: wrapped in chestnut leaves and tied with rafia

Selection:
  Appearance: slightly sticky rind
  Feel: firm, supple texture
  Smell: faint lactic smell (when fresh), strong smell (when cured)
  Taste: mild lactic flavor to mild nutty flavor (2–3)
What to watch out for: surface sweating, bad odor, grainy texture, saltiness
Uses: end of meals; additional uses: in the preparation of Fromage Fort du Mont Ventoux
Appropriate wines: all fruity and lively reds, whites and rosés of Mont Ventoux and the slopes of Durance
Origin of name: town with most important market
A good buy in season

  Note: There is also a Banon flavored with summer savory called BANON AU PEBRE D'AI (*see* this listing).

Related cheeses: all other goat's-milk and and sheep's-milk cheeses cured in leaves
  Differences: character of milk, flavor, origin

BANON AU PEBRE D'AI

Province: PROVENCE
(*See* POIVRE-D'ANE)

BARBEREY

Also known as: FROMAGE DE TROYES or TROYEN CENDRE
Province: CHAMPAGNE
Source: has shifted in recent times because of urban sprawl into Champagne
Made in or by: small dairies
Best seasons: summer, autumn; these are periods of manufacture, end of curing for the last batches
Milk: cow's milk, skimmed
Fat content: 20% to 30%
Type: soft

Rind: natural, coated with ash
Curing: dry, in wood ashes, in humid cellars for month or longer
Form: flat cylinder
Dimensions: 4½ in. in diameter, 1 in. thick
Weight: 9 oz.
Packaging: box
Selection:
  Appearance: regular shape, dry surface
  Feel: dry surface, yielding texture
  Smell: no strong smell, musty smell
  Taste: slightly saponified to sharp (4–5)
What to watch out for: desiccation, smoky taste
Uses: end of modest rural meals
Appropriate wines: robust, full-bodied reds: the Riceys
Origin of name: place where cheese was made in past and method of
  curing

  Note: Nowadays locally produced Camemberts are also
  cured in ashes.

A good buy
Related cheeses: other low-fat or moderate-fat ash cheeses of Champagne
  (the Riceys) or of the Ardennes (Rocroi) or of the Orléans region
  (Olivet)
  Differences: origin, shape, flavor, fat content

BEAUFORT

Also known as: GRUYERE DE BEAUFORT
Province: SAVOIE BEAUFORTIN (HAUTE TARENTAISE)
Source: the high mountains of Beaufort; additional sources: Haute
  Tarantaise, Col de la Madeleine in Maurienne (Label of origin
  regulated by law)
Made in or by: in high mountain chalets
Best seasons: winter, spring, summer; best milk from summer pasturing
  (herds may graze at heights of 10,000 feet); end of the curing and
  ripening period
Milk: cow's milk
Fat content: 50%
Type: pressed, cooked or hard

Rind: natural, brushed
Curing: in cool and humid cellars, with damp brushings, minimum of
    6 months
Form: flattened cylinder, concave on the sides
Dimensions: 2 ft. in diameter, 4½ to 5 in. thick
Weight: 88 lb. to 132 lb.
Packaging: bare wheels
Selection:
    Appearance: slightly rough, evenly parallel rind; when cut, almost
        complete absence of holes and smooth appearance with small
        horizontal cracks
    Feel: firm, supple and buttery
    Smell: distinct, fruity smell
    Taste: very fruity and salty flavor (3–4)
What to watch out for: cracked rind, penetration by mold, too many
    holes, rubbery or sandy texture
Uses: end of meals, snacks; additional uses: in the local cuisine, in fon-
    dues, crusts, pies, gratins, seasoning of various dishes
Appropriate wines: all fruity white wines of Savoie, Roussette, Chignin;
    all sturdy and fruity reds
Brief history: probably akin to the cheese of the "Centronian Alps"
    known in Roman times
Related cheeses: other big Gruyères from the Jura Comtois

BEAUMONT

Province: SAVOIE
Source: Beaumont
Made in or by: commercial plants
Best seasons: summer, autumn, best quality milk and end of the curing
    period
Milk: cow's milk, non-pasteurized
Fat content: 50%
Type: pressed, uncooked
Curing: humid, in cool cellars, 1½ months
Form: flattened disk
Dimensions: 8 in. in diameter, 1½ to 2 in. thick
Weight: about 3 lb. 5 oz.
Packaging: paper, brand name

Selection:
  Appearance: regular light-yellow rind
  Feel: delicate supple rind
  Smell: no special smell
  Taste: mild, creamy flavor (2–3)
What to watch out for: swelling, heat spoilage, desiccation, bitterness, accidents due to improper or extended storage
Uses: end of meals; additional uses: cheese crusts
Appropriate wines: the same as for Reblochon: Crépy, Ripaille, Roussette
Origin of name: most prominent town in neighboring region
Brief history: an original product of Girod and Co.
A good buy
Related cheeses: all Saint-Paulins and other monastery cheeses, especially Tamié
  Differences: origin, form, size, flavor, fineness of texture

BELLELAY

Country: SWITZERLAND
Province: JURA BERNOIS
A monastery cheese also called TETE-DE-MOINE (*see* this listing)
Related to Beaufort

BEL PAESE

Country: ITALY
Region: LOMBARDY
Source: Melzo; additional sources: Certosa di Pavia, Corteolona, etc.
Made in or by: commercial plant (Galbani)
Best seasons: all year; manufacture is standardized
Milk: cow's milk, pasteurized
Fat content: 45% to 50%
Type: pressed, not cooked
Rind: washed
Curing: damp, in humid cellars, 2 months
Form: thickish disk
Dimensions: 8 in. in diameter, 1½ to 2 in. thick
Weight: 4 lb. 6 oz.

Packaging: foil with trademark
Selection:
   Appearance: cream-colored interior
   Feel: soft consistency
   Smell: a pleasant lactic smell
   Taste: mildly fruity flavor (2–3)
What to watch out for: heat spoilage of the rind, sharpness
Use: end of meals, sandwiches; additional uses: in *croque-madame, croustines au Bel Paese*
Appropriate wines: light, fruity wines with some bouquet: Valpolicella
Origin of name: factory trademark
Brief history: introduced into France in 1927 (originated in monastery: the Charterhouse of Pavia)
A good buy
Related cheeses: Saint-Paulin
   Differences: origin, manufacturing process, fineness of texture, flavor

BELVAL

Also known as: TRAPPISTE DE BELVAL
Province: PICARDY
Source: Abbey of Belval
Made in or by: entirely by monks of Abbey of Belval
Best seasons: all year; pressed-curd cheeses are not sensitive to changes in temperature and keep well
Milk: cow's milk
Fat content: 40% to 42%
Type: pressed, uncooked
Rind: washed
Curing: humid, 2 months
Form: thick disk
Dimensions: 8 to 10 in. in diameter, 1 to 1½ in. thick
Weight: about 4 lb. 6 oz.
Selection:
   Appearance: very glossy rind, straw-yellow to grayish yellow; ivory-white inside
   Feel: supple, fine consistency
   Smell: faint lactic smell
   Taste: not very pronounced flavor (2–3)

What to watch out for: dried-out rind, grayish color, mottled interior ranging from yellow to pinkish gray, too many openings, bitterness, heat spoilage

Use: end of meals; additional use: in *croustines au fromage*

Appropriate wines: all light and fruity red wines: Bouzy Rouge, Beaujolais-Villages, Bourguère, Chinon, Champigny

Origin of name: site of monastery

Brief history: linked with the foundation of the abbey

A good buy locally

Related cheeses: all the monastery cheeses, all the Saint-Paulins
  Differences: dimensions, origin, flavor, manufacturing processes

BERGUES

Province: FLANDERS

Source: immediate vicinity of town of Bergues

Made in or by: homes, farms

Best seasons: all year; low-fat cheeses can be stored indefinitely

Milk: cow's milk, skimmed

Fat content: 15% to 20%

Type: soft

Rind: washed

Curing: in humid cellars, with washings of brine and beer, 2 months or longer

Form: thick disk or flattened ball

Dimensions: 6½ to 8 in. in diameter, 1½ to 2 in. thick

Weight: average 4 lb. 6 oz.

Packaging: unwrapped

Selection:
  Appearance: smooth rind, possibly sticky
  Feel: soft or hard, depending upon the method of curing
  Smell: faint to strong smell, depending upon age
  Taste: always somewhat sharp in flavor (4–6)

What to watch out for: excessive dryness

Use: end of meals, snacks; additional uses: grated into local dishes (dry cheeses)

Appropriate wines: usually beer

Origin of name: place of origin and sale

A good buy

Related cheeses: all low-fat cheeses, particularly the home-made cheeses
of Creuse
   Differences: origin, form, size, flavor

BETHMALE

Also known as: OUSTET
Province: COMTE DE FOIX
Source: Bethmale; additional sources: valleys of Lez and Salat
Made in or by: villages, farms, mountain cabins
Best seasons: spring, summer for cheeses made from milk from valley
   pastures; made in the villages during winter
Milk: cow's milk
Fat content: 45%
Type: hard
Rind: natural
Curing: 3 to 4 months with damp brushings
Form: flattened cylindrical disk, thick, slightly convex on sides
Dimensions: 12 to 16 in. in diameter, 2½ to 3 in. thick
Weight: 11 lb. to 15½ lb.
Packaging: unwrapped
Selection:
  Appearance: fine, flat, parallel rind
  Feel: firm texture with some give in a young cheese, harder when it
    is older
  Smell: little smell on the outside
  Taste: flavor ranging from pronounced to sharp (3–5)
What to watch out for: swelling, cracks in the rind, sharpness
Use: end of meals; additional use: grated as a condiment in local dishes
Appropriate wines: all the fruity and robust wines of Fitou, Corbières,
   Roussillon, Madiran
Origin of name: region in which cheese is made
A fairly good buy locally
Related cheeses: cheeses from the valleys of Valais (Switzerland),
   Bagnes, Conches, Anniviers, etc; Toupin de Savoie
   Differences: grain, aroma, bouquet, origin, flavor

BETHUNE

Also known as: FROMAGE FORT DE BETHUNE (*see* this listing)
Province: ARTOIS (GOHELLE)
Milk: cow's milk
Fat content: 45%

BIBBELSKÄSE

Province: ALSACE
Made in or by: traditionally on farms and in private homes in Alsace; not sold
Best season: all year
Milk: cow's milk
Fat content: usually whole rather than skimmed milk, 45%
Type: fresh; seasoned with horseradish, herbs, salt
Curing: none; eaten fresh
Flavor: mild (1–2)

> *Recipe:* The fresh, drained cheese is put in bowls, beaten, salted, peppered, and mixed with horseradish and herbs. It is then left to stand for one or two days for the flavor of the herbs to develop. It is served as a dessert or as a snack.

BLEU D'AUVERGNE

Province: AUVERGNE
Source: mountains of Cantal, Aurillac, Vic-sur-Cère; additional sources: scattered areas in Departments of Cantal and Puy-de-Dôme. (Cheese protected by legislation defining the producing regions)
Made in or by: commercial dairies; still made on mountain farms in a few places such as THIEZAC (*see* this listing)
Best seasons: farm cheeses: summer, autumn because of availability of milk from herds in summer mountain pasture, end of the curing period for the last batches; dairy cheeses: all year because pasteurized milk is used
Milk: cow's milk
Fat content: 45%

Type: soft, with internal molds
Curing: dry, in humid cellars, with scraping of the surface
Form: flattened cylinder
Dimensions: 7 to 8 in. in diameter, 3½ to 4 in. thick
Weight: 5 lb. to 5½ lb.
Packaging: foil, with label of origin
Selection:
   Appearance: if the cheese is cut, veins well distributed throughout the
     entire body
   Feel: firm but greasy
   Smell: rather strong smell
   Taste: very sharp, engaging flavor (4–6)
What to watch out for: sticky rind, sharpness, granular texture
Appropriate wines: all lively, well-balanced wines, Cornas, Hermitage
Origin of name: province of origin and manufacturing process
Brief history: an imitation of Roquefort substituting cow's milk for
   sheep's milk
A good buy
Related cheeses: Bleus of Laqueuille, Causses and Quercy
   Differences: origin, fineness of texture, flavor

BLEU DE BRESSE

Province: PAYS DE L'AIN
Source: La Bresse; best source: Servas (Ain)
Made in or by: commercial plants
Best seasons: all year because of availability of good quality milk, pas-
   teurization
Milk: cow's milk, pasteurized
Fat content: 50%
Type: soft, blue veins
Curing: dry, in cool and humid cellars, for periods varying according to
   size
Form: cylindrical; long loaf with circular cross-section
Dimensions: small: 2½ in. in diameter, 1½ in. thick; medium: 3 in. in
   diameter, 2 in. thick; large: 4 in. in diameter, 2½ in. thick
Weight: 4½ oz., 9 oz., 17½ oz., 4 lb. 5 oz., respectively for small,
   medium, large cylinders and long loaf
Packaging: foil, cardboard box

Selection:
  Appearance: (after unwrapping) fine smooth blue rind
  Feel: supple consistency
  Smell: no specific smell, a hint of moldiness
  Taste: medium to pronounced savoriness (3–4)
What to watch out for: excessive surface fermentation, reddish gray
  interior, sharpness, saponification
Use: end of meals
Appropriate wines: light and fruity wines from Beaujolais, Côtes-Lyon-
  naises, Côtes-du-Rhône, Côtes-Roannaises
Origin of name: character of cheese and place of origin
Brief history: created in 1950 by making the large (13 lb.) Saingorlon
  in smaller sizes that could easily be sold whole
A good buy
Related cheeses: Sain Gorlon, Gorgonzola
  Differences: origin, flavor

BLEU DES CAUSSES

Province: AQUITAINE (ROUERGUE)
Source: the dairying sections of Rouergue; best source: the sections with
  the best pasturelands. (Cheese legally protected by label of quality)
Made in or by: commercial dairies
Best seasons: summer, autumn; availability of milk from summer pastur-
  ing, end of the curing period for the last batches
Milk: cow's milk
Type: soft, internal molds
Rind: natural
Curing: dry, in humid cellars similar to those used for Roquefort
Form: flat cylinder
Dimensions: 7 to 8 in. in diameter, 3½ to 4 in. thick
Weight: 5 lb. 3 oz. to 5 lb. 13 oz.
Packaging: foil, with label of quality
Selection:
  Appearance: if the cheese is cut: veins well distributed throughout
  Feel: firm and fatty
  Smell: rather strong smell
  Taste: savory to very savory, with some bouquet (4–5)
What to watch out for: sticky rind, graininess, sharpness
Use: end of meals, snacks

Appropriate wines: all lively well-balanced reds with an aromatic note:
Cornas
Origin of name: producing area and manufacturing process
Brief history: linked with that of all the blues of the Massif Central
A good buy
Related cheeses: blues of Auvergne, Laqueuille, Quercy, etc.
  Differences: origin, fineness of grain

BLEU DE CORSE

Province: CORSICA
Source: the high plateaus of northern Corsica; additional sources: adjacent central plateaus
Made in or by: shepherds' cabins
Best seasons: end of spring, summer (availability of sheep's milk from summer pastures), beginning of autumn; end of curing period
Milk: sheep's milk
Fat content: 45%
Type: soft
Rind: natural
Curing: in cool, damp caves, 3 months
Form: tall cylinder
Dimensions: 8 in. in diameter, 4 in. high
Weight: about 5 lb. 13 oz.
Packaging: foil
Selection:
  Appearance: pale surface
  Feel: firm and buttery
  Smell: faint smell of the cow shed
  Taste: very savory, light sharpness (4–5)
What to watch out for: crumbling, lack of veining, gray color, excessive sharpness
Use: end of meals; additional uses: in canapés, salad dressing, *croustades,* etc.
Appropriate wines: all the major reds of the island: Cap Corse, Patrimonio, Sciaccarello; all very robust and aromatic wines of the Continent; Madiran
Origin of name: place where cheese is made and nature of the curd
Brief history: white cheeses are sent to the caves of Roquefort to undergo the prescribed curing

Related cheese: Roquefort
  Differences: fineness of texture, flavor, which depends upon the place
    where cheese is cured

BLEU DE COSTAROS

(*See* BLEU DE LOUDES, an identical cheese)

BLEU DE GEX

Legal definition: BLEU DU HAUT JURA
Province: FRANCHE-COMTE (PAYS DE GEX)
Source: the Ain slopes of the producing region; best source: Saint-Germain-de-Joux
Made in or by: small, traditional dairies; small amount still made on
    farms
Best seasons: summer, autumn; availability of milk, end of curing period
    for last batches
Milk: cow's milk
Fat content: 45%
Type: blue-veined, slightly pressed
Rind: natural, brushed
Curing: dry, in cool and humid cellars, 2 to 3 months
Form: thick disk with convex edges
Dimensions: 12 in. in diameter, 3 to 3½ in. thick
Weight: 11 lb. to 13 lb. 3 oz.
Packaging: unwrapped
Selection:
  Appearance: dry, slightly rough rind, light gray in color; dense and
      well-defined veins
  Feel: some, but not too much give
  Smell: no special smell
  Taste: slightly bitter and savory (3–4)
What to watch out for: crumbling, veins a bit too dense, excessive bitterness or sharpness
Use: end of meals; additional uses: in *fondue nantuatienne*

Appropriate wines: fruity and lively reds of the Jura, Beaujolais, Burgundy and Côtes du Rhône
Origin of name: town to which the cheeses were brought from the mountainous regions of Ain
Related cheeses: Bleu de Septmoncel, Bleu de Sassenage
  Differences: origin

BLEU DU HAUT JURA

Province: FRANCHE-COMTE
(Legally defined name for BLEU DE GEX and BLEU DE SEPTMONCEL)

BLEU DE LAQUEUILLE

Province: AUVERGNE
Source: Laqueuille and environs
Made in or by: commercial dairies
Best seasons: summer, autumn; mountain milk preferable, end of the curing period
Milk: cow's milk
Fat content: 45%
Type: soft, with internal mold
Rind: natural
Curing: dry, in humid cellars, 3 months
Form: cylindrical
Dimensions: 8 to 9 in. in diameter, 4 in. thick
Weight: about 5 lb.
Packaging: foil, with label of quality
Selection:
  Appearance: if the cheese is cut; veins well distributed throughout a homogeneous mass
  Feel: soft
  Smell: a penetrating but pleasant, forthright smell
  Taste: highly savory (4–5)
What to watch out for: sticky rind, sharpness, strong smell

Use: end of meals, snacks
Appropriate wines: all lively, well-balanced, somewhat aromatic wines
Origin of name: place of origin
Brief history: developed about a century ago by M. Roussel
A fairly good buy

> In the 19th century, the peasants of the Laqueuille region made a modest cheese which they sold in Rochefort-Montagne under the name Fourme de Rochefort. In 1850, a clever farmer named Antoine Roussel worked on their recipe and perfected a cheese 8 in. in diameter and 4 in. thick that ripened well and developed a nice blue veining when he sprinkled the curds with blue molds that he found growing on rye bread. This is how the blue cheese of Laqueuille was born. It is much superior to the original Fourme, and its invention earned for M. Roussel the distinction of a memorial bust in the town of Laqueuille, done by a Canadian sculptor and donated by an appreciative Parisian doctor.

Related cheeses: blues of Auvergne, Quercy, Causses
  Differences: origin, appearance, quality, flavor

BLEU DE LOUDES

Also known as: BLEU DU VELAY
Province: AUVERGNE (VELAY)
Source: Loudes; additional sources: Cantons of Cayres, Langeac and Solignac (southern part of Haute-Loire Department)
Made in or by: farms
Best seasons: summer, autumn; availability of good milk, end of curing period
Milk: cow's milk
Fat content: 25% to 35%
Type: blue-veined, slightly pressed
Rind: natural
Curing: dry, in humid cellars, about 2 months
Form: cylindrical
Dimensions: 5 in. in diameter, 5 to 6 in. high; also shorter
Weight: 1 lb. 5 oz. to 2 lb. 3 oz.
Packaging: unwrapped

Selection:
   Appearance: clean rind without cracks
   Feel: firm but supple, may harden as it ages
   Smell: no special smell
   Taste: savory to very savory (4–5)
What to watch out for: cracked rind, crumbly texture
Use: end of meals, snacks
Appropriate wines: all fruity, lively reds: Côtes-du-Rhône or Costières-du-Gard
Origin of name: character of the cheese and its place of origin
A good buy locally
Related cheeses: Bleus from small mountain farms: Fourmes du Livradois, Bleu de Tignes, Bleu de Sainte-Foy
   Differences: origin, dimensions, fineness of texture, milk

BLEU DU PELVOUX

Province: DAUPHINE
Milk: cow's milk
Fat content: 45%
Type: soft, with internal molds

   Note: Former brand name of a small blue cheese made in Briançon

BLEU DU QUERCY

Province: AQUITAINE (QUERCY)
Source: Quercy; best source: Arrondissements of Figeac and Gourdon (Lot); additional sources: districts bordering on Corrèze Department. (Cheese protected by label of quality)
Made in or by: commercial dairies
Best season: autumn, winter; best milk, end of curing period
Milk: cow's milk
Fat content: 45%
Type: soft, blue veining
Rind: natural

Curing: dry, in humid caves
Form: cylindrical
Dimensions: 7 to 8 in. in diameter, 3½ to 4 in. thick
Weight: 5 to 5½ lb.
Packaging: foil bearing label of quality
Selection:
  Appearance: if the cheese is cut, veins well distributed throughout
  Feel: firm, greasy and homogeneous
  Smell: rather strong smell
  Taste: savory to very savory (4–5)
What to watch out for: sticky rind, granular texture, sharpness
Use: end of meals, snacks
Appropriate wines: all well-knit lively, aromatic wines: Cahors
Origin of name: producing area
A fairly good buy
Related cheeses: Bleu d'Auvergne, Bleu de Laqueuille, Bleu des Causses
  Differences: imperceptible to the eye, origin, fineness of texture

BLEU DE QUEYRAS

Province: DAUPHINE
Milk: cow's milk
Type: soft, internal mold

Note: Former brand name of a small Bleu made in Briançon

BLEU DE SAINTE-FOY

Province: SAVOIE (HAUTE TARENTAISE)
Source: Sainte-Foy and its environs; additional source: Tignes
Made in or by: mountain chalets, farms
Best seasons: Summer, autumn; milk from summer mountain pastures,
    end of curing period
Milk: cow's milk
Fat content: 40% to 45%
Type: slightly pressed, internal molds
Rind: natural
Curing: dry, in cool and humid cellars, 2 to 3 months

Form: flat cylinder
Dimensions: 6½ to 8 in. in diameter, 3 to 4 in. thick
Weight: 4 lb. 6 oz. to 6 lb. 9 oz.
Packaging: unwrapped
Selection:
  Appearance: flawless rind; smooth veined interior
  Feel: easily broken
  Smell: no special smell
  Taste: savory (4–5)
What to watch out for: cracked rind, excessive crumbliness, sharpness
Use: end of meals, snacks
Appropriate wines: fruity, lively, well-balanced wines: Ex-mondeuse
Origin of name: nearest town
A good buy locally
Related cheeses: Bleu de Tignes, Bleu du Mont-Cenis, various blue
    Fourmes, Bleu de Loudes or Bleu du Velay
  Differences: origin, form and size, quality of the milk, fineness of
    texture, flavor

BLEU DE SASSENAGE

Province: DAUPHINE
Source: Le Villard-de-Lans (Isère); additional sources: neighboring pla-
    teaus of Vercors
Made in or by: traditional dairies
Best seasons: summer (quality of milk from summer pastures); autumn,
    end of curing period
Milk: cow's milk
Fat content: 45%
Type: slightly pressed, internal veins
Rind: natural
Curing: dry, in humid cellars, 2 or 3 months
Form: thick disk with convex edges
Dimensions: 12 in. in diameter, 3 to 3½ in. thick
Weight: 11 lb. to 13 lb. 4 oz.
Packaging: unwrapped
Selection:
  Appearance: fairly smooth rind; fine grained, light-colored, veins well
    distributed
  Feel: supple texture

Smell: little smell

Taste: savory, shading toward bitter (3–4)

What to watch out for: desiccation, heat spoilage of rind, grainy texture with insufficient veining, sharpness, bitterness

Use: end of meals

Appropriate wines: robust, lively Beaujolais-Villages and Côtes-du-Rhône-Villages

Origin of name: town where the market was held

Brief history: mentioned more than 300 years ago by Olivier de Serres in his *Le Théâtre d'Agriculture* (1600)

A fairly good buy

Related cheeses: Bleu de Gex, Bleu de Septmoncel, and all cow's-milk Bleus

> *Differences:* origin, fineness of grain, tang, flavor

BLEU DE SEPTMONCEL

Legal definition: BLEU DU HAUT JURA

Province: FRANCHE-COMTE

Source: Septmoncel (Jura); best source: Les Bouchoux (Jura); additional sources: nearby mountain regions

Made in or by: small dairies; a small amount still made in the traditional way in chalets and on farms

Best seasons: summer, autumn; availability of milk, end of the curing

Milk: cow's milk

Fat content: 45%

Type: blue-veined

Rind: natural

Curing: dry, in cool cellars, 2 to 3 months

Form: thick disk with convex edges

Dimensions: 12 in. in diameter, 3 to 3½ in. thick

Weight: 11 lb. to 13 lb. 4 oz.

Packaging: unwrapped

Selection:

> *Appearance:* fairly smooth gray rind, fine texture; cut; well-distributed veins
>
> *Feel:* supple texture
>
> *Smell:* no special smell
>
> *Taste:* savory, slightly bitter (3–4)

What to watch out for: crumbling, poorly distributed or insufficient veining, bitterness or sharpness
Use: end of meals; additional uses: like Gex, in *fondue nantuatienne*
Appropriate wines: fruity, lively reds of Jura, Beaujolais, Burgundy, Côtes-du-Rhône and Côtes du Jura
Origin of name: nature of cheese and place of origin
A fairly good buy
Related cheeses: Bleu de Gex and Bleu de Sassenage
   Differences: origin

BLEU DE THIEZAC

Province: AUVERGNE
Source: upper valley of the Cère and the Jordanne; best source: Thiézac (Cantal); additional sources: nearby countryside
Made in or by: mountain farms, exclusively
Best seasons: summer (quality of milk produced during summer mountain pasturing), autumn; end of the curing period
Milk: cow's milk
Fat content: 45%
Type: soft, interior veining
Rind: natural
Curing: dry, in humid cellars
Form: flattened cylinder
Dimensions: 7 to 8 in. in diameter, 3 to 3½ in. thick
Packaging: foil
Selection:
   Appearance: if the cheese is cut, veins well distributed throughout
   Feel: firm but fatty
   Smell: rather strong smell
   Taste: savory to very savory (4–5)
What to watch out for: sticky rind, graininess, sharpness
Use: end of meals, snacks
Appropriate wines: all lively, well-balanced, aromatic reds: Cornas, Cahors
Origin of name: central region of producing area
A good buy locally
Related cheeses: Bleus of Laqueuille, Auvergne, Causses, Quercy
   Differences: origin, less smooth, although fatty

BLEU DE TIGNES

Also known as: TIGNARD
Province: SAVOIE (HAUTE TARENTAISE)
Source: Tignes and its environs; additional sources: nearby pasture-
     lands
Made in or by: mountain chalets, farms
Best seasons: summer, autumn; milk from alpine pastures, end of curing
     period
Milk: cow's milk
Fat content: 40% to 45%
Type: blue-veined, slightly pressed
Rind: natural
Curing: dry, in cool and humid cellars
Form: flat cylinder
Dimensions: 6½ to 7 in. in diameter, 4 in. thick
Weight: 6 lb. 9 oz. to 8 lb. 12 oz.
Packaging: unwrapped
Selection:
   Appearance: flawless rind; smooth, veined interior
   Feel: even texture
   Smell: no special smell
   Taste: savory (4–5)
What to watch out for: cracked rind, crumbling, sharpness
Use: end of meals, snacks
Appropriate wines: all well-balanced, full-bodied reds: Cornas, Saint-
     Joseph, Hermitage
Origin of name: place name
A fairly good buy
Related cheeses: Bleu du Mont-Cenis, Bleu de Sainte-Foy, various blue
     Fourmes
   Differences: origin, form and size, fineness of texture

BLEU DU VELAY

Province: AUVERGNE
Milk: cow's milk
Fat content: 30% to 40%
(See BLEU DE LOUDES and BLEU DE COSTAROS)

BOERENKAAS

Also known as: PRESENT (French name) (*see* this listing)
Country: HOLLAND
Province: ZUID HOLLAND
Source: environs of Gouda; additional sources: several places in Zuid Holland
Made in or by: farms, exclusively
Best seasons: summer, autumn; milk from grazing herds, end of curing period
Milk: cow's milk, unpasteurized
Fat content: 45%
Type: pressed, semi-hard
Rind: natural, brushed
Curing: in dry cellars, with sprinklings and brushings, 4 months
Form: wheel with very convex rim
Dimensions: 14 in. in diameter, 3½ to 5 in. thick
Weight: 17 lb. 9 oz. to 26 lb. 6 oz.
Packaging: unwrapped, with label of origin and fat content
Selection:
  Appearance: regular shape, glossy rind
  Feel: firm, but without toughness
  Smell: faint smell of the cellar
  Taste: nutty flavor, with a pleasant bouquet (2–3)
What to watch out for: internal holes or fissures; external blemishes
Use: breakfast, lunch, end of meals; additional uses: toasted sandwiches, canapés
Appropriate wines: all light and fruity reds and rosés with character
Origin of name: from the fact that it is made on farms, which is exceptional in Holland
A fairly good buy
Related cheeses: Mimolette, Friesekaas
  Differences: origin, form, size, quality, flavor

BONBEL

Country: FRANCE
Flavor: 1–2

Brand name of a commercial Saint-Paulin (Etablissements Bel)
(*See* SAINT-PAULIN)

BONDARD

Also known as: proprietary cheese
Province: NORMANDY (PAYS DE BRAY)
Source: environs of Neufchâtel-en-Bray; additional source: entire Bray
    region
Made in or by: farms, from evening milk
Best seasons: late autumn; intensive curing of cheeses for holiday market
    at year end
Milk: cow's milk, enriched
Fat content: 60%
Type: soft, double cream
Rind: bloomy
Curing: dry, in humid cellars, 4 months
Form: long cylinder
Dimensions: 7 oz. size: 2½ in. in diameter, 3 in. long; 10½ oz. size: 3
    in. in diameter, 3½ in. long
Weight: 7 oz. to 10½ oz.
Packaging: unwrapped, or foil
Selection:
  Appearance: gray to purplish red rind
  Feel: soft and buttery
  Smell: strong smell of fermentation
  Taste: very pronounced fruity flavor (5–7)
What to watch out for: sharpness, saponification
Use: end of special holiday meals
Appropriate wines: all the great well-balanced, full-bodied reds: Bour-
    geuil, red wines of the Loire
Origin of the name: shape of cheese, which vaguely resembles bung
    (bonde) of a cider barrel
Related cheeses: Bondon, Coeur, Briquette, Gournay
  Differences: origin, form, size, quality, flavor

BONDAROY AU FOIN

Also known as: PITHIVIERS AU FOIN
Province: ORLEANAIS
Source: Bondaroy; additional sources: Orléanais, region of Pithiviers
Made in or by: farms, small traditional dairies
Best seasons: summer, autumn, availabilitity of milk, end of curing pe-
riod
Milk: cow's milk
Fat content: 40% to 45%
Type: soft
Rind: natural
Curing: dry, in hay-filled bins, 5 weeks
Form: rather thin disk
Dimensions: 5 in. in diameter, 1 in. thick
Weight: 10½ oz.
Packaging: unwrapped, covered with wisps of hay
Selection:
  Appearance: gray and unblemished rind beneath the hay
  Feel: supple texture
  Smell: slight smell of fermenting vegetation
  Taste: tang with some bouquet (3–4)
What to watch out for: excessive fermentation, gray interior, ammonia
  odor, excessive saltiness
Use: end of meals, snacks
Appropriate wines: the pale red Pinots of Orléanais and the fruity, lively
  light red wines of Orléanais and Touraine
Origin of name: place of origin
A fairly good buy
Related cheeses: Dreux à la Feuille, Olivet, Vendôme
  Differences: origin, form, quality, flavor

BONDON DE NEUFCHATEL

Also known as: NEUFCHATEL
Province: NORMANDY (PAYS DE BRAY)
Source: environs of Neufchâtel; additional sources: entire western part
  of Pays de Bray
Made in or by: partly commercialized dairies; small factories

Best seasons: summer, autumn, winter; best quality milk, best conditions for curing and storage

Milk: cow's milk

Fat content: 45%

Type: soft

Rind: bloomy

Curing: dry, 3 weeks

Form: small cylinder

Dimensions: 1½ to 2 in. in diameter, 2½ in. long

Weight: average 3½ oz.

Packaging: unwrapped, on straw

Selection:

  Appearance: very downy rind, white with sparse touches of reddish pigments

  Feel: supple and smooth

  Smell: slight smell of mushrooms

  Taste: (salted) only slightly fruity to very fruity flavor (3–4)

What to watch out for: dry and grayish rind, excessive saltiness, granular texture

Use: end of meals, snacks

Appropriate wines: all lively and fruity reds

Origin of name: most important market in Pays de Bray and resemblance of cheese form to the bung *(bonde)* of a barrel

Brief history: a cheese with at least a thousand-year history in upper Normandy; has numerous descendants

A good buy

Related cheeses: Gournay, Bondard, Briquette, Coeur

  Differences: form and size, length of curing period, flavor, fineness of grain

BOSSONS MACERES

Province: LANGUEDOC (BAS VIVARAIS)

Made in or by: homes, using local produce; practically unavailable in markets and stores

Best seasons: late autumn, winter

Milk: goat's milk

Fat content: 45%

Type: soft

Rind: natural
What to watch out for: cheeses "melted" during maceration (a desirable
    quality to many lovers of these cheeses)
Use: snacks, end of meals
Appropriate wines: very well-balanced, very full-bodied Costières-du-
    Gard, Côtes-du-Rhône
Origin of name: local dialect

Bossons are obtained by macerating dry Tommes de Chèvre (the
ordinary goat's-milk cheese of the region) in a mixture of olive oil, white
wine and marc. The macerating is done in sealed crocks, set in cool, dark,
well-ventilated cellars for 3 months.

These cheeses are prepared for consumption on the farm and are
usually not for sale.

Related cheeses: all goat's-milk cheeses macerated in crocks, *fromage fort*
    of Burgundy and Dauphiné, etc.

  Differences: origin, basic cheeses, flavorings, soaking medium, flavor
    (6–7)

BOUGON

Province: POITOU
Source: Bougon
Made in or by: commercial plants
Best seasons: spring, summer, autumn; best quality milk, high standards
    of curing
Milk: goat's milk
Fat content: 46%
Type: soft
Rind: bloomy
Curing: dry, 2 to 3 weeks
Form: flat cylinder
Dimensions: 4½ in. in diameter, 1 in. thick
Weight: 9 oz.
Packaging: box

Selection:
  Appearance: white rind; smooth, homogeneous texture
  Feel: supple
  Smell: pronounced goat smell
  Taste: nutty flavor (3)
What to watch out for: gray spots on rind, granular texture, excessive
    saltiness
Use: end of meals
Appropriate wines: all fruity, lively wines of Poitou, Beaujolais, Côtes-du-
    Rhône
Origin of name: place of origin
Brief history: linked with that of the La Mothe-Bougon cooperative
A fairly good buy
Related cheeses: La Mothe-Saint-Héray

BOUILLE, LA

Province: NORMANDY
Source: La Bouille (Seine-Maritime)
Made in or by: small dairies
Best seasons: summer, autumn, winter; best possibilities for curing
Milk: cow's milk, enriched
Fat content: 60%
Type: soft, double cream
Rind: bloomy
Curing: dry, 2 to 3 months
Form: thick cylinder
Dimensions: 3 in. in diameter, 2 in. thick
Weight: about 8 oz.
Packaging: unwrapped
Selection:
  Appearance: downy white rind sprinkled with red
  Feel: firm, inelastic texture
  Smell: penetrating smell, considerable bouquet
  Taste: highly fruity flavor (4)
What to watch out for: sticky rind, excessive redness, ammonia smell,
    saponification
Use: end of meals
Appropriate wines: well-balanced, spiritous, full-bodied reds

Origin of name: place of origin
Brief history: invented at the turn of the century by Monsieur Fromage; a parallel variety of Fromage de Monsieur, differing in size, longer curing and fuller development of flavor.
Related cheeses: Monsieur-Fromage, Chaource, Brie de Melun
  Differences: origin, size, quality, flavor

BOULE DE LILLE or VIEUX LILLE

Also known as: MIMOLETTE (*See* Mimolette)
Province: FLANDERS

BOULETTE D'AVESNES

Region: FLANDRE-HAINAUT
Source: Thiérache, Avesnois
Made in or by: formerly farms; today to a small extent factories
Best seasons: summer, autumn, winter; high quality of the basic cheeses, end of the curing period
Milk: cow's milk
Fat content: 50%
Type: soft, mashed, kneaded, flavored with parsley, tarragon and pepper
Rind: natural, tinted red
Curing: in moist cellars, 3 months
Form: irregular, hand-shaped cone
Dimensions: 2½ to 3 in. in diameter, 3½ to 4 in. high
Weight: 7 to 10½ oz., depending upon maker
Selection:
  Appearance: brick-red color, grayish interior
  Feel: doughy, without elasticity
  Smell: strong, penetrating smell
  Taste: very sharp flavor (6–7)
What to watch out for: overpowering flavor, excessive fermentation due to age
Use: end of meals
Appropriate wines: all very well-knit, very full-bodied wines, Cahors; but a shot of gin is best

Origin of name: shape of cheese and place of origin

Brief history: in the past made exclusively from buttermilk and eaten only by farmers themselves; nowadays made from imperfect Maroilles cheeses, which are mashed and flavored with parsley, tarragon and pepper

A fairly good buy locally

Related cheeses: mashed and flavored strong cheeses of Burgundy, Beaujolais, Lyonnais, Dauphiné

> *Differences:* shape, size, packaging, origin, flavor

BOULETTE DE CAMBRAI

Region: FLANDERS

Source: Cambrésis

Made in or by: farms, homes

Best seasons: all year; cheese prepared in homes

Milk: cow's milk

Fat content: about 45%

Type: fresh, drained, flavored with parsley, tarragon and chives; salted and peppered; eaten fresh

Form: hand-molded ball

Dimensions: variable: from 2½ to 3 in. in diameter, 3 to 4 in. high

Weight: average 10 oz.

Packaging: unwrapped

Selection:

> *Appearance:* pure white
>
> *Feel:* smooth, soft texture
>
> *Smell:* faint flavored-milk smell
>
> *Taste:* mild aromatic flavor (2–3)

What to watch out for: excessive aging

Use: end of meals, snacks, sandwiches

Appropriate wines: all light and fruity reds: Beaujolais

Origin of name: shape of cheese and its place of manufacture

A good buy locally

Related cheeses: fresh, flavored cheeses of all origins

> *Differences:* origin, appearance, quality, flavor, type of milk

BOULETTE DE LA PIERRE-QUI-VIRE

Province: BURGUNDY
Source: Abbey of La Pierre-Qui-Vire, Saint-Léger-Vauban (Côte-d'Or)
Made in or by: monastery
Best seasons: summer, autumn; most abundant and best milk
Milk: cow's milk
Fat content: 45%
Type: fresh, drained, flavored with herbs
Rind: none
Curing: none
Form: nearly spherical ball
Dimensions: 3 in. in diameter
Weight: 5 oz. to 7 oz.
Packaging: unwrapped
Selection:
  Appearance: fine unblemished surface
  Feel: firm and supple consistency
  Smell: herb fragrance
  Taste: mild aromatic flavor (3–4)
What to watch out for: overaging
Use: end of meals
Appropriate wines: all fruity, lively wines of Burgundy and Beaujolais
Origin of name: shape of cheese and place of origin
Brief history: invented by monks in order to increase their sales of fresh
  cheeses
Related cheeses: Boulette de Cambrai; other part-fresh, flavored cow's-
  milk cheeses
  Differences: herbs, origin, flavor

BOURSAULT

(*See* LUCULLUS)

BOURSIN

Provinces: ILE-DE-FRANCE, NORMANDY
Made in or by: commercial plants
Milk: cow's milk, enriched and pasteurized
Fat content: 70%
Type: soft, flavored or unflavored
Appropriate wines: slightly dry white wines or light reds and rosés usually
    served with triple-cream cheeses

BOUTON-DE-CULOTTE

Also known as: CHEVRETON DE MACON (*see* Mâconnais this list-
    ing)
Made in or by: farms, homes; not sold
    Boutons-de-culotte (breeches-buttons) are small Chèvreton du
Mâconnais that are stored in cupboards during the autumn for winter
use. By winter they become dark brown and hard and are ready to b'e
grated into the local *fromage fort*
Selection:
    Appearance: dark brown to grayish black rind
    Feel: hard and brittle
    Smell: rancid smell
    Taste: saponified, sharp flavor (5–6–7)
Appropriate wines: all the powerful full-bodied vintages of Mâconnais
    and Côte Chalonnaise
Origin of name: local dialect

BRESSAN

Also known as: PETIT BRESSAN
Province: PAYS DE L'AIN (BRESSE, VALROMEY)
Source: Bresse Louhannaise; additional sources: Pays de l'Ain
Made in or by: farms
Best seasons: summer, autumn; availability of goat's milk, end of curing
    period
Milk: goat's milk or half goat's milk

Fat content: 40% to 45%
Type: soft
Rind: natural
Curing: dry, in ventilated cellars, about 3 weeks
Form: truncated cone
Dimensions: 1½ in. in diameter, 1 to 1½ in. high
Weight: 2 oz.
Packaging: unwrapped
Selection:
  Appearance: unblemished light rind
  Feel: firm and homogeneous
  Smell: light goat smell
  Taste: slightly savory to very fruity (3–5)
What to watch out for: brittle texture, saponification
Use: end of meals, snacks; additional uses: may be substituted for Rame-
    quin de Lagnieu in *fondue bugiste* or for Mâconnais in *fromage fort*
Appropriate wines: all light, subtle and fruity whites, reds and rosés of
    Beaujolais, Jura and Bugey
Origin of name: producing region
Related cheeses: Chèvre du Bugey, Chèvre du Mâconnais, Chèvre du
    Charolais
  Differences: origin, size, shape, fineness of grain, flavor

BRICQUEBEC

Also known as: TRAPPISTE DE BRICQUEBEC
Province: NORMANDY (COTENTIN)
Source: Abbey of Bricquebec (Manch)
Made in or by: monks, using traditional methods
Best seasons: all year; availability of milk, end of curing period
Milk: cow's milk
Fat content: 45%
Type: pressed, not cooked
Rind: washed
Curing: humid in humid cellars, 2 months
Form: flat disk
Dimensions: 8¾ in. in diameter, 1½ in. thick
Weight: about 3 lbs.
Packaging: unwrapped, trademark "Providence"

Selection:
  Appearance: smooth, yellowish gray rind
  Feel: supple
  Smell: slight smell of cellar
  Taste: mild (2–3)
What to watch out for: hard rind, graininess, bitterness, superficial heat
    spoilage
Use: end of meals; additional uses: in *croustines,* toasts, *croque-madame*
Appropriate wines: all lively white wines, rosés, light and fruity reds,
    Muscadet, Saint-Emilion
Origin of name: site of monastery
Brief history: associated with that of the monastery
A good buy
Related cheeses: all monastery cheeses and Saint-Paulin
  Differences: origin, shape, composition, quality, taste

BRIE DE COULOMMIERS

Also known as: BRIE PETIT MOULE
Province: ILE-DE-FRANCE
Source: Coulommiers; additional sources: environs of Coulommiers
Made in or by: originally, farms; today, more and more in factories
Best seasons: autumn, winter, spring; milk from cows kept in stalls, easy
    curing, good storage
Milk: cow's milk
Fat content: 45%
Type: soft
Rind: bloomy
Curing: dry, 1 month
Form: flat disk
Dimensions: 10 in. in diameter, 1 in. thick
Weight: 2 lb. 12 oz.
Packaging: unwrapped, or foil
Selection:
  Appearance: downy white rind sprinkled with reddish pigments
  Feel: supple throughout the entire mass, not runny
  Smell: faint mushroom smell with agreeable bouquet
  Taste: fruity with a pronounced tang (3)

What to watch out for: grayish or excessively red rind, excessive hardness, runniness, excessive saltiness

Use: end of meals; additional use: cheese croquettes

Appropriate wines: fruity, lively reds: Beaujolais-Villages, Pommard, Volnay, Savigny-les-Beaune

Origin of name: chief town of the district, where the most important market was held

Brief history: linked with the history of Brie de Meaux

Fairly inexpensive

Related cheeses: Brie de Meaux, Coulommiers, Chevru

   Differences: size, place of manufacture

BRIE LAITIER

Source: Ile-de-France; additional sources: Burgundy, Champagne, Lorraine; foreign sources: Belgium, Switzerland, etc.

Made in or by: commercial plants

Best seasons: all year; pasteurized milk used

Milk: cow's milk, pasteurized

Type: soft

Rind: bloomy

Curing: dry, 3 weeks

Form: flat disk

Dimensions: big mold: 14 in. in diameter, 1¼ in. thick; medium mold: 11 in. in diameter, 1 to 1¼ in. thick

Weight: big mold: 6 lb. 10 oz.; medium mold: 4 lb. to 4 lb. 6 oz.

Packaging: unwrapped, trademarked, if whole; or else in a box, divided into portions of 1/16, 1/12, 1/10, 1/8, or 1/6

Selection:

   Appearance: downy white rind lightly sprinkled with reddish molds; straw-yellow interior

   Feel: supple

   Smell: faint smell of mold and fermentation.

   Taste: rather pronounced flavor (3)

What to watch out for: rind too white or too red, hardness, brittleness, graininess, flakiness, excessive saltiness, bitterness

   The sloping board on which Bries are drained produces a slight distortion in their shape, making part of the cheese thicker than the rest. The thicker portion takes longer to ripen. For this reason it is always best to choose the thinner side.

Use: end of meals; additional uses: in croquettes, canapés, *bouchées*
Appropriate wines: all fruity reds with some bouquet: Fleurie
Origin of name: traditional name of the Brie region
A good buy
Related cheeses: various Bries, Coulommiers
  Differences: origin, size, quality, flavor

BRIE DE MEAUX FERMIER

Province: ILE-DE-FRANCE (BRIE)
Source: Arrondissement of Meaux: valley of Grand Morin and Petit Morin, district of Crécy and La Ferté-sous-Jouarre; Arrondissement of Coulommiers: Rozoy-en-Brie, La Ferté-Gaucher
Best seasons: summer (shipping difficult), autumn, winter; quality of the feed, end of curing period
Milk: cow's milk
Fat content: minimum 45%
Type: soft
Rind: bloomy
Curing: dry, 1 month
Form: flat disk
Dimensions: big mold: 14 in. in diameter; small mold: 10½ to 11 in. in diameter; 1 in. thick
Weight: big mold: 4 lb. 6 oz. after curing; small mold: 2 lb. 10 oz.
Packaging: unwrapped, or foil
Selection:
  Appearance: regular shape; downy white rind dusted with reddish pigments; straw-yellow interior
  Feel: supple but not runny
  Smell: full bouquet
  Taste: fruity tang
What to watch out for: grayish or overly red rind, excessive hardness or runniness, saltiness, ammonia smell
Use: end of meals; additional uses: in canapés, croquettes
Appropriate wines: lively, fruity red wines of Burgundy, aromatic Bordeaux of Pomerol or Saint-Emilion

Origin of name: town closest to place of origin where the principal
   market was held
Brief history: presumed to be older than the 8th century; Charlemagne's
   chronicler, Eginhard de Saint Gall, reported that the emperor tasted
   it at the priory of Rueil in Brie in 774.
A fairly good buy

> One would be much surprised to learn that the General
Assembly of the United Nations had unanimously passed
a resolution declaring Brie "the king of cheeses," but this
is just about what happened at the Congress of Vienna
which brought the representatives of 30 nations together
after the Battle of Waterloo and reconstructed the map of
Europe in 1815.
> To relieve the seriousness of their debates, these gentle-
men held balls and above all dinners. At such dinners they
would discuss the merits of various cheeses. Each had
decided to present a cheese. Monsieur de Talleyrand
brought a Brie, and this Brie (made, it is said, by a certain
Baulny of Villeroy) was immediately and unanimously pro-
claimed "king of cheeses."
> France had lost a war, but the world had gained a
cheese.

Related cheeses: Coulommiers, Chevru, Fougerus
   Differences: size, origin, quality, flavor

BRIE DE MELUN AFFINE

Province: ILE-DE-FRANCE
Source: plains region surrounding Melun
Made in or by: small dairies, fewer each year
Best seasons: summer, autumn, winter; availability of milk, end of curing
   period
Milk: cow's milk
Fat content: 40% to 45%
Type: soft
Rind: natural
Curing: moist, in humid cellars, 2½ months
Form: rather thick disk
Dimensions: 9½ in. in diameter, 1¼ in. thick

Weight: about 3 lb. 5 oz.
Packaging: unwrapped, or foil
Selection:
    Appearance: brick-red rind pigmented here and there with traces of
        white molds; golden yellow and homogeneous within
    Feel: supple and elastic without being soft
    Smell: strong smell of fermentation
    Taste: very fruity flavor with some bouquet
What to watch out for: spoiled rind, gray interior, ammonia smell
Use: end of meals
Appropriate wines: all red wines of Burgundy and Bordeaux, and Côtes-
    du-Rhône that are lively and full-bodied and have bouquet
Origin of name: nearest town where the market was held
Brief history: may be ancestor of all Bries
Related cheeses: Brie de Montereau, Feuille de Dreux
    Differences: origin, form, size, quality, flavor

BRIE DE MELUN BLEU

Province: ILE-DE-FRANCE
Milk: cow's milk
Fat content: average 45%
Type: fresh, salted, sprinkled with powdered charcoal
Same characteristics as BRIE DE MELUN FRAIS (*see* this listing)

BRIE DE MELUN FRAIS

Province: ILE-DE-FRANCE
Source: environs of Melun
Made in or by: farms, small factories
Best seasons: all year; fresh curds are about the same in any season
Milk: cow's milk
Fat content: 45%
Type: fresh, salted; sometimes sprinkled with powdered charcoal and
    called BRIE DE MELUN BLEU (*see* this listing)
Rind: none
Curing: none

Form: flat disk
Dimensions: 10½ in. in diameter, 1½ in. thick
Weight: 4 lb. 15 oz. to 5 lb. 8 oz.
Packaging: foil
Selection:
  Appearance: very white
  Feel: supple, elastic
  Smell: lactic smell
  Taste: mild sour milk taste (1–2)
What to watch out for: defects almost undetectable when the cheese is very fresh, but there should be no fissures, so that a clean cut can be made
Use: end of meals
Appropriate wines: all light and fruity reds, whites and rosés, still Champagne
Brief history: linked with that of aged Melun cheese; no doubt always consumed fresh
A good buy
Related cheeses: all soft cheeses in their fresh state
  Differences: origin, packaging, form, flavor, consistency and quality

BRIE DE MONTEREAU

Also known as: VILLE-SAINT-JACQUES
Province: ILE-DE-FRANCE
Source: Ville-Saint-Jacques; additional sources: region of Montereau-Seine, left bank
Made in or by: small traditional dairies
Best seasons: summer, autumn, winter; availability of milk, end of curing period
Milk: cow's milk
Fat content: 40% to 45%
Type: soft
Rind: natural
Curing: moist, in humid cellars, 6 weeks
Form: flat disk
Dimensions: 7 in. in diameter, 1 in. thick
Weight: 14 oz.
Packaging: unwrapped, or foil

Selection:
  Appearance: reddish fermented rind
  Feel: tender, without being soft
  Smell: rather strong smell
  Taste: very fruity flavor with some bouquet (3–4)
What to watch out for: spoiled rind, ammonia smell, excessive saltiness
Use: end of meals
Appropriate wines: all aromatic, full-bodied reds
Origin of name: market nearest to producing region
Related cheeses: Brie de Melun, Olivet and Vendôme Bleu
  Differences: origin, size, quality, flavor

BRIE DE NANGIS

Province: ILE-DE-FRANCE
(No longer produced; similar to BRIE DE MELUN)

BRILLAT-SAVARIN

Province: NORMANDY (PAYS DE BRAY)
Source: Forges-les-Eaux
Made in or by: a small factory: Ets Dubuc in Rouvray-Catillon
Best seasons: all year; good overall conditions of manufacture, aging and
    storing
Milk: cow's milk
Fat content: 75%
Type: soft, triple cream
Curing: 3 weeks
Form: thick disk
Dimensions: 5 in. in diameter, 1½ in. thick
Packaging: box, or unwrapped
Selection:
  Appearance: downy white rind, little mold, quite firm (Note: some
      people age it longer until it becomes soft and oily and the rind
      becomes red)
  Feel: buttery texture without elasticity

Smell: light smell of mold and of cream

Taste: milk flavor, slightly sour (2)

What to watch out for: dried-out surface, saponification, rancidity, phenol smell

Use: end of meals; additional uses: variously flavored spreads for canapés and sandwiches

Appropriate wines: all light fruity wines; in particular Champagnes with some character

Origin of name: invented by Henri Androuet sometime between First and Second World Wars

Brief history: descendant of a somewhat smaller and coarser Excelsior

Related cheeses: all triple-cream cheeses: Excelsior (72% butterfat), Magnum, Délice de Saint-Cyr, Explorateur, Boursin, aged Boursin, Grand-Vatel

Differences: size, quality, origin

BRINDAMOUR

Also known as: FLEUR DU MAQUIS (*see* this listing)

Province: CORSICA

Source: the plateau of Niolo; additional sources: central Corsica

Made in or by: small mountain dairies

Best seasons: summer; goat's milk from summer pasture, end of curing period

Milk: goat's milk

Fat content: 45%

Type: soft, flavored with savory and rosemary

Rind: natural, barely formed

Curing: in a cool and humid place with aromatic herbs, 3 months

Form: square, with rounded corners

Dimensions: 5 to 5½ in. square, 1½ to 2 in. thick

Weight: 1 lb. 5 oz. to 1 lb. 12 oz.

Packaging: none; with herbs

Selection:

Appearance: light gray surface covered with herbs

Feel: firm, rather hard texture

Smell: slight smell of the cow shed and of aromatic herbs

Taste: moderately pronounced flavor, aromatic

What to watch out for: fissures, presence of parasites

Use: end of meals

Appropriate wines: all the robust and full-bodied wines of Cap Corse, Sciaccarello, Patrimonio

Origin of name: brand name

Related cheeses: the other cheeses of Niolo, Asco and Venaco when consumed young

   Differences: origin, curing period, method of curing

BRIQUE DU FOREZ

Also known as: CHEVRETON D'AMBERT or CABRION DU FOREZ

Province: AUVERGNE (LIVRADOIS)

Source: Ambert Arrondissement; additional sources: neighboring regions, Canton of Viverols

Made in or by: farms, entirely

Best seasons: summer, autumn; best milking period for goats, high quality milk

Milk: goat's milk or mixed goat's and cow's milk

Fat content: 40% to 45%, depending upon amount of goat's milk used

Type: soft

Rind: natural

Curing: dry, in humid cellars, on rye hay, 2 or 3 months

Form: rectangular loaf with rectangular cross section

Dimensions: 5 to 5½ in. long, 1½ to 2½ in. wide, 1 in. thick

Weight: 12 oz. to 14 oz.

Packaging: unwrapped

Selection:

   Appearance: regular shape, smooth rind with bluish molds (all goat's milk) or grayish molds (mixed milks)

   Feel: firm with some give

   Smell: slight mold smell

   Taste: nutty flavor (3)

What to watch out for: rind too dry or too sticky, graininess, excessive saltiness, saponification

Use: end of meals

Appropriate wines: all light and fruity whites, rosés and reds of Auvergne, Roanne, Beaujolais, etc.

Origin of name: shape of cheese, region in which it is made or type of
    milk used
A good buy locally
Related cheeses: all country goat's-milk cheeses, pure or mixed
    Differences: form, size, origin, fineness of texture, flavor

BRISE-GOUT or BRISEGO

Province: SAVOIE (HAUTE TARENTAISE)
Source: mountainous region of Beaufort
Made in or by: mountain chalets; but not marketed: farm families make
    it for their own use during the winter
Best seasons: autumn, winter; summer pasturing, long curing period
Milk: cow's milk, completely or partly skimmed
Fat content: not guaranteed; 15% to 25%
Type: pressed, cooked
Curing: in cool and humid cellars, with brushings, 4 to 6 months
Form: tallish cylinder
Dimensions: 8 to 9 in. in diameter, 7 to 8 in. high
Weight: 6 lb. 10 oz. to 11 lb.
Packaging: unwrapped
Selection:
    Appearance: sound rind, rough, but without uneven patches
    Feel: soft, supple texture
    Smell: strong smell
    Taste: very fruity to sharp flavor (4–6)
What to watch out for: cracked rind, hard or crumbly texture (some
    people of the region prefer a cheese with these characteristics)
Use: end of meals, or snack
Appropriate wines: fruity, lively wines of Savoie and Beaujolais
Origin of name: Savoyard dialect
Related cheeses: Tomme de Montagne from Savoie, Revard, Belleville,
    Beauges, etc.
    Differences: origin, form, size, quality, richness, flavor

BROCCIO BROCCIU

Province: CORSICA
Source: plateaus of central Corsica
Made in or by: farms, exclusively
Best seasons: fresh cheeses: late autumn, winter, beginning of spring; dry
    cheeses: all year
Milk: sheep's milk, heated and churned
Fat content: minimum 45%
Type: fresh, unsalted
Rind: none
Curing: none; generally eaten fresh
Form: irregular mass molded in a basket
Dimensions: variable
Weight: 2 lb. 3 oz.
Packaging: drip baskets
Selection:
  Appearance: as fresh as possible
  Feel: greasy
  Smell: slight goat smell
  Taste: mild flavor (1–2) or sharp (5–7) (*See* Note)
What to watch out for: excessive draining
Use: end of meals: additional uses: served mixed with fresh or stewed
    fruit; in a cake called *fiadone*
Appropriate wines: light and accommodating whites and rosés; rosés of
    Provence when the cheese is fresh or of Patrimonio when it is dry

    Note: May be salted to permit drying and storage (6 months).
In this case, the cheeses are washed periodically with brine and left
to ferment in vessels that protect them from insects. The flavor
develops and becomes very pronounced and sharp.

Related cheeses: mainland Brousses of Rove and Vésubie

BROCQ

Province: LORRAINE
District: METZ
Made in or by: homes
Milk: cow's milk

Fat content: approximately 45%
Type: fresh
Flavor: 1–2
Recipe: Curdle some milk, let it drain slowly for one whole day. Mix in an amount of fresh milk equal to the amount of whey drained off, stirring it with a spoon. Slice some bread into the mixture and let it soak for an hour or two.
Use: local farm workers' snack called *mérande.* (Other names for this dish: BROCKEL in the Boulay region and BRACQ in the Thionville region)

BROODKAAS

Country: HOLLAND
Milk: cow's milk, pasteurized
Fat content: 30% to 40%
Type: pressed, semi-hard
(In Dutch, synonymous with slicing cheese)

BROUSSE DU ROVE

Province: PROVENCE
Source: Rove peninsula
Made in or by: farms; only slightly commercialized
Best seasons: end of autumn, winter, beginning of spring; availability of sheep's milk
Milk: sheep's milk, unsalted
Fat content: 45%
Type: fresh
Rind: none
Curing: none
Form: shape of drip basket
Dimensions: variable
Packaging: in bulk in baskets
Selection:
  Appearance: as fresh and white as possible
  Feel: tender and creamy

Smell: smell of cream with a slight sheep smell

Taste: mild flavor (1–2)

What to watch out for: lack of freshness and heaviness of flavor

Use: served mixed with fresh or stewed fruits; may also be treated as a regular cheese, salted and flavored

Appropriate wines: Palette; soft, fruity Coteaux d'Aix, white or rosé

Origin of name: word *brousser* in the Provençal dialect meaning stir or beat, and place of production

Related cheeses: Brousse de la Vésubie, fresh Corsican Broccio

Differences: origin, fineness of texture

BROUSSE DE LA VESUBIE

Province: PROVENCE (COMTE DE NICE)

Source: Vésubie valley; additional sources: nearby valleys

Made in or by: farms

Best seasons: spring, beginning of summer; availability and quality of milk

Milk: sheep's or goat's milk

Fat content: 45% minimum

Type: fresh

Rind: none

Curing: none

Dimensions: depend upon the container

Weight: variable

Packaging: in bulk in baskets

Selection:

Appearance: as fresh and white as possible

Feel: very creamy

Smell: smell of sweet cream

Taste: mild flavor (1–2)

What to watch out for: lack of freshness and lightness

Use: sweetened as dessert; additional uses: served mixed with fresh or stewed fruits: may also be salted and flavored

Appropriate wines: all the soft, fruity whites and rosés of Provence

Origin of name: Provençal dialect and place of origin

Related cheeses: Brousse du Rove, fresh Corsican Broccio

Differences: origin, quality, bouquet

BURRINO

Country: ITALY
Region: MOLISE
Province: CAMPOBASSO
Milk: cow's milk
Fat content: 45%
Type: semi-hard, twisted, lump of butter in the center
Rind: natural, spontaneous
Flavor: mild (1–2)
(*See* SCAMORZE)

CABECOU D'ENTRAYGUES

Province: AQUITAINE (ROUERGUE)
Source: Entraygues-sur-Truyère (Aveyron); additional sources: immediate vicinity
Made in or by: farms
Best seasons: end of autumn, winter, beginning of spring; availibility of milk
Milk: sheep's, goat's or mixed goat's and cow's milk
Fat content: average 45%
Type: soft
Rind: natural
Curing: dry, in ventilated drying rooms, 1 month
Form: small, very flat disk
Dimensions: 1½ in. in diameter, a bit less than ½ in. in thickness
Weight: 1¼ oz. before drying
Packaging: unwrapped
Selection:
  Appearance: fine, smooth rind, bluish
  Feel: firm, but not excessively so
  Smell: little aroma
  Taste: very characteristic bouquet, from mild to nutty (2–4)
What to watch out for: excessive hardness, saponification
Use: end of meals, snacks, light meals
Appropriate wines: all local fruity red wines: Marcillac, Le Fel; and other wines with similar characteristics

Origin of name: contraction of Langue d'Oc word meaning "little goat"
Related cheeses: all the Cabécous of the uplands of Gramat and Limogne
  Differences: origin, quality, types of milk used

CABECOU DE LIVERNON

Province: AQUITAINE (QUERCY)
(*See* LIVERNON, also known as ROCAMADOUR or CABECOU DE
  ROCAMADOUR)

CABECOU DE ROCAMADOUR

(*See* ROCAMADOUR)

CABRION DU FOREZ

Also known as: BRIQUE DU FOREZ
(*See* this listing)

CABRION DE MACON

Province: BURGUNDY
Milk: goat's milk
(*See* MACONNAIS or CHEVRETON DE MACON)

CACHAT

Also known as: TOMME DU MONT VENTOUX
Province: PROVENCE
Source: Malaucene; additional sources: Massif of Mount Ventoux
Made in or by: farms
Best seasons: summer; end of the lactation period for sheep, storage

Milk: sheep's milk
Fat content: 45%
Type: fresh, salted
Rind: none
Curing: drained several days in fine cheesecloth
Packaging: bulk, in baskets
Selection:
  Appearance: white and fresh
  Feel: very soft
  Smell: light lactic smell
  Taste: sweet and creamy flavor (2)
What to watch out for: excessive draining
Use: end of meals; additional uses: as ingredient of Fromage Fort du
    Mont Ventoux
Appropriate wines: whites and rosés from the slopes of Mount Ventoux
Origin of name: from Provençal
A fairly good buy locally when in season
Related cheeses: Provençal and Corsican Brousses
  Differences: origin, texture, flavor

CACIOCAVALLO

Country: ITALY
Source: southern Italy; additional sources: central and northern Italy
Made in or by: small and medium-sized factories
Best seasons: all year
Milk: cow's milk
Fat content: 44%
Type: pressed, often smoked
Rind: self-forming, dry and oily
Curing: in dry cellars or storage rooms, with sprinklings and brushings,
    3 to 4 months; curing is speeded up by storage in warm cellars
Form: shaped like a gourd with a narrow end to permit the cheese to be
    attached to other cheeses with a cord
Dimensions: 5 to 5½ in. in diameter at widest, 14 to 16 in. long
Weight: 6 lb. 10 oz. to 8 lb. 13 oz.
Packaging: unwrapped, with a cord attaching it to another cheese

Selection:
   Appearance: fine, smooth, glossy rind ranging in color from golden to grayish yellow; ivory-white interior
   Feel: dense, but with some give
   Smell: light smell of smoke
   Taste: mild smoky flavor, delicate, not fruity (3)
What to watch out for: holes in the cheese, sharpness (although some like this)
Use: end of meals: addtional uses: grated, as a condiment, when the cheese is fairly old
Appropriate wines: all fruity wines with good keeping qualities and some bouquet: Chianti, Valpolicella
Origin of name: there are three theories for "on horseback": the cheeses were set to dry on top of one another; the cheese was originally made from mare's milk; the cheese was stamped with the seal of the kingdom of Naples—a galloping horse
Brief history: believed to have been introduced into the West by the barbarian invaders
A fairly good buy
Related cheese: Provolone
   Differences: origin, form, size, flavor, absence of smoking

CAHORS

Province: AQUITAINE (QUERCY)
(*See* CABECOU)

CAILLEBOTE

Province: POITOU
Source: region of Niort, Thouars; additional sources: Brittany, Anjou, Maine
Made in or by: farms, homes
Best seasons: end of spring, summer; greater abundance of milk
Milk: cow's milk
Fat content: variable
Type: fresh, unsalted

Rind: none
Curing: none
Packaging: rush mat, or wooden mold
Selection:
  Appearance: white and fresh
  Feel: very tender, fatty
  Smell: lactic smell
  Taste: mild, creamy flavor (1–2)
What to watch out for: lack of homogeneity, granular curds
Use: end of meals; additional uses: served mixed with stewed or ripe fruit
Appropriate wines: none
Origin of name: from nature of the cheese (*caille* means curdled milk) and from the name for the open-work shelves on which it is set to drain *(caillebotis)*
A fairly good buy locally
Related cheeses: all fresh cheeses made from cow's milk
  Differences: none besides name and packaging

CAILLEBOTE D'AUNIS

Province: AUNIS
Source: Marans; additional sources: Serigny, Andilly (Charente-Maritime)
Made in or by: farms
Best seasons: winter, spring, summer; availability of milk
Milk: sheep's milk
Type: fresh, unsalted
Form: bulk
Packaging: wicker or rush basket
Selection:
  Appearance: pure white
  Feel: very soft, not very much drained
  Smell: light sheep smell
  Taste: creamy, very mild (1–2)
What to watch out for: excessive drying
Use: end of meals, snacks; additional uses: served mixed with fresh or stewed fruit
Appropriate wines: all dry and fruity white wines of Charente and Ile d'Oléron

Origin of name: packaging and place of origin

> *Note:* When molded and drained, this cheese is called PI-GOUILLE (*see* this listing)

Related cheeses: Sableau or Trois Cornes, other rush-basket cheeses, other sheep's or goat's-milk Caillebotes
> *Differences:* origin, quality, flavor

CAMEMBERT FERMIER

Province NORMANDY (PAYS D'AUGE)
Source: Pays d'Auge; additional sources: department of lower Normandy
Made in or by: farms; increasingly rarely
Best seasons: end of spring, summer, autumn; availability of higher quality milk
Milk: cow's milk, unpasteurized
Fat content: 45% to 50%
Type: soft
Rind: bloomy
Curing: dry, in cellars, 1 month
Form: flat disk
Dimensions: 4½ in. in diameter, 1¼ in. thick
Weight: 9 oz.
Selection:
> *Appearance:* regular shape, very even surface, downy white surface with touches of red
> *Feel:* supple, not soft
> *Smell:* tangy fragrance with some bouquet
> *Taste:* fruity flavor, not very pronounced (3)

What to watch out for: rind too white or too red, vermiculated (wrinkled) surface, grayish edges, gray interior with black spots, odor of mildew or ammonia, excessive hardness, runniness
Use: end of meals: additional uses: in croquettes and canapés
Appropriate wines: all suave fruity and elegant wines of Burgundy, Bordeaux and Côtes-du-Rhône
Origin of name: village where a cheese was made that was presented to Napoleon III at the opening of the World's Fair of 1855

Brief history: perfected by Marie Harel around 1790 near Vimoutiers
A good buy

It is said that around 1791 Marie Harel, née Fontaine, a farm woman of Camembert (in the Orne region), invented this cheese and gave the recipe to her daughter Marie, the wife of Victor Paynel. To commemorate her invention a statue was erected in Vimoutiers in 1928 at a cost of $2,-800, donated by "400 men and women who make cheese in Van Wert, Ohio (U.S.A.)."

No doubt the full truth about the "invention" of Camembert will never be known. The most important invention was that of the cylindrical box by Monsieur Ridel in 1890. Before this, Camembert was sold in a wrapping of straw and spoiled if shipped farther than Paris. The box made possible shipment over long distances. Thanks to M. Ridel, Marseilles and Bayonne discovered Camembert and so did New York, Buenos Aires and Saigon.

Related cheeses: Brie de Meaux, raw-milk Coulommiers
  Differences: origin, shape, size, quality, flavor

CAMEMBERT PASTEURISE

Source: Normandy; additional sources: 67 cheese-producing departments in France; foreign sources: Belgium, Holland, Switzerland, Ireland, Great Britain, German Federal Republic, U.S.
Made in or by: commercial plants
Best seasons: all year, pasteurized
Milk: cow's milk, pasteurized
Fat content: 45% to 50%
Type: soft
Rind: bloomy
Curing: dry, 2 months
Form: small flat disk
Dimensions: 4½ in. in diameter, 1¼ in. thick
Weight: 9 oz.
Selection:
  Appearance: geometrically regular shape, white rind
  Feel: firm texture with some give

Smell: dominant aroma of mold

Taste: from neutral milky flavor to fruity (3)

What to watch out for: malformed, concave rind, excessive redness, graininess, excessive saltiness, hardness or runniness

Use: end of meals, snacks

Appropriate wines: red table wines of good quality

Origin of name: see CAMEMBERT FERMIER

> *Note:* Also available as DEMI-CAMEMBERT and CAMEMBERT EN PORTIONS (*see* these listings)

Related cheeses: commercial Bries, Coulommiers and Carrés de l'Est made from pasteurized milk

Differences: origin, form, size, quality, flavor

CAMEMBERT EN PORTIONS

This packaging was developed for distant markets and for food retail chains.

There are also half Camemberts (*see* DEMI-CAMEMBERT).

There are 4, 6 or 8 individual portions in each box; the average is 6.

CAMPENEAC

or TRAPPISTE DE CAMPENEAC

Province: BRITTANY

Source: Abbey of Campénéac

Made in or by: nuns of Campénéac convent

Best seasons: all year; pressed cheeses are not sensitive to fluctuations in temperature and keep well

Milk: cow's milk

Fat content: 40% to 42%

Type: pressed, uncooked

Rind: washed

Curing: humid, 2 months

Form: thick disk

Dimensions: 10 in. in diameter, 1½ in. thick

Weight: about 4 lb. 6 oz.

Packaging: unwrapped
Selection:
  Appearance: very smooth rind, ochre to grayish yellow; light-yellow
      interior with very fine holes
  Feel: supple and elastic
  Smell: rather penetrating smell
  Taste: not very pronounced lactic taste (3)
What to watch out for: dry tough rind, grayish tinge; interior of indeter-
    minate color, too many openings, bitterness, heat spoilage
Use: dessert; additional uses: cheese crisps
Appropriate wines: all light fruity red wines: Muscadet and Saint-Emilion
Origin of name: site of Trappist convent
Brief history: this cheese supersedes the one that was previously made
  by the same Trappist nuns in their Sainte-Anne-d'Auray Convent.
  This cheese is relatively recent, dating from the foundation of the
  present monastery
A good buy
Related cheeses: all monastery cheeses of the semi-soft type, all Saint-
  Paulins
  Differences: origin, form, size, fineness of texture, flavor

CANCOILLOTTE

Province: FRANCHE-COMTE
Prepared from METTON (*see* this listing)
Flavor: very fruity (4)
Recipe: Put some well "rotted" (golden ripe) Metton in a cast-iron pot
  with 30% of its weight of salt water (3% solution or 2 tablespoons
  of salt to a quart of water). Warm over low heat or in a double
  boiler, stirring to blend. Then add an amount of fresh butter equivalent to 30% of the weight of the cheese. Stir again to blend. When
  the mixture is smooth and uniform, pour into serving dishes.

    Note: Cancoillotte is eaten warm at any time of the day in
sandwiches or on slices of toast.
    In accordance with family traditions it is flavored with garlic or
white wine. It does not keep well and must be remelted periodically.
    The skin that forms on the top when it is cooled should be as

little wrinkled as possible and on the inside the Cancoillotte should be light yellow or slightly greenish. If it is gray, it is no longer fresh.

A very good buy

CANTAL

Also known as: FOURME DU CANTAL, SALERS, or FOURME DE SALERS

Province: AUVERGNE

Source: upland pastures of Cantal; best source: the region above Mauriac; additional sources: a large region comprising the Department of Cantal and adjoining areas (Label of origin regulated by law)

Made in or by: mountain farms in summer, commercial plants all year round

Best seasons: summer (better milk from summer pastures), autumn; end of curing period

Milk: cow's milk

Fat content: 45%

Type: pressed, uncooked

Rind: natural, brushed

Curing: dry, in humid cellars, with brushings, 3 to 6 months

Form: tall cylinder

Dimensions: 14 to 18 in. in diameter; 14 to 16 in. high

Weight: 77 lb. to 99 lb.

Packaging: unwrapped

Selection:

  Appearance: light gray unbroken rind or a bit darker gray with slight cracks

  Feel: springy to firm

  Smell: faint smell of the cellar, pronounced lactic aroma when cut

  Taste: mild nutty flavor (3)

What to watch out for: cracked rind, porous and uneven texture, sharpness

Use: end of meals, snacks: additional uses: as a condiment in the local cuisine: in soups, purées, sauces and au gratin dishes

Appropriate wines: all light fruity wines: Côtes-d'Auvergne, Côtes-Roannaises, Beaujolais

Origin of name: Cantal Mountains

A very good buy

Related cheeses: Fourmes de Laguiole and Fourmes de Rochefort-Montagne
  Differences: origin, shape, fineness of texture, flavor

CANTALON

Province: AUVERGNE
Source: Mauriac region, Marmanhac; additional source: a large part of Auvergne
Best seasons: summer, autumn
Milk: cow's milk
Fat content: 45%
Type: pressed, uncooked
Rind: natural, brushed
Curing: dry, in humid cellars, 2 to 3 months
Form: tall cylinder
Dimensions: 6 to 8 in. in diameter, 10 to 12 in. high
Weight: 8 lb. 13 oz. to 22 lb.
In other respects resembles CANTAL
Flavor: 3
Origin of name: diminutive of Cantal

> *Note*: Fourme de Rochefort is a Cantalon.

A very good buy

CAPRICE DES DIEUX

Province: CHAMPAGNE (BASSIGNY)
Source: Ets Bongrain
Best seasons: all year; pasteurized milk used
Milk: cow's milk, enriched and pasteurized
Fat content: 60%
Type: soft, double cream
Rind: bloomy
Curing: dry, in ventilated cellars
Form: small oval loaf
Dimensions: 5½ in. long, 2½ in. wide, 1½ in. high

Weight: 7 oz.
Packaging: cardboard box with brand name
Selection: no possibility of selection; the wrapping hides the product
Uses: end of meal
Appropriate wines: all light and fruity table wines: Beaujolais
Origin of name: factory trademark
Related cheeses: all the commercial pasteurized double-cream cheeses
    with bloomy rinds
  Differences: origin, shape, size, texture, flavor

CARRE DE BONNEVILLE

Province: NORMANDY
(*See* MOYAUX, or PAVE DE MOYAUX, or PAVE D'AUGE)

CARRE DE BRAY

Province: NORMANDY (PAYS DE BRAY)
Source: Forges-les-Eaux region, Gournay-en-Bray; additional sources:
    all of Pays de Bray
Made in or by: small dairies
Best seasons: end of spring, summer; milk from pasturelands, end of the
    curing period
Milk: cow's milk
Fat content: 45%
Type: soft
Rind: bloomy
Curing: in a somewhat humid place, 2 weeks
Form: small square
Dimensions: 2¾ in. square, ¾ in. thick
Weight: 3½ oz.
Packaging: unwrapped, on straw
Selection:
  Appearance: uniformly white rind
  Feel: somewhat yielding
  Smell: distinct mushroom smell
  Taste: somewhat grainy and salty, slightly astringent (3)

What to watch out for: excessive saltiness, excessive graininess due to overdrying
Use: end of meals
Appropriate wines: all lively fruity or full-bodied wines: Beaujolais-Villages
Origin of name: shape of cheese and place of origin
Brief history: probably the ancestor of Demi-Sel or Carré Frais
A good buy
Related cheeses: Bondon, Bondard, Coeur de Bray and all cheeses of the region
  Differences: local origin, shape, size, texture

CARRE DE L'EST

Province: CHAMPAGNE or LORRAINE
Source: departments of eastern France
Made in or by: commercial dairies
Best seasons: all year round, pasteurized milk used
Milk: cow's milk, pasteurized
Fat content: 45% to 50%
Type: soft
Rind: bloomy
Curing: in air-conditionned cellars, 3 weeks
Form: square
Dimensions: 3¼ to 4 in. square, 1 to 1¼ in. thick
Weight: 4½ oz. to 9 oz.
Packaging: box
Selection:
  Appearance: very white and downy rind
  Feel: supple without being soft
  Smell: slight mushroom smell
  Taste: bland flavor (3)
What to watch out for: grayish rind, excessive reddish discoloration on surface, dried out or runny inside
Use: end of meals
Origin of name: shape of cheese and region of origin

> *Note:* Small Carrés de l'Est for export are divided into portions.

A very good buy
Related cheeses: Coulommiers and Brie ae l'Est
  Differences: shape, size, origin, flavor

CASTILLON

Province: COMTE DE FOIX
(*See* BETHMALE)

CENDRE D'AISY

Province: BURGUNDY
Source: Montbard (Côte-d'Or) and vicinity; additional sources: Armançon Valley
Best seasons: autumn, winter, spring; stocks of cheese kept for the period when production is slow or has ceased
Milk: cow's milk
Fat content: 45%
Type: soft
Rind: washed
Curing: humid, 2 months in marc, then stored in wood ashes
Form: thick disk or truncated cone
Dimensions: 4 to 5 in. in diameter, 1½ to 2½ in. thick
Weight: 12 oz. to 1 lb. 5 oz.
Packaging: covered with ashes
Selection:
  Feel: firm
  Smell: faint smell on the outside, very strong smell within
  Taste: very fruity savor, tangy aroma (5)
What to watch out for: gray interior, saponification, sharpness (enjoyed by some local consumers)
Use: end of meals
Appropriate wines: only the most robust and full-bodied: Corton
Origin of name: invented name for a specialty produced not far from Aisy-sur-Armançon
Not a very good buy

Related cheeses: all the whole or partly skimmed cow's-milk Cendrés of
Champagne and Orléanais
Differences: nature of the curd, origin, shape and flavor

CENDRE D'ARGONNE

Province: CHAMPAGNE
Milk: cow's milk, partly skimmed
Fat content: 30% to 35%
Type: soft
Rind: natural, coated with ashes
Generic name of several Cendrés such as HEILTZ-LE-MAURUPT,
NOYER-EN-VAL
Rare

CENDRE DE CHAMPAGNE

Also known as: CENDRE DES RICEYS
Province: CHAMPAGNE
Source: Châlon-sur-Marne, Vitry-le-François and Sainte-Menehould re-
gion
Made in or by: farms, and small dairies
Best seasons: summer, autumn; available milk, end of curing period
Milk: cow's milk, skimmed
Fat content: 20% to 30%
Type: soft
Rind: natural, coated with ashes
Curing: in humid cellars, in cases filled with wood ashes, 6 to 8 weeks
Form: flat disk
Dimensions: 8½ in. in diameter, 1¼ in. thick
Weight: 9 oz.
Packaging: unwrapped
Selection:
  Appearance: regular shape
  Feel: some give
  Smell: not strong on the outside
  Taste: ranges from very nutty to rank, depending upon age (4–7)

What to watch out for: desiccation
Use: snacks
Appropriate wines: all solid, full-bodied wines: red Bouzy, Les Riceys
Origin of name: producing region and method of curing
A good buy locally
Related cheeses: Cendrés of Orléanais, Ardennes and other sections of
    Champagne
  Differences: origin, shape, size, texture, flavor

CERVELLE DE CANUT

Also known as: CLAQUERET LYONNAIS
Province: LYONNAIS
Recipe: Take some partly drained curds and beat them thoroughly with
    a spoon. When very smooth, add pepper, salt, shallots, herbs and
    a very small amount of minced garlic. Let the mixture ferment for
    a day or two. Then add a pony of vinegar, a glass of white wine and
    2 tablespoons of oil. Serve chilled as an hors d'oeuvre or as a dessert.
Flavor: 3
(*See* CLAQUERET)

CHABICHOU FERMIER

Province: POITOU
Source: plateau of Neuville-de-Poitou; additional sources: Poitiers region
Made in or by: scattered farms
Best seasons: end of spring, summer, autumn; availability of goat's milk
Milk: goat's milk
Fat content: 45%
Type: soft
Rind: natural
Curing: dry, in dry cellars, 3 weeks
Form: small truncated cone
Dimensions: 2½ in. in base diameter, 2 in. in top diameter, 2½ in. high
Weight: maximum 3½ oz.
Packaging: unwrapped

Selection:
   Appearance: thin blue-gray rind with reddish pigmentation
   Feel: firm, but not hard
   Smell: pronounced goat smell
   Taste: highly pronounced to sharp flavor
What to watch out for: gray rind, blackish pigmentation, grainy texture, excessive saltiness, sharpness
Use: end of meals
Appropriate wines: lively, fruity reds of Neuville-de-Poitou, Dissay, Saint-Martin-la-Rivière
Origin of name: local dialect
Related cheeses: Mothais, Saint-Maixent, Couhé-Vérac, Sainte-Maure, etc.
   Differences: origin, shape, size, texture, flavor

CABRICHOU LAITIER

Also known as: CABICHOU, CHABI, CABRICHIU, etc.
Province: POITOU
Source: Poitou; additional sources: Charentes, Touraine
Made in or by: dairies
Best seasons: end of spring, summer; availability of goat's milk
Milk: goat's milk
Fat content: 45%
Type: soft
Rind: bloomy
Curing: dry, 2 weeks
Form: small truncated cone
Weight: 3 oz. to 3½ oz.
Packaging: paper container
Selection:
   Appearance: white rind
   Feel: firm with some give
   Smell: rather strong goat smell
   Taste: very fruity to sharp (4)
What to watch out for: grayish rind, blackish pigmentation, discoloration just beneath the rind, graininess, excessive saltiness
Use: dessert
Appropriate wines: all durable fruity reds of Poitou and elsewhere

Origin of name: Poitou dialect
Brief history: linked with the history of the farm-produced cheese
A fairly good buy
Related cheeses: all dairy goat's-milk cheeses of the region
   Differences: origin, shape, size, texture, flavor

CHABRIS

Province: BERRY
Milk: goat's milk
Fat content: 45%
(*See* VALENÇAY or LEVROUX)

   Note: Name of a brand of Valençay or Levroux.

CHAMBARAND

Also known as: TRAPPISTE DE CHAMBARAND
Province: DAUPHINE
Source: Roybon (Isère)
Made in or by: monks, using traditional methods
Best seasons: summer, autumn, winter; availability of high-quality milk,
   end of curing period
Milk: cow's milk
Fat content: 45%
Type: slightly pressed curd
Rind: washed
Curing: in humid cellars, 3 to 6 weeks
Form: small disk, convex on the sides
Dimensions: 3 in. in diameter, 1 in. thick
Weight: about 5½ oz.
Packaging: paper
Selection:
   Appearance: smooth rind, light yellow to pink
   Feel: tender and supple
   Smell: no special smell
   Taste: mild and creamy (2–3)

What to watch out for: swelling, heat spoilage, grainy texture, bitterness or desiccation
Use: end of meals
Appropriate wines: all light and fruity wines of Savoy, Mâconnais, Sancerre, Pouilly-sur-Loire (Chasselas)
Origin of name: name of Trappist monastery
Brief history: linked with that of the monastery
A fairly good buy
Related cheeses: Reblochon, Saint-Paulin, other Trappist cheeses: Echourgnac, Entrammes, etc.
  Differences: origin, shape, size, texture, flavor

CHAMBÉRAT

Province: BOURBONNAIS
Source: Chambérat (Allier); additional sources: Achignat, Treignat (Allier)
Made in or by: farms, but disappearing
Best seasons: summer, autumn; availability of milk, end of curing period
Milk: cow's milk
Fat content: 40% to 45%
Type: pressed, uncooked
Rind: washed
Curing: under humid conditions, 2 months; also consumed semi-fresh
Form: flat disk
Dimensions: 6½ to 8 in. in diameter, 1½ to 2 in. thick
Weight: 2 lb. 3 oz. to 3 lb. 5 oz
Packaging: unwrapped
Selection:
  Appearance: sound brownish yellow surface
  Feel: firm, but not excessively so
  Smell: no special odor
  Taste: somewhat strong to very fruity (3–5)
Use: end of meals, snacks
Appropriate wines: all fruity lively reds of Saint-Pourcain, Côtes-d'Auvergne and Côtes-Roannaises
Origin of name: place name
A fairly good buy locally

Related cheeses: all Trappist cheeses
　Differences: coarser and much firmer

CHANTEMERLE-LES-BLES

Province: DAUPHINE
(*See* PICODON)

CHAOURCE

Province: CHAMPAGNE
Source: Chaource; additional sources: surrounding region. (Label of
　origin regulated by law)
Made in or by: small dairies
Best seasons: summer, autumn; best production of milk, end of curing
　period
Milk: cow's milk
Fat content: 45% to 50%
Type: soft
Rind: bloomy
Curing: dry, 2 to 3 weeks (semi-cured) or 1 to 2 months (cured)
Form: cylinder
Dimensions: 5 in. in diameter, 2½ in. thick
Weight: 1 lb. 5 oz. to 1 lb. 7 oz.
Packaging: paper
Selection:
　Appearance· white, downy rind
　Feel: supple without softness
　Smell: faint mushroom smell
　Taste: milky to fruity flavor (2–3)
What to watch out for: grainy texture
Uses: end of meals
Appropriate wines: fruity white wines of Saint-Bris-le-Vineux, Chablis
　and Irancy; fruity durable reds and rosés of Irancy
Origin of name: town which was the most important market and the
　center of the producing region
A good buy

Related cheeses: Ervy-le-Châtel, Epoisses Demi-affiné
  Differences: origin, shape, quality

CHAROLAIS

Province: BURGUNDY
Source: environs of Charolles; additional sources: mountain regions of
    Charolais
Made in or by: farms; very limited production of pure goat's milk
    cheese
Best seasons: goat's milk cheese: summer, autumn, depending on availa-
    bility of goat's milk, end of storage period; cow's-milk cheese: all
    year
Milk: goat's milk, half goat's milk or all cow's milk
Fat content: 40% to 45%
Type: soft
Rind: natural
Curing: dry, 2 or 3 weeks
Form: tall cylinder; pure goat's milk cheeses shorter and narrower,
    truncated cone
Dimensions: 2 in. in diameter, 3 in. high
Weight: 7 oz.; pure goat's milk cheese, about 4 oz.
Packaging: unwrapped
Selection:
  Appearance: grayish white to pale blue rind
  Feel: hard
  Smell: faint aroma
  Taste: nutty to pronounced flavor (3–4); may be eaten fresh: in this
      case the flavor is milk and nutty.
What to watch out for: grainy texture, vermiculate rind of mixed-milk
    cheeses
Use: end of meals, snacks; additional uses: in Burgundy or Lyon *fromage
    fort* (strong cheese)
Appropriate wines: all dry white wines of the Mâcon region or Aligotés
    of Burgundy
Origin of name: name of producing region
Related cheeses: all dry goat's-milk or half goat's-milk cheeses of Mâcon-
    nais, Bresse, Nivernais

CHATEAUBRIAND

Province: NORMANDY (PAYS DE BRAY)
   Name invented by some retailers and applied to a triple-cream cheese made in the Canton of Forges-les-Eaux, Normandy

CHATEAUROUX

Province: BERRY
(*See* VALENÇAY or LEVROUX)

CHAUMONT

Province: CHAMPAGNE
Source: Neuilly-sur-Suize
Made in or by: traditional methods
Best seasons: summer, autumn; milk from pastured cows, end of the curing period
Milk: cow's milk
Fat content: 45%
Type: soft
Rind: washed
Curing: humid, in humid cellars, periodic washings, 2 months
Form: small, relatively tall truncated cone with a shallow depression on top surface
Dimensions: 3 in. in diameter, 2 in. high
Weight: about 7 oz.
Packaging: unwrapped
Selection:
  Appearance: light brick-red to red-brown rind
  Feel: supple
  Smell: rather robust smell
  Taste: spicy savor (4–5)
What to watch out for: hard rind, solidity, granular texture, sharp or bitter taste, excessive saltiness
Use: end of meals

Appropriate wines: all lively full-bodied Burgundies and Bordeaux or Côtes-du-Rhône

Origin of name: invented name applied to a type of Langres cheese

Related cheeses: Langres, Epoisses, Soumaintrain, Munster, Gérômé

   Differences: origin, shape, size, flavor

CHAUNAY

Province: POITOU

Made in or by: commercial dairies

(See CHABICHOU)

CHAVIGNOL-SANCERRE

Province: BERRY

Source: Chavignol; additional sources: all of Sancerrois (Cher)

Made in or by: farms

Best seasons: summer, autumn; periodic nature of goats' lactation, good storage during these periods

Milk: goat's milk

Fat content: 45%

Type: soft

Rind: natural

Curing: dry, 2 weeks

Form: small flattened ball

Dimensions: 2 in. in diameter, 1 inch thick

Weight: 2 oz. to 3 oz.

Packaging: unwrapped

Selection:

  Appearance: delicate bluish rind; inside white, fine-grained and smooth

  Feel: firm and dense

  Smell: slight goat smell

  Taste: mild and nutty (2–3)

What to watch out for: superficial and internal desiccation, granulation, excessive saltiness

Use: dessert

Appropriate wines: all white wines of Sauvignon-de-Sancerre, all frank and fruity local Pinot Gris wines

Origin of name: name of place where it is mainly produced and perhaps from the name of the well-known wine

> *Note:* Chavignol is often incorrectly called Crottin ("horse-dung") de Chavignol when it is still blue. The real Crottins are old cheeses that have turned brown from age, desiccation, or maceration in white wine.

Related cheeses: Crézanzy, Santranges
   Differences: origin, shape, texture

CHECY

Province: ORLEANAIS
(*See* OLIVET)

CHEDDAR

Country: GREAT BRITAIN
County: SOMERSET
Made in or by: large factories; more rarely on farms
Best seasons: all year round; predominantly continuous industrial production
Milk: cow's milk
Fat content: 45%
Type: pressed, uncooked, uncolored
Rind: natural, untreated, oiled
Curing: dry, in dry cellars, about 6 months
Form: tall cylinder
Dimensions: 14 to 16 in. in diameter; 14 to 16 in. high
Weight: 66 lb. to 77 lb.
Packaging: cloth wrapper
Selection:
   Appearance: smooth even rind; slightly waxy, homogeneous interior despite natural granulation
   Feel: firm and oily with some degree of suppleness

Smell: light bouquet
Taste: pronounced, not very spicy savor (3)
What to watch out for: graininess, crumbly texture, excessive hardness, sharpness
Use: end of meals, breakfasts, snacks; additional uses: cheese toasts, seasoning of dishes
Appropriate wines: all fruity lively wines: Bordeaux (Médoc), Port; also pale export ale
Origin of name: place of origin
Brief history: linked with that of Cheshire
A fairly good buy
Related cheeses: Cheshire, Leicester, Gloucester, etc.
  Differences: origin, shape, color, packaging, texture, savor

CHESHIRE

Country: GREAT BRITAIN
County: CHESHIRE
Source: Cheshire; additional sources: Shropshire and other counties
Made in or by: factories, almost entirely
Best seasons: all year round; bulk of production from factories
Milk: cow's milk
Fat content: 45%
Type: pressed, uncooked
Rind: natural, oiled, colored red
Curing: dry, in dry cellars, 6 months to 2 years
Form: tall cylinder
Dimensions: 14 in. in diameter, 16 in. high average
Weight: 77 lb. to 88 lb.
Packaging: cloth wrapper
Selection:
  Appearance: smooth even rind, slightly waxy; homogeneous interior despite natural granulation
  Feel: firm and oily with some suppleness
  Smell: faint smell with some bouquet
  Taste: pronounced, not very spicy savor
What to watch out for: grainy texture
Use: end of meals; additional uses: in Welsh rarebit

Appropriate wines: all durable fruity wines: Bordeaux (Médoc), Port; also pale export ale
Brief history: goes back to the beginning of the 17th century
A fairly good buy

> *Note:* Cheshires from countries other than the British Isles (from Canada, Australia, New Zealand, and the U. S.) are inaccurately called Cheddar.
> The English age Cheshires until bluish veins begin to form; these cheeses, aged for 2 years, are sold under the name Blue Cheddar.

Related cheeses: Cheddar, Leicester, Gloucester, etc.
  Differences: origin, size, texture, color, packaging

CHESTER

Country: FRANCE
Made in or by: commercial plants in France, in Castres in Tarn Department (Solafro)
Best seasons: all year; commercial production all year
Milk: cow's milk, pasteurized
Fat content: 45%
Type: pressed, uncooked
Rind: natural, untreated, oiled, colored red
Curing: dry, in dry cellars, about 6 months
Form: tall cylinder
Dimensions: 14 to 16 in. in diameter, 16 to 18 in. high
Weight: 70 lb. to 110 lb.
Packaging: unwrapped, or cloth wrapper
Selection:
  Appearance: smooth, even, slightly waxy rind; homogeneous interior despite natural granulation
  Feel: firm with a touch of suppleness
  Smell: bouquet, but some residual lactic odor
  Taste: pronounced, not very spicy savor (3)
What to watch out for: grainy, crumbly or brittle texture; rancidity
Use: in cheese dishes such as Welsh rarebit, cheese toasts and crisps; additional uses: end of meals, snacks, canapés
Appropriate wines: durable fruity wines: Bordeaux (Médoc), Port; also pale export ale

Origin of name: capital of county of Cheshire
Brief history: manufacture begun in France after World War II
A fairly good buy

>*Note:* French-made Cheshire style cheese is often called "Cheddar," as are similar products made in U.S., Canada and New Zealand.

Related cheeses: English Cheshire and Cheddar
  Differences: origin, size, color, texture, savor

CHEVRE A LA FEUILLE

Province: POITOU
Milk: goat's milk
Fat content: 45%
Type: soft
Rind: natural
Flavor: 3
(*See* MOTHAIS)

CHEVRE LONG

Provinces: ANJOU, CHARENTES, POITOU, TOURAINE
Milk: goat's milk
Fat content: 45%
Type: soft
Rind: bloomy
Flavor: 3
Generic name of SAINTE-MAURE LAITIER (*see* this listing)

CHEVRET

Province: FRANCHE-COMTE
Source: mountainous areas of Jura and upper Doubs; high Jura plateau: Mijoux, La Faucille; additional sources: districts of Ain
Made in or by: farms, chalets, by traditional methods; rare

Best seasons: summer, autumn; availability of goat's milk, end of curing period

Milk: goat's milk

Fat content: 45%

Type: soft

Rind: natural

Curing: dry, in ventilated cellars, 4 to 5 weeks

Form: small flat disk, small square, or rectangular loaf

Dimensions: 3½ in. by 1 in. high or 3 in. by 1½ in. high on average

Weight: average 5 oz.

Packaging: unwrapped

Selection:

  Appearance: delicate bluish rind, pink spots

  Feel: smooth, homogeneous texture

  Smell: faint goat smell

  Taste: nutty flavor (3)

What to watch out for: thick, vermiculated rind, friability, rancidity

Use: end of meals, snacks

Appropriate wines: all choice, light and fruity white, rosé and red wines of Jura, Savoy, Beaujolais

Origin of name: type of milk used

Related cheeses: all country goat's-milk cheeses, particularly Tomme de Belley, Brique du Forez

CHEVRETON D'AMBERT

Also known as: BRIQUE DU FOREZ
Province: AUVERGNE (LIVRADOIS)

Brique du Forez may be considered the generic type of Chèvreton d'Ambert

CHEVRETON DE VIVEROLS

Also known as: BRIQUE DU FOREZ
Province: AUVERGNE (LIVRADOIS)

Brique du Forez may be considered the generic type of Chèvreton de Viverols

CHEVRETTE DES BAUGES

Province: SAVOIE
Source: Le Châtelard (Savoie); additional sources: the immediate neighborhood
Made in or by: chalets; production dying out
Best seasons: summer, autumn; availability of goat's milk, end of curing period
Milk: goat's milk
Fat content: 45%
Type: pressed, uncooked
Rind: washed
Curing: humid, in cool cellars, 2 to 3 months
Form: thick disk
Dimensions: 7 in. in diameter, 2 in. thick
Weight: 2 lb. 10 oz.
Packaging: unwrapped
Selections:
  Appearance: thin, glossy, light-colored rind
  Feel: supple
  Smell: faint smell of the barn
  Taste: light nutty flavor (3)
What to watch out for: swelling, desiccation, grainy texture
Use: end of meals, snacks
Appropriate wines: all dry and fruity wines of Chablais, the upper Rhone valley: Roussette de Seyssel, Roussette de Frangy, Crépy
Origin of name: composition of cheese and place of origin
Related cheeses: Tomme de Chèvre de Tarantaise: Allues, Courchevel, Beaufort, Grataron d'Arêches, Tomme d'Annot
  Differences: origin, size, texture, flavor

CHEVRINE DE LENTA

Province: SAVOIE (HAUTE MAURIENNE)
Source: pasture areas of Lenta; pasture around Bonneval-sur-Arc, above
    6,000 feet high
Made in or by: chalets; consumed exclusively in Bonneval
Best season: summer; summering of flocks in mountain pastures
Milk: goat's milk
Fat content: 45%
Type: pressed, uncooked
Rind: none
Dimensions: 4 in. in diameter, 3¼ in. high
Weight: 1 lb. to 1 lb. 2 oz.
Packaging: unwrapped
Selection:
    Appearance: very sound, white or yellowish white in color
    Feel: hard, brittle texture
    Smell: faint barn smell
    Taste: very nutty to sharp flavor (3–4 or 6–7)
What to watch out for: overaging, excessive dryness, sharpness (qualities
    preferred locally)
Use: end of meals, snacks
Appropriate wines: whatever you have or fruity lively wines of Savoy and
    Beaujolais
Origin of name: name of pasture areas and type of milk used
A good buy locally
Related cheeses: Grataron d'Arêches, pressed mountain Tommes de
    Chèvre
    Differences: origin, shape, texture, flavor

CHEVROTIN DES ARAVIS

Province: SAVOIE
Sources: massif of Aravis
Made in or by: chalets
Best seasons: summer, autumn; availability of goat's milk, end of curing
    period
Milk: goat's milk, or mixed goat's and cow's milk
Fat content: 45%

Type: pressed, uncooked
Rind: natural
Curing: dry, in humid cellars, with slight dampenings, 2 months
Form: flat disk
Dimensions: 5 in. in diameter, 2 in. thick; often smaller
Weight: 1 lb. 5 oz. to 1 lb. 8 oz., sometimes 14 oz.
Packaging: unwrapped
Selection:
   Appearance: gray sound rind, rough-surfaced but delicate
   Feel: firm
   Smell: no special smell
   Taste: mild, slight goat flavor (3–4)
What to watch out for: excessive desiccation, grainy texture
Use: end of meals, snacks
Appropriate wines: Mondeuse, Chignin-Bergeron
Origin of name: type of milk used and producing region
Related cheeses: other Tomme de Chèvre de Savoie, Tomme de Beaufort,
      Grataron d'Arêches, etc.

CHEVROTIN DU BOURBONNAIS

Province: BOURBONNAIS
Source: Conne, Souvigny; additional sources: Ygrand and out-skirts of
      Moulin
Made in or by: farms
Best seasons: summer, autumn; availability of goat's milk, good curing
      period
Milk: goat's milk
Fat content: 45%
Type: soft
Rind: natural
Curing: very brief, dry 1 or 2 weeks; eaten fresh or semi-dry
Form: trucated cone
Dimensions: 2½ to 3 in. at base, 2 to 2½ in. high
Weight: 3½ oz. to 4 oz.
Packaging: unwrapped
Selection:
   Appearance: delicate or barely formed rind
   Feel: supple or firm but oily

Smell: no special smell, possibly lactic smell when fresh

Taste: from creamy to very nutty (3–4)

What to watch out for: grainy texture

Use: end of meals, snacks

Appropriate wines: all fruity whites of Sancerrois; all light, fruity whites, rosés and reds of Saint Pourcain

Origin of name: type of milk and place of origin

Note: Chevrotin de Bourbonnais is the generic type of CHEVROTIN DE CONNE, CHEVROTIN DE MOULINS and CHEVROTIN DE SOUVIGNY

Related cheeses: all goat's-milk cheeses of Mâconnais, Charolais, Nivernais

Differences: origin, texture, shape and size

CHEVROTIN DE CONNE

Province: BOURBONNAIS
Milk: goat's milk
Fat content: 45%
(*See* CONNE)

CHEVROTIN DE MOULINS

Province: BOURBONNAIS
Milk: goat's milk
Fat content: 45%

CHEVROTIN DE SOUVIGNY

Province: BOURBONNAIS
Milk: goat's milk
(*See* SOUVIGNY)

CHEVRU

Province: ILE-DE-FRANCE
Source: Ile-de-France
Made in or by: small traditional cheese factories
Best seasons: summer, autumn, winter; best quality milk in summer, best
     storage conditions at the end of season
Milk: cow's milk
Fat content: 45% to 50%
Type: soft
Rind: bloomy
Curing: dry, on beds of fern, about 1 month
Form: thick disk
Dimensions: 6½ in. in diameter, 1½ in. thick
Weight: 1 lb. 2 oz.
Selection:
   Appearance: downy white rind dotted with reddish pigments; straw-
        yellow interior
   Feel: supple throughout
   Smell: faint mold smell; full bouquet
   Taste: fruity flavor with pronounced tang (3)
What to watch out for: see Brie de Meaux
Use: end of meals
Appropriate wines: lively, fruity reds of Beaujolais, Burgundy, Côtes-du-
     Rhône, and Bordeaux
Origin of name: village in which cheese originated
Brief history: a very ancient farmer's cheese with good keeping qualities
     that has been revived in recent times
A fairly good buy
Related cheeses: Coulommiers, Brie de Meaux
   Differences: thickness, savor, curing

CIERP DE LUCHON

Also known as: BETHMALE (*see* this listing)
Province: COMTE DE FOIX

CITEAUX

Also known as: TRAPPISTE DE CITEAUX
Province: BURGUNDY
Source: Monastery of Cîteaux, Saint-Nicolas-les-Cîteaux (Côte-d'Or)
Made in or by: monks, in the traditional way; rather rare
Best seasons: summer, autumn; best and most abundant milk, end of
    curing period
Milk: cow's milk
Fat content: 45%
Type: pressed, uncooked
Rind: washed
Curing: in humid cellars; 2 months
Form: thick disk
Dimensions: 7 in. in diameter, 1½ in. thick
Weight: about 2 lb. 3 oz.
Packaging: paper
Selection:
  Appearance: light grayish yellow rind
  Feel: springy
  Smell: faint smell
  Taste: fruity flavor, pronounced tang (2–3)
What to watch out for: too many holes, grainy texture, strong taste, barn
    odor
Use: end of meals
Appropriate wines: all light fruity wines of Burgundy and elsewhere
    (Volnay)
Origin of name: name of monastery where cheese was invented
Brief history: goes back to the renewal of farming on monastery lands
A fairly good buy
Related cheeses: all pressed, uncooked monastery cheeses with washed
    rinds
  Differences: origin, shape, size, texture

CIVRAY

Province: POITOU
(*See* CHABICHOU)

CLAQUEBITOU

Province: HAUTE BOURGOGNE
Source: uplands of Beaune; additional source: Hautes Côtes region
Made in or by: farms, for domestic use; rarely commercialized
Best seasons: summer, autumn; availability of goat's milk
Milk: goat's milk
Fat content: slight variations, minimum 45%
Type: fresh, flavored with fresh herbs and garlic (parsley)
Rind: none
Curing: none
Packaging: bulk
Selection:
  Appearance: fresh and semi-drained
  Feel: tender and velvety-smooth
  Smell: goat's-milk smell
  Taste: mild, slightly acid, aromatic (2–3)
What to watch out for: excessive drainage (not serious), grainy texture
Use: end of meals, snacks
Appropriate wines: Aligotés or Passe-Tout-Grain de la Côte
Origin of name: dialectal
A good buy
Related cheeses: all flavored fresh cheeses: particularly Claqueret Lyonnais
  Differences: flavoring materials, fineness of texture, type of milk

CLAQUERET LYONNAIS

Also known as: CERVELLE DE CANUT
Province: LYONNAIS
Source: Lyons region
Made in or by: homes; very little commercialization
Best seasons: all year round; milk used can come from anywhere in any season
Milk: cow's milk
Fat content: variable
Type: fresh, flavored with herbs
Rind: none

Curing: none
Form: any earthenware or ceramic vessel
Dimensions: of no particular importance; according to need
Packaging: bulk, in crock or tub
Selection: according to freshness and seasoning
  Appearance: freshness
  Taste: degree of flavor imparted by seasonings
What to watch out for: lack of freshness or seasoning
Use: end of meals; additional uses: snacks
Appropriate wines: Beaujolais
Origin of name: traditional in Lyons
A good buy locally
Related cheeses: all other fresh, flavored cheeses
  Differences: origin, spices and flavorings used, smoothness of texture

CLOVIS

Province: ILE-DE-FRANCE
  Old brand name of a double-cream cheese made in the Soissons region

COEUR D'ARRAS

Provinces: PICARDY, ARTOIS
Best seasons: end of spring, summer, autumn
Milk: cow's milk
Fat content: 45%
Type: soft
Rind: washed
Curing: humid, in humid cellars, 2 months
Flavor: 4
A fairly good buy

> *Note:* Like QUART MAROILLES, except for the heart shape, or ROLLOT; same weight.

COEUR DE BRAY

Province: NORMANDY (PAYS DE BRAY)
Source: upper Normandy
Made in or by: often in factories
Best season: summer; best quality milk, best curing conditions
Milk: cow's milk
Fat content: 45%
Type: soft
Rind: bloomy
Curing: dry, 3 weeks
Form: heart
Weight: 3½ oz. to 10½ oz.
Selection:
   Appearance: very downy white rind with a touch here and there of
        reddish pigmentation
   Feel: smooth, supple consistency
   Smell: very slight moldy smell
   Taste: astringent, fruity flavor (3)
What to watch out for: desiccation of rind, exaggerated saltiness, grainy
        texture
Use: end of meals
Appropriate wines: all well-knit fruity reds: red wines of the Loire, Bor-
        gueil
Origin of name: from shape of cheese and name of place of origin
Brief history: a specialty of Pays de Bray
A fairly good buy
Related cheeses: Gournay, Neufchâtel, Bondon, Bondard, Briquettes
   Differences: shape and size

COLOMBIERE

Province: SAVOIE (PLATEAU DES ARAVIS)
Source: massif of Colombière
Made in or by: farms, exclusively
Best seasons: summer, autumn; best quality milk from mountain pas-
        tures, end of curing period
Milk: cow's milk
Fat content: 50%

Type: soft, lightly pressed
Rind: washed
Curing: under cold, humid conditions, 6 to 8 weeks
Form: flat disk
Dimensions: 6 to 6½ in. in diameter, 1¼ to 1½ in. thick
Weight: 1 lb. 5 oz. to 1 lb. 7 oz.
Packaging: set on a thin board, wrapped in paper
Selection:
   Appearance: smooth, mat pink-white rind
   Feel: very supple
   Smell: slight odor of mold
   Taste: mild flavor (2–3)
What to watch out for: hard or sticky rind; hard, granular texture; bitter
   taste
Use: end of meals
Appropriate wines: all choice fruity white wines of Savoie: Crépy, Rous-
   sette, Abymes; light and fruity reds: Mondeuse, Gamay de Chan-
   tagne, Beaujolais
Origin of name: name of mountain area where cheese is produced
Brief history: connected with history of Reblochon, of which it is a
   variety
Not a good buy
Related cheeses: Reblochon, Trappiste de Chambarand
   Differences: origin, size, texture, flavor

COMTE

Also known as: GRUYERE DE COMTE
Province: FRANCHE-COMTE
Source: second plateau of the upper Doubs and of the Jura; best source:
   Verrières-de-Joux; additional sources: a large area including the
   Departments of Doubs, Jura and Haute-Saône, and parts of Depart-
   ments of Ain, Haute-Marne, Vosges and Côte-d'Or
Best seasons: end of summer, autumn, winter; 3 to 6 months after pro-
   duction
Milk: cow's milk
Fat content: 45%
Type: pressed, cooked
Rind: natural, brushed

Curing: dry, with sprinklings in cool and humid cellars, 3 to 6 months
Form: flattened cylindrical wheel with slightly convex rim
Dimensions: 25 to 26 in. in diameter, 4 to 4½ in. thick
Weight: about 77 lb.
Packaging: unwrapped
Selection:
    Appearance: relatively smooth, parallel-sided or very slightly bulging
        rind; holes ranging in size from that of a hazelnut to that of a
        cherry
    Feel: firm with a bit of give
    Smell: little odor
    Taste: fruity, salty or gritty with a strong bouquet (3–4)
What to watch out for: pronounced bulging rind, elastic texture, holes too
    close together, insipid or sharp taste
Use: end of meals, snacks; additional uses: as condiment in cooking, in
    canapés, fondues, gratins, *croque-monsieur,* fritters
Appropriate wines: light, fruity whites, reds or rosés of Mâconnais, Jura,
    Savoy
Origin of name: olden times in France the "fruit" of the mountains was
    subject to a tax collected by *agents gruyers,* whence name *Gruyère*
Brief history: known since the 13th century, when the first fruitery or
    voluntary mountain village cooperative was formed; produced in
    the fruitery dairies
Related cheeses: Gruyère, Emmental Fruité, Beaufort
    Differences: origin, shape, size, texture, flavor

CONCHES

Also known as: FROMAGE A RACLETTE
Country: SWITZERLAND
Canton: VALAIS
Source: valley of Conches (upper Rhône); additional sources: cheeses
    from other places are marked with place names
Best seasons: summer (milk from summer pastures), autumn, winter; end
    of curing period
Milk: cow's milk
Fat content: 45%
Type: pressed, cooked (hard)
Rind: brushed

Curing: humid, in cool cellars, 3 months
Flavor: 3–4
In other respects identical with BAGNES

CONNE

Also known as: CHEVROTIN DU BOURBONNAIS (*see* this listing)
Province: BOURBONNAIS
Source: Conne; additional sources: vicinity of Moulins, Souvigny
Made in or by: farms
Best seasons: end of spring, summer, autumn; most abundant and best quality goat's milk
Milk: goat's milk
Fat content: 45%
Type: soft
Rind: natural, dried
Curing: in dry cellars, 6 weeks
Form: frustum of cone
Dimensions: 3 in. in diameter at base, 2½ in. at top, 2½ in. thick
Weight: about 7 oz.
Packaging: unwrapped
Selection:
  Appearance: finely downed, light-blue rind
  Feel: firm and smooth
  Smell: light goat smell
  Taste: mild nutty flavor (3)
What to watch for: excessive hardness, rancidity, saltiness
Use: end of meals
Appropriate wines: choice fruity whites, rosés and reds of all origins: Pouilly-sur-Loire
Origin of name: place where cheese originated
Related cheeses: various Chevrotins, goat's milk cheeses of Sancerrois
  Differences: origin, fineness of grain, shape, size

COSTAROS

Also known as: BLEU DE COSTAROS or BLEU DU VELAY
(*See* BLEU DU VELAY)

> *Note:* Bleu du Velay is the generic name for BLEU DE COS-
> TAROS, BLEU DE LOUDES, FOURME DE MEZENC.

COUHE-VERAC

Province: POITOU
Source: Couhé-Vérac; additional sources: the immediate vicinity
Made in or by: farms
Best seasons: end of spring, summer, beginning of autumn; best milk after
weaning of the kids, storage conditions, duration of curing period
Milk: goat's milk
Fat content: 45%
Type: soft
Rind: natural
Curing: dry, 3 to 4 weeks
Form: square
Dimensions: 3½ by 3½ in., 1 in. thick
Weight: 8 to 9 oz.
Packaging: plane-tree leaves or chestnut leaves
Selection:
  Appearance: thin rind lightly pigmented with blue
  Feel: firm and homogeneous
  Smell: distinct goat smell
  Taste: pronounced nutty flavor (3)
What to watch out for: heat spoilage, granulation, excessive saltiness,
excessive sharpness
Use: end of meals
Appropriate wines: all robust, full-bodied red wines of Poitou and else-
where: Marigny-Brizay
Origin of name: town nearest to the center of production
Not a good buy

Related cheeses: all farm cheeses of Poitou, in particular La Mothe-Saint-Héray, Saint-Maixent, Chabis, Chabichou
   Differences: origin, shape, size, texture, flavor

COULANDON or CHAUCETIER

Province: BOURBONNAIS
Milk: cow's milk, partly skimmed
Type: soft, eaten fresh, reminiscent of fresh Coulommiers

COULOMMIERS

Region: ILE-DE-FRANCE
Source: Ile-de-France; additional sources: Champagne, Lorraine, Burgundy
Made in or by: farms; increasingly in factories
Best seasons: summer, autumn, winter, end of spring; best quality milk, end of curing period, best storage
Milk: cow's milk
Fat content: 45% to 50%
Type: soft
Rind: bloomy
Curing: dry, 1 month
Form: flat disk
Dimensions: 5 in. in diameter, 1 to ½ in. thick
Weight: 1 lb. 2 oz.
Packaging: unwrapped
Selection:
   Appearance: downy white rind dotted with reddish ferments
   Feel: supple, homogeneous
   Smell: distinct Brie smell, pleasant bouquet
   Taste: rather pronounced tang (3)
What to watch out for: excessive moldiness (overly covered with white down), excessive redness, runniness
Use: end of meals; additional uses: in croquettes, canapés
Appropriate wines: lively fruity reds: Côtes-de-Beaune
Origin of name: town where market was held

Brief history: a smaller version of Brie de Meaux, less vulnerable to injury during shipment

A fairly good buy

Related cheeses: Chevru, Pithiviers

  Differences: size, thickness, curing conditions and flavor, origin

CREMET NANTAIS

Province: BRITTANY (upper)
Source: upper Brittany; additional sources: Anjou, Maine
Best seasons: all year; fresh cheeses are not seasonal in nature
Milk: cow's milk
Fat content: 45% to 50%
Type: fresh, unsalted
Rind: none
Curing: only draining
Form: any sort of mold
Weight: variable, according to container used
Selection:
  Appearance: pure white
  Feel: very soft
  Smell: lactic smell
  Taste: mild, creamy flavor (1–2)
What to watch out for: staleness, excessive dryness
Use: end of meals; additional uses: as dessert with fresh fruit and sugar, compote, etc.; served with fresh whipped cream
Appropriate wines: none necessary
Origin of name: appearance and consistency of cheese
Brief history: traditional dessert cheese in the western provinces under various names

A good buy locally

Related cheeses: all unsalted fresh cheeses, cottage cheese, Jonchées
  Differences: none, except smoothness of texture

CREUSOIS

Province: MARCHE
Milk: cow's milk, skimmed
Fat content: about 10%
Type: soft, dry
Flavor: 3 or 6
(*See* GUERET)

CREZANCY-SANCERRE

Province: BERRY
Source: Crézancy; additional sources: Menetou-Ratel, Subligne, etc.
Made in or by: farms
Best seasons: end of spring, summer, beginning of autumn; periodic nature of goat lactation, good storage during warm weather
Milk: goat's milk
Fat content: 45%
Type: soft
Rind: natural
Curing: dry, 2 to 3 weeks
Form: small flattened ball
Dimensions: 2½ in. in diameter, 1½ in. thick
Weight: 3 oz. to 3½oz.
Packaging: unwrapped
Selection:
  Appearance: delicate, bluish rind; pure white interior
  Feel: firm
  Smell: faint goat smell
  Taste: mild goat flavor (2–3)
What to watch out for: desiccation, vermiculated rind, rancidity, granulation, excessive saltiness
Use: end of meals
Appropriate wines: all white wines of Sauvignon, clean and fruity local Pinot Gris
Origin of name: place of manufacture
Related cheeses: Chavignol, Santranges, other goat's-milk cheeses
  Differences: origin, size, texture, flavor

CROTTIN DE CHAVIGNOL

(*See* CHAVIGNOL)
Province: BERRY
Source: Chavignol; additional sources: Sancerrois area
Made in or by: farms
Best seasons: winter; dried Chavignol is intended for winter
Milk: goat's milk
Fat content: 45%
Type: soft
Rind: natural
Curing: dry, in cool cellars or in tubs, 2 to 3 months
Form: small flattened ball
Dimensions: smaller than the regular cheese
Weight: about 2 oz.
Packaging: unwrapped
Selection: these cheeses are usually not sold in stores, they must be obtained directly from the farmer
  Appearance: red-brown to dark gray rind
  Feel: hard and brittle
  Smell: rancid smell (when dried) or confined fermentation smell (when in tubs)
  Taste: sharp (4–5, sometimes 7)
What to watch out for: defects are often the same as desirable qualities, especially sharpness
Use: farmers' and grape-harvesters' snack, end of meals
Appropriate wines: heartiest, most robust wines are counterbalance; personally, I like the cheese best with a Sancerre-Sauvignon
Origin of name: place of origin and appearance of cheese when it reaches maturity (*crottin* means horse dung)

> *Note:* Nowadays all cheeses of Chavignol are incorrectly called Crottin; only the old, dry cheeses, blackened with age are entitled to the name.

Related cheeses: all dry, aged goat's-milk cheeses of Berry, Touraine, Poitou
  Differences: size, hardness, texture, flavor, origin

DU CURE

Province: BAS POITOU (VENDEE)
Place of origin of NANTAIS cheese, called FROMAGE DU CURE
(*see* this listing)

DAUPHIN

Province: FRENCH HAINAUT
Source: Avesnois, Thiérache
Best seasons: summer, autumn, winter; best milk from pasturelands, end
of the curing period for cheeses made from this milk
Milk: cow's milk
Fat content: minimum 50%
Type: soft, seasoned with tarragon and pepper
Rind: washed
Curing: humid, 2 to 3 months, according to size
Form: crescent; stylized fish; long, thin loaf
Dimensions: variable, but thickness remains constant at 1½ to 2 in.
Weight: 7 oz. to 18 oz.
Packaging: unwrapped, or transparent wrapper
Selection:
   Appearance: smooth brown rind
   Feel: supple without being soft
   Smell: rather penetrating aroma
   Taste: spicy, aromatic flavor with a bouquet like Maroilles (4–5)
What to watch out for: dry, crackled rind; bitterness; runniness; ammonia
odor
Use: end of meals
Appropriate wines: robust, full-bodied Burgundies, Côtes-du-Rhône-Vil-
lages; eaten locally with strong beer
Origin of name: It is said that Louis XIV and the Dauphin made a
stopover in the region on the way to Nijmegen. They liked the taste
of the local cheese and the inhabitants decided to name it for the
Dauphin.

Note: Legend has it that this name was bestowed upon it by
the son of Louis XIV when he visited the region and was served
flavored Maroilles. The legend arose when a scholar noticed that
there was no mention of Dauphin in the monastery records before

1670. As the eminent historian of Maroilles, Leon-Albert Ruelle, has pointed out: "The creation of a new cheese or the modification of an older one does not take place overnight."

It has been proved that, according to a royal order fixing the privileges of the Dauphin, the carters of Maroilles were exempted from the payment of a duty that was to be levied on behalf of the Dauphin on each cart entering Cambrai from Hainaut.

We may assume that the name of Dauphin was given to the cheese as a sign of the carters' gratitude for this exemption.

The cheese is molded in the shape of a heart, a shield or a crescent; the latter form gives it the appearance of a tiny whale.

Related cheeses: flavored, soft-type, washed-rind cheeses, Boulette d'A-vesnes

Differences: shape, size, flavor, origin, texture

DELICE DE SAINT-CYR

Province: ILE-DE-FRANCE (BRIE)
Source: Saint-Cyr-sur-Morin
Made in or by: small factories
Best seasons: all year; good conditions for production, curing and storage
Milk: cow's milk, enriched
Fat content: 75%
Type: soft, triple cream
Rind: bloomy
Curing: in dry cellars, 3 weeks
Form: thick disk
Dimensions: 5 in. in diameter, 1½ in. thick
Weight: 1 lb. 2 oz.
Packaging: unwrapped
Selection:
  Appearance: white rind sprinkled with slight reddish spots
  Feel: buttery texture without elasticity
  Smell: light smell of mold and cream
  Taste: mild and slightly nutty (2–3)
What to watch out for: dried-out surface, rancidity, carbolic acid smell
Use: end of meals; additional uses: in canapés, sandwiches
Appropriate wines: all light fruity wines: red Bouzy; fruity Champagne is excellent

Origin of name: trademark of creator, M. Boursault
Related cheeses: all triple-cream cheeses: Excelsior (72% butterfat), aged
  Boursin, Brillat-Savarin, Explorateur, Grand-Vatel
  Differences: dimensions, origin, fineness of texture

DEMI-BAGUETTE LAONNAISE

Province: ILE-DE-FRANCE
Best seasons: summer, autumn, winter; best milk, end of the curing of
  the last batches
Milk: cow's milk
Fat content: 45% to 50%
Type: soft
Rind: washed
Curing: in humid cellars, washings with brine, 3 months
Form: parallelepiped with square or rectangular cross-section
Dimensions: 5½ in. long, cross-section 1½ by 1½ in.
Weight: 9 oz.
Packaging: box
Flavor: 4
A fairly good buy

> *Note:* In other respects identical with BAGUETTE LAON-
> NAISE *(see* this listing).

DEMI-CAMEMBERT

Province: NORMANDY
Milk: cow's milk, pasteurized or unpasteurized
Fat content: 45%
Type: soft
Rind: bloomy
Flavor: 3
A good buy

> *Note:* Same characteristics as CAMEMBERT, but packaged in
> "half-moon" boxes.
> Demi-camembert is also available in a small size measuring 3 in.
> in diameter and 1 in. thick.

DEMI-COULOMMIERS

Province: CHAMPAGNE or LORRAINE
Source: Champagne; additional sources: Lorraine
Best seasons: all year; standardized industrial production
Milk: cow's milk
Fat content: 45% to 50%
Type: soft
Rind: bloomy
Form: flat half disk
Dimensions: 5 in. in diameter, 1 in. thick
Packaging: semicircular box
Flavor: 3
A good buy

Note: In other respects similar to COULOMMIERS *(see* this listing).

DEMI-ETUVE

Countries: FRANCE; HOLLAND
Milk: cow's milk
Fat content: 30% to 40%
Type: pressed, uncooked
Flavor: 3

Note: Name of French or Dutch cheeses of the EDAM or GOUDA type *(see* these listings).

DEMI-PONT-L'EVEQUE

Province: NORMANDY
Made in or by: factories
Milk: cow's milk
Fat content: 50%
Type: soft
Rind: washed
Form: small parallelepiped with a rectangular cross-section

Dimensions: 4 in. long, 2 in. wide, 1 in. high
Weight: average 5 oz. or 6 oz.
Packaging: box
Flavor: 3–4

> *Note:* Identical with Pont-l'Evêque except for size and shape; cheese is generally obtained by cutting a Pont-l'Evêque in half lengthwise.

A fairly good buy

DEMI-REBLOCHON

Also known as: REBLOCHONNET
Province: SAVOIE
Source: Haute-Savoie
Best seasons: all year; commercial production, use of pasteurized milk
Milk: cow's milk
Fat content: 45%
Type: soft, slightly pressed
Rind: washed
Curing: under humid conditions, 4 weeks
Form: small flattened cylinder
Dimensions: 8½ in. in diameter, 1 in. thick
Weight: 9 oz.
Packaging: unwrapped, or paper with brand name
Flavor: 2–3
Same as REBLOCHON
A fairly good buy

DEMI-SEL

Province: originally NORMANDY
Source: Normandy; additional sources: all regions
Made in or by: medium and large commercial dairies
Best seasons: all year; pasteurized milk used
Milk: cow's milk, pasteurized
Fat content: 40% to 45%

Type: fresh, salted
Rind: none
Curing: none
Form: small square
Dimensions: 3 by 3 in., 1 in. thick
Weight: 2½ oz. to 3½ oz.
Packaging: foil
Selection:
  Appearance: fresh, white and smooth
  Feel: tender but not elastic
  Smell: light lactic smell
  Taste: mild, slightly acid (2)
What to watch out for: lack of freshness, excessive dryness
Use: end of meals
Appropriate wines: none
Origin of name: weak salinity (1.5%) of cheese
Brief history: created in the 19th century by M. Pommel
A good buy
Related cheeses: all fresh, smooth-textured, salted cheeses
  Differences: none besides origin and quality of milk

DORNECY

Province: NIVERNAIS
Source: Dornecy; additional sources: the immediate vicinity, and Corbigny (Nièvre)
Made in or by: farms, exclusively
Best seasons: summer, autumn; availability of goat's milk, end of curing period
Milk: goat's or half goat's milk
Fat content: 45%
Type: soft
Rind: natural
Curing: dry, in ventilated cellars, 3 to 4 weeks
Form: truncated cone
Dimensions: 3 in. at the base, 2 or 2½ in. high
Weight: about 9 oz.
Packaging: unwrapped

Selection:
   Appearance: delicate bluish rind; pure white interior
   Feel: firm
   Smell: light goat smell
   Taste: rather pronounced flavor with some bouquet (3)
What to watch out for: excessive dryness, granular texture, rancidity
Use: end of meals, snacks
Appropriate wines: white and rosés of Sancerre and Tannay
Origin of name: place of origin
A good buy locally; not much commercialized
Related cheeses: Lormes, Valençay, Levroux, Sainte-Maure, Tournon-Saint-Pierre, all Chabis
   Differences: origin, shape, size, texture, flavor

DREUX A LA FEUILLE

Province: NORMANDY (THYMERAIS)
Milk: cow's milk, partly skimmed
Fat content: 28% to 35%
(See FEUILLE DE DREUX)

DUCS

Province: BURGUNDY (TONNERROIS)
Source: La Chapelle-Vieille-Forêt (Yonne)
Best seasons: all year round; pasteurized milk used
Milk: cow's milk, pasteurized
Fat content: 50%
Type: soft, separated curds
Rind: bloomy
Curing: in humid cellars, 2 weeks
Form: cylindrical
Dimensions: 3 in. in diameter, 2 in. high
Weight: 8 oz.
Packaging: cardboard, with brand name
Selection: no choice; packaging prevents seeing the cheese
Use: end of meals

Appropriate wines: Chablis, white and rosé Irancy, Saint-Bris, and all
fruity, supple wines
Origin of name: factory trademark
A fairly good buy
Related cheeses: all cheeses of the same type
Differences: origin, shape, size, flavor

ECHOURGNAC

or TRAPPISTE D'ECHOURGNAC
Province: AQUITAINE (PERIGORD)
Source: Echourgnac
Made in or by: monks of monastery
Best season: all year; the cheese stands up under high summer tempera-
tures and keeps well
Milk: cow's milk
Fat content: 45%
Type: pressed, uncooked
Rind: washed
Curing: under humid conditions, 3 weeks
Form: small, thick disk with very convex rim
Dimensions: 4 in. in diameter, 1 in. thick
Weight: 10½ oz.
Packaging: paper, with brand name
Selection:
Appearance: smooth ochre-yellow to grayish yellow rind; ivory-yellow
interior with very tiny holes
Feel: supple and delicate
Smell: little smell
Taste: mild lactic flavor with bouquet (2–3)
What to watch out for: dry rind, gray color, grayish or mixed yellow and
pinkish gray interior, bitterness, heat spoilage
Use: end of meals; additional uses: in cheese crisps
Appropriate wines: all fruity lively reds of Bergéracois and elsewhere; dry
and fruity white wines
Origin of name: monastery site
Brief history: connected with the founding of the monastery
Related cheeses: all monastery cheeses
Differences: origin, size, smoothness of texture

EDAM

Country: NETHERLANDS
Province: NOORD HOLLAND
Source: Noord Holland; additional sources: other provinces of Netherlands
Made in or by: factories
Best seasons: all year; pasteurized milk used
Milk: cow's milk, pasteurized
Fat content: 30% to 40%
Type: pressed, semi-hard
Rind: tinted, paraffined, red or yellow
Curing: in dry cellars, 2 to 3 months for the young (fat) cheeses
Form: ball slightly taller than its diameter
Dimensions: 5 to 5½ in. at widest, 4½ to 5 in. at narrowest
Weight: 3 lb. 5 oz. to 3 lb. 12 oz.
Packaging: unwrapped, with label of origin and fat content
Selection:
  Appearance: nice geometrical shape, very smooth rind
  Feel: supple, elastic
  Smell: faint lactic smell
  Taste: mild, nutty flavor (2)
What to watch out for: overly large holes (rarely)
Use: breakfast, snacks; additional uses: toasts, canapés, patties
Appropriate wines: all light and fruity white wines, reds of Beaujolais; or strong beer
Origin of name: town of Edam, a small port in Noord Holland
Brief history: connected with the history of Dutch overseas trade
A good buy
Related cheeses: Gouda, Broodkaas
  Differences: shape, color, packaging, texture, origin

EDAM DEMI-ETUVE

Countries: FRANCE; NETHERLANDS; BELGIUM
Sources: Netherlands: Noord Holland; France: Flanders; Belgium: Flanders, Hainaut; additional sources: Netherlands: other provinces; France: western provinces, Burgundy
Made in or by: commercial plants

Best seasons: all year; pasteurized milk used
Milk: cow's milk, pasteurized
Fat content: 30% to 40%
Type: pressed, semi-hard
Rind: tinted, paraffined, red or yellow
Curing: in dry cellars, at least 6 months; shorter time in specially heated drying rooms
Form: ball a little taller than its diameter
Dimensions: 5 in. in diameter, 5½ in. high
Weight: 3 lb. 5 oz. to 3 lb. 12 oz.
Packaging: unwrapped, with label of origin and fat content
Selection:
  Appearance: nice geometrical shape; smooth, flawless rind
  Feel: hard and brittle
  Smell: rather penetrating aroma
  Taste: slightly sharp flavor (4)
What to watch out for: holes, excessive crumbling, excessive sharpness (rarely imperfect)
Use: breakfast, snacks, end of meals; additional uses: grated as a seasoning in Dutch dishes
Appropriate wines: all rosés and reds with body and character: Moulin-à-Vent
Origin of name: town of Edam, where the cheeses were loaded on boats for shipment overseas (the cheese keeps indefinitely)
A fairly good buy
Related cheeses: dried or partially dried Dutch Goudas, French cheeses of the same type; distant resemblance to aged Parmesan
  Differences: origin, shape, size, texture

EDAM ETUVE

Countries: FRANCE; NETHERLANDS; BELGIUM
Source: Netherlands: Noord Holland; France: Flanders; Belgium: Flanders, Hainaut; additional sources: Netherlands: all other provinces; France: Provinces of l'Ouest, Bourgogne
Made in or by: commercial plants
Best seasons: all year; pasteurized milk used, supplies in storage
Milk: cow's milk, pasteurized
Fat content: 30% to 40%

Type: pressed

Rind: colored, red or yellow paraffin

Curing: in dry cellars, at least 12 months (less in special warm drying rooms)

Form: ball slightly higher than its diameter

Dimensions: 4¼ to 5 in. in diameter, 5 to 5¼ in. high

Weight: 2 lb. 13 oz. to 3 lb. 4 oz.

Packaging: unwrapped, with label of origin and fat content

Selection:

  Appearance: well shaped; smooth, flawless rind

  Feel: hard, brittle

  Smell: quite penetrating smell

  Taste: slightly sharp (4)

What to watch out for: holes, excessive brittleness, excessive sharpness

Use: breakfast, snacks, ends of meals; additional uses: grated as condiment in Dutch cooking

Appropriate wines: all full-bodied reds and rosés with character: Moulin-à-Vent

Origin of name: city of Edam, from where cheese was shipped overseas (cheese keeps indefinitely)

A fairly good buy

Related cheeses: all aged and semi-aged Dutch Gouda and similar French cheeses; distant resemblance to half-aged Parmesan

  Differences: origin, shape, composition, quality

EDAM FRANÇAIS

Country: FRANCE

Source: Flanders; additional sources: Ouest, Bordelais, Charentes, Burgundy

Made in or by: commercial plants

Best seasons: all year; pasteurized milk used

Milk: cow's milk, pasteurized

Fat content: 40%

Type: pressed, reheated

Rind: tinted red, paraffined

Curing: dry, in dry cellars, 2 to 3 months

Form: small ball, slightly thicker along the vertical axis

Dimensions: 5 in. at widest, 4½ in. at narrowest

Weight: 3 lb. 5 oz.
Packaging: unwrapped, with label of origin and fat content
Selection:
  Appearance: nice geometric shape; smooth shiny rind; interior without
      holes or with only very tiny holes
  Feel: supple and elastic
  Smell: no special smell
  Taste: mild lactic taste (2)
What to watch out for: lack of homogeneity in texture, over-large holes,
    sharpness
Use: end of meals, snacks; additional uses: sandwiches, toasts, crisps
Appropriate wines: all light and fruity reds, whites and rosés
Origin of name: Dutch homonym
Brief history: the first Edams were made in France in 1670 at the instiga-
    tion of Colbert after the conclusion of a treaty against Louis XIV
    by England, Sweden and the Netherlands
A good buy

> *Note:* This Edam is also molded in the shape of a GALANTINE
> (*see* this listing).

Related cheeses: Gouda, Galantine
  Differences: shape, size, color, texture, origin

EMMENTAL

Country: SWITZERLAND
Cantons: mountain cantons of central Switzerland
Source: Emmental (valley of the Emme), Bern plateau; additional
    sources: lower mountain areas of central Switzerland
Made in or by: fruiteries
Best seasons: all year; continuous cycle of production and aging; at
    certain times cheeses are older and fruitier
Milk: cow's milk, raw, pasteurized or irradiated
Fat content: 45%
Type: pressed, cooked
Rind: brushed, oiled
Curing: humid, in cool cellars, 6 to 10 months
Form: big wheel with convex rim and slightly convex sides
Dimensions: 32 to 34 in. in diameter, 9 in. thick at edges

Weight: 176 lb. to 220 lb.

Packaging: unwrapped, with the mark "Switzerland" and label on side

Selection:

> *Appearance:* unblemished smooth rind; light ivory-yellow interior; spherical holes evenly distributed throughout and not too close together
>
> *Feel:* firm, inelastic, oily
>
> *Smell:* good smell of mountain pastures
>
> *Taste:* fruity without sharpness (3)

What to watch out for: too numerous or too large holes, fissures, cracks, sharpness

Use: end of meals; additional uses: grated as a condiment, as ingredient of certain fondues, in mixed salads

Appropriate wines: all fruity reds and whites: Gamay-de-Chantagne, Mondeuse

Origin of name: valley of Emme, a tributary of Aar

Brief history: unknown, connected with the need to stock up milk products for winter

A fairly good buy

Related cheeses: French cheeses of the same name

> *Differences:* origin, texture, maturity, flavor

EMMENTAL FRANÇAIS

Province: FRANCHE-COMTE, SAVOIE

Source: Haute-Savoie; additional sources: Franche-Comté, Burgundy, etc.

Made in or by: commercial dairies, cooperatives

Best seasons: cheeses aged 6 months: November to May; cheeses aged 2 months, all year; cheeses cured at low temperatures generally come from mountain areas and are affected by regional seasonal cycle; cheeses made in the lowlands are not so affected

Milk: cow's milk, raw, pasteurized or irradiated

Fat content: 45%

Type: pressed, cooked

Rind: brushed, oiled

Curing: humid, in cool cellars, 6 months; in warm cellars, 2 months

Form: big wheel with convex rim and convex to very convex sides
(cheeses with the greatest convexity are those aged for 3 months in
warm cellars)

Dimensions: 32 to 34 in. in diameter, 8½ to 10 in. thick (at edges)

Weight: 176 lb. to 220 lb. (density is not great because of the holes)

Packaging: unwrapped, with mark of country of origin, label on side

Selection:

Appearance: cheeses that have not "risen" too much, with the smooth-
est, least swollen rinds, and holes not too close together

Feel: not too rubbery

Smell: slightly lactic but fruity smell

Taste: mild to fruity, spicy (2–4)

What to watch out for: exaggerated swelling, oval holes too close-set,
elastic texture, sharp flavor without bouquet, hollows

Use: end of meals; additional uses: grated for use as a condiment, in
canapés

Appropriate wines: all light and fruity wines

Origin of name: place of origin of the similar Swiss cheese

Brief history: began in France in the 19th century, thanks to the immigra-
tion of German Swiss cheesemakers

A good buy

Related cheeses: Swiss Emmental, large-holed Comté

Differences: size, flavor, texture and sometimes origin

ENTRAMMES

Province: MAINE

Source: Monastery of Entrammes

Best seasons: all year; cheeses are stable and keep well in all seasons

Milk: cow's milk

Fat content: 40% to 42%

Type: pressed, uncooked

Rind: washed

Curing: humid, 1 month or longer

Form: thick disk

Dimensions: 4 in. in diameter, 1½ in. thick

Weight: 12½ oz. to 14 oz.

Selection:
  Appearance: smooth light ochre-yellow rind; ivory-white to light-yellow interior
  Feel: supple
  Smell: no specific smell
  Taste: fruity flavor (2–3)
What to watch out for: dry, leathery rind; grayish coloration; toughness and graininess, bitterness; heat spoilage
Use: dessert
Appropriate wines: Jasnières and all light, fruity red wines
Origin of name: site of the Port-du-Salut monastery at Entrammes (Mayenne)
Brief history: the monastery, which was founded in the 19th century, perfected a cheese that was at first called Port-Salut and then, after that name was sold to a dairy firm, was called by the name of the locality
Related cheeses: all unpasteurized monastery cheeses
  Differences: size, technique, origin, flavor, shape

ENTRAYGUES

Province: AQUITAINE
(*See* CABECOU D'ENTRAYGUES)

EPOISSES

Province: BURGUNDY
Source: area around Epoisses; additional source: Auxois
Best seasons: summer, autumn, winter; start of production and end of curing of the last batches
Milk: cow's milk
Fat content: 45%
Type: soft
Rind: washed
Curing: humid, in humid cellars, 3 months; washings with burgundy marc, 1 month
Form: flat cylinder

incipal cheeses of France. By shelf, left to right, top to bottom; Roquefort,
rénées, Processed cheese, Bleu d'Auvergne, Fourme d'Ambert, Pont l'Evêque,
erb and garlic cheese, Crottin de Chavignol, Port Salut, Beaufort, Goat Log,
member t, Valencay, Brie

French soft cheese varieties. By shelf, left to right, top to bottom; Munster, Carré de l'Est, Livarot, Reblochon, Pont l'Evêque, Epoisses, Munster, Camembert, Brie, Coeur Neufachâtel, Camembert, Brillat-Savarin

ench hard & semi-hard cheese varieties. By shelf, left to right, top to bottom; St
ulin, Morbier, Pyrénées, Comté, Mimolette, Emmental, Cantal, Beaufort

French goat's and ewe's milk cheese varieties. By shelf, left to right, top to bottom; Chevre Log, Roquefort, Brebis, Small Log, Valencay, Crottin de Chavignol, Sainte Maure, Lingot du Berry, Valencay, St Chevrier, Banon, Crottin de Chavignol

French blue cheese varieties. By shelf, left to right, top to bottom; Fourme d'Ambert, Bleu de Bresse, Roquefort, Bleu de Causses, Blue veined soft cheese, Bleu d'Auvergne, Bleu de Bresse, Blue Brie

The open-air market at Trouville

Dimensions: 4 in. in diameter, 2 to 2½ in. thick
Weight: 9 oz.
Packaging: unwrapped
Selection:
  Appearance: smooth, shiny, brick-colored rind
  Feel: supple and resilient
  Smell: rather penetrating smell with bouquet
  Taste: very spicy tang (4–5)
What to watch out for: granular texture, grayish appearance, sharpness
Use: end of meals; additional uses: in *fromage fort* (strong cheese) macerated in burgundy marc or kept in wood ashes for the winter
Appropriate wines: well-knit and full-bodied wines of Burgundy, Nuits and Beaunes.
Related cheeses: Saint-Florentin, Soumaintrain, La Pierre-Qui-Vire, Les Laumes, Langres
  Differences: origin, shape, size, flavor, texture

ERCE

Province: COMTE DE FOIX
(See BETHMALE)

ERVY-LE-CHATEL

Province: CHAMPAGNE
Source: Ervy-le-Châtel (Aube); additional sources: immediate vicinity
Made in or by: small dairies, farms
Best seasons: end of spring, summer, autumn; best milk, end of curing period
Milk: cow's milk
Fat content: 45% to 50%
Type: soft
Rind: bloomy
Curing: dry, in cellars, 4 to 5 weeks
Form: truncated cone
Dimensions: 5 in. in base diameter, 2½ to 3 in. thick
Weight: 1 lb. 1½ oz. to 1 lb. 3 oz.

Packaging: paper
Selection:
  Appearance: white, velvety surface
  Feel: firm
  Smell: light mushroom smell
  Taste: milky flavor with some bouquet, not spicy (3)
What to watch out for: grainy texture
Use: end of meals
Appropriate wines: fruity wines of Saint-Bris-le-Vineux, Chablis, Irancy;
    fruity, lively reds and rosés
Origin of name: central market town nearest to the producing region
A fairly good buy
Related cheeses: Chaource, partly aged Epoisses
  Differences: origin, size and shape, texture, flavor

ESBAREICH

Province: PAYS BASQUE (BIGORRE)
Source: upper valley of Lourse and of Cuzon; additional sources: valleys
    adjacent to upper Barousse
Made in or by: mountain cottages
Best seasons: end of spring, summer, autumn; cheese made during sum-
    mer pasturing in mountains, end of curing period
Milk: sheep's milk
Fat content: 45%
Type: pressed, uncooked
Rind: natural
Curing: dry, with a touch of humidity, 2 to 6 months
Form: big, round, flattened loaf
Weight: 8 lb. 13 oz. to 11 lb.
Packaging: unwrapped
Selection:
  Appearance: delicate, smooth light-ochre rind; dense and homogene-
    ous interior with few holes
  Feel: resilient
  Smell: faint, tangy sheep smell
  Taste: not very pronounced to pronounced flavor with some bouquet
    (3–4)

What to watch out for: excessive hardness, brittleness, smokiness or
  sharpness
Use: snacks, dessert; additional uses: as condiment in the local cuisine
  when aged and sharp
Appropriate wines: well-knit, lively wines of Madiran
Origin of name: most important center of production
Related cheeses: sheep's milk cheeses from the Béarn region of Pays
  Basque (Laruns, Iraty)
  Differences: consistency, origin

ETUVE

Countries: FRANCE; NETHERLANDS
Quality like that of certain EDAMS and GOUDAS (*see* these listings)

EXCELSIOR

Province: NORMANDY
Source: upper Normandy
Made in or by: small dairies
Best seasons: summer, autumn; no need for elaborate curing, always very
  good
Milk: cow's milk, enriched
Fat content: 72%
Type: soft, double cream
Rind: bloomy
Curing: in drying room, 2 weeks
Form: irregular small cylinder
Dimensions: 4 in. in diameter, 1 in. thick
Weight: 8 oz.
Packaging: box
Selection:
  Appearance: downy white rind with very little mold
  Feel: dense, firm, without elasticity
  Smell: light aroma of cream and molds
  Taste: very mild, slightly nutty flavor (2)

What to watch out for: sticky rind, reddishness; saponification, unpleasant odor, occasionally carbolic acid smell when kept too long

Use: end of meals

Appropriate wines: light, fruity red wines: Beaujolais; also very solid Champagne from black grapes

Origin of name: from trademark registered by inventors

Brief history: invented around 1890, it has become almost a classic speciality: Ets. Dubuc (Rouvray-Catillon)

Related cheeses: Magnum (trademark), Brillat-Savarin, Fin-de-Siècle, Parfait, Suprême (all invented names applied to specialties of the same origin or of the same composition)

   Differences: origin, shape, size, packaging, texture, flavor

EXPLORATEUR

Province: ILE-DE-FRANCE (BRIE)

Source: La Trétoire (Seine-et-Marne)

Made in or by: small commercial plants

Best seasons: all year; availability of milk in all seasons, industrial production

Milk: cow's milk, enriched

Fat content: 75%

Type: triple cream

Rind: bloomy

Curing: dry, in humid cellars, 3 weeks

Form: cylindrical

Dimensions: 3 in. in diameter, 2 to 2½ in. high

Weight: 10 oz. to 10½ oz.

Packaging: unwrapped, or paper with brand name

Selection:

   Appearance: delicate, white-downed surface

   Feel: firm, little elasticity

   Smell: light mold smell

   Taste: mild and creamy flavor (2)

What to watch out for: overaging, saponification

Use: end of meals

Appropriate wines: all light and fruity reds: red, white or rosé Bouzy

Origin of name: trade name

Related cheeses: Excelsior, Boursin, Délice de Saint-Cyr, Brillat-Savarin, Magnum

    Differences: origin, shape, size, texture, flavor

FEUILLE DE DREUX

Also known as: DREUX A LA FEUILLE
Province: ILE-DE-FRANCE
Made in or by: small traditional cheese factories
Best seasons: end of summer, autumn, winter
Milk: cow's milk, partly skimmed
Fat content: 30% to 40%
Type: soft
Rind: bloomy
Form: very flat disk
Dimensions: 6 to 7 in. in diameter, increasingly only 4 to 4½ in. in diameter, 1 to 1½ in. thick
Weight: 10½ oz. to 1 lb. 2 oz (frequently now only 5½ oz.)
Packaging: unwrapped, 3 chestnut leaves on each side
Selection:
    Appearance: blue-gray rind sprinkled with reddish pigments, leaves firmly adhering to the cheese; grayish-yellow interior
    Feel: supple consistency
    Smell: strong smell but no smell of ammonia
    Taste: very fruity flavor (3–4)
What to watch out for: sticky rind, rotting leaves; distinctly gray interior, harsh ammonia smell
Use: farmers' snack
Appropriate wines: fruity, lively red wines: Chinon
Origin of name: town where the market was held; the most famous place: Marsauceux (Eure-et-Loire)
Brief history: a very ancient household cheese that has continued to be a purely local item
A good buy
Related cheeses: Ville-Saint-Jacques, Brie de Melun, Olivet Bleu, Vendôme Bleu
    Differences: origin, shape, appearance, texture, flavor

FIN-DE-SIECLE

Province: NORMANDY (PAYS DE BRAY)
Source: Forges-les-Eaux
Best seasons: end of spring, summer, autumn; best quality milk from summer pastures
Milk: cow's milk, enriched
Fat content: 72%
Type: soft, double cream
Rind: bloomy
Curing: in ventilated drying-room, 2 weeks
Form: irregular small thick disk
Dimensions: 4 in. in diameter, 1 in. thick
Weight: 8 oz.
Packaging: unwrapped
Flavor: 2

> *Note:* In all other respects the same as EXCELSIOR (*see* this listing)

Related cheeses: see Excelsior; invented name given to a similar cheese

FIORE SARDO

Also known as: PECORINO SARDO (*see* this listing)
Country: ITALY
Province: SARDINIA
Source: Sardinia; additional sources: Latium, Campagna
Made in or by: traditional factories
Best seasons: fresh: end of autumn, winter, and spring because of seasonal production of sheep's milk; aged: all year
Milk: sheep's milk
Fat content: 45%
Type: soft, slightly pressed
Rind: spontaneous, brushed, coated with oil or fat
Curing: dry, in dry cellars, 2 months for young cheeses, longer for aged sharp cheeses
Form: small cylindrical wheel with convex rim
Dimensions: 8 in. in diameter, 6 in. high
Weight: 11 lb. to 13 lb. 3 oz.

Packaging: unwrapped
Selection:
   Appearance: rind white and smooth or yellowish and oily; consistency
      from firm to brittle
   Feel: hard when aged more than 2 months
   Smell: distinct sheepfold smell
   Taste: young: light nutty flavor (2–3); aged: sharp and saponified (6–7)
What to watch out for: rarely imperfect after desiccation
Use: end of meals or snack when fresh or semi-aged; additional uses:
   aged cheese grated as condiment
Appropriate wines: all robust and sappy wines of southern Italy and Sicily
Origin of name: type of milk and province of origin
Brief history: was brought to Sardinia from Latium at the end of the last
   century
A fairly good buy
Related cheeses: other Pecorinos: Siciliano, Romano
   Differences: size, fineness of grain, degree of savoriness

FLEUR DU MAQUIS

Province: CORSICA
Milk: goat's milk or sheep's milk or both mixed
Type: soft
Flavor: 2–3
Origin of name: invented name given to a cheese also called BRIN-
   DAMOUR (*see* this listing)

FONDU AU MARC

Also known as: FONDU AU RAISIN
Province: SAVOIE
Made in or by: commercial plants
Best seasons: all year; standardized industrial product not dependent
   upon seasonal ingredients
Milk: cow's milk
Fat content: average of the various cheeses and other products that go
   into this cheese, 45%

Type: processed
Rind: artificial, formed of toasted grape pits
Curing: none
Form: big thick disk
Dimensions: 8 in. in diameter, 2 in. thick
Weight: approximately 5 lb. 4 oz.
Packaging: unwrapped, trademarked
Selection: no risk; production is standardized and uniform
What to look out for: desiccation and fissuring due to faulty storage
Use: end of meals, snacks; additional uses: canapés, toasts
Appropriate wines: all lively fruity wines
Origin of name: type of coating and character of cheese
Brief history: its invention is linked with the problems of marketing
    processed cheeses
Flavor: 3
A good buy

Note: not to be confused with TOMME AU MARC (*see* this
listing).

FONTAINEBLEAU

Province: ILE-DE-FRANCE
Made in or by: commercial plants; may be made at home
Best seasons: all year; fresh cheeses can be made in every season
Milk: cow's milk
Fat content: 60%
Type: fresh, unsalted, mixed with whipped cream
Rind: none
Curing: none
Form: that of the container
Weight: according to capacity of container
Packaging: cardboard cartons with cheesecloth
Selection: as fresh as possible
Flavor: 1
What to watch out for: lack of freshness, lack of lightness
Uses: with sugar for dessert, with or without fruit
Appropriate wines: wine is unnecessary

Origin of name: place name
A fairly good buy
Related cheeses: all creamy fresh cheeses
  Differences: not noticeable when very fresh

FONTAL

Countries: ITALY; FRANCE
Region: NORTHERN ITALY, EAST OF FRANCE
Source: Northern Italy; additional sources: eastern regions of France, Ain region
Made in or by: commercial dairies
Best seasons: all year; lowland cheese manufactured on a large scale
Milk: cow's milk
Fat content: 45%
Type: pressed, uncooked
Rind: brushed
Curing: in cool and humid cellars, with sprinklings, 3 to 4 months
Form: flat cylindrical wheel with flat sides and slightly convex rim
Dimensions: 16 in. in diameter, 3½ in. thick
Weight: 22 lb. to 26 lb. 6 oz.
Packaging: unwrapped
Selection:
  Appearance: fairly smooth, even rind; interior ivory-white almost without holes
  Feel: supple yet dense
  Smell: not much bouquet
  Taste: mild and only very slightly fruity, to fruity and slightly nutty (2–3)
What to watch out for: too many or too large holes, swelling, sharpness
Use: end of meals; additional uses; in Piedmontese fondues and *raclette valaisane* when cheese from the valleys is in short supply
Appropriate wines: light, supple and fruity wines, red or white
Origin of name: invented name replacing the name Fontina, which is regulated by law in Italy
Brief history: supplemented Fontina when legal restrictions of the producing area in Val d'Aosta kept that production too small to satisfy demand
A good buy

Related cheeses: cheeses from the valleys of Valais; Bagnes, Conches, Anniviers, Tomme d'Abondance, Fontina
Differences: origin, size, texture, flavor

FONTINA

Country: ITALY
Region: PIEDMONT
Section: VAL D'AOSTA
Source: Val d'Aosta
Made in or by: chalets, at altitudes up to 8,500 feet
Best seasons: production: May to September; consumption: September to December; production of milk in summer mountain pastures, end of curing for the last batches
Milk: cow's milk
Fat content: 45% to 50%
Type: pressed, cooked
Rind: brushed
Curing: dry, with sprinklings, in humid cellars, about 4 months
Form: small flat cylindrical wheel with flat sides and convex rim
Dimensions: 16 to 18 in. in diameter, 3 to 3½ in. thick
Weight: 22 lb. to 22 lb. 6 oz.
Packaging: unwrapped
Selection:
   Appearance: thin, fairly smooth rind; interior of cheese shows very tiny holes
   Feel: supple
   Smell: pleasant bouquet
   Taste: delicate flavor, slightly fruity to fruity (2–3)
What to watch out for: sandy texture, swelling, exaggerated holes
Use: end of meals; additional uses: in Piedmontese fondue; very old cheeses grated and served as condiment
Appropriate wines: light fruity wines of Piedmont with bouquet
Origin of name: oily character of cheese
Brief history: served at the table of the Dukes of Savoy as early as the 13th century
A fairly good buy

Related cheeses: Fontal, Valais cheeses from the valleys of Anniviers, Bagnes, Conches
   Differences: origin, texture, flavor

FOUDJOU

Province: LANGUEDOC (VIVARAIS)
Flavor: 6–7

A *fromage fort* composed of Tommes de Chèvre or "toummo" cheeses of lower Ardèche, half of which is fresh and just barely drained, and the other half sharp and grated. These ingredients are kneaded together with pepper, salt, brandy and crushed garlic. The mixture is eaten with potatoes.

In Viviers the recipe is different: layers of fresh Tomme and sharp, dry grated cheese are alternated. The whole is doused with equal parts of brandy and olive oil and seasoned with salt, pepper and garlic. Cheese is ready to eat when it forms a reddish skin.

It is best made in the autumn and eaten in February or March. The crock should never be emptied. Some cheese should be left to "feed" the cheese that is added to the crock. The bottoms of some cheese crocks have not seen the light of day for years.
Reference: Forot: *Odeurs et fumet de table*

FOUGERU

Cheese of the COULOMMIERS type (*see* this listing)

FOURME D'AMBERT

Also known as: FOURME DE MONTBRISON, FOURME DE PIERRE-SUR-HAUTE
Province: AUVERGNE (LIVRADOIS)
Source: mountain areas of Livradois; additional source: plains of Forez
Made in or by: farms, dairies
Best seasons: summer, autumn; quality of the milk, end of curing period
Milk: cow's milk

Fat content: 45%
Type: soft, lightly pressed, internal molds
Form: tall cylinder
Dimensions: 4½ in. in diameter, 9 in. high
Weight: 3 lb. 5 oz.
Packaging: unwrapped
Selection:
  Appearance: sound dark-gray rind dotted with light-yellow and
    bright-red molds
  Feel: firm and homogeneous
  Smell: light cellar smell
  Taste: very pronounced savor with some bitterness (4–5)
What to watch out for: cracked, thick or sticky rind; grainy texture;
  excessive bitterness
Use: end of meals, snacks
Appropriate wines: Coteaux-d'Auvergne, Beaujolais; in general, all light
  wines with some bite
Origin of name: shape (*fourme* in Langue d'Oc) of cheese and place of
  origin
A fairly good buy
Related cheeses: Fourme de Pierre-sur-Haute, Fourme de Montbrison,
  Bleu de Gex, Bleu de Septmoncel, etc.
  Differences: origin, shape, size, flavor

FOURME DU CANTAL

Also known as: FOURME DE SALERS
Province: AUVERGNE
(*See* CANTAL)

FOURME DE LAGUIOLE

Also known as: LAGUIOLE-AUBRAC
Province: AQUITAINE (ROUERGUE)
(*See* LAGUIOLE-AUBRAC)

FOURME DU MEZENC

Province: LANGUEDOC (VIVARAIS)
(*See* BLEU DU VELAY)

FOURME DE MONTBRISON

Province: FOREZ
Source: plateau of upper Forez
Made in or by: small traditional dairies
Best seasons: summer, autumn; availability of good quality milk, end of
    curing period
Milk: cow's milk
Fat content: 45%
Type: semi-pressed, internal molds
Rind: natural
Curing: dry, in humid cellars, 3 months
Form: tall cylinder
Dimensions: 4½ in. in diameter, 9 in. high
Weight: 3 lb. 5 oz.
Packaging: unwrapped
Selection:
    Appearance: sound, dark-gray rind, dotted with light-yellow and
        bright-red molds
    Feel: firm and homogeneous
    Smell: light cellar smell
    Taste: very pronounced savor with some bitterness (4–5)
What to watch out for: cracked and infiltrated or thick and sticky rind;
    granular texture; excessive bitterness
Uses: end of meals, snacks
Appropriate wines: Coteaux-d'Auvergne, Coteaux-du-Forez, Côtes-
    Roannaises, full-bodied Beaujolais
Origin of name: shape (*fourme* in Langue d'Oc) of cheese and place of
    origin
A fairly good buy
Related cheeses: Fourme d'Ambert, Fourme de Pierre-sur-Haute
    Differences: origin, quality

FOURME DE PIERRE-SUR-HAUTE

Province: AUVERGNE (MONTS DU FOREZ)
Source: high mountains of Livradois
Best seasons: summer, autumn; milk from the mountains, end of curing
  period
Milk: cow's milk
Fat content: 45%
Type: soft, lightly pressed, internal veining
Rind: natural
Curing: dry, 2 to 3 months
Form: tall cylinder
Dimensions: 4½ in. in diameter, 9 in. high
Weight: 3 lb. 5 oz.
Packaging: unwrapped
Flavor: 4–5
  In other respects like Fourme d'Ambert
A fairly good buy
Related cheeses: Fourme de Montbrison, Fourme d'Ambert

FOURME DE ROCHEFORT

Province: AUVERGNE
Source: Rochefort-Magne (Puy-de-Dôme); additional sources: the im-
  mediate vicinity
Made in or by: upland farms
Best seasons: summer, autumn; best milk from the mountains, end of
  curing period
Milk: cow's milk
Fat content: 45%
Type: pressed, uncooked
Rind: natural
Curing: dry, in humid cellars, 2 to 3 months
Form: tall cylinder
Dimensions: 6 to 8 in. in diameter, 6 to 8 in. high
Weight: 11 lb. to 22 lb.
Packaging: unwrapped

Selection:
    Appearance: unblemished and regular light-gray rind
    Feel: supple but not excessively so
    Smell: no particular smell on the surface, but a lactic smell released
        when the cheese is cut
    Taste: mild to pronounced flavor, tangy (2–3)
What to watch out for: cracked rind, infiltration by molds, grainy texture,
    sharpness
Use: end of meals, snacks; additional use: grated as condiment in local
    cuisine
Appropriate wines: Côtes-d'Auvergne, Côtes-Roannaises, Beaujolais; all
    light and fruity wines
Brief history: linked with the history of Salers (or Cantal) but of smaller
    size because the daily yields of milk are not large enough; made on
    smaller farms
A fairly good buy
Related cheeses: Fourme du Cantal and Fourme de Laguiole
    Differences: origin, size, grain

FREMGEYE

Province: LORRAINE
Made in or by: farm households for domestic use; not sold
Best seasons: all year
Milk: cow's milk
Fat content: full fat
Type: fresh, salted
Rind: none
Use: spread on bread, with sliced onions or minced shallots
Flavor: 5–6
Recipe: drained, salted and peppered white cheese is left to ferment for
    one month in closed vessel, preferably an earthenware crock.
Reference: Auricoste de Lazarque: *La Cuisine messine*

FRINAULT

Province: ORLEANAIS
Source: Orléans
Best seasons: summer, autumn; best quality milk, good storage conditions during curing period
Milk: cow's milk
Fat content: 50%
Type: soft
Rind: natural
Curing: dry, in humid cellars, 3 weeks
Form: small, very flat disk
Dimensions: 3½ in. in diameter, ½ in. thick
Weight: 4½ oz.
Packaging: unwrapped
Selection:
   Appearance: regular shape; delicate, bluish rind
   Feel: tender
   Smell: little smell
   Taste: pronounced flavor with bouquet (3–4)
What to watch out for: superficial heat spoilage, too grayish interior, desiccation
Use: end of meals
Appropriate wines: pale red wines of the Orléans region (Vins Gris); all light and fruity wines of Loire Valley: Bourgeuil, Chinon
Origin of name: name of manufacturer who invented the cheese
Brief history: factory trade name of a small very fatty Olivet made in the suburbs of Orléans
Related cheeses: Olivet Bleu and Vendôme Bleu, Villebarou
   Differences: origin, size, texture, flavor

FRINAULT CENDRE

Province: ORLEANAIS
Source: Orléans
Made in or by: traditional dairies
Best seasons: summer, autumn; best quality milk, simple storage requirements
Milk: cow's milk

Fat content: 50%
Rind: natural, coated with ashes
Curing: dry, in boxes of wood ashes, 4 weeks
Form: small thin disk
Dimensions: 3½ in. in diameter, ½ in. thick
Weight: 4½ oz.
Packaging: unwrapped, or paper with trademark
Selection:
   Appearance: regular shape
   Feel: supple without softness
   Smell: faint smell
   Taste: fruity, slightly saponified flavor (3–4)
What to watch out for: desiccation or excessive saponification due to too
    lengthy storage
Use: end of meals
Appropriate wines: pale red wines of the Orléans region; fruity wines of
    the Loire Valley: Champigny, Bourgeuil, Chinon
Origin of name: name of manufacturer-inventor
Brief history: small whole-milk Olivet invented by M. Frinault
Related cheeses: ash-coated Olivet and Vendôme; in general, all ash-
    coated cheeses
   Differences: origin, size, texture, flavor

FROMAGE CUIT

Province: LORRAINE (BOULAY)
Made in or by: homes
Milk: cow's milk
Fat content: about 45%
Type: fresh
Flavor: 4
Recipe: Take undrained white cheese, set it on the fire and let it cook for
    a few minutes. Drain off the whey, and turn the cheese into a cloth
    hung by the corners in a dry place. Let it dry for 3 to 5 days.

    At the end of this time, crumble it into an earthenware crock and
    salt it slightly: 1 tablespoon of salt to the pound. Mash it down into
    the bottom of the crock with a wooden pestle. Cover it to prevent
    contamination and to concentrate the fermentation. In 2 weeks the
    fermentation will have done most of its work. Put cheese back into

a pan, adding a bit of butter to help it melt and a few tablespoons of milk to thin it. Mix in two egg yolks, add salt and freshly ground pepper to taste. When the cheese is fully melted pour it into a serving dish.

Reference: Auricoste de Lazarque: *La Cuisine messine*
Not marketed

FROMAGE FORT DU BEAUJOLAIS

Province: LYONNAIS
Type: worked in crock
Selection:
   Appearance: by the eye: smooth, homogeneous texture
   Smell: strong smell of fermentation
   Taste: sharp flavor (5–6)
Use: end of meals
Appropriate wines: see FROMAGE FORT A LA LYONNAIS
Ordinarily not marketed commercially
Recipe: Take 8 very dry boutons-de-culotte and ½ lb. of slightly fruity Gruyère, 1 tablespoon of oil, ½ lb. of unsalted butter, 1 pony of old fruity marc.

   Grate the boutons-de-culotte and the Gruyère finely, put them through a sieve, add the oil and the butter and put the mixture in a crock. Work it thoroughly together, seal the crock and wait 2 or 3 weeks.
Related cheeses: Fromage Fort à la Lyonnaise, Bourgogne, Fremgeye (Lorraine), Poustagnacq (Landes), Pétafine (Dauphiné), Fromage Fort du Mont Ventoux (Provence), Pottekees (Belgium) *(see* these listings)
   Differences: origin, spices and flavorings, texture, strongness of flavor

FROMAGE FORT DE BETHUNE

Province: ARTOIS (GOHELLE)
Source: Thiérache, French Hainaut; additional source: Avesnois
Made in or by: homes; not marketed
Best seasons: autumn, winter, spring; use of overage Maroilles cheeses as a means of saving them

Milk: cow's milk
Fat content: 45%
Type: soft, seasoned with parsley, tarragon and pepper
Rind: none
Curing: none; keeps in crocks for 2 to 3 months
Form: no clearly defined shape, heaped into crocks and served loose
Selection:
  Appearance: not too deep color
  Feel: doughy consistency
  Smell: very strong smell
  Taste: very sharp and aromatic (6–7)
What to watch out for: too strong taste (which some people like); sticky, blackish appearance
Use: miners' snack
Appropriate wines: any wine, as long as it is strong; locally a glass of gin is preferred
Origin of name: character of cheese and the place where it is usually eaten
Brief history: most likely introduced by the miners of northeastern France
Related cheeses: Boulette d'Avesnes and other cow's-milk *fromages forts:* Fromage Fort de Bourgogne, Fromage Fort de Lorraine
  Differences: quality and flavorings

FROMAGE FORT A LA LYONNAISE

Province: LYONNAIS
Source: Lyonnais, Beaujolais
Made in or by: homes; not much on market
Best seasons: summer, autumn, winter; best cheeses, customary preference
Milk: cow's milk, goat's milk or mixture of both
Fat content: undetermined
Rind: none
Selection:
  Appearance: homogeneous texture
  Feel: smooth and creamy

Smell: strong smell of fermentation

Taste: extremely aromatic and sharp (6–7)

Use: snack, end of meals

Appropriate wines: all stout and well-knit local wines or else a glass of old Beaujolais marc

Origin of name: intensity of cheese flavor

Recipe: Take dry and fruity goat cheeses, grate them finely into a crock, moisten them with hot or lukewarm leek water, macerate for 2 weeks with a pony of old Beaujolais, tarragon, thyme, bay leaf, salt and pepper, seal the crock. Set it aside for another 2 to 3 weeks, open, remove the herbs and work it with a spoon. Serve, reseal. With age cheese becomes explosive.

Related cheeses: fromage fort of other parts of Burgundy, crocked cheese from Lorraine, Pétafine from Dauphiné, Fromage Fort du Mont Ventoux, Foudjou du Vivarais, Belgian Pottekees, etc.

Differences: origin of the component cheeses, spices and flavorings, method of preparation, flavor

FROMAGE FORT DU MONT VENTOUX

Province: PROVENCE

Source: Mont Ventoux

Made in or by: homes; not marketed

Best seasons: spring, summer, autumn; availability of sheep's or goat's milk, fermentation time

Milk: sheep's milk or goat's milk

Fat content: undetermined

Type: kneaded, based on fresh crocked Cachat cheese

Rind: none

Selection:

Appearance: homogeneous texture

Feel: smooth

Smell: strong fermentation smell

Taste: saponified, sharp flavor (5–7)

Use: snacks, end of meals

Appropriate wines: all stout wines of Provence and the South of France: Fitou, Corbières du Roussillon; small glass of brandy quite appropriate

Recipe: Take some freshly drained Cachat. Mash it and place it in a *toupin,* a Provençal earthenware crock. Add salt and pepper and cover.

From time to time stir back into the cheese on the bottom the cream that rises to the surface. The longer it is left, the sharper and stronger flavored the mixture becomes.

When cheese is ready, it is eaten with onion slices and stout, full-bodied red wines of Côtes-du-Rhône or Châteauneuf-du-Pape.

To lend variety, one may add at the last minute a pony of vinegar or marc brandy.

Related cheeses: Fromage Fort à la Lyonnaise, crocked cheese from Lorraine, Pétafine from Dauphiné, Foudjou du Vivarais, Belgian Pottekees, etc.

Differences: origin of component cheeses, spices and flavorings, method of preparation, flavor

FROMAGE EN POT

Province: LORRAINE
Source: vicinity of Metz
Made in or by: homes; not marketed
Best seasons: all year; availability of milk
Milk: cow's milk
Fat content: minimum 45%
Type: kneaded
Rind: none
Selection:
  Appearance: homogeneous texture, pinkish-yellow color
  Feel: smooth
  Smell: strong fermentation smell
  Taste: very strong saponified sharp flavor (5–7)
Use: snack, end of meals
Appropriate wines: any very full-bodied red wine, preferably Côtes-du-Rhône
Recipe: Take fresh cheese that has drained for five days, put it in a crock to the depth of about 1 inch, sprinkle it with salt, pepper and fennel seeds; add another layer of cheese, season it in the same way and continue until all the cheese is used up. Seal the crock as tightly as possible and set it in a cool dry place for 6 weeks.

At the end of this time, open the crock, remove the film of mold that has formed, and work the cheese with a wooden spoon. Cover it with a cloth to keep out flies.

Note: This recipe is the same as the recipe for Belgian POT-TEKEES.

Related cheeses: Fromage Fort à la Lyonnaise, Pétafine Dauphinoise, Foudjou du Vivarais, Fromage Fort du Mont Ventoux, etc.

Differences: origin and nature of component cheeses, spices and flavorings, method of preparation, flavor

GALANTINE

Also known as: EDAM, GALANTINE FRANÇAIS
Countries: FRANCE; NETHERLANDS
Source: Flanders; additional sources: all dairy regions
Best seasons: all year; pasteurized milk used
Milk: cow's milk, pasteurized
Fat content: 40%
Type: pressed, semi-hard, reheated
Rind: paraffined, tinted red or yellow
Curing: dry, in humid cellars, about 2 months
Form: loaf
Dimensions: 12 in. in rectangular cross-section or 4 in. in square cross-section
Weight: 4 lb. 6 oz. to 6 lb. 10 oz.
Packaging: unwrapped with label of origin

Cheeses of the EDAM type *(see* this listing) molded in the shape of a parallelepiped with a square or rectangular cross-section.

The Dutch version of this cheese is called BROODKAAS *(see* this listing).

GALETTE DE LA CHAISE-DIEU

Province: AUVERGNE (HAUT VELAY)
Source: La Chaise-Dieu (Haute-Loire); additional sources: Velay plateau
Made in or by: farms; not commercialized

Best seasons: end of spring, autumn; availability of goat's milk, end of
    curing period
Milk: goat's milk or half goat's milk
Fat content: 45%
Type: soft
Rind: natural
Curing: dry, 3 weeks in cool and humid cellars
Form: small brick or very thin disk
Dimensions: 6 in. long, 3 in. wide, 1 in. thick
Weight: about 9 oz.
Packaging: unwrapped
Selection:
    Appearance: regular shape; delicate rind, bluish molds (pure goat's
        milk) or gray molds (mixed goat's and cow's milk)
    Feel: firm with some give
    Smell: faint mold smell
    Taste: very nutty flavor (4)
What to watch out for: dry or sticky rind, grainy texture, too strong flavor
Uses: end of meals, snacks
Appropriate wines: all light and fruity reds, whites and rosés of Coteaux
    d'Auvergne, Roanne, Beaujolais
Origin of name: thinness (GALETTE means flat cake) of cheese and
    place of origin
Related cheeses: Brique de Forez, Chèvreton d'Ambert
    Differences: slight, depending upon origin

GAPRON or GAPERON

Province: AUVERGNE
Region: HAUTE AUVERGNE
Source: upland Auvergne; additional source: plains region
Made in or by: recently in small factories; in the past, exclusively on
    farms
Best seasons: not sharply defined, end of the curing period; period of
    abundant milk, best period for storage in hay or rye straw
Milk: cow's milk, skimmed, or buttermilk (casein extracted by heat from
    buttermilk)
Fat content: very low
Type: pressed, uncooked, flavored with garlic

Rind: natural
Curing: dry, touches of humidity, about 2 months
Form: flattened ball on a base
Dimensions: 3½ in. in diameter, 2½ to 3 in. high
Weight: 12½ oz. to 1 lb. 2 oz.
Packaging: unwrapped, tied with a cord
Selection:
  Appearance: the rind should not be too fermented
  Feel: supple to soft
  Smell: neutral to light garlic smell
  Taste: pronounced flavor with taste of garlic (4)
What to watch out for: overripeness, sticky rind, powerful odor

> *Note:* The cheeses of the past, made exclusively on farms, were allowed to ripen in the cellars for very long periods of time and for this reason necessarily took on an appearance and characteristics which we would today consider defective.

Use: snacks
Appropriate wines: all robust, full-bodied wines: Côtes-du-Rhône
Origin of name: dialect word *gap* or *gape* meaning buttermilk
Brief history: the number of these cheeses hanging in the kitchen or the storeroom was at one time a sign of a farmer's wealth and as such might influence the marriage of his daughter
A good buy

GAUVILLE

Province: NORMANDY (PAYS D'OUCHE, PAYS DU PERCHE)
Milk: cow's milk
Type: soft
Flavor: 4–5

This *fromage fort* of Laigle is now extremely rare and is fast disappearing

GERARDMER

Also known as: LORRAINE or GROS LORRAINE *(see* this listing)
Province: LORRAINE

Milk: cow's milk
Fat content: 45% to 50%
Type: soft
Rind: washed
Flavor: 4–5

GEROME

Province: LORRAINE
Source: high valleys of the Lorraine side of the mountain ridge; additional sources: entire Vosges Massif
Made in or by: commercial dairies
Best seasons: summer, autumn, winter; if made with pasteurized milk, all year
Milk: cow's milk, usually pasteurized
Fat content: 45% to 50%
Type: soft
Rind: washed
Curing: humid, in humid cellars with washings, 1 to 3 months, according to size
Form: thick disk
Dimensions: 4½ to 8 in. in diameter, 1 to 1½ in. thick
Weight: 9 oz. to 3 lb. 5 oz.
Packaging: box
Selection:
  Appearance: smooth, reddish rind
  Feel: supple
  Smell: strong and penetrating smell, bouquet
  Taste: spicy to very spicy, depending upon thickness (4–5)
Locally Gérômé is eaten fresh or partly cured
What to watch out for: chalky and grainy texture, sticky rind
Use: end of meals, snacks
Appropriate wines: all full-bodied lively wines of Bordeaux, Burgundy, Côtes-du-Rhône
Origin of name: dialectal pronunciation of Gérardmer
Brief history: related to that of Munster
A fairly good buy

Related cheeses: farm and dairy Munsters, Langres, Epoisses, Soumaintrain
   Differences: origin, size, packaging, quality, flavor

GEROME ANISE

Province: LORRAINE
Milk: cow's milk, usually pasteurized
Fat content: 45% to 50%
Type: soft, flavored with seeds of *carum carvi* (caraway)
Flavor: spicy to very spicy, depending upon thickness (4–5)
(See GEROME)

GIEN

Province: ORLEANAIS
Source: Gien, Châtillon-sur-Loire; additional sources: immediate
   vicinity
Made in or by: farms, exclusively
Best seasons: end of spring, summer, autumn; availability of milk, best
   manufacturing, good storage
Milk: goat's milk, cow's milk, or a mixture of both
Fat content: goat's milk, 45%; goat's and cow's milk, 40% to 50%
Type: soft
Rind: natural
Curing: dry, in leaves or ashes, about 3 weeks
Form: cylinder or truncated cone
Dimensions: 3 in. in diameter, 2 in. thick
Weight: 7 oz.
Packaging: unwrapped; or plane-tree leaves or ashes
Selection:
   Appearance: goat's milk cheeses: delicate bluish colored rind; mixed-
      milk cheeses: thick, vermiculated and gray rind
   Feel: firm to hard
   Smell: no specific smell
   Taste: nutty to very nutty (3–4)

What to watch out for: grainy texture, excessive saltiness, moisture
  beneath rind
Use: end of meals, snacks
Appropriate wines: Pinots Meuniers and Vins Gris of Orléanais, Tou-
  raine; all light fruity wines
Origin of name: town nearest to the producing region
A fairly good buy locally
Related cheeses: cow's-milk cheeses: Olivet, Vendôme, Saint-Benoît, Vil-
  lebarou
  Differences: origin, fineness of texture, flavor

GORGONZOLA

Country: ITALY
Province: LOMBARDY
Sources: Gorgonzola region; additional sources: formerly the Provinces
  of Como and Bergamo; nowadays the Provinces of Brescia, Como,
  Cremona, Cuneo, Milano, Novara, Pavia, Vercelli
Made in or by: commercial plants
Best seasons: all year; commercial dairy product using milk from a wide
  range of sources
Milk: cow's milk
Fat content: 48%
Type: soft, with internal blue molds
Rind: natural
Curing: dry, in cold and humid cellars, intermittently scraped and
  washed
Form: cylindrical
Dimensions: 10 to 12 in. in diameter, 6 to 8 in. high
Weight: 13 lb. 3 oz. to 17 lb. 10 oz.
Packaging: foil, with trademark
Selection:
  Appearance: fairly smooth reddish gray rind; evenly distributed vein-
    ing
  Feel: soft and tender, almost runny
  Smell: rather fully developed smell
  Taste: savory to very savory, verging on sharp (3–5)
What to watch out for: hardness, fewness of veins, sharp flavor
Use: end of meals

Appropriate wines: well-knit sappy red wines of Bordeaux, Burgundy, Côtes-du-Rhône, Barolo

Origin of name: place where cheese is thought to have been invented, an old halting place on the drive to summer pasturelands

Brief history: the cheese, at least in so far as the blue veining is concerned, must have been an accidental invention of the 11th century, comparable to the legendary invention of Roquefort

A good buy

Related cheeses: Bleu de Bresse, Sain-Gorlon, Bleu de Laqueuille

  Differences: origin, shape, size, flavor, texture

GOUDA

Country: NETHERLANDS

Province: ZUID HOLLAND

Source: Zuid Holland; additional sources: other provinces

Made in or by: commercial plants

Best seasons: all year; pasteurized milk used

Milk: cow's milk, pasteurized

Fat content: 30% to 40%

Type: pressed, reheated

Rind: paraffined, tinted yellow

Curing: dry, in dry cellars, 2 to 3 months; specially constructed drying rooms speed the aging process

Form: small wheel with very convex rim

Dimensions: 10 to 12 in. in diameter, 3 in. thick

Weight: 6 lb. 10 oz. to 11 lb.

Packaging: unwrapped, with label of origin and fat content

Selection:

  Appearance: smooth, shiny rind

  Rind: very firm

  Smell: no special smell

  Taste: not very pronounced, not very spicy (3)

What to watch out for: excessive crumbling, sharpness

Use: breakfast, snacks, teas, end of meals

Appropriate wines: all light and fruity wines: Beaujolais; beer goes very well

Origin of name: small river port that markets and ships cheese

A good buy

Related cheeses: Edam, Mimolette, Boerenkaas
  Differences: origin, shape, color, texture, flavor

GOUDA DEMI-ETUVE

Countries: FRANCE; NETHERLANDS; BELGIUM
Sources: Netherlands: Zuid Holland; Belgium: Flanders, Hainaut; France: Flanders; additional sources: all dairying regions of France and the Netherlands
Made in or by: commercial plants
Best seasons: all year; a commercial cheese made from pasteurized milk and stabilized by drying
Milk: cow's milk, pasteurized
Fat content: 30% to 40%
Type: semi-hard, reheated
Rind: tinted red, paraffined
Curing: dry, in dry cellars, 4 to 6 months; heated drying rooms shorten aging period
Form: thick disk with very convex edge
Dimensions: 10 to 12 in. in diameter, 3 in. thick
Weight: 6 lb. 10 oz. to 11 lb.
Packaging: unwrapped, with label of origin and fat content
Selection:
  Appearance: smooth, shiny rind; perfect shape
  Feel: very firm
  Smell: no special smell
  Taste: pronounced flavor (4)
What to watch out for: holes, sharp flavor
Uses: snacks, breakfast, end of meals; additional uses: sandwiches, toasts
Appropriate wines: all light and fruity wines: Beaujolais-Villages; beer goes very well
Origin of name: Dutch port where cheese was marketed
A fairly good buy
Related cheeses: Edam, Mimolette, Boerenkaas
  Differences: origin, shape, size, color, flavor, texture

GOUDA ETUVE

Countries: FRANCE; NETHERLANDS; BELGIUM
Sources: Netherlands: Zuid Holland; Belgium: Flanders, Hainaut; France: Flanders; additional sources: all dairying regions of France, the Netherlands and Belgium
Made in or by: commercial plants
Best season: all year; pasteurized milk used, stock carried over
Milk: cow's milk, pasteurized
Fat content: 30% to 40%
Type: semi-hard, pressed
Rind: tinted yellow, paraffined
Curing: dry, in dry cellars, 10 to 12 months
Form: thick disk with very convex edges
Dimensions: 10 to 12 in. in diameter, 3 in. thick
Weight: 6 lb. 10 oz. to 11 lb.
Packaging: unwrapped, with label of origin and fat content
Selection:
  Appearance: smooth, shiny rind; perfect shape
  Feel: very hard
  Smell: no special smell
  Taste: very pronounced flavor (4)
Uses: snacks, breakfast, end of meals; additional uses: sandwiches, toasts
Appropriate wines: all fruity wines with some body: Moulin-à-Vent; beer goes very well
Origin of name: small Dutch port from which the cheeses were shipped to the Far East
Related cheeses: Edam, Mimolette, Boerenkaas
  Differences: origin, shape, size, color, flavor, texture

GOUDA FRANÇAIS

Country: FRANCE
Source: Flanders; additional sources: western provinces, Burgundy
Made in or by: commercial plants
Best seasons: all year; pasteurized milk used
Milk: cow's milk, pasteurized
Fat content: 30% to 40%
Type: pressed, reheated
Rind: paraffined, tinted yellow (occasionally red)

Curing: dry, in dry cellars, 2 to 3 months for young (fat) cheeses
Form: small wheel with very convex rim
Dimensions: 10 in. in diameter, 3 in. thick
Weight: 7 lb. 11 oz. to 8 lb. 13 oz.
Packaging: unwrapped, with label of origin and fat content
Selection:
   Appearance: smooth, shiny, flawless rind
   Feel: young cheese: supple and elastic
   Smell: no special smell
   Taste: mild and slightly lactic flavor (2–3)
What to watch out for: large holes
Use: snacks, end of meals; additional uses: sandwiches, canapés, toasts
Appropriate wines: light and fruity wines of Beaujolais, light wines of
   Bordeaux
Origin of name: Dutch cheese of the same name
A good buy
Related cheeses: Edam, Mimolette
   Differences: shape, color, texture, flavor, origin

GOURNAY AFFINE

Province: NORMANDY (PAYS DE BRAY)
Source: Gournay and vicinity; additional sources: Pays de Bray
Made in or by: commercial dairies
Best seasons: end of spring, summer, autumn; milk from the pastured
   herds
Milk: cow's milk
Fat content: 45%
Type: soft
Rind: bloomy
Curing: in cellars until the appearance of the "moss" or bloom, which
   is a fine white down; about 1 week
Form: small round disk
Dimensions: 3 in. in diameter, 1 in. thick
Weight: 3½ oz.
Packaging: unwrapped, on straw tray
Selection:
   Appearance: white, downy rind
   Feel: supple, smooth

Smell: light lactic smell and smell of molds
Taste: mild, slightly salty, slightly acid (3)
What to watch out for: grainy texture, excessive saltiness
Uses: end of meals
Appropriate wines: all light and fruity red wines: red wines of Loire: Bourgueil
Origin of name: place where cheese was first made
Brief history: ancestor of the cheeses of upper Normandy of the Caserette type, also called Malakoff
A good buy
Related cheeses: Neufchâtel (Bondon, Briquette, Coeur)
  Differences: shape, size, amount of aging, origin, texture

GOURNAY FRAIS

Also known as: MALAKOFF
Province: NORMANDY (PAYS DE BRAY)
Source: Gournay and vicinity; additional sources: Pays de Bray
Made in or by: commercial plants
Best seasons: all year; fresh cheese based on pasteurized milk
Milk: cow's milk, pasteurized
Fat content: 45%
Type: fresh, salted
Rind: none
Form: small round disk
Dimensions: 3 in. in diameter, 1 in. thick
Weight: 4 oz.
Packaging: unwrapped, on straw tray
Selection:
  Appearance: white surface without mold
  Feel: soft and a trifle elastic
  Smell: lactic smell
  Taste: mildly sour flavor (2)
What to watch out for: grainy texture
Use: end of meals
Appropriate wines: all light reds, whites and rosés: Gros-Plant, Burgundy Aligoté
Origin of name: place of origin

Brief history: connected with that of the other cheeses of Pays de Bray
A good buy
Related cheeses: all fresh cheeses of Pays de Bray
   Differences: shape, size, aging, fineness of texture, origin

GRAÇAY

Province: BERRY
Sources: Arnon Valley; additional sources: Berry area of Champagne
Made in or by: small traditional dairies
Best seasons: end of spring, summer, autumn; periodic nature of goat
    lactation, high quality milk, good storage
Milk: goat's milk
Fat content: 45%
Type: soft
Rind: natural, dusted with powdered charcoal
Curing: dry, 6 weeks
Form: truncated cone
Dimensions: 4 in. in diameter at base, 2½ in. high
Weight: 1 lb.
Packaging: unwrapped
Selection:
   Appearance: delicate rind, dark blue to blue-gray; regular shape; pure
      white interior
   Feel: firm, no elasticity
   Smell: light goat smell
   Taste: nutty flavor (3)
What to watch out for: excessive hardness, sticky rind, moisture between
    rind and cheese, grainy texture, saponification, exaggerated saltiness
Use: end of meals
Appropriate wines: Sauvignon of Reuilly, Quincy, Memetou-Salon, Pi-
    nots Gris or any fruity thoroughbred wines of Touraine
Origin of name: invented name given to a cheese of rather recent origin
Related cheeses: Selles-sur-Cher, Levroux, Valençay
   Differences: shape, size, origin, fineness of texture

GRAND VATEL

Province: ILE-DE-FRANCE
Region: BRIE
Flavor: 2–3
  Invented name given to DELICE DE SAINT-CYR (*see* this listing)

GRATARON D'ARECHES

Province: SAVOIE (BEAUFORTIN)
Sources: Doron Valley in Beaufort; additional sources: Roseland and
    plateau of Cormet de Roseland
Made in or by: mountain chalets
Best seasons: summer, autumn; availability of goat's milk from summer
    pastures, end of curing period
Milk: goat's milk
Fat content: 45%
Type: pressed, uncooked
Rind: washed
Curing: dry, with touches of humidity, about 1 month
Form: small thick cylinder
Dimensions: 2½ in. to 3 in. in diameter, 2 to 2½ in. thick
Weight: 7 oz. to 10½ oz.
Packaging: unwrapped
Selection:
    Appearance: smooth brownish-gray rind; homogeneous interior
    Feel: firm
    Smell: no special smell
    Taste: very pronounced tang (3–4)
What to watch out for: grainy texture, brittleness, sharpness
Uses: snacks
Appropriate wines: all fruity and lively wines of Savoie and elsewhere:
    Abymes-de-Myans, Aspremont
A good buy locally
Related cheeses: other Tommes de Chèvre de Beaufort, Allues, Pralog-
    nan, Courchevel

GRIS DE LILLE

Also known as: PUANT DE LILLE or PUANT MACERE
Region: ARTOIS, FLANDERS, HAINAUT
Source: Flanders, Hainaut; additional source: Artois
Made in or by: farms, small dairies
Best seasons: autumn, winter, spring; end of curing from the first batches
    to the last
Milk: cow's milk
Fat content: 45%
Type: soft
Rind: washed
Curing: dry, in humid cellars, with washings for 2 months, then im-
    mersed in pickling brine for up to 3 months in the case of the largest
    cheeses
Form: slab
Dimensions: 4½ to 5 in. square, 2 to 2½ in. thick
Selection:
  Appearance: sticky pinkish gray rind; homogeneous texture
  Feel: tender, not soft
  Smell: very powerful fermentation smell
  Taste: very spicy and very salty (5)
What to watch out for: excessive saltiness, cracking; infiltration of mold
Use: snacks, end of meals
Appropriate wines: all strong, very solid wines: Cahors; a glass of Wam-
    brechies gin quite suitable
Origin of name: color, strong odor and place where cheese is cured and
    eaten (Lille and vicinity)
Brief history: derived from Maroilles; origin is the same, but the curing
    process is different
A fairly good buy
Related cheeses: Maroilles and similar cheeses, well aged
  Differences: methods of curing, lower salt content, appearance

GRUYERE

Country: FRANCE
Provinces: BURGUNDY, FRANCHE-COMTE, PAYS DE L'AIN, SAVOIE

> *Note:* In France, Gruyère is the generic name for all the big cheeses: BEAUFORT, COMTE, EMMENTAL (*see* these listings).
> The origin of these cheeses goes back, it is said, to a distant time when Saint Louis ruled over France and none of the four provinces had as yet been added to the realm. Diderot describes the manufacture of the cheese in his *Encyclopédie*.

GRUYERE

Country: SWITZERLAND
Cantons: FRIBOURG, NEUFCHATEL, VAUD
Source: La Gruyère (fore-Alps of Fribourg); additional sources: Jura of Vaud and Neufchâtel
Made in or by: mountain fruiteries
Best seasons: from September to February; production in mountain chalets and end of curing period
Milk: cow's milk
Fat content: 45%
Type: pressed, cooked
Rind: brushed
Curing: in humid cellars, with brushings, 6 months on the average
Form: wheel with slightly convex rim and flat sides
Dimensions: 24 to 26 in. in diameter, 4 in. thick
Weight: 66 lb. to 88 lb.
Packaging: unwrapped, with label of origin
Selection:
  Appearance: sound, fairly smooth rind; interior ivory-yellow to light amber, holes small and far apart, from the size of a pea to the size of a small cherry
  Feel: firm, but crushes between the fingers
  Smell: considerable bouquet
  Taste: fruity to very fruity. Sometimes salty (3–4)
What to watch out for: clefts and splits (oblique and longitudinal fissures beneath the rind that may cause cracks to form on the surface);

sandy texture; sharpness (a desirable quality for some lovers of the cheese)

Use: in fondues, cheese steaks, toasts, seasoning in various dishes and in some classical sauces, salads

Appropriate wines: preferably the charming light and fruity white wines of Neufchâtel, Dorin Vaudois and Fendant du Valais; Beaujolais and other light and fruity red wines

Origin of name: Gruyère, a region of Fribourg Canton

Brief history: origins are obscured in the distant past, but the cheese was definitely in existence by the beginning of the 13th century

Related cheeses: Comtés Français de Montagne

   Differences: origin; rim convexity generally less pronounced than in French cheeses; the holes, with rare exception, always smaller

GUERBIGNY

Province: PICARDIE
Flavor: 4
Invented name given to a ROLLOT shaped like a heart (*see* ROLLOT)

GUERET

Also known as: CREUSOIS or COUPI
Province: MARCHE
Source: La Souterraine, additional sources: the department of Creuse
Made in or by: farms, for domestic use
Best seasons: summer, autumn, winter; prepared during the summer when milk is plentiful, set aside for haymaking and harvest time and winter uses
Milk: cow's milk, almost completely skimmed
Fat content: about 10%
Type: soft
Rind: natural
Curing: warm and dry, under confined conditions, in sealed crock or vessel, for an indefinite period but not more than 6 months
Form: thick, irregular disk
Dimensions: 4½ to 6 in. in diameter, 1 to 2 in. thick

Weight: 13 oz. to 1 lb. 2 oz.
Packaging: unwrapped
Selection:
   Appearance: very smooth surface; translucent interior
   Feel: hard, slightly sticky rind
   Smell: aged: very penetrating smell
   Taste: not very pronounced flavor (4–6)
What to watch out for: desiccation
Use: snack, end of meals; additional uses: grated on pasta and local
   dishes
Appropriate wines: all fruity wines with bouquet: Pécharmant, wines of
   Bergeracois
Origin of name: province or department of origin (Creuse)
A good buy locally
Related cheeses: Bergues (Flanders)
   Differences: origin, shape, size, texture, flavor

GUEYIN

Province: LORRAINE (PAYS MESSIN)
Type: fermented in crocks, based on TRANG'NAT (*see* this listing)
Flavor: 5–7
Recipe: Take Trang'nat after 15 or 20 days of drying under the ceiling(!),
   put it in an earthenware crock, cover it with a cloth, and place
   it in a dark and draft-free corner of the cellar. Some farmers hang
   it up in the cow barn directly over the livestock so that cheese will
   ferment in their heat. The Trang'nat "turns" quickly, taking on a
   creamy consistency and a yellowish color.
     When this last transformation has taken place, the Trang'nat has
   become Gueyin.
Only very slightly commercialized

HAUTELUCE

Also known as: GRATARON DE HAUTELUCE
Province: SAVOIE
Milk: goat's milk

Fat content: 45%
Type: pressed, uncooked
Rind: natural
Curing: humid in cool cellars
Flavor: 3–4
Similar to GRATARON D'ARECHES (*see* this listing)

HEILTZ-LE-MAURUPT

Also known as: CENDRE D'ARGONNE
Province: CHAMPAGNE (ARGONNE)
Source: Heiltz-le-Maurupt; additional sources: Argonne
Made in or by: farms, production dying out; not commercialized
Best seasons: summer, autumn; cheeses are prepared for the hay harvest
   or for the grape harvest in Champagne
Milk: cow's milk, partly skimmed
Fat content: 30% to 35%
Type: soft
Rind: natural, coated with ashes
Curing: in boxes of ashes, under dry conditions, 2 to 3 months
Form: small thick disk
Dimensions: 4½ to 5½ in. in diameter, 1½ in. thick
Weight: 10½ to 12½ oz.
Packaging: unwrapped
Selection:
   Appearance: surface well coated with ashes
   Feel: firm with some give
   Smell: little smell
   Taste: very spicy (4–5)
What to watch out for: desiccation
Use: harvesters' lunch, end of farmers' meals
Appropriate wines: stout and lively wines: Côteaux-de-Toul
Origin of name: region or the province where the cheese originated and
   method of preserving
Related cheeses: ash-coated cheeses of Champagne (Les Riceys) and of
   Orléanais (Olivet Vendôme)
   Differences: origin, size, richness and smoothness of texture, flavor,
      bouquet

HERVE

Country: BELGIUM
Province: LIEGE
Source: Hervé; additional source: Hervé plateau
Made in or by: small traditional dairies; commercial dairies
Best seasons: end of spring, summer, autumn; herds are in pasture; curing
   is over
Milk: cow's milk
Fat content: 45%
Type: soft
Rind: washed
Curing: humid, in cool and·humid cellars, 2 to 3 months
Form: small cube
Dimensions: 2½ in. to side
Weight: 8 or 9 oz.
Packaging: label of origin
Selection:
   Appearance: sleek, unblemished, rosy-ochre rind
   Feel: supple, tender
   Smell: powerful smell
   Taste: very strong taste (5)
What to watch out for: overripeness, desiccation of rind, insufficient
   curing, grainy texture, lack of homogeneity
Use: end of meals or snacks
Appropriate wines: well-knit, sappy reds: Cornas
Origin of name: region and town where cheese is marketed
A fairly good buy
Related cheeses: Remoudou, Limburg, Maroilles
   Differences: origin, shape, size, texture, bouquet

IGNY

Also known as: TRAPPISTE D'IGNY
Province: CHAMPAGNE
Source: Monastery of Igny (Marne)
Made in or by: monks, using traditional methods
Best seasons: end of spring, summer, autumn; more and better milk
   available, end of curing period

Milk: cow's milk
Fat content: 42% to 45%
Type: pressed, uncooked
Rind: washed
Curing: in humid cellars, with washings, 2 months
Form: flat disk
Dimensions: 8 in. in diameter, 1½ in. thick
Weight: 2 lb. 10 oz. to 2 lb. 14 oz.
Packaging: unwrapped
Selection:
  Appearance: very smooth, light-yellow rind
  Feel: supple
  Smell: little smell
  Taste: not very spicy flavor (2–3)
What to watch out for: dry, hard rind, grainy texture; superficial heat
    spoilage
Uses: end of meals; additional uses: in *croustines, croque-madame*
Appropriate wines: plain wines of Champagne: fruity, light and lively
    whites, rosés and reds
Origin of name: site of monastery
Brief history: linked with that of the foundation of the monastery
Related cheeses: all monastery cheeses
  Differences: origin, size, texture, flavor

IRATY

Region: BASQUE COUNTRY
Section: BASSE NAVARRE
Source: pasturelands along the Spanish border, not far from the pass of
    Roncevaux
Made in or by: mountain homes
Best seasons: end of spring, summer, autumn; cheese made during sum-
    mer pasturing period, good milk yields good cheese, end of curing
    period
Milk: sheep's milk mixed with cow's milk
Fat content: 45%
Type: pressed, uncooked
Rind: natural
Curing: dry, with washings in humid cellars

Form: big flattened loaf
Dimensions: 11 to 12 in. in diameter; 2½ to 3 in. thick
Weight: 8 lb. 13 oz. to 11 lb.
Packaging: unwrapped
Selection:

   Appearance: smooth rind; homogeneous texture
   Feel: supple
   Smell: not much smell
   Taste: pronounced flavor (4)
What to watch out for: excessive dryness, overaging, hardness and brittle-
   ness (desirable qualities for local lovers of the cheese)
Use: snack, end of meals; additional uses: as condiment in cooking
Appropriate wines: harsh, well-knit wines of Madiran or Irurozqui
Origin of name: town near the pasturelands, near Spanish border and
   Roncevaux
A fairly good buy
Related cheeses: cheeses of the Basque country—Béarn region: Laruns,
   Esbareich
   Differences: lower quality, mixture of milks

JONCHEE NIORTAISE

Province: POITOU
Source: vicinity of Niort; additional sources: Vendée, Charentes
Made in or by: farms
Best seasons: end of spring, summer, autumn; goat's milk plentiful
Milk: goat's milk
Fat content: 45%
Type: unsalted
Rind: none
Curing: none
Dimensions: not set
Weight: variable
Packaging: loose, on rush mat
Selection:

   Appearance: very fresh and pure white
   Feel: very soft
   Smell: lactic smell
   Taste: mild and creamy (1–2)

What to watch out for: insufficient drainage, lack of homogeneity
Use: savory or sweet dessert
Appropriate wines: unnecessary
Origin of name: packaging and place of origin
A good buy locally
Related cheeses: all fresh goat's-milk cheeses, Lusignan
  Differences: packaging, origin

JONCHEE D'OLERON

Also known as: BREBIS D'OLERON or OLERON (*see* this listing
Province: AUNIS
Flavor: 1–2

LAGUIOLE-AUBRAC

Also known as: FOURME DE LAGUIOLE
Province: AQUITAINE (ROUERGUE)
Source: Aubrac mountains (Label of origin regulated by law)
Made in or by: mountain "burons" or creameries
Best seasons: summer (milk from summer pastures), autumn, winter; end
    of curing of the last batches
Milk: cow's milk
Fat content: 45%
Type: pressed, uncooked
Rind: natural, brushed
Curing: dry, in humid cellars, 3 months (6 months for local aficionados)
Form: big cylinder with slightly convex sides
Dimensions: 16 in. in diameter, 14 to 16 in. high
Weight: 66 lb. to 88 lb.
Packaging: unwrapped, with protective hoops
Selection:
  Appearance: gray rind: delicate, regular light-gray rind (3 months);
      thick, slightly cracked dark-gray rind (6 months); light straw-
      yellow interior
  Feel: homogeneous, supple to somewhat firm

Smell: light lactic smell, penetrating bouquet

Taste: pronounced tang (3–4)

What to watch out for: infiltration of molds, grainy texture, accidental internal fermentation

Use: end of meals, snacks; additional uses: grated in local cuisine

Appropriate wines: all fruity red wines of Marcillac, du Fel, Costières du Gard

Origin of name: principal market center

Brief history: among most ancient cheeses of Gaul

Related cheeses: Cantal, Rochefort

Differences: origin, size, texture, flavor

LANGRES

Province: CHAMPAGNE (BASSIGNY)

Source: Poiseul; additional source: all of Bassigny

Made in or by: small dairies; farm-produced cheese gradually disappearing

Best seasons: end of spring, summer, autumn; best milk, end of curing

Milk: cow's milk

Fat content: 45%

Type: soft

Rind: washed

Curing: humid, in humid cellars, with washings, 3 months

Form: truncated cone slightly hollowed on the top

Dimensions: 4 in. in diameter, 2 in. thick

Weight: about 11 oz.

Packaging: wrapped in marked paper

Selection:

Appearance: delicate, smooth, brown-red to light-brown rind

Feel: supple

Smell: strong smell, penetrating bouquet

Taste: spicy tang (4–5)

What to watch out for: hardness, lack of homogeneity, cracked rind, sharpness, gray interior

Use: end of meals

Appropriate wines: all very well-knit and full-bodied wines of Bordeaux (Saint-Emilion), Burgundy, Côtes-du-Rhône

Origin of name: chief market town

Related cheeses: Chaumont, Epoisses, Saint-Florentin, Soumaintrain
   Differences: origin, shape, size, texture, flavor

LARRON D'ORS

Province: FLANDERS (AMBRISIS)
Source: Ors (Nord)
Made in or by: locally; limited production
Best seasons: spring, winter; milk from cows that have not yet been
   driven to summer pasture
Milk: cow's milk, partly skimmed
Fat content: 30%
Type: soft
Rind: washed
Curing: humid, in humid place, 6 to 7 weeks
Form: a square or cross
Dimensions: 3 to 5 in. square, 1 to 2 in. thick
Weight: 9 oz. to 1 lb. 9 oz. (square), 7 to 14 oz. (cross)
Packaging: unwrapped
Selection:
   Appearance: smooth, shiny, red-brown rind
   Feel: supple, elastic
   Smell: very strong bouquet
   Taste: spicy tang (4–5)
What to watch out for: insufficient homogeneity, hard and grainy texture,
   desiccation or runniness
Use: end of meals
Appropriate wines: very well-knit, full-bodied red wines: Côtes-du-
   Rhône-Villages
Origin of name: brand name and place of origin
A fairly good buy
Related cheeses: all Maroilles and Baguettes du Laonnais
   Differences: origin, shape, size, flavor

LARUNS

Province: BEARN
Source: valley of Ossau; additional sources: adjacent valleys
Made in or by: mountain cottages
Best seasons: end of spring, summer, autumn; cheeses made while flocks are in summer pasture are of high quality; end of curing period
Milk: sheep's milk
Type: pressed, semi-cooked (2 heatings)
Fat content: 45%
Rind: natural
Curing: humid, 2 to 6 months
Form: big round flattened loaf
Dimensions: 12 in. in diameter, 3½ in. thick
Weight: 11 lb. to 13 lb. 4 oz.
Packaging: unwrapped
Selecting:
  Appearance: smooth, thin, straw-yellow to ochre-yellow rind
  Feel: supple, tender at 2 months, hard and brittle at 6 months
  Smell: little smell except slight smoky smell
  Taste: mild and nutty at 3 months (2–3), very pronounced and sharp at 6 months (4–5–6)
What to watch out for: thick rind; hard, brittle texture; sharpness (deemed a desirable quality locally)
Use: snacks, end of meals; additional uses: in home cooking when the cheese is very aged and fruity
Appropriate wines: Basque wines in Irurozqui; Béarn wines of Madiran, fruity and rich in tannin (reds); all other well-knit, lively wines
Origin of name: chief market town

   Note: for the table, 2 months curing is enough; 6 months (3 of which under dry conditions) for kitchen use

Related cheeses: sheep cheeses of the Pays Basque (Arpéguy) and of Pays Bigourdan (Oloron)
  Differences: consistency, quality, grain, origin

LAUMES, LES

Province: BURGUNDY
Source: Les Laumes
Made in or by: farms; production dying out
Best seasons: autumn, winter; beginning of production and end of curing
   period
Milk: cow's milk
Fat content: 45%
Type: soft
Rind: washed
Curing: humid, in humid cellars, washings with water and coffee or wine,
   3 months
Form: big brick with square base
Dimensions: 4½ to 5 in. square at base, 2½ to 3 in. thick
Weight: 1 lb. 14 oz. to 2 lb. 4 oz.
Packaging: unwrapped
Selection:
   Appearance: smooth, shiny, light-brown rind
   Feel: supple
   Smell: very penetrating smell when fully aged
   Taste: very spicy taste, slightly smoky (4–5)
   It is also eaten when white and creamy
What to watch out for: lack of homogeneity, cracked rind
Use: end of meals
Appropriate wines: well-knit, full-bodied Burgundies: Nuits and Beaune
Origin of name: place of origin
Related cheeses: Epoisses, Saint-Florentin, Pierre-Qui-Vire, Soumain-
   train
   Differences: origin, shape, size, texture, flavor

LAVAL

Also known as: TRAPPISTE DE LAVAL
Province: MAINE
Source: Maine
Made in or by: monks, at monastery
Best seasons: end of spring, summer, autumn; best quality milk, good
   storage, end of curing

Milk: cow's milk
Fat content: 40% to 42%
Type: pressed, uncooked
Rind: washed
Curing: humid, about 2 months
Form: thick disk
Dimensions: 10 in. in diameter, 1½ in. thick
Weight: approximately 4 lb. 7 oz.
Packaging: unwrapped
Selection:
　Appearance: smooth light-yellow to grayish yellow rind; ivory-yellow
　　interior with very tiny holes
　Feel: supple and elastic
　Smell: fermentation smell
　Taste: pronounced tang (3), not very spicy
What to watch out for: dry, thickened, or sticky rind; gray or reddish
　color; murky-colored interior tinging on pink; too many holes, bit-
　terness; heat spoilage
Use: end of meals; additional uses: in cheese crisps
Appropriate wines: all light and fruity red wines: Saint-Emilion; dry white
　wines: Muscadet
Origin of name: site of monastery
Brief history: connected with the founding of the Trappist monastery at
　Laval
A fairly good buy
Related cheeses: all monastery cheeses
　Differences: origin, dimensions, quality, flavor

LEIDSE KAAS

Country: NETHERLANDS
Province: ZUID HOLLAND
Milk: cow's milk
Fat content: 40%
Flavor: 3–4
Dutch name of LEYDEN *(see* this listing)

LEIDSE NAGELKAAS

Country: NETHERLANDS
Province: ZUID HOLLAND
Milk: cow's milk
Fat content: 40%
Flavor: 3–4
Origin of name: Dutch for Leyden with cloves *(see* LEYDEN WITH
 CLOVES)

LEVROUX

Province: BERRY
Milk: goat's milk
Fat content: 45%
Packaging: unwrapped
Flavor: nutty (3)
Identical with VALENÇAY *(see* this listing) but produced in the neigh-
 borhood of the fortified town that has lent its name

LEYDEN

Also known as: LEIDSE KAAS (Dutch name)
Country: NETHERLANDS
Province: ZUID HOLLAND
Source: Zuid Holland; additional sources: surrounding area
Made in or by: commercial plants
Best seasons: all year; standardized production using pasteurized milk
Milk: cow's milk
Fat content: 40%
Type: pressed, reheated, flavored with *carum carvi* (caraway)
Rind: brushed, washed periodically before paraffining
Curing: 1st stage: humid, damp brushings; 2nd stage: dry, 3 months
Form: flat cylinder with slightly convex sides
Dimensions: 14 to 16 in. in diameter, 3 to 4 in. thick
Weight: 11 lb. to 22 lb.
Packaging: unwrapped, with mark of origin and label of fat content

Selection:
>*Appearance:* smooth, delicate, grayish yellow rind; caraway seeds evenly distributed throughout cheese
>
>*Feel:* firm with some degree of suppleness
>
>*Smell:* little smell
>
>*Taste:* mild flavor with an aromatic caraway note (3)

What to watch out for: seldom anything

Uses: end of meals, breakfast, snacks

Appropriate wines: all light and fruity wines: Beaujolais-Villages; beer also goes well

Origin of name: city of Leyden where it was originally marketed and from which it was shipped

A fairly good buy

Related cheeses: other Dutch cheeses: Edam, Gouda, Mimolette
>*Differences:* origin, shape, size, absence of *carum carvi*

LEYDEN WITH CLOVES

Also known as: LEIDSE NAGELKAAS (Dutch name)

Country: NETHERLANDS

Province: ZUID HOLLAND

Source: Zuid Holland; additional sources: surrounding area

Made in or by: commercial plants

Best seasons: all year; pasteurized milk used

Milk: cow's milk

Fat content: 40%

Type: pressed, semi-soft, reheated, flavored with cloves

Rind: brushed, washed periodically before paraffining

Curing: 1st stage: damp brushings; 2nd stage: dry, 3 months

Form: flat cylinder with slightly convex sides

Dimensions: 14 to 16 in. in diameter, 3 to 4 in. thick

Weight: 11 lb. to 22 lb.

Packaging: unwrapped, with mark of origin and label of quality

Selection:
>*Appearance:* smooth, delicate, grayish yellow rind
>
>*Feel:* some degree of suppleness
>
>*Smell:* distinct smell of cloves
>
>*Taste:* predominant aromatic flavor of cloves (3–4)

What to watch out for: seldom anything

Use: breakfast, snacks, end of meals
Appropriate wines: all light and fruity wines: Beaujolais-Villages; beer
    goes very well, too
Origin of name: city of Leyden, where it was originally marketed and
    from which it was shipped, as well as from the flavoring
A fairly good buy
Related cheeses: Edam, Gouda, Mimolette, Leyden
  Differences: origin, shape, dimensions, texture, flavor

LIGUEIL

Province: TOURAINE
Made in or by: commercial dairy
Milk: goat's milk
Fat content: 45%
Type: soft
Rind: bloomy
Flavor: 3
Packaging: unwrapped
Origin of name: brand name of commercial dairy
In other respects the same as SAINTE-MAURE *(see* these listings)

LIMBURGER

Countries: BELGIUM, NETHERLANDS
Province: LIMBURG
Source: Campine plateau; additional sources: other parts of Belgian
    Limburg
Made in or by: commercial plants
Best seasons: end of summer, autumn, winter; herds in pastures, end of
    curing period
Milk: cow's milk
Fat content: 30% to 40%
Type: soft
Rind: washed
Curing: humid, in humid cellars, 3 months
Form: rectangular parallelepiped with square cross-section

Dimensions: 6 in. long, 2½ to 3 in. wide and high
Weight: 1 lb. 2 oz. to 1 lb. 5 oz.
Packaging: unwrapped, with band or label
Selection:
  Appearance: regular, delicate, brick-red rind; smooth, fine-textured, yellow interior
  Feel: supple
  Smell: powerful smell, fully developed bouquet
  Taste: very spicy and hearty flavor (4–5)
What to watch out for: firm, granular texture; underripeness, cracked rind; excessive ammonia flavor
Use: end of meals
Appropriate wines: all stout and sappy red wines: Châteauneuf-du-Pape
Origin of name: province of origin
Brief history: no doubt linked with that of the Maroilles-type cheeses, Hervé, Remoudou; their invention has been ascribed to monks of the many monasteries that existed in this region during the Middle Ages
A fairly good buy
Related cheeses: Hervé, Remoudou, Maroilles
  Differences: origin, shape, size, quality, flavor

LIVAROT

Province: NORMANDY
Source: Livarot; additional source: Viette Valley
Made in or by: farms, primarily, but production dying out; cautious attempts by commercial producers, preferred localities are Viette and Vie valleys
Best season: end of spring, autumn, winter; best herd feed, best conditions for curing
Milk: cow's milk
Fat content: 40% to 45%
Type: soft
Rind: washed
Curing: humid, 3 months
Form: cylinder
Dimensions: 4½ to 5 in. in diameter, 1½ to 2 in. thick

Weight: 12 oz. to 1 lb. 2 oz.
Packaging: unwrapped, banded with sedge (marsh grass), or box
Selection:
   Appearance: very smooth, glossy rind, brown to dark brown; well-defined shape
   Feel: not hollow, fine texture, elastic
   Smell: normally strong smell
   Taste: strong, spicy flavor (4–5)
What to watch out for: dry or sticky rind, chalky consistency, holes, putrid odor, runniness
Use: snacks, end of meals
Appropriate wines: all fairly well-knit red wines for a perfectly ripe cheese; locally big glass of homemade hard cider or even a shot of Calvados
Origin of name: nearest important town (Livarot, Calvados), where the market was in part held; there was also a market in Vimoutiers (Orne)
Brief history; probably one of the most ancient cheeses of Normandy, indistinguishable from the Angelots of the past and in all probability invented by monks who lived nearby

   Note: It is jokingly called a Livarot-colonel or five-striper in allusion to the "service stripes" of sedge running around the outside of the cheese

A fairly good buy
Related cheeses: Petit Lisieux, Pavé de Moyaux, Pont-l'Evêque
   Differences: shape, size, flavor, texture

LIVERNON

Also known as: CABECOU DE LIVERNON
Province: AQUITAINE (QUERCY)
Milk: goat's milk
Type: soft
Rind: natural
Packaging: unwrapped
Flavor: 3
(See CABECOU)

LIVRON

Also known as: TOMME DE LIVRON
Province: DAUPHINE
Made in or by: commercial plants
Milk: goat's milk
Fat content: 45%
Type: soft
Rind: bloomy
Packaging: paper, with trade name
Flavor: 3
Origin of name: trade name of commercial dairy
(See SAINTE-MAURE*)*

LOCHE

Province: TOURAINE
Made in or by: commercial plants
Milk: goat's milk
Fat content: 45%
Type: soft
Rind: bloomy
Packaging: trademarked label
Flavor: 3
Origin of name: brand name of commercial dairy *(see* SAINTE-MAURE*)*

LORMES

Province: NIVERNAIS
Source: Lormes (Nièvre); additional sources: vicinity of Clamecy
Made in or by: farms
Best seasons: end of spring, summer, autumn; availability of goat's milk, end of curing period
Milk: goat's or half goat's milk
Fat content: 45%
Type: soft

Rind: natural
Curing: dry, in ventilated cellars, 3 to 4 weeks
Form: truncated cone
Dimensions: 3 in. at base, 2 in. high
Weight: approximately 9 oz.
Packaging: unwrapped
Selection:
  Appearance: delicate, bluish rind
  Feel: firm and supple
  Smell: light goat smell
  Taste: pronounced flavor, some bouquet (3–4)
What to watch out for: excessive dryness, graininess, rancidity
Use: end of meals, snacks
Appropriate wines: fruity whites and rosés: Pouilly-sur-Loire; whites and
    rosés of Tannay
Origin of name: place of origin
A fairly good buy locally
Related cheeses: Valençay, Levroux, Sainte-Maure, Tournon-Saint-
    Pierre, Chabis, etc.
  Differences: origin, shape, size, texture, flavor

LORRAINE

Also known as: GERARDMER *(see* this listing) or GROS LORRAINE
Province: LORRAINE
Source: Gérardmer region
Made in or by: commercial dairies
Best seasons: summer, autumn; best milk from pastured herds
Milk: cow's milk
Fat content: 40% to 45%
Type: soft; usually sold as white cheese
Rind: washed
Curing: in humid cellars, about 1 month
Form: thick cylinder
Dimensions: 12 in. in diameter, 3 in. thick
Weight: 13 lb. 3 oz.
Packaging: box

Selection:
 Appearance: barely pink rind; white interior
 Feel: firm
 Smell: penetrating lactic smell
 Taste: mild lactic flavor, slightly acidulous (4–5)
What to watch out for: rarely anything at this stage of curing
Use: end of meals, snacks
Appropriate wines: dry and fruity whites or rosés of Côtes de Toul; supple
 and fruity reds of Beaujolais
Origin of name: center of production and dialectal pronunciation of
 Gérardmer
Brief history: linked with that of Munster and Gérômé
A good buy
Related cheeses: fresh Gérômés and Munsters
 Differences: slight: fineness of texture

LOUDES

Also known as: BLEU DE LOUDES
Packaging: unwrapped
Flavor: 4
(See BLEU DE LOUDES)

LUCULLUS

Province: ILE-DE-FRANCE and NORMANDY
Source: Grand Morin Valley and plain of Evreux
Made in or by: commercial plants
Best seasons: autumn, winter; low temperature curing
Milk: cow's milk, enriched and pasteurized
Fat content: 75%
Type: soft
Rind: bloomy
Curing: in a slightly humid place, 3 weeks to 1 month
Form: small, tallish cylinder
Dimensions: 3 in. in diameter, 2 in. tall
Weight: 8 oz.
Packaging: unwrapped

Selection:
  Appearance: downy pinkish rind
  Feel: tender without elasticity
  Smell: pronounced fermentation smell
  Taste: mild nutty flavor (2–3)
What to watch out for: excessive surface redness, runniness
Use: end of meals; additional uses: in canapés
Appropriate wines: light fruity wines with bouquet: red Bouzy
Origin of name: invented name used by some retailers for similar triple-
    cream cheeses
Related cheeses: all triple-cream cheeses with bloomy rinds
  Differences: fineness of texture, origin, size

LUSIGNAN

Province: POITOU
Source: Lusignan; additional sources: immediate vicinity
Made in or by: farms
Best seasons: end of spring, summer, autumn; availability of milk
Milk: goat's milk
Fat content: 45%
Type: fresh, drained, and occasionally molded
Rind: nonexistent; filmy skin
Curing: 1 to 2 weeks
Form: flat disk
Dimensions: 3½ to 4 in. in diameter, 1 in. thick
Weight: 7 to 9 oz.
Packaging: unwrapped, or as curds in bulk
Selection:
  Appearance: fresh and pure white
  Feel: tender and velvety
  Smell: goat's milk smell
  Taste: creamy and mild (2)
What to watch out for: lack of homogeneity
Use: eaten as is; additional use: as ingredient in a traditional pastry:
    tourteau fromagé
Appropriate wines: no wine necessary
Origin of name: name of nearest market
A fairly good buy locally

Related cheeses: Jonchée, Caillebotte de Chèvre Frais
  Differences: none save origin

MACONNAIS or CHEVRETON DE MACON

Province: BURGUNDY
Source: Saint-Pierre-de-Cruzille (Saône-et-Loire); additional sources:
  mountains of Mâcon region
Made in or by: farms; small cheese factories
Best seasons: end of spring, summer, autumn because of availability of
  goat's milk; all year for half goat's-milk and cow's-milk cheeses
  because cow's milk is available all year
Milk: goat's milk or half each of goat's milk and cow's milk, or all cow's
  milk
Fat content: 40% to 45%
Type: soft
Rind: natural
Curing: dry, in ventilated cellars, 1 or 2 weeks
Form: small truncated cone
Dimensions: 2 in. in diameter at base, 1½ in. at top, 1 to 1½ in. high
Weight: 2 oz.
Packaging: unwrapped
Selection:
  Appearance: delicate light-blue rind
  Feel: firm, almost hard
  Smell: no special smell
  Taste: faint goat flavor, slightly nutty to nutty (3–4)
    It may be eaten fresh; it is then white and creamy
What to watch out for: brittle, crumbly texture, rancidity (liked by local
  devotees)
Use: end of meals, snacks, light meals; additional uses: in Burgundy or
  Lyons *fromage fort*
Appropriate wines: dry and fruity whites of Mâconnais, Beaujolais and
  light and fruity Mâcon
Origin of name: main market center and producing region
Related cheeses: all firm-textured goat's-milk or mixed-milk cheeses of
  Bresse and Charolais
  Differences: origin, shape, size, texture, flavor

MAGNUM

Province: NORMANDY (PAYS DE BRAY)
Source: Forges-les-Eaux
Best seasons: all year; generally good conditions for curing and storage;
   the cattle graze all year round
Milk: cow's milk, enriched
Fat content: 75%
Type: soft, triple cream
Rind: bloomy
Curing: 3 weeks
Form: thick disk
Dimensions: 5½ in. in diameter, 1½ in. thick
Weight: 1 lb. 2 oz.
Flavor: 2–3
(see BRILLAT-SAVARIN, which is the same cheese aged somewhat
   longer)
Related cheeses: Excelsior, aged Boursin, Délice de Saint-Cyr, etc.
   Differences: name, dimensions, origin, size, etc.

MALAKOFF

Province: NORMANDY (PAYS DE BRAY)
Milk: cow's milk
Fat content: 45%
Type: fresh
Rind: none
Flavor: 1–2
Old brand of fresh GOURNAY; *see* GOURNAY FRAIS

MAMIROLLE

Province: FRANCHE-COMTE
Source: Mamirolle
Made in or by: experimentally, at Mamirolle dairying school
Best seasons: all year; pasteurized milk used
Milk: cow's milk, pasteurized

Fat content: 40%
Type: pressed, uncooked
Rind: washed
Curing: humid, in humid cellars, 2 months
Form: parallelepiped with square cross-section
Dimensions: length 6 in., width and height 2½ to 3 in.
Weight: 1 lb. 2 oz. to 1 lb. 5 oz.
Packaging: trademark
Selection:
  Appearance: delicate, sound, reddish rind
  Feel: supple, elastic
  Smell: little smell
  Taste: somewhat emphatic to hearty flavor (4–5)
What to watch out for: rarely anything
Use: end of meals
Appropriate wines: all light and fruity wines, red or white
Origin of name: place of origin \
A fairly good buy
Related cheese: Limburger
  Differences: origin, manufacturing technique, fineness of texture, milder flavor

MANICAMP

Province: ILE-DE-FRANCE
Milk: cow's milk
Fat content: 40% to 45%
Type: soft
Rind: washed
Flavor: 4
Origin of name: small village of Aisne, part of the Coucy-le-Château Canton, which at one time lent its name to a small cheese of the QUART-MAROILLES type

MARED-SOUS

Country: BELGIUM
Type: Monastery cheese, Trappist, of Saint-Paulin type

MAROILLES

Regions: HAINAUT, FLANDERS (THIERACHE)
Source: Avesnois; additional source: French Hainaut (Label of origin regulated by law)
Made in or by: farms; in the last few years, commercial plants
Best seasons: summer, autumn, winter; milk from pastured herds, end of curing of the last batches
Milk: cow's milk
Fat content: 45% to 50%
Type: soft
Rind: washed
Curing: humid, in humid cellars, 4 months
Form: slab
Dimensions: 5 by 5 in., 2½ in. thick
Weight: 1 lb. 12 oz.
Packaging: unwrapped
Selection:
  Appearance: smooth, shiny red-brown rind
  Feel: supple
  Smell: strong bouquet, strong smell
  Taste: very vigorous, tangy flavor (4–5)
What to watch out for: dried-out rind, chalky texture, ammonia smell
Use: end of meals, snacks; additional uses: in *goyère,* a local cheese pie
Appropriate wines: all very well-knit, vigorous and full-bodied wines
Origin of name: influential monastery where an unknown monk invented Maroilles in the 10th century.

> More than a thousand years ago, the monks of the Monastery of Maroilles, where Saint Hubert is buried, invented the "miracle of Maroilles" in response to the encouragement of the bishop of Cambrai Enguerrand; in the countryside the cheese was called Craquegnon.
> This subtle cheese soon became famous; Philip Augus-

tus, Louis IX, Charles VI, Francis I, Fénélon and Turenne
were all enthusiasts.

Rather inexpensive
Related cheeses: Sorbais, Mignon, Quart, Baguette Laonnaise, which are
different forms of the same product
Differences: origin, shape, size, texture, flavor

MATTONS

Province: LORRAINE
Milk: cow's milk, skimmed
Fat content: 0% to 0.5%
Type: cooked
Rind: none
Flavor: 3
(See METTON*)*

MEILLERAYE DE BRETAGNE, LA

Also known as: ABBAYE DE LA MEILLERAYE or TRAPPISTE DE
LA MEILLERAYE
Province: BRITTANY
Source: Abbey of La Meilleraye
Best seasons: end of spring, summer, autumn; best milk from the pas-
tured herds, end of curing period
Milk: cow's milk
Fat content: 40% to 45%
Type: pressed, uncooked
Rind: washed
Curing: humid, in humid cellars, 2 months
Form: thick slab
Dimensions: 9½ by 9½ in., 2 in. thick
Weight: approximately 4 lb. 6 oz.
Packaging: unwrapped
Selection:
 Appearance: smooth straw-yellow to ochre-yellow rind
 Feel: supple and elastic

Smell: light smell of lactic fermentation

Taste: pronounced tang (3–4)

What to watch out for: superficial heat spoilage, desiccation, grainy texture, bitterness

Use: end of meals, snacks; additional uses: in cheese puffs

Appropriate wines: all light and fruity red country wines: Loire Valley reds; and dry white country wines: Muscadet

Origin of name: site of monastery

A fairly good buy

Related cheeses: all monastery cheeses, commercial Saint-Paulins

Differences: origin, shape, size, texture, flavor

METTON

Province: FRANCHE-COMTE

Source: Besançon; additional sources; all dairying regions of Franche-Comté

Made in or by: small, medium and large dairies

Best seasons: all year; constant availability of whey from curdled milk

Milk: cow's milk, skimmed

Fat content: maximum 1%

Type: hard, grainy, made from recooked whey

Curing: dry, in warm cellars

Form: lumps the size of a hazelnut

Packaging: bulk

Selection:

Appearance: greenish gold color

Feel: elastic

Smell: strong fermentation smell

Taste: not very satisfactory, plain (3)

What to watch out for: underripeness, whitish granulation, overripeness, sticky consistency, foul odor

Use: used in the preparation of CANCOILLOTTE

Appropriate wines: none

Origin of name: dialectal word of undetermined origin

Related cheeses: various recooked, unmolded cheeses, Mattons of Lorraine

Differences: origin

MIGNON MAROILLES or MAROILLES MIGNON

Provinces: HAINAUT, FLANDERS (THIERACHE)
Source: Thiérache; additional source: Avesnois
Made in or by: small dairies
Best seasons: summer, autumn; availability of milk from pastured herds,
    end of curing period
Milk: cow's milk
Fat content: 50%
Type: soft
Rind: washed
Curing: humid, in humid cellars, 6 weeks
Form: square
Dimensions: 5 by 5 in., 1 in. thick
Weight: 14 oz.
Packaging: unwrapped, or box
Selection:
    Appearance: smooth, shiny, red-brown rind
    Feel: supple
    Smell: strong smell, strong bouquet
    Taste: very pronounced tang (4–5)
What to watch out for: desiccation, chalky consistency, runniness, exces-
    sive saltiness, ammonia smell
Use: end of meals; additional uses: in cheese pies, *flamiches, goyères*
Appropriate wines: all well-knit, vigorous, full-bodied wines: Côtes-du-
    Rhône-Villages, Fitou
Origin of name: from prototype, Maroilles
A fairly good buy
Related cheese: Maroilles, Sorbais, Quart, Baguette
    Differences: origin, shape, size, texture, flavor

MIGNOT

Province: NORMANDY (PAYS D'AUGE)
Source: Vimoutiers
Made in or by: farms, exclusively
Best seasons: autumn, winter; milk from herds returned from summer
    pastures, curing at proper time
Milk: cow's milk

Fat content: 40% to 45%
Type: soft
Rind: natural
Curing: in humid cellars, 1 month
Form: thick disk
Dimensions: 4½ to 5 in. in diameter, 1½ in. thick
Weight: 12 oz. to 14 oz.
Packaging: unwrapped
Selection:
  Appearance: unblemished red rind; slightly oily, whitish interior
  Feel: rather firm without being hard
  Smell: rather penetrating and strong smell
  Taste: very fruity flavor with a strong bouquet (4–5)
What to watch out for: difficult to cite because of rustic character of
  cheese
Use: end of meals; additional uses: snacks
Appropriate wines; most often eaten with sweet cider
Origin of name: hamlet in Canton of Vimoutiers
Brief history: probably the latest of the unique farm cheeses still made
  in Normandy
Related cheeses: Livarot
  Differences: origin, more rustic character, more primitive manufactur-
    ing techniques, flavor

MIMOLETTE

Country: NETHERLANDS
Province: NOORD HOLLAND
Source: Noord Holland; additional source: Friesland
Made in or by: commercial plants
Best seasons: all year; industrial production in all seasons
Milk: cow's milk, pasteurized
Fat content: 45%
Type: pressed, reheated, colored orange inside
Rind: brushed
Curing: dry, in dry cellars, 6 months
Form: flattened sphere
Dimensions: 7 in. in diameter, 5 in. high
Weight: 5 lb. 8 oz. to 6 lb. 10 oz.

Packaging: unwrapped, with label of origin
Selection:
  Appearance: slightly rough, very even rind; compact interior without
       holes or very few tiny ones
  Feel: firm
  Smell: little smell
  Taste: pleasantly nutty flavor (3)
What to watch out for: interior a bit too "open"
Use: breakfast, end of meals, snacks; additional uses: canapés, cheese
     toasts
Appropriate wines: all light and fruity wines: Côtes de Beaune; beer goes
     well
Origin of name: from semi-soft *(demi-molle)* texture of cheese

       Note: the market for this famous Dutch cheese is held at
     Alkmaar, in Noord Holland

Related cheeses: Edam, Gouda, Present
  Differences: origin, shape, size, packaging, fineness of texture, flavor

MIMOLETTE FRANÇAISE

Also known as: BOULE DE LILLE or VIEUX LILLE
Region: FLANDERS
Source: Flanders; additional sources: Burgundy, Charente, Normandy
Made in or by: commercial plants
Best seasons: all year; use of pasteurized milk, storage
Milk: cow's milk, pasteurized
Fat content: 45%
Type: pressed, uncooked but reheated, colored orange
Rind: natural, brushed
Curing: dry, 6 to 18 months, according to use
Form: slightly flattened sphere
Dimensions: 8 in. in diameter, 7 in. high
Weight: approximately 6 lb. 10 oz.
Packaging: unwrapped, with label of warranty
Selection:
  Appearance: delicate, regular gray rind
  Feel: firm and oily

Smell: subtle, fruity aroma

Taste: clean, nutty flavor (3)

What to watch out for: cracks in rind, holes in cheese, rancid or sharp flavor

Use: snacks, end of meals; additional uses: cheese toasts, puffs, canapés, grated as a seasoning for certain dishes

Recipe: The cheese is opened at the top and little balls scooped out. The balls are sprinkled with Port or Madeira and allowed to soak for a week or two. They are then mashed and served as canapés or on toast.

Appropriate wines: Madeira, Port and all very full-bodied and generous wines such as Banyuls, Maury, Rivesaltes, etc.

Brief history: introduced from Noord Holland, Netherlands

A fairly good buy

Related cheeses: Edam, Gouda, Dutch Mimolette

Differences: rind appearance (paraffined), origin, flavor, fineness of texture, differences due to aging

MONTSEGUR

Province: COMTE DE FOIX

Source: Pyrenees of Ariège Department

Made in or by: commercial dairies

Best seasons: all year; standardized production using pasteurized milk

Milk: cow's milk, pasteurized

Fat content: 45%

Type: pressed, uncooked

Rind: washed, colored

Curing: in a temperate humid place, 1 month

Form: thick disk with a very convex rim

Dimensions: 9 in. in diameter, 3 in. thick

Weight: 6 lb. 10 oz.

Packaging: unwrapped, labeled

Selection:

Appearance: blackish rind; rather open interior

Feel: very supple

Smell: faintly lactic smell

Taste: very bland (2–3)

Use: end of meals, snacks

Appropriate wines: all light red, rosé or white wines of any origin
Origin of name: nearby place name
Brief history: recent invention
Related cheeses: Saint-Paulin
  Differences: more supple

MONSIEUR

Also known as: MONSIEUR-FROMAGE
Province: NORMANDY (ROUMOIS)
Source: La Bouille
Made in or by: small local dairies
Best seasons: end of spring, summer, autumn; quality of the milk, good
    preparation conditions
Milk: cow's milk, enriched
Fat content: 60%
Type: soft
Rind: bloomy
Curing: dry, 1½ months
Form: rather tall cylinder
Dimensions: 3 in. in diameter, 2 in. high
Weight: 5 oz.
Packaging: if fresh, unwrapped; if aged, box
Selection:
  Appearance: white rind dotted with red
  Feel: firm with some give
  Smell: rather penetrating smell
  Taste: very fruity flavor with some bouquet (4)
What to watch out for: desiccation, sticky rind, excessive redness
Use: end of meals
Appropriate wines: fruity full-bodied reds of Burgundy, Bordeaux, Côtes-
    du-Rhône, etc.
Brief history: invented at the end of the last century by a farmer named
    Fromage, it was perfected by M. Herselin and has slowly become
    a classic specialty
Related cheeses: La Bouille, Chaource, Brie de Melun
  Differences: origin, shape, size, flavor, texture

MONTASIO

Country: ITALY
Region: VENETIA
Province: UDINE
Source: Province of Udine; additional sources: Provinces of Belluno, Treviso, Venezia
Made in or by: small and middle-sized commercial dairies
Best seasons: young cheeses: summer, autumn; because best quality milk from summer mountain pastures; old cheeses: all year because of use of stored supplies
Milk: cow's milk, whole or partially skimmed
Fat content: 30% or 45%
Type: pressed, uncooked
Rind: brushed
Curing: in humid cellars with brushings; table cheeses: 4 months; grating cheese: 2 years, of which only 4 months in humid cellars
Form: small wheel with slightly convex rim
Dimensions: 14 to 16 in. in diameter, 2½ to 3½ in. thick
Weight: 15 lb. 14 oz. to 26 lb. 14 oz.
Packaging: unwrapped
Selection:
  Appearance: fairly smooth rind, ochre yellow to gray; homogeneously textured interior with very tiny holes
  Feel: firm with some give; hard and brittle
  Smell: rather neutral smell
  Taste: young: mild and nutty (2–3); old: rancid and sharp (5–6)
What to watch out for: lack of homogeneity in texture, crumbliness
Use: young: end of meals, snacks; old: grated into regional dishes
Appropriate wines: from light to full-bodied, according to the age of the cheese: from Beaujolais to Châteauneuf-du-Pape
Brief history: developed in the 13th century fief of the Monastery of Moggio, where sheep were pastured; original cheese was in all likelihood made of sheep's milk
A good buy
Related cheeses: Asiago
  Differences: origin, manufacturing, texture, flavor

MONT-DES-CATS

Also known as: ABBAYE DU MONT-DES-CATS, TRAPPISTE DU
   MONT-DES-CATS
Province: FLANDERS
Source: Godwaersvelde
Made in or by: monastery, using commercialized procedures
Best seasons: summer, autumn; quality of milk produced by pastured
   herds
Milk: cow's milk
Fat content: 40% to 45%
Type: pressed, uncooked
Rind: washed
Curing: humid, 2 months
Form: thick disk
Dimensions: 10 in. in diameter, 1½ in. thick
Weight: 4 lb. 6 oz.
Packaging: unwrapped, with trademark
Selection:
   Appearance: straw-yellow to ochre rind; ivory-yellow interior
   Feel: supple, elastic without softness
   Smell: little character
   Taste: pronounced lactic flavor (2–3)
What to watch out for: heat spoilage of rind, too strong odor, grainy
   texture
Use: end of meals, snacks; additional uses: cheese toasts, *croque-madame*
Appropriate wines: all light and fruity wines: reds of the Loire; dry whites:
   Muscadet
Origin of name: name of the hill on which monastery was built
Brief history: linked with that of the founding of the monastery
A good buy
Related cheeses: all monastery cheeses and Saint-Paulins
   Differences: origin, shape, size, texture, flavor

MONT-D'OR

Province: LYONNAIS
Source: Mont d'Or of Lyon
Made in or by: farms; production dying out

Best seasons: cow's milk: all year round because of constant availability of milk; goat's milk: end of spring, summer, autumn because of seasonal availability of goat's milk

Milk: goat's or mixed cow's and goat's or all cow's milk

Fat content: 45%

Type: soft

Rind: natural

Curing: dry, in humid cellars, 2 weeks

Form: very flat disk

Dimensions: 3 to 3½ in. in diameter, ½ in. thick

Weight: 4 oz.

Packaging: unwrapped, flat basket

Selection:

  Appearance: delicate blue rind with reddish pigments

  Feel: tender

  Smell: slight smell of mold and fermentation

  Taste: delicate and savory

What to watch out for: leakage, excessive saltiness

Use: end of meals

Appropriate wines: all the Beaujolais of the Lyons region as well as red Arbois

Origin of name: mountains where cheese is produced

Related cheeses: aged Saint-Marcellin, Rogeret des Cevennes

  Differences: origin, shape, size, texture, flavor

MONTOIRE

Province: **ORLEANAIS (VENDOMOIS)**

Source: Loire Valley

Made in or by: farms

Best seasons: end of spring, summer, autumn; availability of goat's milk

Milk; goat's milk

Fat content: 45%

Type: soft

Rind: natural

Curing: dry, 3 weeks

Form: small truncated cone

Dimensions: 2½ to 3 in. in diameter, at base, 2 in. high

Weight: 3½ oz.
Packaging: unwrapped
Selection:
   Appearance: delicate bluish gray to light-ochre rind
   Feel: fine-textured and firm
   Smell: slight goat smell
   Taste: fruity flavor (3)
What to watch out for: desiccation, grainy texture, excessive saltiness
Use: end of meals, snacks
Appropriate wines: all fruity reds, whites and roses of Loir and Loire
   valleys
Origin of name: invented name given to the cheeses of the region; also
   called Villiers-sur-Loir
Related cheeses: Selles-sur-Cher, Chabichou
   Differences: origin, shape, texture, flavor

MONTRACHET

Province: BURGUNDY
Source: Saint-Gengoux-le-National
Made in or by: small dairy
Best seasons: end of spring, summer, autumn; availability of high-quality
   goat's milk
Milk: goat's milk
Fat content: 45%
Type: soft
Rind: barely formed
Curing: a few days of draining, 1 week in ventilated cellars
Form: tall cylinder
Dimensions: 2 to 2½ in. in diameter, 4 in. tall
Weight: 3 oz. to 3½ oz.
Packaging: chestnut or grape leaves
Selection:
   Appearance: sound surface, bluish beneath the leaves
   Feel: supple
   Smell: light goat smell
   Taste: mild and creamy (3)
What to watch out for: crumbling, sharpness

Use: end of meals
Appropriate wines: Aligotés of Burgundy or light and fruity reds of the Côte: Passe-Tout-Grain, Beaujolais, etc.
Origin of name: brand name suggesting the great wine of the Beaune region
Related cheeses: all semi-fresh goat's-milk cheeses of whatever origin
  Differences: origin, shape, size, texture flavor

MORBIER

Province: FRANCHE-COMTE
Source: Champagne, Saint-Laurent-du-Jura, Morez (Jura), etc.; additional sources: neighboring high plateaus
Made in or by: small fruiteries
Best seasons: spring; made during the winter in low mountain chalets
Milk: cow's milk
Fat content: 45%
Type: pressed, uncooked
Rind: natural
Curing: dry, with brushings in cool, humid cellars, 2 to 3 months
Form: thick disk
Dimensions: 14 to 16 in. in diameter, 3 to 4 in. thick
Weight: 13 lb. 3 oz. to 17 lb. 10 oz.
Packaging: unwrapped
Selection:
  Appearance: light gray rind; black streak running horizontally through middle of cheese
  Feel: firm with some degree of suppleness
  Smell: faint lactic smell
  Taste: rather pronounced flavor (3)
What to watch out for: insufficient suppleness, hardness, bitterness
Use: end of meals, snacks
Appropriate wines: all light and fruity wines of Beaujolais, Burgundy, Côtes-du-Rhône, Jura
Origin of name: village of Morbier, the producing region
A fairly good buy
Related cheeses: small pressed-type cheeses from Valais Alps: Conches, Bagnes; from Ariège section of Pyrenees: Bethmale, Les Orrys
  Differences: origin, texture, packaging

MOTHAIS or CHEVRE A LA FEUILLE

Also known as: LA MOTHE-SAINT-HERAY(*see* this listing)
Province: POITOU
Milk: goat's milk
Fat content: 45%
Type: soft
Rind: natural
Flavor: 3–4

MOTHE-SAINT-HERAY, LA

Province: POITOU
Source: La Mothe-Saint-Héray dairy
Made in or by: dairy, using commercial procedures
Best seasons: end of spring, summer, autumn; availability of goat's milk
Milk: goat's milk
Fat content: 45%
Type: soft
Rind: bloomy
Curing: in dry cellars, 2 weeks
Form: flat disk
Dimensions: 4 in. in diameter; 1 in. thick
Weight: 8 oz. or 9 oz.
Packaging: box
Selection:
   Appearance: even, white rind
   Feel: tender without softness
   Smell: light mold smell
   Taste: rather robust flavor
What to watch out for: excessive fermentation, leakage, grainy texture, excessive saltiness
Use: end of meals
Appropriate wines: all long-lived, full-bodied red wines of Poitou
Origin of name: site of dairy
A fairly good buy

In the La Mothe-Saint-Héray dairy, goat's-milk cheeses are made also in other shapes: pyramids, cylindrical logs, etc.

Related cheeses: all industrial goat's-milk cheeses of Poitou
   Differences: origin, shape, size, texture, flavor

MOYAUX

Also known as: PAVE DE MOYAUX, PAVE D'AUGE
Flavor: 3–4
(*See* PAVE DE MOYAUX)

MOZZARELLA

Country: ITALY
Regions: originally LATIUM, CAMPANIA
Source: Latium, Campania, for buffalo-milk cheese
Made in or by: commercial plants; now also made abroad because of the
   difficulty of export
Best seasons: all year; fresh cheese made all over the country
Milk: cow's milk or buffalo's milk
Fat content: 40% to 45%
Type: pressed, spun fresh
Rind: none
Curing: none; but short storage in salt water
Form: variable: spherical, oval, rectangular loaf, etc.
Dimensions: variable
Weight: 3½ oz. to 2 lb. 3 oz.
Packaging: in a container with salt water
Selection:
   Appearance: immaculate whiteness
   Feel: elastic
   Smell: frank lactic smell
   Taste: mild, creamy flavor (1–2)
What to watch out for: aging, yellowing
Use: in cooking, especially in pizza
Appropriate wines: when the opportunity presents itself with a white or
   rosé from the south of Italy
A good buy

MUNSTER AU CUMIN

Province: ALSACE
Milk: cow's milk
Fat content: 45% to 50%
Type: soft, flavored with seeds of *carum carvi* (caraway)
Rind: washed
Flavor: 4–5
(*See* MUNSTER FERMIER)

MUNSTER FERMIER

Province: ALSACE
Source: upper Munster valley; additional sources: Lapoutroie, Sainte-Marie-aux-Mines, Villé, etc. (Label of origin regulated by law)
Made in or by: farms
Best seasons: summer, autumn; milk from the "high stubble" of the Vosges, end of curing period
Milk: cow's milk
Fat content: 45% to 50%
Type: soft
Rind: bloomy
Curing: humid, in humid cellars, with washings; 5 weeks for small thin cheeses, 2 to 3 months for larger cheeses
Form: flat disk of variable size
Dimensions: 5 to 8 in. in diameter, 1 to 2 in. thick
   Weight: 10 oz. to 3 lb. 5 oz.
Packaging: unwrapped
Selection:
   Appearance: smooth, shiny, brick-red rind
   Feel: supple
   Smell: strong, penetrating smell
   Taste: spicy, very tangy flavor (4–5)
What to watch out for: crumbling, cracking, excessive saltiness due to accidental dehydration (careless handling)
Use: end of meals, snacks
Appropriate wines: in Alsace, where the cheese is eaten less than fully aged, Gewürztraminer; elsewhere, very full-bodied and full-bou-

queted red wines: Côte-Rôtie, Corton, Haut-Médoc, Alsatian Pinot Rouge

Origin of name: city of Munster (name is a contraction of the word for "monastery")

Brief history: Munster is an ancient cheese of monastic origin, in existence since the Middle Ages

Related cheeses: Gérômé, Langres, Chaumont

Differences: origin, shape, size, texture, flavor

MUNSTER LAITIER

Province: ALSACE

Source: eastern slopes of Vosges; additional source: western slopes

Made in or by: medium-sized and large commercial dairies

Best seasons: all year; pasteurized milk used

Milk: cow's milk, pasteurized

Fat content: 45% to 50%

Type: soft

Rind: washed

Curing: humid, with washings; 4 to 6 weeks for small cheeses, 2 to 3 months for large ones

Form: flat cylinder

Dimensions: 4½ to 8 in. in diameter, 1 to 2 in. thick

Weight: 10 oz. to 3 lb. 5 oz.

Packaging: box

Selection:

  Appearance: smooth reddish rind

  Feel: supple

  Smell: strong and penetrating smell

  Taste: spicy to very spicy, depending upon thickness (4–5)

What to watch out for: crumbling, desiccation, overaging (locally Munster is eaten after very little aging)

Use: end of meals, snacks

Appropriate wines: in Alsace, Gewürztraminer; elsewhere, long-lived, full-bodied reds: Côtes-du-Rhône, Beaujolais-Villages, Alsatian Pinot Rouge

Origin of name: name of place that was originally the center of the main manufacturing area

Brief history: linked with that of Munster Fermier

A fairly good buy

Related cheeses: Gérômé, Munster Fermier, Langres, Epoisses, Soumaintrain
   Differences: origin, size, texture, flavor

MUROL

Province: AUVERGNE (MONTS DORE)
Source: Murol and vicinity
Made in or by: small factories
Best seasons: summer, autumn; availability of mountain milk, end of
   curing period
Milk: cow's milk, pasteurized
Fat content: 45%
Type: pressed, uncooked
Rind: washed
Curing: humid, about 6 weeks
Form: flat disk with a 2-inch hole in center
Dimensions: 5 in. in diameter, 1½ in. thick
Weight: 1 lb.
Packaging: unwrapped
Selection:
   Appearance: pink rind
   Feel: supple inside and out
   Smell: no special smell
   Taste: mild (2–3)
What to watch out for: excessively dry rind, toughness
Use: end of meals; additional uses: in cheese puffs
Appropriate wines: Coteaux-d'Auvergne, Côtes-Roannaises, Beaujolais
   and all light and fruity wines
Origin of name: place where cheese was invented
Brief history: invented by M. Jules Bérioux
A good buy
Related cheeses: Saint-Paulin, various Trappist cheeses, commercial
   Saint-Nectaire
   Differences: origin, size, flavor, consistency

NANTAIS

Also known as: FROMAGE DU CURE (PRIEST'S CHEESE)
Province: Brittany
Source: upper Brittany
Made in or by: small factories
Best seasons: all year; even quality of milk, ease of curing in all seasons
Milk: cow's milk
Fat content: 40%
Type: pressed, uncooked
Rind: washed
Curing: humid, 1 month
Form: square with rounded corners
Dimensions: 3½ by 3½ in., 1½ in. thick
Weight: 6 oz. or 7 oz.
Packaging: unwrapped
Selection:
   Appearance: smooth straw-yellow to ochre-yellow rind
   Feel: supple and elastic
   Smell: rather full, strong smell
   Taste: pronounced flavor with a tangy bouquet (3)
What to watch out for: thick, dry rind; grayish coloring; toughness; bitterness; heat spoilage
Use: end of meals
Appropriate wines: Muscadet, Gros-Plant and all long-lived fruity wines: Côteaux-d'Ancenis
Origin of name: from its invention in the 19th century by a priest from Vendée
A fairly good buy
Related cheeses: Saint-Paulin and all other monastery-type cheeses
   Differences: origin, size, texture, flavor

NEUFCHATEL

Province: NORMANDY (PAYS DE BRAY)
Source: Neufchâtel-en-Bray; additional sources: other cantons of Bray region (Label of origin regulated by law)
Made in or by: small factories

Best seasons: farm-produced cheeses: summer, autumn because of best quality milk from pastured cows; commercially produced cheeses: all year round because adequate milk available throughout the year
Milk: cow's milk
Fat content: 45%
Type: soft
Rind: bloomy
Curing: dry, 3 weeks
Form: square, briquette, bung, heart
Packaging: unwrapped
Dimensions: variable according to shape
Weight: average 3½ oz.
Selection:
   Appearance: downy skin, little red pigmentation
   Feel: smooth and velvety
   Smell: slight mold smell
   Taste: savory and salty (2–3)
What to watch out for: desiccation, excessive saltiness, grainy texture
Use: end of meals, snacks
Appropriate wines: all long-lived and fruity red wines: Côtes-du-Rhône-Villages
Origin of name: most important market in region
A good buy
Related cheeses: Gournay
   Differences: shape, size

NIOLO

Also known as: NIOLIN
Province: CORSICA
Source: Niolo plateau
Made in or by: farms, exclusively
Best seasons: summer, autumn; availability of sheep's milk, end of curing period
Milk: sheep's milk
Fat content: minimum 45%
Type: soft
Rind: natural

Curing: humid, with soaking in brine, 3 or 4 months
Form: square with rounded edges, with marks of the basket in which it
    was molded
Dimensions: 5½ by 5½ in., 2 in. thick
Weight: 1 lb. 2 oz. to 1 lb. 9 oz.
Packaging: unwrapped
Selection:
    Appearance: smooth, clean, grayish white surface
    Feel: firm and buttery
    Smell: strong goat smell
    Taste: very sharp flavor, with very full bouquet (6–7)
What to watch out for: breaks, internal fissures
Use: snacks, end of meals
Appropriate wines: natural wines of the Corsican cape: Sciaccarello,
    Madiran, and all rough, stout and spiritous wines
Origin of name: Niolo plateau, where cheese originated

   Note: the same cheese in the fresh state is creamy, mild and
   smoothly oily and is of the same character as Brousses.

Related cheeses: very sharp Roquefort, Venaco
    Differences: origin, shape, size, texture, flavor

NOYERS-LE-VAL

Also known as: CENDRE D'ARGONNE
Province: CHAMPAGNE (ARGONNE)
Source: Argonne; additional sources: Champagne
Made in or by: farms; production dying out
Best seasons: summer, autumn; cheeses are prepared for hay harvest or
    grape harvest in Champagne
Milk: cow's milk
Fat content: 30 % to 35%
Type: soft
Rind: natural, coated with ashes
Curing: in ashes in a dry place, 2 to 3 months
Form: irregular disk
Dimensions: 5 to 5½ in. in diameter, 1 to 1½ in. thick
Weight: 10 oz. to 12 oz.

Packaging: unwrapped
Selection:
  Appearance: surface well coated with ashes
  Feel: firm, with some interior suppleness
  Smell: little smell
  Taste: very spicy and saponified taste (4–6)
What to watch out for: desiccation
Use: snacks, end of meals
Appropriate wines: all solid and very full-bodied wines: red Bouzy
Origin of name: where cheese was first made
Related cheeses: ash-coated cheeses of Argonne, Champagne, Orléanais
  or Beauce
  Differences: origin, shape and size, richness and fineness of texture,
    flavor, bouquet

OELENBERG

Also known as: TRAPPISTE D'OELENBERG
Province: ALSACE
Source: Monastery of Oelenberg
Made in or by: monks, using traditional methods
Best seasons: all year; availability of cow's milk
Milk: cow's milk
Fat content: 45%
Type: pressed, uncooked
Rind: washed
Curing: humid, in humid cellars, 2 months
Form: rather thick disk
Dimensions: 9 in. in diameter, 1½ in. thick, approximately
Weight: 2 lb. 10 oz. to 3 lb. 1 oz.
Packaging: unwrapped
Selection:
  Appearance: smooth light-yellow rind
  Feel: supple
  Smell: light smell of mold and of fermentation
  Taste: mild lactic flavor, not very spicy
What to watch out for: dry rind, grainy texture, bitterness, superficial
  heat spoilage

Use: end of meals; additional uses: cheese toasts
Appropriate wines: all light, fruity wines of Alsace without too pronounced aroma: Pinot, Kniperlé, Zwicker, Sylvaner
Origin of name: monastery where cheese was developed
Brief history: linked with that of the monastery
Related cheeses: all monastery cheeses
  Differences: origin, shape, size, texture, flavor

OLERON

Also known as: JONCHEE D'OLERON or BREBIS D'OLERON
Province: AUNIS
Source: Isle of Oléron
Made in or by: farms
Best season: spring, availability of sheep's milk
Milk: sheep's milk
Fat content: 45% to 50%
Type: fresh
Rind: none
Curing: none; merely drained
Form: no precise form
Dimensions: variable
Weight: variable
Packaging: unwrapped
Selection:
  Appearance: pure white
  Feel: soft
  Smell: fresh and lactic
  Taste: mild and creamy (1–2)
What to watch out for: grainy texture
Use: end of meals
Appropriate wines: the white wine of the island
Origin of name: Isle of Oléron (Charente-Maritime)
Related cheeses: all fresh sheep's-milk cheeses, Caillado of Rouergue and
  upper Limousin
  Differences: origin, aroma, consistency, texture, flavor

OLIVET BLEU

Province: ORLEANAIS
Source: Orléanais
Made in or by: traditional dairies
Best seasons: end of spring, summer, autumn; quality of milk, end of
    curing period
Milk: cow's milk
Fat content: 45%
Type: soft
Rind: natural, blue bloom
Curing: dry, in local chalk caves, approximately 1 month
Form: small disk
Dimensions: 5 in. in diameter, 1 in. thick
Weight: about 11 oz.
Packaging: unwrapped, or waxed paper or plane-tree leaves
Selection:
    Appearance: delicate bluish skin; smooth straw-yellow interior
    Feel: rich, supple, homogeneous
    Smell: light scent of blue mold
    Taste: fruity, not very spicy flavor (3)
What to watch out for: sticky rind, excessive saltiness
Use: end of meals
Appropriate wines: Pinot Meunier from Orléanais or any fruity and
    long-lived red wine: Borgueil, Saint-Emilion
Origin of name: main curing and marketing center
Brief history: linked with that of all Orléans cheeses
A fairly good buy
Related cheeses: Vendôme Bleu, Villebarou
    Differences: origin, size, texture, flavor

OLIVET CENDRE

Province: ORLEANAIS
Source: Orléanais
Made in or by: traditional dairies
Best seasons: summer, autumn, winter; availability of cheeses, good stor-
    age during hot weather, end of storage period
Milk: cow's milk

Fat content: 40%
Type: soft
Rind: natural, coated with ashes
Curing: dry, in cases filled with wood ashes, 3 months
Form: flat disk
Dimensions: 5 in. in diameter, 1 in. thick
Weight: 10½oz.
Selection:
  Appearance: thick and well shaped
  Feel: firm but supple
  Smell: light smell of cellars
  Taste: very savory, saponified (4–5)
What to watch out for: excessive dryness, excessive saponification or saltiness
Use: end of meals, farmers' or grape harvesters' snacks
Appropriate wines: all well-knit, full-bodied wines: Chinon, Saint-Ay
Origin of name: main center of curing and marketing
Brief history: linked with that of all the cheeses of Loire Valley and of Beauce. Ash-coated cheeses are in a sense "cheese preserves" put aside during the period when milk is abundant for use during the summer when demand will be great, especially during mowing and harvesting
A fairly good buy
Related cheeses: Vendôme Cendré, Barberey Cendré, Cendrés of Champagne and Ardennes
  Differences: origin, size, texture, flavor

OLORON-SAINTE-MARIE

Province: PAYS BASQUE (BIGORRE)
Flavor: young, 2–3; old, 4–6
(see ESBAREICH*)*

> Note: Oloron is the central market

ORRYS, LES

Province: COMTE DE FOIX
Source: Les Orrys, Castillon; additional sources: high valleys of Lez and
Salat
Made in or by: mountain cottages
Best seasons: summer, autumn, winter; best quality milk from high sum-
mer pastures, end of curing period
Milk: cow's milk
Fat content: 45%
Type: pressed, uncooked
Rind: natural
Form: flat cylinder with slightly convex sides
Dimensions: 14 to 18 in. in diameter, 3 to 3½ in. thick
Weight: 22 lb. to 24 lb. 7 oz.
Packaging: unwrapped
Selection:
  Appearance: very even wheels, with smooth, fine-grained rind
  Feel: supple without being soft
  Smell: pleasant tangy smell
  Taste: rather pronounced flavor with some bouquet (4)
What to watch out for: swelling, cracks, sandy texture, sharpness
Use: end of meals; additional uses: older cheeses, grated as a condi-
ment
Appropriate wines: all fruity, lively wines of Fitou and Corbières du
Roussillon: Irurozqui, Madiran
Origin of name: mountain village (Les Orrys) in the center of the summer
pasturing area of Ariège
A fairly good buy locally
Related cheeses: Fontina from Val d'Aosta, cheeses from the valleys of
Valais
  Differences: origin, fineness of texture, flavor

OUSTET

Province: COMTE DE FOIX
Milk: cow's milk
(See BETHMALE)

PANNES CENDRE

Province: ORLEANAIS
Source: Orléanais
Made in or by: farms, traditional dairies; not much commercialization
Best seasons: summer, autumn; keeps well in hot weather
Milk: cow's milk, skimmed
Fat content: 20% to 30%
Type: soft
Rind: natural, coated with ashes
Curing: dry, in chests of wood ashes, 3 months
Form: flat disk
Dimensions: 5 in. in diameter, 1 in. thick
Weight: 10½ oz.
Packaging: none
Selection:
  Appearance: thick and well shaped
  Feel: supple
  Smell: mold smell
  Taste: very pronounced flavor, saponified (4–6)
What to watch out for: excessive dryness; excessive saponification or
    saltiness
Use: end of meals, farmers' and harvesters' snacks
Appropriate wines: very pale-red, rough, harsh wines: Côtes-du-Rhône,
    Vinsobres, Cornas
Origin of name: place of manufacture
Brief history: linked with that of all the cheeses of Orléanais *(see*
    OLIVET CENDRE)
A fairly good buy locally
Related cheeses: Olivet Cendré, Vendôme Cendré, and all other Cendrés
  Differences: richness in fat, size, origin, flavor

PARFAIT

Also known as: FIN-DE-SIECLE *(see* this listing) or SUPREME
Province: NORMANDIE (PAYS DE BRAY)
Milk: cow's milk, enriched
Fat content: 72%

Type: soft
Rind: bloomy
Flavor: 2–3
Origin of name: invented name given to a traditional cheese made in the
     Neufchâtel-en-Bray region

PARMESAN

Also known as: PARMIGIANO
Country: ITALY
Region: EMILIA
Province: PARMA
Source: area between Enza and Cristolo rivers and between the hills and
     Aemilian Way; additional sources: Provinces of Bologna and Man-
     tua and part of Modena and Reggio nell'Emilia
Made in or by: commercial plants, from April 15 to November 11 of each
     year
Best seasons: all year; aging of cheese makes possible continuous supplies
Milk: cow's milk
Fat content: 32%
Type: pressed, cooked
Rind: brushed, oiled
Curing: dry, in cool and dry cellars, 2 to 3 years
Form: thick cylindrical wheels with slightly convex sides
Dimensions: 14 to 18 in. in diameter, 7 to 9½ in. tall
Weight: legal minimum, 52 lb. 13 oz.; average, 66 lb.; maximum, 88 lb.
Packaging: unwrapped, blackish coating of mixed oil and umber; for
     certain countries, just oil
Selection:
  Appearance: very regular shape; smooth rind; delicate granular tex-
       ture, straw-yellow color
  Feel: hard, brittle and crumbly
  Smell: faint smell
  Taste: very fruity to sharp flavor (4–5), hard texture, but melts in the
       mouth
What to watch out for: internal fractures, grainy texture, rancidity
Use: in Italy, end of meals; in Italy and elsewhere, used ground as a
     seasoning for many dishes

Appropriate wines: all well-knit, full-bodied wines: Lambrusco
Origin of name "grana": from the granular texture of the cheese
Brief history: goes back most likely to the 11th century
Related cheeses: Sbrinz, Saanen, Passe-l'An, Grana from other sources
  Differences: origin, size, packaging, fineness of texture, flavor

PARTHENAY

Province: POITOU
Milk: goat's milk
Fat content: 45%
Type: fresh
Flavor: 3–4
(See JONCHEE NIORTAISE)

PASSE-L'AN

Province: LANGUEDOC
Source: Montauban (Tarn-et-Garonne); additional sources: central Eastern France
Made in or by: commercial dairies
Best seasons: any; there are always cheeses that are ready to eat
Milk: cow's milk, pasteurized
Fat content: 28% to 32%
Type: hard
Rind: natural, oiled, colored with umber
Curing: in a dry place, at least 2 years
Form: cylindrical wheel with slightly convex sides
Dimensions: 12 to 16 in. in diameter, 14 in. tall
Weight: 77 lb. to 88 lb.
Packaging: unwrapped, coating of oil and umber
Selection:
  Appearance: brittle greenish yellow interior
  Feel: very hard
  Smell: slight smell
  Taste: strong cheese flavor (4–5)

What to watch out for: internal cracks, hollows

Use: grated, in cooking and in cocktail pastries; additional uses: sometimes eaten as is

Appropriate wines: all stout, well-knit wines of Bordeaux (Médoc)

Origin of name: from the legal requirement that it be aged for more than a year to bring out its qualities fully

Brief history: started in France when imports of Italian Parmesan had been cut off

Note: an imitation of Italian Grana

Related cheeses: Italian Grana, Parmigiano, Reggiano, etc.
  Differences: origin, savor, grain

PATAY

Province: ORLEANAIS

Source: Patay; additional sources: immediate vicinity

Made in or by: farms; production dying off

Best seasons: summer, autumn, winter; availability of milk, good preparation conditions, end of the curing of the last batches

Milk: cow's milk

Fat content: 45%

Type: soft

Rind: natural

Curing: dry, either allowed to turn blue or stored beneath ashes in wooden chests, 5 to 6 weeks

Form: flat disk

Dimensions: 10 in. in diameter, 1 in. thick

Weight: 1 lb. 2 oz.

Packaging: unwrapped generally; sometimes wrapped in plane-tree leaves or coated with ashes

Selection:
  Appearance: thin skin characteristic of Bleu cheeses; regular shape characteristic of ash-coated cheeses
  Feel: supple
  Smell: light smell of mold
  Taste: very fruity, saponified flavor (4–5)

What to watch out for: sticky skin, grainy texture, fetid odor, leakage, excessive saltiness

Use: end of meals, snacks

Appropriate wines: pale red wines (Vins Gris) of Orléanais
Origin of name: nearby town where the market was held
A fairly good buy locally
Related cheeses: Olivet, Vendôme, Villebarou
  Differences: origin, size, texture, flavor

PAVE D'AUGE

Province: NORMANDY
Flavor: 3–4
Generic name for various PAVES of lower Normandy
(See PAVE DE MOYAUX, CARRE DE BONNEVILLE)

PAVE DE MOYAUX

Also known as: PAVE D'AUGE
Province: NORMANDY
Source: Moyaux; additional sources: Pont-L'Evêque Canton
Made in or by: farms; small traditional dairies
Best seasons: summer, autumn, winter; best milk, end of curing period
Milk: cow's milk
Fat content: 50%
Type: soft
Rind: washed, sometimes brushed
Curing: humid, with washings in salt water, 2½ to 3 months (longer if
    the cheese is thick); or enclosed for 4 months, treated with damp
    brushings
Form: parallelepiped slab with square base
Dimensions: 4½ by 4½ in., 2 to 2½ in. high
Weight: 1 lb. 9 oz. to 1 lb. 12 oz.
Packaging: unwrapped
Selection:
  Appearance: straw-yellow to ochre-yellow rind, no gray mold
  Feel: firm with some degree of suppleness
  Smell: smell of cellars and mold
  Taste: spicy flavor, strong tang (3–4)
What to watch out for: sticky or leathery rind, granular texture, gray or
    runny interior, bitterness, ammonia smell

Use: end of meals

Appropriate wines: well-knit, full-bodied red wines with some bouquet: Bourgueil, Fleurie, Pomerol

Origin of name: village of Moyaux

Brief history: probably the ancestor of the Angelots and consequently ancestor of the Pont-l'Evéque cheeses

Related cheeses: Pont-l'Evêque, Petit Lisieux, Livarot

   Differences: origin, shape, size, flavor, texture

PECORINO ROMANO

Country: ITALY

Region: LATIUM

Province: ROME

Source: Latium; additional souces: Provinces of Cagliari, Frosinone, Grossetto, Nuoro, Sassari, Viterbo

Made in or by: traditional and commercial dairies

Best seasons: for production: autumn, winter, spring because of the periodicity of sheep lactation; for eating: all year round at different stages of maturity because of stability of product after curing

Milk: sheep's milk

Fat content: 36% minimum

Type: pressed, cooked

Rind: spontaneous, brushed, oiled with olive oil dregs colored with ochre

Curing: dry, in dry and cool cellars, 8 months minimum

Form: cylindrical wheel with flat sides and rim

Dimensions: 8 to 10½ in. in diameter, 5½ to 9 in. tall

Weight: 13 lb. 4 oz. to 26 lb. 8 oz.

Packaging: unwrapped

Selection:

   Appearance: white or ochre-yellow rind; white to light straw-yellow interior

   Feel: compact and hard

   Smell: slightly smoky smell

   Taste: flavor strongly characteristic of sheep's-milk cheeses, sharp (5–7)

What to watch out for: excessive granulation, excessive sharpness (enjoyed by the local users)

Use: young, end of meals; aged, grated as a condiment
Appropriate wines: sappy, full-bodied wines from the south and from Sicily
Origin of name: type of milk and province of origin
Brief history: very ancient, goes back to Roman antiquity
Related cheeses: Pecorino Sardo, Siciliano
   Differences: size, fineness of grain, origin, flavor, packaging

PECORINO SARDO

Country: ITALY
Province: SARDINIA
Milk: sheep's milk
Fat content: 45%
Flavor: 5–7
(See FIORE SARDO)

PECORINO SICILIANO

Also known as: CANESTRATO
Country: ITALY
Region: SICILY
Source: Sicily
Made in or by: traditional and industrial dairies
Best seasons: for production: autumn, winter, spring because of the periodicity of sheep lactation; for eating: all year because of the stabilized nature of the cured cheese
Milk: sheep's milk
Fat content: minimum 40%
Type: pressed, uncooked
Rind: spontaneous, brushed, oiled
Curing: dry, in dry cellars, 4 months minimum
Form: cylinder with flat sides and rim
Dimensions: 8 to 10½ in. in diameter, 4 to 7 in. high
Weight: 13 lb. 4 oz. to 22 lb.
Packaging: unwrapped; cheese bears traces of draining basket or *canestro*

Selection:
> *Appearance:* white to light-yellow rind; compact white or straw-colored interior
> *Feel:* hard
> *Smell:* distinctly characteristic of sheep's-milk cheeses
> *Taste:* sharp and rancid (5–7)

What to watch out for: excessive granulation, crumbling
Uses: young, end of meals; aged, grated as a condiment
Appropriate wines: robust and powerful wines of Sicily
Origin of name: type of milk, and from the draining basket or *canestro* (hence *Canestrato*)
Brief history: known since ancient times
Related cheeses: Pecorino Romano and Pecorino Sardo
> *Differences:* origin, size, packaging, flavor, texture

PELARDON D'ALTIER

Province: LANGUEDOC
Milk: goat's milk
Fat content: 45%
Flavor: 3
(See PELARDON DES CEVENNES)

PELARDON D'ANDUZE

Province: LANGUEDOC
Milk: goat's milk
Flavor: 3
(See PELARDON DES CEVENNES)

PELARDON DES CEVENNES

Province: LANGUEDOC
Source: Cévennes; additional sources: Gévaudan, Vivarais
Made in or by: farms
Best seasons: summer, autumn; quality of the goat's milk, good storage

Milk: goat's milk
Fat content: 45%
Type: soft
Rind: natural
Curing: 2 or 3 weeks
Form: small round disk, fairly thick and irregular
Dimensions: 2½ to 3 in. in diameter, 1 in. thick
Weight: average 3 to 4½ oz. (varies from place to place)
Packaging: unwrapped
Selection:
  Appearance: white, either rindless or very thin-skinned
  Feel: dense
  Smell: almost no smell
  Taste: nutty flavor (3)
What to watch out for: rarely excessive dryness or graininess
Use: end of meals, snacks
Appropriate wines: red Costières-du-Gard, fruity and full-bodied Côtes-du-Rhône
Origin of name: Cévennes dialect

  Note: PELARDON is the generic name for several cheeses of
this type

Related cheeses: Tomme de Chèvre of Chabeuil, Crest
  Differences: origin, fineness of grain, flavor

PERSILLE DES ARAVIS

Also known as: GRAND-BORNAND and PERSILLE DE THONES
Province: SAVOIE
Source: massif of Aravis; additional sources: Thônes and La Clusaz
  cantons (Haute-Savoie)
Made in or by: farms, chalets
Best seasons: summer, autumn; availability of goat's milk, end of curing
  period
Milk: goat's milk
Fat content: 45%
Type: pressed, internal molds
Rind: natural, brushed
Curing: dry, in humid cellars, with sprinklings and scrapings, 2 months

Form: tall cylinder
Dimensions: 3 to 4 in. in diameter, 5 to 6 in. high
Weight: about 2 lb. 4 oz.
Packaging: unwrapped
Selection:
   Appearance: rind ranging from thin and gray to thick and dark brown
   Feel: supple to firm, depending upon age
   Smell: no special smell
   Taste: very savory and sharp (4–5)
What to watch out for: overripeness, hardness and brittleness, graininess, excessive sharpness
Uses: end of meals, snacks
Appropriate wines: all well-knit, full-bodied red wines: Mondeuse, Beaujolais-Villages, Chinon
Origin of name: character of the cheese and the area where it is made

     Note: The Persillés of Grand-Bornand and of Thônes are the Persillés of Aravis

Related cheeses: very few made from goat's milk except the Bleu cheeses of Tignes and of Mont-Cenis made from mixed goat's and cow's milk
   Differences: origin, shape, size, cow's milk mixed with goat's milk

PERSILLE DU GRAND-BORNAND

Also known as: PERSILLE DE THONES
Province: SAVOIE
These cheeses are PERSILLES DES ARAVIS (*see* this listing)

PERSILLE DU MONT-CENIS

Province: SAVOIE
Source: Termignon (Savoie); additional sources: Mont-Cenis Massif
Made in or by: farms, chalets
Best seasons: summer, autumn; summer pasturing gives high quality milk, end of curing period
Milk: mixed cow's and goat's milk

Fat content: 45%
Type: lightly pressed, blue veined
Rind: natural
Curing: dry, in humid and cold cellars, 3 months on average
Form: cylindrical
Dimensions: 12 in. in diameter, 6 in. high
Weight: approximately 17 lb. 9 oz.
Packaging: unwrapped
Selection:
  Appearance: gray, unbroken rind; when cut, smooth and blue
  Feel: hard
  Smell: no special smell
  Taste: very pronounced flavor, approaches bitterness (3–4)
What to watch out for: grainy texture, sharpness (a desirable quality for
  local consumers)
Use: end of meals, snacks
Appropriate wines: all well-knit, somewhat sappy red wines: Beaujolais-
  Villages, Côtes-du-Rhône-Villages
Origin of name: characteristics of cheese and area where it is made
Related cheeses: Persillé des Aravis, Persillé de Tignes
  Differences: origin, size, texture, flavor

PERSILLE DE THONES

Also known as: PERSILLE DU GRAND-BORNAND
Province: SAVOIE
Same cheese as PERSILLE DES ARAVIS (*see* this listing)

PETIT BESSAY

Province: BOURBONNAIS
Source: Bessay and Souvigny (Allier)
Made in or by: farms; production dying out
Best seasons: summer, autumn; availability of high quality milk
Milk: cow's milk
Fat content: 40% to 45%
Type: soft

Rind: natural
Curing: dry, in humid cellars, 3 to 4 weeks
Form: flat disk
Dimensions: 3 to 4 in. in diameter, 1 in. thick
Weight: about 7 oz.
Packaging: unwrapped
Selection:
  Appearance: fresh-looking
  Feel: supple
  Smell: tangy, lactic smell
  Taste: fruity flavor with bouquet (3–4)
Use: end of meals, snacks
Appropriate wines: fruity and supple rosés and reds of Saint-Pourcain, Côteaux d'Auvergne, Côtes-Roannaise
Origin of name: place where cheese is made
A fairly good buy
Related cheeses: all country cow's-milk cheeses with natural rinds that are semi-aged
  Differences: origin, shape, size, texture, flavor

PETIT LISIEUX

Also known as: DEMI-LIVAROT
Province: NORMANDY
Source: Livarot; additional sources: vicinity of Vimoutiers
Made in or by: farms, production dying out; a commercial plant is reviving production
Best seasons: end of spring, summer, autumn; availability of high quality milk, end of curing period
Milk: cow's milk
Fat content: 40% to 45%
Type: soft
Rind: washed
Curing: humid, in warm and humid cellars, 2 months
Form: flattened cylinder
Dimensions: 5 in. in diameter, 1 in. thick
Weight: 10½ oz.
Packaging: unwrapped, surrounded by strips of rush

Selection:
  Appearance: smooth and glossy light brick-red to red-brown rind
  Feel: tender, elastic
  Smell: strong tang
  Taste: spicy flavor (4–5)
What to watch out for: dried-out rind, toughness, graininess, putrid odor, ammonia odor, leakage, bitterness
Appropriate wines: all very robust and solid wines: Hermitage, Cornas, Cahors, Châteauneuf-du-Pape; country cider is quite suitable or a shot of Calvados
Origin of name: most important market town
Brief history: probably one of the oldest cheeses in Normandy, it is undoubtedly the Angelot mentioned in Guillaume de Lorris's *Roman de la Rose* (13th century)
A fairly good buy
Related cheeses: Livarot
  Differences: size, flavor

PETIT-SUISSE

Country: FRANCE
Source: all provinces
Best season: any; pasteurized milk used, cheese sold fresh
Milk: cow's milk, pasteurized and enriched with cream
Fat content: 60% to 75%
Type: fresh, unsalted
Rind: none
Curing: none
Form: small cylinder
Dimensions: 1 in. in diameter, 2 in. long
Weight: 1 oz.
Packaging: sheathed in absorbent paper, or plastic container
Selection: freshness only criterion; always eaten fresh
  Taste: 1
What to watch out for: lack of freshness
Use: end of meals; additional uses: served mixed with fresh or stewed fruit; used for canapés and in various recipes
Appropriate wines: no need for wine

Origin of name: from the nationality of a worker in Mme Héroult's cheese factory who used to transport the cheeses to the markets in Paris and who made some changes in the manufacture of fresh Bondon cheeses in the middle of the last century

A good buy

Related cheeses: all smooth-textured cheeses

PICADOU

Province: AQUITAINE (QUERCY)
Milk: sheep's or goat's milk
Fat content: 45%
Type: soft
Curing: wrapped in leaves, in crocks such cheese is called CABECOU
Selection: choice depends upon individual taste; all very strong and emit a strong odor of alcoholic fermentation
Flavor: 5–6

PICODON DE DIEULEFIT

Province: DAUPHINE (DIOIS)
Source: Montélimar region; best source: Dieulefit; additional source: Diois
Made in or by: farms
Best seasons: end of summer, autumn; availability of goat's milk, end of curing in grape must
Milk: goat's milk
Fat content: 45%
Type: soft
Rind: natural
Curing: dry, in ventilated cellars, then soaked in white wine for 1 month
Form: small irregular disk
Dimensions: 2½ to 3 in. in diameter, 1 in. thick
Weight: 3 oz. to 3½ oz.
Packaging: unwrapped

Selection:
   Appearance: golden to reddish rind
   Feel: firm without being hard
   Smell: smell of alcoholic fermentation
   Taste: moderately sharp
What to watch out for: excessive fermentation (prized by local consumers), brittle or crumbly texture
Use: end of meals, snacks; additional uses: in Fromage Fort de Vivarais, also called FOUDJOU (*see* this listing)
Appropriate wines: lively, full-bodied red and white Côtes-du-Rhône
Origin of name: flavor (*piquant* or sharp) of cheese, and place of origin
Related cheeses: all goat's-milk cheeses soaked in white wine
   Differences: origin, size, texture, flavor

PICODON DE SAINT-AGREVE

Province: LANGUEDOC (VIVARAIS)
Source: Vivarais; best source: Saint-Agrève; additional source: Cévennes mountains
Made in or by: farms
Best seasons: summer, autumn; availability of goat's milk, end of curing period
Milk: goat's milk
Fat content: 45%
Type: soft
Rind: natural
Curing: dry, in ventilated cellars, 2 to 3 weeks
Form: small disk
Dimensions: 3 to 3½ in. in diameter, 1 in. thick
Weight: 4½ oz.
Packaging: unwrapped
Selection:
   Appearance: delicate bluish to golden rind
   Feel: fine-textured and firm
   Smell: faint goat smell
   Taste: very nutty, full bouquet (3–4)
What to watch out for: hardness and brittleness, superficial heat spoilage, too strong odor (preferred by some people)

Use: end of meals, snacks: additional uses: macerated in wine or leek water for kneaded *fromage fort* fermented in crock

Appropriate wines: Côtes-du-Rhône-Villages; all durable, full-bodied reds, rosés or whites

Origin of name: taste (*piquant*) of cheese, and place of origin

Related cheeses: all Picodons and Pélardons of Cévennes, Dauphiné, Comtat Venaissin

Differences: origin, shape, size, texture, flavor

PICODON DE VALREAS

Province: COMTAT VENAISSIN

Source: Valréas; additional sources: immediate vicinity

Made in or by: farms

Best seasons: end of spring, summer, beginning of autumn; availability of goat's milk, end of curing period

Milk: goat's milk

Fat content: 45%

Type: soft, semi-fresh

Rind: natural, thin

Curing: dry, 1 week

Form: small disk

Dimensions: 3 in. in diameter, 1 in. thick

Weight: 3½ oz. to 4½ oz.

Packaging: unwrapped

Selection:

  Appearance: rind barely formed

  Feel: firm and supple

  Smell: no particular smell

  Taste: slightly nutty flavor (2–3)

What to watch out for: grainy texture

Use: end of meals, snacks

Appropriate wines: light and fruity whites and rosés of Côtes-du-Rhône

Origin of name: place of production; main market was Avignon

Related cheeses: all goat's-milk cheeses, fresh or semi-fresh; Picodon with garlic

Differences: origin, size, texture, flavor

A LA PIE

Also known as: FROMAGE BLANC
Country: FRANCE
Source: all regions
Made in or by: homes; commercial plants: production halted and sale of cheese is forbidden
Best seasons: all year; availability of milk in all seasons
Milk: cow's milk, unsalted whole or skimmed
Fat content: variable
Type: fresh, partly drained
Rind: none
Curing: none
Form: circular wicker cheese draining basket
Dimensions: 16 in. in diameter, 2½ in. thick
Weight: 13 lb. 3 oz. to 17 lb. 10 oz.
Packaging: unwrapped, sold in bulk
Selection: always select freshest and softest cheese
What to watch out for: too thorough drainage
Use: end of meals: additional uses: served with fresh or stewed fruits; in cooking
Appropriate wines: no wine necessary

Note: the name COTTAGE CHEESE has dropped out of use

Related cheeses: all partly drained fresh cheeses
  Differences: type and richness of milk

PIERRE-QUI-VIRE

Province: BURGUNDY
Source: Monastery of La Pierre-Qui-Vire, Saint-Léger-Vauban (Côte-d'Or)
Made in or by: monks, using traditional methods
Best seasons: summer, autumn; best milk, end of curing period
Milk: cow's milk
Fat content: 45%
Type: soft
Rind: washed
Curing: 2 months after drying, in humid cellars, with washings

Form: flat disk
Dimensions: 4 in. in diameter, 1 in. thick
Weight: 7 oz.
Packaging: unwrapped, on straw
Selection:
  Appearance: reddish rind
  Feel: supple
  Smell: rather penetrating smell
  Taste: not very spicy flavor with a strong tang (3–4)
It may also be eaten fresh after draining
What to watch out for: vermiculated rind, granular texture
Use: end of meals
Appropriate wines: all lively, full-bodied red burgundies
Origin of name: Monastery of La Pierre-Qui-Vire
Brief history: connected with the return to use of the monastery lands
Related cheeses: Epoisses, Saint-Florentin, Soumaintrain, Langres
  Differences: shape, size, origin, fineness of texture, flavor

PIGOUILLE

Provinces: CHARENTES, POITOU (MARAIS POITEVIN)
Source: Marans
Best seasons: sheep's-milk cheese: end of autumn, winter; goat's-milk cheese: end of spring, summer, beginning of autumn; cow's-milk cheese: all year round; periodic availability of sheep's and goat's milk, and nonseasonality of cow's milk
Milk: cow's, goat's or sheep's milk
Fat content: about 45%
Type: soft
Rind: natural
Curing: draining, brief drying
Form: small round disk
Dimensions: 4½ in. in diameter, 1 in. thick
Weight: about 9 oz.
Packaging: unwrapped, on straw
Selection:
  Appearance: delicate white rind
  Feel: tender

Smell: light lactic smell
Taste: creamy flavor (2–3)
What to watch out for: granular texture, sourness
Use: end of meals, snacks
Appropriate wines: all light and fruity red or white wines
Origin of name: dialect word
Fairly inexpensive to expensive, according to the type of milk used
Related cheeses: various fresh sheep's-milk and goat's-milk cheeses
　　Differences: origin, shape, size, texture, flavor

PITHIVIERS AU FOIN

Also known as: BONDAROY AU FOIN (*see* this listing)
Province: ORLEANAIS
Section: GATINAIS
Flavor: 3–4

POIVRE-D'ANE

Also known as: PEBRE D'AI (in patois)
Province: PROVENCE
Source: Lure mountains; additional sources: Comtat Venaissin, Dauphiné
Made in or by: sheep's-milk cheese: farms; goat's-milk cheese: farms, small dairies
Best seasons: sheep's-milk cheese: spring; goat's-milk cheese: end of spring, summer, beginning of autumn; cow's-milk-cheese: all year; milk becomes available in accordance with the productive cycles of the different species
Milk: sheep's, goat's or cow's milk or mixed cow's and goat's milk
Fat content: 45%
Type: soft
Rind: natural, covered with sprigs of savory
Curing: 1 month
Form: small disk
Dimensions: 3 in. in diameter, 1 in. thick
Weight: 3½ oz. to 4 oz.

Packaging: unwrapped; in baskets or boxes filled with savory
Selection:
  Appearance: beneath the herbs, bluish white to yellowish white rind
  Feel: dense and fine-grained
  Smell: aromatic perfume, light lactic aroma in fresh cheeses
  Taste: mild and aromatic (2–3)
What to watch out for: granular texture
Appropriate wines: lively, fruity whites and rosés of Mont Ventoux on the
  slopes of Durance
Origin of name: patois word *pebre d'ai* for the herb savory
Brief history: it is a Banon cheese
Related cheeses: all cheeses aged in aromatic herbs in southeastern
  France
  Differences: origin, shape, size, flavor, texture, aroma

PONT-L'EVEQUE

Province: NORMANDIE
Source: Pays d'Auge (Normandy)
Made in or by: farms, almost entirely; commercial producers just getting
  started
Best seasons: summer, autumn, winter; best milk, best storage
Milk: cow's milk
Fat content: 50%
Type: soft
Rind: washed, sometimes merely brushed
Curing: humid, in humid cellars, 1½ months; or else sealed curing in
  humid cellars
Form: small parallelepiped with square base
Dimensions: 4 by 4 in., 1 in. high
Weight: 12 oz. to 13 oz.
Packaging: box, or unwrapped
Selection:
  Appearance: very smooth golden rind
  Feel: tender, supple consistency, homogeneous
  Smell: savory with some bouquet
  Taste: pronounced tang (3–4)
What to watch out for: hard rind, grayish color, grainy texture, cow-barn
  odor, leakage

Use: end of meals
Appropriate wines: stout, full-bodied reds with some bouquet from Bordeaux, Burgundy, or Côtes-du-Rhône; Bouzy, Pomerol, Volnay
Origin of name: nearest large market town, Pont-L'Evêque (Calvados)
Brief history: probably one of the oldest cheeses of Normandy, mentioned as Angelot by Guillaume de Lorris in his 13th-century *Roman de la Rose*
A fairly good buy
Related cheeses: Pavé de Moyaux, Pavé d'Auge
   Differences: shape, size, flavor

PORT-SALUT

Country: FRANCE

   Note: Brand name sold by the monks of the Monastery of Port-du-Salut in Entrammes to a firm (S.A.F.R.).

Flavor: 2–3
(*See* SAINT-PAULIN)

POTTEKEES

Country: BELGIUM
Province: BRABANT
Milk: cow's milk
Type: fresh
Curing: drained for approximately 5 days
Flavor: 4–5
(*See* FROMAGE EN POT)

POULIGNY-SAINT-PIERRE

Province: BERRY
Source: Pouligny-Saint-Pierre; additional source: neighboring area
Made in or by: farms

Best seasons: end of spring, summer, beginning of autumn; availability of goat's milk, end of curing period

Milk: goat's milk

Fat content: 45%

Type: soft

Rind: natural

Curing: dry, 4 to 5 weeks

Form: pyramid

Dimensions: 3 by 3 in. at the base, 3½ in. high

Weight: 7 oz. to 9 oz.

Packaging: unwrapped

Selection:

  Appearance: delicate, bluish rind

  Feel: firm with some degree of suppleness

  Smell: light goat smell

  Taste: pronounced tang (3)

What to watch out for: grainy texture, dryness

Use: end of meals

Appropriate wines: dry and fruity white Chenin or Sauvignon from Touraine and Berry

Origin of name: convenient name given to cheeses collected from area around village of Pouligny-Saint-Pierre

Related cheeses: Tournon-Saint-Pierre, Chabis de Touraine, Sainte-Maure

  Differences: origin, shape, size, texture, flavor

POURLY

Province: BURGUNDY

Source: Essert (Yonne)

Made in or by: small traditional dairies

Best seasons: end of spring, summer, autumn; availability of goat's milk, end of curing

Milk: goat's milk

Fat content: 45%

Type: soft

Rind: natural

Curing: dry, in ventilated cellars, 1 month

Form: cylinder with convex surfaces

Dimensions: 4 in. in diameter; 2½ in. high
Weight: about 11 oz.
Packaging: unwrapped
Selection:
  Appearance: delicate bluish rind; smooth interior
  Feel: some degree of suppleness
  Smell: light goat smell
  Taste: not very pronounced nutty flavor (3)
What to watch out for: grainy curds, vermiculated rind
Use: end of meals
Appropriate wines: fine white wines of Chablis with bouquet, Aligotés of
    Burgundy and other light and fruity red wines
Origin of name: trade name taken from name of nearest hamlet
Related cheeses: all pure goat's-milk cheeses: Levroux, Valançay, Tour-
    non-Saint-Pierre, Sainte-Maure, etc.
  Differences: origin, shape, size, texture, flavor

POUSTAGNACQ

Province: AQUITAINE (LANDES)
Best seasons: end of autumn, winter, beginning of spring (old cheeses
    may be eaten later)
Milk: sheep's milk
Type: fresh, flavored
Curing: fermented in sealed crocks

PRESENT

Country: NETHERLANDS
Province: ZUID HOLLAND
Source: Gouda; additional source: Zuid Holland
Made in or by: largely commercial plants, farms somewhat less
Best seasons: all year; pasteurized milk, standardized production
Milk: cow's milk: pasteurized for commercial production, unpasteurized
    for farm cheeses
Fat content: 40% or 45%
Type: pressed, reheated

Rind: brushed

Curing: humid in the beginning, then dry in dry cellars, minimum of 3
months (may be much longer: 6–8 months)

Form: small wheel with convex sides

Dimensions: 14 in. in diameter, 2½ to 3 in. thick

Weight: 13 lb. 3 oz. to 15 lb. 7 oz. (farm cheeses as heavy as 22 lb. have
been recorded)

Packaging: unwrapped; trademark, label of fat content

Selection:

  Appearance: smooth grayish yellow rind; very dense

  Feel: firm with some degree of suppleness

  Smell: little smell

  Taste: delicate and nutty (3)

What to watch out for: rarely anything

Use: breakfast, end of meals, snacks; additional uses: in cheese toasts,
canapés

Appropriate wines: all light and fruity wines: Beaujolais; beer goes well

Brief history: linked with that of the other Dutch cheeses

A good buy

Related cheeses: Edam, Gouda, Mimolette

  Differences: origin, fineness of texture, shape, size

PROVIDENCE

Also known as: BRICQUEBEC or TRAPPISTE DE BRICQUEBEC
(*see* these listings)

Province: NORMANDY

Section: COTENTIN

Milk: cow's milk

Fat content: 45%

Brand name of the Monastery of Bricquebec

PROVOLA

Also known as: SCAMORZE (*see* this listing)

Country: ITALY

Region: MOLISE

Province: CAMPOBASSO
Flavor: 2–3

PROVOLONE

Country: ITALY
Province: CAMPANIA
Source: Campania; additional source: southern Italy
Made in or by: commercial plants
Best seasons: all year; production method not seasonal
Milk: cow's milk
Fat content: 44%
Type: pressed, hard, uncooked
Rind: smooth, spontaneous
Curing: dry, in dry cellars, 2 or 3 months to 6 months
Form: molded by hand, it assumes various shapes: most typical a bulging
    truncated cone ending in a ball supported by the cords that hold the
    cheese; apex and base usually flattened
Dimensions: 6 in. in diameter at widest, 14 to 18 in. long
Weight: 8 lb. 13 oz. to 11 lb. (there are small ones as well: 2 lb. 3 oz.
    to 6 lb. 10 oz.)
Packaging: unwrapped, in a net of cords and tied two together
Selection:
    Appearance: smooth, thin, glossy golden-yellow rind; dense creamy-
        white interior
    Feel: dense, smooth and supple
    Smell: light lactic smell
    Taste: delicate, mild to sharp, according to age (2–3 or 5–6)
What to watch out for: internal fermentation (holes)
Use: end of meals; additional uses: when aged, grated into dishes as a
    seasoning
Appropriate wines: all light and fruity wines: Beaujolais
Origin of name: from the word *prova* in Campanian dialect, meaning a
    fresh cheese of spherical shape

> *Note:* in Campania some cheeses are still made from buffalo's
> milk

A fairly good buy

Related cheeses: Provola, Provolette
  Differences: origin, shape, size, flavor

PUANT DE LILLE, or GRIS PUANT, or GRIS DE LILLE

Province: FLANDERS, HAINAUT
Milk: cow's milk
Fat content: 45% to 50%
Flavor: 4–5
(*See* GRIS DE LILLE)

PUANT MACERE

Cheese of the Maroilles type soaked in brine and occasionally after that
  in beer

PYRAMIDE

Provinces: ANJOU, CHARENTES, POITOU, TOURAINE
Milk: goat's milk
Fat content: 45%
Type: soft
Rind: bloomy
Flavor: 3
Generic name of VALENÇAY LAITIER (*see* this listing)

QUARTIROLO

Country: ITALY
Region: LOMBARDIE
Best season: autumn; milk from cows pastured on third-growth grass
  (*erba quartirola*)
Milk: cow's milk
Fat content: 48%
Type: pressed, not cooked

Rind: washed
Curing: in humid cellars, with washings, 7 to 8 weeks
Origin of name: Italian phrase *erba quartirola* describing third-growth
    autumn pasturage for cows
Flavor: 2–3

QUART MAROILLES

Also known as: MIGNONNET
Province: HAINAUT, FLANDERS
Source: French Hainaut; additional sources: Flanders, Champagne
Made in or by: semi-commercialized makers
Best seasons: end of spring, summer, autumn; quality of milk from
    pastured cows
Milk: cow's milk
Fat content: 45% to 50%
Type: soft
Rind: washed
Curing: humid, in humid cellars, 6 to 8 weeks
Form: square
Dimensions: 3 in. to a side, 1 to 1½ in. thick
Weight: 7 oz. to 8 oz.
Selection:
  Appearance: smooth, glossy red-brown rind
  Feel: supple
  Smell: strong bouquet
  Taste: rather strong tang (4–5)
What to watch out for: chalky, dried-out surface; leakage, ammonia smell
Use: end of meals; additional uses: in *goyère* and *flamiche,* local cheese
    pies
Appropriate wines: all well-knit, full-bodied and sappy wines (*see* MA-
    ROILLES)
Origin of name: from the relationship of cheese size to the size of the
    original Maroilles
A fairly good buy

Related cheeses: all cheeses of the Maroilles family: Maroilles, Sorbais, Mignon, Baguette Laonnaise
Differences: origin, shape, size, flavor

RAMEQUIN DE LAGNIEU

Province: PAYS DE L'AIN (BUGEY)
Source: Lagnieu; additional sources: Ambérieu-en-Bugey and lower Bugey
Made in or by: farms; very little marketed
Best seasons: end of spring, summer, autumn; availability of goat's milk, end of curing period
Milk: goat's milk or half goat's milk
Fat content: 30% to 45%
Type: soft
Rind: natural
Curing: dry, in ventilated cellars, 2 to 3 weeks
Dimensions: 2 in. in diameter, 2 in. high
Weight: 2 oz. to 2½ oz.
Packaging: unwrapped
Selection:
  Appearance: unblemished, light-colored rind; homogeneous
  Feel: hard with some degree of suppleness
  Smell: light goat smell
  Taste: a bit nutty (3)
What to watch out for: brittle texture, rancidity
Use: end of meals, snacks; additional uses: in ramequin bugiste
Appropriate wines: fruity whites of Montagnieu and Virieu
Origin of name: a Bugey dialect word and place of origin
Related cheeses: goat's milk cheeses of Bresse, Mâconnais, Charolais
  Differences: origin, shape, size, texture, flavor

REBLOCHON

Province: SAVOIE (ARAVIS)
Source: Le Grand-Bornand; additional sources: districts adjacent to the

main curing center, Thônes, on the Aravis Massif (Label of origin regulated by law)

Made in or by: farms; fruiteries; commercial dairies

Best seasons: summer, autumn; milk from high mountain pastures, end of curing period

Milk: cow's milk

Fat content: 50%

Type: soft, slightly pressed

Rind: washed

Curing: in humid conditions, in cold cellars, 4 to 5 weeks

Form: flattened disk

Dimensions: 5 in. in diameter, 1 in. thick

Weight: 1 lb. 2 oz.

Packaging: on a very thin circular wooden board

Selection:

   Appearance: smooth, mat, pinkish white skin

   Feel: very supple

   Smell: light smell of the cellar

   Taste: mild and creamy flavor (2–3)

What to watch out for: tough rind, grainy texture, bitterness

Use: end of meals

Appropriate wines: all fine fruity wines of Savoy: Crépy, Roussette, Abymes; light and fruity reds: Mondeuse, Gamay de Chautagne, Beaujolais

Origin of name: the patois word (*reblocher*) for the milk dripping from cows after milking

Brief history: Goes back to the time when the herdsmen would not milk the cows dry on the days when the stewards came to inspect yield. The withheld milk or *lait de rebloche* was for the herders' personal use. For this reason few people knew of this cheese, even though it is a very ancient one.

Related cheeses: Colombière, Trappiste de Chambarand

   Differences: origin, size, fineness of texture

REBLOCHONNET

Also known as: DEMI-REBLOCHON or PETIT REBLOCHON
Province: SAVOIE

Flavor: 2–3
(See DEMI-REBLOCHON and REBLOCHON)

RECOLLET

Province: LORRAINE
Flavor: 3
Brand name of a CARRE DE L'EST with a bloomy rind

REMOUDOU

Also known as: PIQUANT
Country: BELGIUM
Province: LIEGE
Source: Hervé; additional source: Hervé plateau
Made in or by: small or middle-sized commercial dairies
Best seasons: end of summer, autumn, winter; pasturing of herds, end of
     curing period
Milk: cow's milk
Fat content: 45%
Type: soft
Rind: washed
Curing: humid, in cool and humid cellars, 3 to 4 months
Form: cube
Dimensions: 3 or 3½ in. to side
Weight: 1 lb. 5 oz. to 1 lb. 8 oz.
Packaging: paper, with trademark
Selection:
   Appearance: healthy, shiny red-brown rind
   Feel: supple without being soft
   Smell: very powerful smell
   Taste: very spicy tang (4–5)
What to watch out for: desiccated rind, grainy texture
Use: end of meals
Appropriate wines: all well-knit, sappy red wines: Châteauneuf-du-Pape,
     Gigondas

Origin of name: old Germanic word with the same root as the word *Rahm* (cream)

Brief history: no doubt linked with the invention of monastery cheeses in the great Benedictine abbeys of Western Europe

A fairly good buy locally

Related cheeses: Hervé, Limburger, Maroilles

  Differences: origin, shape, size, texture, bouquet

RICEYS, LES

Also known as: CENDRE DES RICEYS
Province: CHAMPAGNE
Source: grape-growing region of Aube
Made in or by: small dairies
Best seasons: summer, autumn; production period and end of curing period
Milk: cow's milk, skimmed
Fat content: 30% to 40%
Type: soft
Rind: natural, coated with ashes
Curing: dry, in humid cellars, in grapevine ashes, 1 to 2 months
Form: flat disk
Dimensions: 5 in. in diameter, 1 in. thick
Weight: 12 oz. to 14 oz.
Packaging: unwrapped
Selection:
  Appearance: very regular shape
  Feel: still supple
  Smell: no strong smell
  Taste: very fruity, saponified flavor (3–4)
What to watch out for: desiccation, rancidity
Use: hay-mowers' and grape-harvesters' snack, end of meals
Appropriate wines: fairly full-bodied local rosés or lively, well-knit reds: Médoc, Borgueil, Les Riceys rosés
Origin of name: chief market located in center of producing region, and method of curing and storing
A fairly good buy

Related cheeses: all skim or part-skim milk ash-coated cheeses of Champagne, Ardennes, Orléanais
  Differences: origin, size, texture, flavor

RIGOTTE DE CONDRIEU

Province: LYONNAIS
Source: Ampuis, Condrieu; additional sources: Lyons region, Rhône-Loir plateau
Made in or by: small dairies
Best seasons: all year; dairy cheese
Milk: cow's milk
Fat content: 45% to 50%
Type: soft
Rind: natural, colored red (tinted with annatto)
Curing: in a drying room, 2 weeks
Form: small cylinder
Dimensions: 1½ in. in diameter, 1½ in. high
Weight: 2 oz.
Packaging: unwrapped
Selection:
  Appearance: reddish almost nonexistent rind
  Feel: firm with some degree of suppleness
  Smell: no particular smell
  Taste: not very pronounced flavor, sometimes lactic (3)
What to watch out for: desiccation, rancidity
Use: end of meals; other uses: in Fromage Fort à la Lyonnaise
Appropriate wines: light and fruity wines of Côtes-du-Lyonnais, Beaujolais, Côtes-du-Rhône
Origin of name: place of origin of cheese
A good buy
Related cheeses: small cow's-milk or half goat's-milk cheeses of Mâconnais, Charolais or Bresse
  Differences: origin, shape, size, texture, flavor

RIGOTTE DE PELUSSIN

Province: AUVERGNE
Section: FOREZ (upper part)
Source: Pelussin; additional sources: immediate vicinity
Made in or by: farms; small traditional dairies
Best seasons: end of spring, summer, autumn; availability of goat's milk
Milk: goat's or half goat's milk
Fat content: 40% to 45%
Type: soft
Rind: natural
Curing: dry, 2 weeks
Form: small cylinder or truncated cone
Dimensions: 2 in. in diameter at base, 1 in. high
Weight: 2½ oz. to 3 oz.
Packaging: unwrapped
Selection:
  Appearance: delicate bluish rind
  Feel: firm
  Smell: light goat smell
  Taste: slightly nutty (3)
What to watch out for: dryness, graininess, sharpness
Use: end of meals, snacks
Appropriate wines: light and fruity wines of Côtes-du-Rhône, Beaujolais, Côtes-Roannaises; all dry and fruity white wines
Origin of name: place of origin
A good buy locally
Related cheeses: Rigottes of Ampuis and Condrieu
  Differences: origin, type of milk, flavor, texture

ROCAMADOUR or CABECOU DE ROCAMADOUR

Province: AQUITAINE
Source: limestone plateau of Gramat; additional sources: other plateaus of Quercy
Made in or by: farms only
Best seasons: sheep's-milk cheese: spring; goat's-milk cheese: summer, autumn; availability of good milks, good storage
Milk: sheep's or goat's milk

Fat content: 45%
Type: soft
Rind: natural
Curing: dry, 1 week
Form: small thin disk
Dimensions: like a large coin
Weight: 1 oz.
Packaging: unwrapped
Selection:
  Appearance: regular shape, delicate bluish skin, sometimes pink in
    spots
  Feel: tender (sheep's milk) or rather firm (goat's milk)
  Smell: little odor (sheep's milk) or light goat odor (goat's milk)
  Taste: slightly nutty flavor (sheep's milk) to very nutty (goat's milk)
    (3)
What to watch out for: dryness, smoky taste
Use: end of meals, snacks
Appropriate wines: fruity and durable reds of the region (Cahors) or from
  elsewhere
Origin of name: patois for little goat (*cabécou*) and from the best known
  market in the region: Rocamadour

> *Note:* When wrapped in leaves, sprinkled with wine or
> brandy, and aged in crocks, these cheeses are called PICADOU
> (*see* this listing).

Related cheeses: other Cabécous of Quercy and Rouergue
  Differences: origin, dimensions, flavor

ROCROI

Also known as: ROCROI CENDRE or CENDRE DES ARDENNES
Province: CHAMPAGNE, ARDENNES
Source; Rocroi (Ardennes); additional sources: a few places in Meuse
  Valley
Made in or by: farms; very seldom marketed
Best seasons: summer, autumn; availability of milk, end of curing period
Milk: cow's milk, skimmed
Fat content: 20% to 30%
Type: soft

Rind: natural, coated with ashes
Curing: dry, in humid cellars, in wood ashes, 1 or 2 months
Form: flat disk or flat square slab
Dimensions: 5 in. in diameter, 1 in. thick, or 5 by 5 in. square, and 1 in.
　　thick
Weight: 12 oz. to 14 oz.
Packaging: unwrapped
Selection:
　Appearance: regular shape
　Feel: still supple
　Smell: light mold smell
　Taste: very fruity to saponified flavor (4–6)
What to watch out for: desiccation, rancidity
Use: end of meals
Appropriate wines: all well-knit, full-bodied wines: Mercurey, Médoc,
　　Bourgueil
Related cheeses: all ash-coated cheeses of Champagne, Argonne, or Or-
　　léanais
　Differences: origin, size, shape, texture, flavor

ROGERET DES CEVENNES

Province: LANGUEDOC
Source: Lamastre; additional sources: surrounding area
Made in or by: farms
Best seasons: end of spring, summer, autumn; availability of highest
　　quality goat's milk
Milk: goat's milk
Fat content: 45%
Type: soft
Rind: natural
Curing: in humid conditions (no washings), 4 weeks
Form: small thick disk
Dimensions: 2½ in. in diameter, 1 in. thick
Weight: 3 oz.
Packaging: unwrapped
Selection:
　Appearance: delicate reddish and bluish rind
　Feel: very tender

Smell: strong goat smell

   Taste: pronounced, very nutty flavor (3–4)

What to watch out for: rind too red and sticky, sharpness, leakage

Use: end of meals

Appropriate wines: fruity, lively, full-bodied wines of Côtes-du-Rhône

Origin of name: appearance of cheese and place of origin

Related cheeses: Pélardon des Cévennes, Picodon du Tricastin

   Differences: origin, texture, size, flavor

ROLLOT

Province: PICARDY

Source: Montdidier Arrondissement

Made in or by: small dairies

Best seasons: end of spring, summer, autumn; best milk from the pasture, end of curing period

Milk: cow's milk

Fat content: 45%

Type: soft

Rind: washed

Curing: humid, with washing; 2 months

Form: small flat cylinder or heart

Dimensions: 3 in. in diameter, 1½ in. thick

Weight: average 7 oz. to 10 oz.

Selection:

   Appearance: smooth, glossy, light ochre-yellow rind

   Feel: supple

   Smell: rather full aroma with some bouquet

   Taste: spicy tang (4)

What to watch out for: grainy or runny texture, superficial desiccation

Use: end of meals

Appropriate wines: all lively and fruity reds: Sauvigny-les-Beaune, Saint-Emilion, Côte-Rôtie

Origin of name: village of Rollot

Related cheeses: Quart Maroilles, Guerbigny

   Differences: origin, shape, size, texture, flavor

ROMANS

Also known as: TOMME DE ROMANS (*see* this listing)
Province: DAUPHINE

ROQUEFORT

Province: AQUITAINE
Source: causse (limestone plateau) of Larzac; additional sources: high
    plateaus with similar flora and climate: Corsica (Label of origin
    regulated by law)
Made in or by: caves
Best seasons: end of winter, spring, summer, autumn; availability of
    sheep's milk, end of curing period
Milk: sheep's milk
Fat content: 45%
Type: soft
Rind: natural
Curing: in the humid natural cave of Cambalou, 3 months
Form: tall cylinder
Dimensions: 7 in. in diameter, 4 in. high
Weight: approximately 5½ lb.
Packaging: foil
Selection:
    Appearance: after the foil is removed: unblemished rind; after cutting:
        uniform mold marbling throughout
    Feel: firm, smooth, buttery
    Smell: light smell of mold, very distinct bouquet
    Taste: pronounced sheep flavor (4–5, occasionally 6)
What to watch out for: crumbling edges, interior too white and lacking
    in veins, grayish color, excessive sharpness
Use: end of meals; additional uses: in canapés, salad dressings, cheese
    toasts and sandwiches
Appropriate wines: all great red wines that are very well knit and sappy:
    Châteauneuf-du-Pape, Madiran, Cahors, etc.
Origin of name: Roquefort-sur-Soulzon (Aveyron) where the cheeses are
    aged in natural caves
Brief history: presumably one of the ancient cheeses of the Gauls, men-
    tioned by Pliny the Elder

Although Pliny the Elder had already mentioned it and Charlemagne had made it his favorite cheese, it was not until April, 1411, that Charles VI signed a charter granting the inhabitants of Roquefort "the monopoly of curing the cheese as has been done in the caves of the aforesaid village since time immemorial." These famous caves were called *cabanes* (huts) and the women who work in them are still called *cabanières*. The French law of July 26, 1925, merely spells out the terms of Charles VI's charter: it recognizes (after Charles VI, Henry IV, Louis XII, Louis XIV, who also signed charters) a cheese prepared exclusively from pure, whole sheep's milk, manufactured and aged according to authentic and unchanging local custom in the natural cave of the mountains of Cambalou. The Stresa convention, signed June 1, 1951, protects the name Roquefort at the international level.

Related cheeses: none except Corsican Bleu made from sheep's milk
Differences: the place of curing determines the quality of the finished product

ROUY

Province: BURGUNDY
Source: Dijon
Made in or by; commercial plants
Best seasons: all year; pasteurized milk used
Milk: cow's milk, pasteurized
Type: soft
Rind: washed
Curing: under humid conditions, 1 month
Form: square with rounded corners
Dimensions: 4 by 4 in., 1 in. thick
Weight: 8 oz.
Packaging: labeled box
Selection:
  Appearance: smooth and unblemished rind
  Feel: supple
  Smell: full, rather strong smell of Burgundy
  Taste: pronounced tang (4)
What to watch out for: lack of suppleness, overfermentation

Use: end of meals
Appropriate wines: all lively, fruity red wines: Beaune, Morgon, Saint Emilion
Origin of name: trade name assigned by inventor and manufacturer
A good buy
Related cheeses: Saint-Rémy, Langres, Epoisses
   Differences: origin, shape, size, texture, flavor

RUFFEC

Province: POITOU
Source: Ruffec and vicinity; additional sources: northern part of Charente Department
Made in or by: farms
Best seasons: end of spring, summer, autumn; availability of milk, good manufacturing conditions
Milk: goat's milk
Type: soft-
Rind: natural
Curing: dry, 1 month
Form: thick disk
Dimensions: 4 in. in diameter, 2 in. thick
Weight: 9 oz.
Packaging: unwrapped
Selection:
   Appearance: delicate, bluish rind
   Feel: smooth
   Smell: some goat smell
   Taste: fruity flavor (3)
What to watch out for: grainy texture, oversalting
Use: end of meals, snacks
Appropriate wines: all lively, full-bodied red wines: Loudun, Champigny, Bourgueil, Chinon
Origin of name: town nearest producing region
Related cheeses: Mothais, Saint-Maixent, Chef-Boutonne, Couhé-Vérac, various Chabis
   Differences: origin, shape, size, texture, flavor

SAANEN

Also known as: FROMAGE A REBIBES or SPALEN KASE
Country: SWITZERLAND
Canton: FRIBOURG
Source: Saanen; additional sources: En-Haut region (in Gruyère)
Made in or by: chalets; not commercialized
Best seasons: all year; always available because of aging
Milk: cow's milk
Fat content: 40% to 45%
Type: pressed, cooked
Rind: brushed, oiled
Curing: dry, with damp brushings in humid cellars, aged as long as
    possible (5 years and longer)
Form: large wheel with straight sides
Dimensions: 24 in. in diameter, 5½ in. high
Weight: average 88 lb.
Packaging: unwrapped
Selection: no choice; these cheeses are set aside for family use on occa-
    sions of certain feasts or ceremonies. Flavor is very fruity with
    considerable bouquet (3–4).
What to watch out for: no apparent defects
Uses: hors d'oeuvres or snacks, shaved into very thin slices with a special
    parer; additional uses: as condiment in certain dishes, but the scar-
    city of the cheese generally precludes this
Appropriate wines: all fruity, lively reds and rosés: wines of the Jura
Origin of name: center of production
Related cheeses: Sbrinz, Italian Grana
    Differences: origin, size, manufacturing technique, flavor

SABLEAU

Also known as: TROIS CORNES
Province: POITOU
Source: Le Sableau, near Fontenay-la-Comte (Vendée); additional
    source: Chaillé-les-Marais
Made in or by: farms, exclusively; production dying out
Best seasons: end of spring, summer, autumn; availability of goat's milk
Milk: goat's milk

Fat content: 45%
Type: fresh
Rind: none
Curing: drained at least 1 week
Form: triangular
Dimensions: 4½ to 5 in. on side, 1 in. thick
Weight: 7 oz. to 10 oz.
Packaging: unwrapped, on a rush mat
Selection:
   Appearance: very fresh and pure white
   Feel: smooth and oily
   Smell: light lactic aroma
   Taste: mild goat's milk flavor (2)
What to watch out for: overdrainage, granulation
Use: end of meals
Appropriate wines: all light, fruity and lively reds, whites and rosés: Muscadet, local wines
Origin of name: hamlet in which cheese originated, and shape of cheese
Related cheeses: Jonchées, goat's-milk Caillebottes from Poitou and Charente-Maritime
   Differences: origin, fineness of texture

SAINGORLON

French cheese with internal molds made in imitation of Italian Gorgonzola

SAINT-BENOIST or SAINT-BENOIT

Province: ORLEANAIS
Source: Saint-Benoît-sur-Loire; additional sources: Jargeau, Sully-sur-Loire
Made in or by: farms
Best seasons: end of spring, summer, autumn; availability of high quality milk, good storage conditions
Milk: cow's milk, partly skimmed
Fat content: 40%

Type: soft
Rind: natural
Curing: 1 month
Form: small thick disk
Dimensions: 5 in. in diameter, 1 in. thick
Weight: 14 oz.
Packaging: unwrapped
Selection:
   Appearance: ivory to yellow rind, not highly colored
   Feel: firm
   Smell: little smell
   Taste: fruity flavor (3)
What to watch out for: chalkiness; brittleness
Use: end of meals; eaten semi-aged
Appropriate wines: fruity pale reds (Vins Gris) of Orléanais, fruity reds of Champigny, Chinon and Borgueil
Origin of name: neighboring abbey
Brief history: might be of monastery origin
A good buy locally
Related cheeses: Olivet, Vendôme, Bleus, Pannes, Patay
   Differences: origin, size, texture, flavor

SAINT-CYR

Province: POITOU
Flavor: 3
Source and factory brand name of goat's-milk cheeses of various sizes and shapes produced in Dissay (Vienne)

SAINTE-MARIE

Province: BURGUNDY
Source: Les Laumes and vicinity
Made in or by: farms; production dying out
Best seasons: end of spring, summer; best milk available
Milk: cow's milk
Fat content: 45%

Type: fresh, salted or unsalted
Rind: none
Curing: none
Form: truncated cone
Dimensions: 5 in. in diameter at base, 2½ to 3 in. high
Weight: 14 oz. and over
Packaging: unwrapped, on board
Selection:
  Appearance: pure white
  Feel: supple
  Smell: lactic smell
  Taste: slightly lactic, mild, creamy
What to watch out for: crumbling (too much rennet)
Use: salted, at end of meals: sweetened, as dessert
Appropriate wines: all light and fruity reds, whites and rosés of Burgundy
    and Beaujolais
Origin of name: probably feast day in period when cheese is made
Related cheeses: all fresh cheeses of Burgundy: Les Laumes, Epoisses,
    Saint-Florentin, La Pierre-Qui-Vire
  Differences: origin, size, shape, fineness of grain

SAINTE-MAURE FERMIER

Province: TOURAINE
Source: Sainte-Maure plateau; additional sources: Anjou, Charentes,
    Poitou
Made in or by: farms; still very active production
Best seasons: end of spring, summer, autumn; availability of goat's milk,
    end of curing period
Milk: goat's milk
Fat content: 45%
Type: soft
Rind: natural
Curing: in dry cellars, 1 month
Form: elongated cylinder
Dimensions: 6 in. long, 1½ in. in diameter
Weight: 10½ oz.
Packaging: unwrapped

Selection:
   Appearance: delicate bluish rind dotted with pink
   Feel: firm, oily
   Smell: rather pronounced goat smell
   Taste: very full flavor with some bouquet (3)
What to watch out for: grainy texture, excessive saltiness, leakage
Use: end of meals
Appropriate wines: all fruity, lively whites and reds of Touraine: dry Vouvray, dry Montlouis, Champigny, Chinon, Borgueil
Origin of name: nearest central market
Brief history: an anecdote says the straw that runs through the cheese is no indication of its origin; it just means that the cheese, which is difficult to unmold, was stuck back together again
Related cheeses: Tournon-Saint-Martin, Pouligny-Saint-Pierre, Chabis
   Differences: origin, shape. size, texture, flavor

SAINTE-MAURE LAITIER

Also known as: CHEVRE LONG
Province: TOURAINE
Source: Sainte-Maure plateau; additional sources: Anjou, Charentes, Poitou
Made in or by: commercial plants; use of a straw at the center, as in farm cheese, optional
Best seasons: end of spring, summer, autumn; availability of goat's milk, end of curing period
Milk: goat's milk
Type: soft
Rind: bloomy
Curing: in dry and cool cellars, 1 month
Form: elongated cylinder
Dimensions: 1½ in. in diameter, 6 in. long
Weight: 10½ oz.
Packaging: paper, with trademark
Selection:
   Appearance: very regular shape; white moderately downy rind
   Feel: firm with a little give
   Smell: rather strong mold smell
   Taste: full goat flavor (3)

What to watch out for: graininess, excessive saltiness, leakage
Uses: end of meals
Appropriate wines: all dry, fruity, lively whites or reds of Touraine and
 Anjou
Origin of name: the farm cheese which is parent of Sainte-Maure Laitier
 and principal market, Sainte-Maure
A good buy
Related cheeses: all industrial goat's milk cheeses of Anjou, Berry, Cha-
 rente, Poitou
 Differences: origin, shape, size, texture, flavor

SAINT-FLORENTIN

Province: BURGUNDY
Source: Beugnon (Yonne); additional sources: Soumaintrain and vicinity
Made in or by: farms, production dying out; commercial plants, produc-
 tion rising
Best seasons: summer, fall, beginning of winter; quality of milk, length
 of curing, end of curing period
Milk: cow's milk
Fat content: 45%
Type: soft
Rind: washed
Curing: humid, in humid cellars, with washings with salted water, 2
 months
Form: flat disk
Dimensions: 5 to 5½ in. in diameter, 1 in. thick
Weight: 1 lb. to 1 lb. 2 oz.
Packaging: unwrapped
Selection:
 Appearance: smooth, shiny rind, red-brown in color
 Feel: supple
 Smell: penetrating smell with some bouquet
 Taste: spicy, very pronounced tang (4)
What to watch out for: granular texture, lack of homogeneity
Uses: end of meals
Appropriate wines: well-knit, full-bodied Burgundies: Nuits, Beaune,
 Reuilly, etc.
Origin of name: place of origin

Related cheeses: Epoisses, Soumaintrain, La Pierre-Qui-Vire, Les
Laumes, Langres
Differences: origin, shape, size, texture, flavor

SAINT-GELAIS

Province: POITOU
Flavor: 3
(*See* SAINT-MAIXENT)

SAINT-GILDAS-DES-BOIS

Province: BRITTANY
Source: Saint-Gildas-des-Bois
Best seasons: all year; pasteurized milk used
Milk: cow's milk, enriched and pasteurized
Fat content: 75%
Type: soft, triple cream
Rind: bloomy
Curing: dry, 2 weeks
Form: tallish cylinder
Dimensions: 3 in. in diameter, 2 in. high
Weight: average 7 oz.
Packaging: box
Selection:
  Appearance: nearly immaculate, downy white rind
  Feel: tender, but not excessively so
  Smell: faint mushroom smell
  Taste: creamy flavor (2–3)
What to watch out for: red rind, leakage, grainy texture
Use: end of meals
Appropriate wines: Beaujolais
Origin of name: place of manufacture; trade name "Le Roi"
A fairly good buy
Related cheeses: all triple-cream cheeses: Bourain, Délice de Saint-Cyr,
  Excelsior, Magnum, Tarare
  Differences: origin, shape, size, texture, flavor

SAINT-LIZIER

Province: COMTE DE FOIX
Flavor: 3–5
(*See* BETHMALE)

SAINT LOUP

Province: POITOU
Flavor: 3
Source and trade name of industrially manufactured goat's-milk cheeses
of various sizes and shapes

SAINT-MAIXENT

Province: POITOU
Source: immediate vicinity of Saint-Maixent
Made in or by: farms; production dying out
Best seasons: end of spring, summer, autumn; best milk, good storage
conditions
Milk: goat's milk
Fat content: 45%
Type: soft
Rind: natural
Curing: dry, 6 weeks
Form: square
Dimensions: 4 by 4 in., 1 in. thick
Weight: 10 oz. to 12 oz.
Selection:
  Appearance: bluish gray rind lightly sprinkled with red
  Feel: firm, without hard or soft spots
  Smell: strong goat smell
  Taste: spicy flavor with a penetrating tangy bouquet (3–4)
What to watch out for: excessive redness, sticky rind, grainy texture,
excessive saltiness
Use: end of meals

Appropriate wines: all well-knit, full-bodied reds: Chinon, Bourgueil, Champigny

Origin of name: name of the principal market

Related cheeses: La Mothe-Saint-Héray, Couhé-Vérac, Chabis, Chabichous

   Differences: origin, shape, size, texture, flavor

SAINT-MARCELLIN

Also known as: TOMME DE SAINT-MARCELLIN

Province: SAINT-MARCELLIN DAUPHINÉ

Source: Isère Valley; additional sources: slopes of Vercors

Best seasons: all year; cow's milk available in all seasons (best in summer and in autumn)

Milk: cow's milk

Fat content: 50%

Type: soft

Rind: natural

Curing: in humid cellars, 2 weeks; in ventilated drying rooms, 2 weeks

Form: small disk

Dimensions: 3 in. in diameter, 1 in. thick

Weight: 3 oz.

Packaging: paper, or on a board

Selection:

   Appearance: delicate, bluish gray rind

   Feel: supple

   Smell: light lactic smell

   Taste: mild flavor, slight lactic acidity (2–3)

What to watch out for: lack of homogeneity, saltiness, grainy texture

Use: end of meals; additional uses: in Fromage Fort à la Lyonnaise

Appropriate wines: light and fruity Beaujolais; soft, fruity Côtes-du-Rhône

Origin of name: place where the largest market was held

Brief history: formerly produced on farms from pure goat's milk, this cheese is now made commercially from pure cow's milk. A few goat farms still exist here and there, but farm production is fast disappearing.

A good buy

Related cheeses: cow's-milk or half-goats's milk Tommes of Dauphiné
   or Languedoc
Differences: origin, size, texture, flavor

Louis XI and Saint-Marcellin

Is there any truth to the story that has been handed down
from father to son in Dauphiné and especially in Vercors?

It dates to 1445, a year when the future King Louis XI
was living in Dauphiné. The Dauphin Louis used to hunt to
pass the time of day; in Vercors he hunted wolves, boar,
and foxes. One day as he was pursuing a wolf near the
massifs of Vercors and Diois, deep in the forest of Lenta,
he strayed away from his companions, became lost in the
thick undergrowth of boxwood and suddenly found himself confronted by a giant bear. It was a difficult situation
to be in alone.

Thinking himself lost, as a religious man he called upon
the Virgin and made a vow. If he were to come out alive
and whole, he would institute a charitable foundation in
the village for whoever might save him.

He cried out for help. Two woodcutters heard him and
came to his aid. They routed the bear and brought the
Dauphin back to their log cabin. The future Louis XI was
famished and the woodcutters had nothing to offer him
besides some bread and some local cheese, the Saint-
Marcellin made in the valley. The Dauphin found it excellent.

After he had satisfied his hunger, his next action was to
proceed to the nearest village, Saint-Laurent-en-Royans,
and fulfill his promise to the Madonna. In 1447, the two
woodcutters, Richaud and Bouillane, received titles of nobility. Their coat of arms was azure with a bear's paw set
on a bend of or. The Dauphin, however, proved as miserly
as he was timorous. Neither of them saw a penny of the
10,000 ecus that he had promised to them.

On the other hand, to square his accounts with heaven,
he instituted the "Reinage" custom in Saint-Laurent-en-
Royans. It still exists and it never cost him one penny.

On the third Sunday after Easter, the anniversary of his
misadventure, the future King Louis XI authorized by letter
patent the parish priest and his successors ad infinitum "to
sell at auction to the highest bidders, for a term of one year,
the titles of king, queen, prince, princess, and constable of

Royans." The proceeds of the auction, not his own money, were to go to charities of the parish.

Was it because of this first experience of Saint-Marcellin, which comforted him in his adventure? Was it because of his sojourn in Dauphiné? Whatever the reason, and this is certain, the first mention of Saint-Marcellin is found in Louis XI's account books. Beyond the shadow of a doubt Saint-Marcellin had already appeared upon the royal tables of Plessis-les-Tours and the Louvre as early as 1461.

And thus it was that Louis XI, one of the most important figures in history and one of the most remarkable architects of French might, gave Saint-Marcellin its first titles of nobility.

Henri Ballouhey

SAINT-NECTAIRE

Province: AUVERGNE (MONTS DORE)
Source: high pasture of the Monts Dore; additional sources: upper Auvergne (Label of origin of farm cheese regulated by law)
Made in or by: farms and commercial dairies
Best seasons: summer, autumn; mountain milk, end of curing period
Milk: cow's milk
Fat content: 45%
Type: pressed, uncooked
Rind: natural
Curing: on a bed of rye straw, 8 weeks
Form: flat disk
Dimensions: 8 in. in diameter, 1½ in. thick
Weight: 3 lb. 5 oz.
Packaging: unwrapped, trademarked
Selection:
  Appearance: violet or grayish rind, may be pigmented with light yellow or bright red molds
  Feel: supple, no softness
  Smell: mold smell predominant
  Taste: mild tang, with pronounced bouquet (2–3)
What to watch out for: sticky or dried-out rind, excessive firmness and toughness, bitterness
Use: end of meals; additional uses: for cheese toasts

Appropriate wines: Côteaux-d'Auvergne, Côtes-Roannaises; all light, fruity wines
Origin of name: largest town in the producing region
Brief history: very ancient cheese
A fairly good buy
Related cheeses: Savaron, Vachard and all semi-soft cheeses
  Differences: origin, shape, size, flavor, texture

SAINT-PAULIN

Country: FRANCE
Source: Maine, Anjou, Brittany; additional sources: all France
Made in or by: small, middle-size and large commercial plants
Best seasons: all year; pasteurized milk used
Milk: cow's milk, pasteurized
Fat content: 45% to 50%
Type: pressed, uncooked
Rind: washed
Curing: humid, in a humid and cool place, 2 months
Form: thick disk
Dimensions: 8 to 9 in. in diameter, 2 in. thick
Weight: about 4 lb. 7 oz.
Packaging: unwrapped, labeled
Selection:
  Appearance: smooth rind and interior
  Feel: tender and velvety smooth
  Smell: light smell of lactic fermentation
  Taste: mild flavor (2–3)
What to watch out for: heat spoilage of rind (spots of fermentation), desiccation, granular texture
Use: all table uses; additional uses: in cheese pastries; sandwiches
Appropriate wines: all popular light and fruity wines
Origin of name: administrative decision
Brief history: derived from monastery sources
A good buy
Related cheeses: all other commercial or monastery Saint-Paulins
  Differences: origin, quality of milk, flavor, texture

SAINT-REMY

Province: LORRAINE
Source: Meuse Department; additional sources: neighboring pasture-
    lands
Made in or by: local factories
Best seasons: end of spring, summer, autumn; availability of high quality
    milk, end of curing period
Milk: cow's milk
Fat content: 40% to 45%
Type: soft
Rind: washed
Curing: humid, in humid cellars, with washings, 6 weeks
Form: square
Dimensions: 4 by 4 in., 1 in. thick
Weight: 7 oz. to 9 oz.
Packaging: unwrapped
Selection
    Appearance: smooth, light red-brown rind
    Feel: supple
    Smell: penetrating smell
    Taste: rather spicy flavor (3–4)
What to watch out for: firmness, graininess, lack of suppleness
Use: end of meals
Appropriate wines: all full-bodied and sappy red wines, Moulin-à-Vent,
    Côtes-du-Rhône, Saint-Emilion
Origin of name: trade name of local factory
A good buy
Related cheeses: Munster, Gérômé, Langres
    Differences: origin, shape, size, texture, flavor

SAINT-SAVIOL

Province: POITOU
Flavor: 3
Source and trade name of commercially produced goat's-milk cheeses in
    various sizes and shapes

SAINT-VARENT

Province: POITOU
Flavor: 3
Source and trade name of commercially produced goat's-milk cheeses in
    various sizes and shapes

SALERS or FOURME DE SALERS

Also known as: CANTAL-SALERS
Province: AUVERGNE (Label of origin regulated by law)
Milk: cow's milk
Fat content: 45%
Type: pressed, uncooked
Rind: natural, brushed
Flavor: 3–4

SANCERRE

Province: BERRY
Milk: goat's milk
Fat content: 45%
Type: soft
Rind: natural
Flavor: 3
Sancerre is the generic name of three varieties: CHAVIGNOL, CRE-
    ZANCY, SANTRANGES (*see* these listings)

SANTRANGES-SANCERRE

Province: BERRY
Source: Santranges; additional sources: neighboring villages
Made in or by: farms
Best seasons: end of spring, summer, autumn; availability of goat's milk,
    end of curing period
Milk: goat's milk

Fat content: 45%
Type: soft
Rind: natural
Curing: dry, 4 weeks
Form: flattened ball
Dimensions: 2½ in. in diameter, 1½ in. thick
Weight: 5 oz. to 6 oz.
Packaging: unwrapped
Selection:
   Appearance: delicate bluish skin; delicate white interior
   Feel: firm and homogeneous texture
   Smell: light goat smell
   Taste: pronounced tang (3)
What to watch out for: superficial and internal desiccation, rancidity,
   granulation, excessive saltiness
Use: end of meals
Appropriate wines: all the white wines of Sauvignon; clean-tasting, fruity
   local Pinot Blanc and Pinot Gris
Origin of name: place of origin
Related cheeses: Chavignol, Crézancy, other goat's-milk cheeses
   Differences: origin, size, texture

SARRASSON or SARRASSOU

Province: LANGUEDOC
Milk: buttermilk, naturally or centrifugally skimmed
Flavor: 2–3
Recipe: Sarrassou may be made from whey, but the best is obtained by
   pouring hot water on the buttermilk left in the churn after butter
   has been made.

     Mixed with milk it yields a tangy "cream" which serves as a
   healthy accompaniment to the delicious potatoes of the mountains.
Reference: Forot: *Odeur et fumet de table*

SARTENO

Province: CORSICA
Source: Sartène; additional sources: high plateaus of southwestern Corsica
Made in or by: farms
Best seasons: end of spring, summer, autumn; availability of goat's milk or sheep's milk, end of curing period
Milk: goat's or sheep's milk or both mixed
Type: pressed, uncooked
Rind: natural film
Curing: dry, 3 months
Form: roughly flattened ball
Dimensions: 5 in. in diameter, 4 in. thick
Weight: 2 lb. 3 oz. to 4 lb. 5 oz.
Packaging: unwrapped, covered with natural casein film
Selection:
  Appearance: delicate, smooth, glossy light-yellow rind
  Feel: firm with a touch of suppleness
  Smell: light rancid smell
  Taste: sharp (5–6)
What to watch out for: pebbly texture, overaging (both considered good qualities by local people who seek a strong, brittle cheese)
Use: snacks and end of meals; additional uses: grated as a condiment in local dishes
Appropriate wines: stout, full-bodied, well-knit wines: Cahors, Madiran, Châteauneuf-du-Pape and Corbières du Roussillon
Origin of name: nearest and largest market
Brief history: probably dates to Roman antiquity
Related cheeses: distantly related to Italian Caciocavallo and Provolone
  Differences: the Italian cheeses are shaped like gourds and are made of cow's or buffalo's milk and dried or smoked

SASSENAGE

Also known as: BLEU DE SASSENAGE
Province: DAUPHINE (VERCORS)
Source: Villars-de-Lans (Isère); additional sources: Vallonnais (Vercors)
Made in or by: traditional dairies; not much developed

Best seasons: end of spring, summer, autumn; high quality milk from herds in summer pasture
Milk: cow's milk with some goat's milk added
Fat content: 45%
Type: soft, lightly pressed, internal molds
Rind: natural
Curing: dry, with damp brushings, 2 to 3 months
Form: big loaf with convex sides
Dimensions: 12 in. in diameter, 3 to 4 in. thick
Weight: 11 lb. to 13 lb.
Packaging: unwrapped
Selection:
  Appearance: smooth, perfect rind
  Feel: supple
  Smell: faint mold smell
  Taste: spicy flavor, slightly bitter (4)
What to watch out for: grainy texture, sharpness
Use: end of meals
Appropriate wines: sappy and full-bodied Côtes-du-Rhône-Villages
Origin of name: chief township of Canton of Sassenage (Isère)
A fairly good buy locally
Related cheeses: Bleu de Gex, Bleu de Septmoncel and all other cow's-milk Bleus
  Differences: origin, fineness of grain, tang, flavor

SAUZE-VAUSSAIS

Province: POITOU
Flavor: 3
Source and trade name of commercially manufactured goat's-milk cheeses of various sizes and shapes

SAVARON

Province: AUVERGNE
Source: Auvergne
Made in or by: small, middle-sized and large commercial dairies

Best seasons: all year; pasteurized milk used
Milk: cow's milk, pasteurized
Fat content: 45%
Type: pressed, uncooked
Rind: washed in the beginning, mildewed in humid cellars, 3 months
Form: thick disk
Dimensions: 8 in. in diameter, 1½ to 2½ in. thick
Weight: 3 lb. 5 oz. to 3 lb. 12 oz.
Packaging: unwrapped, labeled
Selection:
  Appearance: gray rind pigmented with mildew
  Feel: supple
  Smell: strong mold smell
  Taste: moderately pronounced flavor (3)
What to watch out for: insufficient curing in the special cellars (inside looks like a Saint-Paulin and is bland in taste)
Use: end of meals; additional uses: in cheese toasts
Appropriate wines: light and fruity reds or rosés of Côtes d'Auvergne or Saint-Pourcain
Brief history: developed because of a shortage of the original Saint-Nectaire
Related cheeses: Saint-Nectaire, Saint-Paulin
  Differences: origin, size, fineness of texture, flavor

SBRINZ

Also known as: FROMAGE A RAPER (grating cheese)
Country: SWITZERLAND
Cantons: SCHWYZ, UNTERWALD, URI
Source: Schwyz, Unterwald and Uri cantons; additional sources: other cantons of central Switzerland
Made in or by: small dairies
Best seasons: all year; large stocks provide a continuous supply
Milk: cow's milk
Fat content: 45%
Type: pressed, cooked
Rind: washed, brushed, oiled
Curing: in dry cellars, 2 or 3 years
Form: large flattened cylindrical wheel

Dimensions: 2 ft. in diameter, 5½ in. thick
Weight: 80 lb. to 132 lb.
Packaging: unwrapped, oiled; engraved trademark
Selection:
  Appearance: dark yellow rind; dense yellow interior
  Feel: hard and brittle
  Smell: light rancid smell
  Taste: very pronounced flavor tending toward saponification (3–4)
What to watch out for: crumbly, grainy texture; excessive saponification
Use: grated as seasoning in certain dishes; additional uses: occasionally
    end of meals
Appropriate wines: all well-knit, full-bodied wines: Dôle from Valais,
    Merlot du Tessin
Brief history: undoubtedly manufactured to do away with the need to
    import Grana
A good buy locally
Related cheeses: Italian Grana, Parmesan, Reggian
  Differences: origin, fineness of texture, richness in fat, flavor

SCAMORZE

Country: ITALY
Region: CAMPANIA
Source: Campania (St. Gregorio, Onna); additional sources: Abruzzi e
    Molise (Campobasso, Frosolone, etc.)
Made in or by: small local industry, now spreading throughout Italy
Best seasons: all year; cow's milk is available all year
Milk: cow's milk or buffalo's milk
Fat content: 44%
Type: pressed, roped
Rind: natural, spontaneous
Curing: in dry cellars, 4 to 6 weeks
Form: gourd-shaped; narrow neck tied with a cord, four little loops on
    top
Dimensions: 3 in. in diameter, 4 in. high
Weight: about 7 oz.
Packaging: unwrapped, tied together in clusters

Selection:
  Appearance: glossy golden-yellow skin
  Feel: firm but malleable
  Smell: slightly rancid smell
  Taste: delicate, nutty flavor (3)
What to watch out for: excessive dryness, sharpness
Use: end of meals, snacks; additional uses: in pizza
Appropriate wines: all light and fruity wines

> *Note:* There are farms where Scamorze cheeses are still made from goat's milk by the traditional methods. The manufacturing period extends from late spring to late autumn and the flavor differs with the season. These cheeses are best eaten fresh.

Related cheeses: Provolette, Provola, Provolone

SCHABZIEGER

Country: SWITZERLAND
Canton: GLARIS
Source: Canton of Glaris
Made in or by: commercial plants
Best seasons: all year; product is stabilized by dehydration
Milk: by-product of cow's milk (reheated whey)
Fat content: 1% maximum
Type: cooked, pressed, flavored with powdered fenugreek
Rind: incorporated into the product
Curing: unnecessary; the product is dried
Form: small, tallish truncated cone
Dimensions: 2 in. in diameter at base, 1½ in. in diameter at apex, 3 in. high
Weight: 3½ oz. (there are also 1¾ oz. and 7 oz. sizes)
Packaging: foil, Geska brand name
Selection; none possible because of wrapping
  Appearance: olive-greenish color
  Feel: hard and dry
  Smell: strong aromatic smell
  Taste: sharp flavor (5–6)
Uses: grated, as a condiment for various dishes
Appropriate wines: all potent, full-bodied red wines

Brief history: no doubt introduced from the Orient when the barbarian invasions reached the Urals, introduced into Switzerland for the purpose of commercial exchange with Russia

A good buy

Related cheeses: none

SCOURMONT

Country: BELGIUM
Type: Monastery cheese comparable to Saint-Paulin

SELLES-SUR-CHER

Province: ORLEANAIS, BERRY
Region: SOLOGNE
Source: southern Sologne; additional sources: Berry
Best seasons: end of spring, summer, autumn; availability of goat's milk
Milk: goat's milk
Fat content: 45%
Type: soft
Rind: natural, tinted blue with powdered charcoal
Curing: dry, 3 weeks
Form: very flat truncated cone
Dimensions: 3 in. in diameter at base, 1 in. thick
Weight: 4½ oz. to 5 oz.
Packaging: unwrapped
Selection:
  Appearance: neat shape; dark blue skin; pure white interior
  Feel: firm and fine-textured
  Smell: light goat smell
  Taste: mild, nutty flavor (2–3)
What to watch out for: leakage, grainy texture, excessive saltiness
Uses: end of meals, snacks
Appropriate wines: all dry whites and rosés of Blésois; light and fruity reds of Touraine: Chinon, Bourgeuil
Origin of name: invented name, taken from name of nearest commercial center; cheese is also known as Romorantin

Related cheeses: Chablis, Levroux, Valençay, Pouligny
   Differences: origin, shape, size, texture, flavor

SORBAIS

Provinces: FLANDERS, HAINAUT
Source: Avesnois, Thiérache; additional sources: Champagne, Laonnais
Made in or by: semi-commercialized makers
Best seasons: end of spring, summer, autumn; milk from pastured cows
Milk: cow's milk
Fat content: 45% to 50%
Type: soft
Rind: washed
Curing: humid, in humid cellars, 3 months
Form: block or slab
Dimensions: 4¾ in. to side, 1¾ in. thick
Weight: 1 lb. 5 oz.
Packaging: unwrapped, or box
Selection:
   Appearance: smooth, shiny, brownish-red rind
   Feel: supple
   Smell: strong bouquet, strong smell
   Taste: pronounced tang (4–5)
What to look out for: superficial desiccation; chalkiness, ammonia odor
Use: end of meals, snacks; additional uses: in *goyère,* a local cheese tart
Appropriate wines: all full-bodied, sappy wines (*see* MAROILLES)
Origin of name: administrative decision to attribute cheese to a small
    village in Aisne
A fairly good buy
Related cheeses: Maroilles, Mignon, Quart, Baguette
   Differences: origin, form, composition, quality, taste

SOUMAINTRAIN

Province: BOURGOGNE
Source: Soumaintrain (Yonne)
Made in or by: farms; production dying off

Best seasons: end of spring, summer, autumn; best milks, end of curing
   period
Milk: cow's milk
Fat content: 45%
Type: soft
Rind: washed
Curing: humid, in humid cellars, washings in salt water, 6 weeks
Form: flat disk
Dimensions: 5 in. in diameter, 1 in. thick
Weight: about 12 oz.
Packaging: unwrapped
Selection:
   Appearance: smooth and shiny red-brown rind
   Feel: supple
   Smell: penetrating smell
   Taste: spicy tang (4–5)
   It may also be eaten white and creamy
What to watch out for: graininess
Use: end of meals
Appropriate wines: all well-balanced, full-bodied Burgundies: Nuits,
   Beaune, etc.
Origin of name: place of origin
Related cheeses: Epoisses, Les Laumes, Saint-Florentin, La Pierre-Qui-
   Vire, Langres
   Differences: origin, shape, size, texture, flavor

SPALEN KASE

Also known as: SAANEN (*see* this listing) (In the patois it is also called
   FROMAGE À REBIBES)
Country: SWITZERLAND
Canton: FRIBOURG

STEENWOORDE

Province: FLANDERS
Origin of name: trade name of a commercial dairy in Steenwoorde (Nord) producing Dutch-style cheeses as well as Saint-Paulins and fresh cheeses

STILTON

Country: GREAT BRITAIN
County: LEICESTERSHIRE
Source: originally Stilton, Leicestershire; additional sources: neighboring counties
Made in or by: farms, primarily; little commercialization
Best seasons: autumn, winter, spring; best quality milk, end of curing period
Milk: cow's milk, enriched
Fat content: 55%
Type: soft, with internal molds
Rind: natural, brushed
Curing: in cool and humid cellars, 6 months
Form: tall cylinder
Dimensions: 6 in. in diameter, 10 in. high
Weight: 8 lb. 13 oz. to 9 lb. 15 oz.
Packaging: unwrapped
Selection:
  Appearance: fairly even, unblemished gray rind; fairly dense internal veining
  Feel: firm, with a touch of suppleness
  Smell: fairly strong mold smell
  Taste: very pronounced flavor, strong spicy bouquet (4)
What to watch out for: graininess, excessive sharpness, bitterness
Uses: end of meals; additional uses: soaked in Sherry, Madeira or Port, used for canapés and toasts
Appropriate wines: well-balanced full-bodied wines; when soaked, Sherry, Madeira or Port
Origin of name: town of Stilton, where the main market was originally held

Related cheeses: French mountain Bleus, blue Fourmes
   Differences: origin, shape, size, fineness of texture, flavor

STRACCHINO

Country: ITALY
Region: LOMBARDY
Source: plains of Lombardy, principally the Provinces of Milan, Bergamo, Brescia, Como, Pavia
Best seasons: autumn, winter; production in summer or autumn, end of curing period
Milk: cow's milk
Fat content: 48%
Type: pressed, uncooked
Rind: washed
Curing: in humid cellars, with washings, 7 to 8 weeks
Form: square slab
Dimensions: 6 to 8 in. square, 2 in. thick
Weight: 2 lb. 3 oz. to 4 lb. 7 oz.
Packaging: paper, with trademark
Selection:
   Appearance: smooth pinkish surface and rind; light-yellow interior
   Feel: tender and supple
   Smell: rather full, characteristic smell
   Taste: somewhat emphatic fruity flavor (3)
What to watch out for: lack of suppleness, mishaps in fermentation, sharpness
Use: end of meals
Appropriate wines: popular light and fruity table wines: Italian Piedmont wines (Barbera)
Origin of name: stracco, meaning soft
Brief history: monastery cheese with a very ancient reputation; its origins go back to the 9th century
Related cheeses: Taleggio, Quartirolo, other brands of pressed, uncooked cheese (Bel Paese)
   Differences: origin, shape, size, texture, flavor

SUISSE

Also known as: GROS SUISSE
Country: FRANCE
Source: all France
Best seasons: all year; pasteurized milk used
Milk: cow's milk, enriched and pasteurized
Fat content: 60% to 75%
Type: fresh, unsalted
Rind: none
Curing: none
Form: log
Dimensions: 1½ in. in diameter, 2 in. long
Weight: 2 oz.
Packaging: sheathed in plastic
Selection: freshness only criterion; always eaten fresh
  Flavor: 1
What to watch out for: lack of freshness
Use: end of meals; additional uses: served mixed with fresh or stewed
    fruit; used in canapés and in certain recipes
Appropriate wines: no need for wine
Origin of name: nationality of one of the workmen in Mme. Héroult's
    cheese factory who brought the cheese to the markets in Paris and
    who introduced certain changes in its manufacture around 1850
A good buy
Related cheeses: all fresh, whipped, double- and triple-cream cheeses
    (with a fat content of 60% to 75%)

SUPREME

Province: NORMANDY (PAYS DE BRAY)
Flavor: 2–3
Origin of name: invented name given to a double-cream cheese made in
    Canton of Neufchâtel-en-Bray
(*See* FIN-DE-SIECLE)

TALEGGIO

Country: ITALY
Region: LOMBARDY
Source: high valleys of Bergamo; additional sources: fore-Alps of the
    Lombard plain
Best seasons: summer, autumn; best quality milk (commercial Taleggios
    made from pasteurized milk are good all year)
Milk: cow's milk
Fat content: 48%
Type: pressed, uncooked
Rind: washed
Curing: in humid cellars, with washings, 7 weeks
Form: thick slab
Dimensions: 8 in. square, 2 in. thick
Weight: 2 lb. 3 oz.
Selection:
    Appearance: smooth pinkish surface; light straw-yellow interior
    Feel: tender and supple
    Smell: rather full characteristic smell
    Taste: somewhat emphatic, fruity (3)
What to watch out for: lack of suppleness, mishaps in fermentation
Uses: end of meals
Appropriate wines: all light and fruity table wines
Origin of name: place of origin
Brief history: linked with that of all Stracchino cheeses
A fairly good buy locally
Related cheeses: all Stracchino and Bel Paese cheeses
    Differences: origin, shape, size, flavor, texture

TAMIE

Also known as: TRAPPISTE DE TAMIE
Province: SAVOIE
Source: Monastery of Tamié
Made in or by: monks, using traditional methods
Best seasons: summer, autumn; milk from the pastures
Milk: cow's milk
Fat content: 40% to 45%

Type: pressed, uncooked
Rind: washed
Curing: in humid cellars, with washings, 2 months
Form: thick disk
Dimensions: 7 in. in diameter, 2 in. thick
Weight: 1 lb. 10 oz.
Packaging: unwrapped, or paper
Selection:
  Appearance: smooth, light-colored rind
  Feel: tender and elastic
  Smell: no special smell
  Taste: rather pronounced lactic flavor (2–3)
What to watch out for: excessive desiccation of rind, lack of suppleness
    and homogeneity
Use: end of meals; additional uses: cheese toppings
Appropriate wines: all light and fruity reds, whites and rosés of Savoy,
    Gamay de Chautagne, Beaujolais
Origin of name: Monastery of Tamié
Brief history: connected with the founding of the Trappist monastery at
    Tamié
A fairly good buy
Related cheeses: Reblochons, Trappiste de Chambarand, other Trappist
    cheeses, Saint-Paulin
  Differences: origin, size, texture, flavor

TARARE

Province: LYONNAIS
Milk: cow's milk
Fat content: 75%
Type: soft, triple cream
Rind: bloomy
Flavor: 1–2

TARDETS

Province: PAYS BASQUE
Flavor: 3–4
(*See* ESBAREICH)

TETE-DE-MOINE

Country: SWITZERLAND
Canton: BERN
Source: Bellelay; additional sources: Jura Mountains of the Bern Canton
Made in or by: small traditional dairies
Best seasons: autumn, winter; made in the mountains, length of curing
    period
Milk: cow's milk
Fat content: 45% to 50%
Type: pressed, uncooked
Rind: washed
Curing: dry, in humid cellars, damp brushings, 3 months
Form: small cylinder of equal height and diameter
Dimensions: 4 to 5 in. in diameter, 4 to 5 in. high
Weight: 1 lb. 5 oz. to 3 lb. 5 oz.
Packaging: unwrapped
Selection:
  Appearance: delicate, slightly sticky, yellowish rind
  Feel: firm but somewhat supple
  Smell: bouquet
  Taste: spicy, very fruity flavor (4)
What to watch out for: insufficient smoothness, coarse grain
Use: end of meals (thin slivers are shaved from the surface and the whole
    cheese assumes the shape of a dome); additional uses: canapés,
    snacks
Appropriate wines: all lively fruity reds: red wines of Neufchâtel: Saint
    Blaise
Origin of name: from the old custom at the Monastery of Bellelay of
    giving the prior one cheese for each monk ("per head")
Related cheeses: Valais cheeses, Tilsit, Jura Gruyère
  Differences: origin, shape, size, texture, flavor

THIONVILLE

Province: LORRAINE
Flavor: 4
Process cheese derived from Mattons
(See CANCOILLOTTE)

TIGNARD

Also known as: BLEU DE TIGNES (*see* this listing)
Province: SAVOIE
Flavor: 3–4

TILSIT

Country: SWITZERLAND
Cantons: SAINT GALL, THURGAU
Source: Cantons of Saint Gall and Thurgau; additional sources: neighboring cantons
Made in or by: small factories
Best seasons: all year; made in the lowlands
Milk: cow's milk
Fat content: 45%
Type: pressed, uncooked
Rind: brushed
Curing: humid, in humid cellars, 4 months
Form: small wheel with slightly convex rim
Dimensions: 14½ in. in diameter, 3 in. thick
Weight: 8 lb. 13 oz. to 11 lb.
Packaging: unwrapped
Selection:
  Appearance: regular brownish ocher rind without rough spots
  Feel: supple without being soft
  Smell: strong cellar smell
  Taste: very fruity flavor (4)

What to watch out for: sandy texture, insufficient aging

Use: end of meals, snacks; additional uses: canapés, sandwiches, as a condiment when aged

Appropriate wines: all light, fruity red wines with character

Origin of name: name of a Dutch-style cheese formerly imported from East Prussia

Brief history: believed to have been introduced into Switzerland in the 18th century

A good buy locally

Related cheeses: Valais cheeses, Toupin

  Differences: origin, shape, size, texture, flavor

TOMME DES ALLUES

Province: SAVOIE (HAUTE TARENTAISE)

Source: Miribel; additional sources: neighboring pasturelands

Made in or by: mountain chalets

Best seasons: autumn; availability of goat's milk, summer pasturing in the mountains, end of curing period

Milk: goat's milk

Fat content: 45%

Type: pressed, uncooked

Rind: washed

Curing: humid, in cool cellars, about 2 months

Form: flattened disk

Dimensions: 8 to 10 in. in diameter, 2½ to 3 in. thick

Weight: 6 lb. 10 oz. to 8 lb. 13 oz.

Packaging: unwrapped

Selection:

  Appearance: smooth and delicate gray to light-yellow rind

  Feel: supple and velvety smooth

  Smell: light goat smell; penetrating aroma

  Taste: mild flavor with mild bouquet

What to watch out for: grainy texture, dryness, sharpness (resulting from overaging and enjoyed by local consumers)

Use: end of meals, snacks

Appropriate wines: all fruity and lively wines

Origin of name: producing region
Related cheeses: mountain goat's-milk cheeses of Courchevel, Pralognan, Beaufort, Arêches

TOMME ARLESIENNE

Also known as: TOMME DE CAMARGUE (*see* this listing)
Province: PROVENCE
Milk: sheep's milk
Fat content: 45%
Flavor: 2

TOMME DE BAUGES

One of the countless varieties of gray Tommes from the mountains of Savoy
(*See* TOMME DE SAVOIE)

TOMME DE BELLEVILLE

Province: SAVOIE (TARENTAISE)
Source: Saint-Martin-de-Belleville; additional sources: Saint-Jean-de-Belleville, valley of Doron de Belleville
Made in or by: chalets
Best seasons: summer, autumn; availability of milk from summer mountain pastures
Milk: cow's milk, partly skimmed
Fat content: 30% to 40%
Type: pressed, uncooked
Rind: natural brushed
Curing: humid, in humid and cool cellars, with washings and brushings, about 2 months
Form: disk
Dimensions: 7 to 9 in. in diameter, 1½ to 2½ in. thick
Weight: 3 lb. 5 oz. to 6 lb. 10 oz.

Packaging: unwrapped
A good buy
Related cheeses: all Tommes de Savoie

TOMME DE BELLEY

Department: AIN (PAYS DE BUGEY)
Source: Belley region (Ain); additional sources: mountainous section of Bugey
Made in or by: farms; production dying out
Best seasons: summer, autumn; availability of goat's milk, end of curing period
Milk: goat's milk or mixed cow's and goat's milk
Fat content: 40% to 45%
Type: soft
Rind: natural
Curing: dry, in ventilated cellars, 4 weeks
Form: small flat disk or brick with a square or rectangular base and a rectangular cross-section
Dimensions: 3 to 4 in. in diameter, 1 in. thick; 3½ by 3½ in., 1 in. thick
Weight: 5 oz. to 7 oz.
Packaging: unwrapped
Selection:
  Appearance: delicate bluish rind with reddish spots
  Feel: smooth and homogeneous
  Smell: light goat smell
  Taste: nutty flavor, full bouquet (3)
What to watch out for: thick rind, crumbling, smoky flavor
Use: end of meals, snacks
Appropriate wines: all light, delicate and fruity reds, whites and rosés of the Jura, Savoy and Beaujolais
Origin of the name: nearest town, which served as a market for the cheese
A fairly good buy locally
Related cheeses: small country goat's-milk Tommes d'Auvergne, Brique de Forez, Chèvrets from the Jura
  Differences: origin, shape, size, texture, flavor

TOMME BOUDANE

Province: SAVOIE
Milk: cow's milk
Fat content: 20% to 30%
Type: pressed, uncooked
Rind: natural
Flavor: 3
In other respects similar to other TOMMES DE SAVOIE (*see* this
　listing)
The name BOUDANE is given to household Tommes in some parts of
　Savoie
A good buy

TOMME DE BRACH

Also known as: CAILLADA DE VOUILLOS
Region: CORREZE
Source: Canton of Tulle
Made in or by: farms; little or no commercial production
Best seasons: spring, summer; lactation period of sheep, end of curing
　period
Milk: sheep's milk
Fat content: 45%
Type: soft
Rind: natural
Curing: dry, 2 to 4 months
Form: tall cylinder
Dimensions: 4 in. in diameter, 3 in. high
Weight: 1 lb. 5 oz. to 1 lb. 12 oz.
Packaging: unwrapped
Selection:
　Appearance: clean, unblemished rind; no veining inside
　Feel: firm and oily
　Smell: distinct smell of the sheepfold
　Taste: pronounced flavor (4)
What to watch out for: sticky rind, cracking, grainy texture
Use: dessert, snacks
Appropriate wines: all well-balanced, lively red wines

Origin of the name: dialect term
Related cheeses: fresh drained Roquefort cheeses, salted and dried Broccio
  Differences: origin, texture, flavor, shape, size

TOMME DE CAMARGUE

Also known as: TOMME ARLESIENNE
Province: PROVENCE
Source: Arles; additional source: Camargue
Made in or by: small dairy, "Lou Gardian" brand
Best seasons: winter, spring; availability of sheep's milk
Milk: sheep's milk
Fat content: 45%
Type: fresh, drained, flavored with ground thyme and bayleaf
Rind: none
Curing: drainage, 1 week
Form: small square
Dimensions: 2½ by 2½ in., ½ in. thick
Packaging: unwrapped, band covering the bayleaf
Selection:
  Appearance: thin film of ivory-colored skin
  Feel: soft
  Smell: aroma of herbs
  Taste: mild and creamy taste, herb flavor (2)
What to watch out for: overaging (changes the taste but increases the aromatic character and is preferred by certain users)
Use: end of meals
Appropriate wines: "Listels" of Camargue, Clairette of Bellegarde
Origin of name: place of origin

TOMME DE COMBOVIN

Province: DAUPHINE (VALENTINOIS)
Source: Combovin (Drôme)
Made in or by: farms

Best seasons: end of spring, summer, autumn; availability of goat's milk, end of curing period
Milk: goat's milk
Fat content: 45%
Type: soft
Rind: natural
Curing: dry, in ventilated cellars, 4 weeks
Form: round disk
Dimensions: 4 in. in diameter, 1 in. thick
Weight: 8 oz. or 9 oz.
Packaging: unwrapped
Selection:
  Appearance: delicate bluish rind with some red pigmentation; smooth, fine-grained interior
  Feel: firm without being tough
  Smell: light goat smell
  Taste: nutty flavor with some bouquet (3)
What to watch out for: grainy texture, sharpness (preferred by local users)
Use: end of meals, snacks; additional uses: in crocked *fromage fort*
Appropriate wines: all fruity and lively wines of southern Côtes-du-Rhône
Origin of name: place of origin
Related cheeses: goat's-milk Tommes from Romans, Picodons, Pélardons
  Differences: origin, size, texture, flavor

TOMME DE CORPS

Province: DAUPHINE
Source: La Salette; additional sources: valleys draining into the Drac
Made in or by: farms; rare
Best seasons: end of spring, summer, autumn; availability of goat's milk
Milk: goat's milk
Fat content: 45%
Type: soft, slightly pressed
Rind: natural
Curing: in cold and dry cellars, 3 to 4 weeks
Form: cylinder

Dimensions: 4 in. in diameter, 2½ to 3 in. high
Weight: 14 oz. to 1 lb. 2 oz.
Packaging: unwrapped
Selection:
  Appearance: smooth and delicate rind, bluish to pinkish gray in color
  Feel: firm, hard
  Smell: rather strong goat smell
  Taste: nutty, not very spicy flavor (3)
What to watch out for: crumbling, saponification
Use: snacks, end of meals
Appropriate wines: all light and fruity reds, whites and rosés: Côtes-du-
  Rhône-Villages
Origin of name: town where it is marketed
Related cheeses: Grataron d'Arêches, goat's-milk Tommes of Maurienne
  (Chevrine de Lenta)
  Differences: origin, shape, size, texture, flavor

TOMME DE COURCHEVEL

Province: SAVOIE
Region: HAUTE TARENTAISE
Source: Praslin pasturelands
Made in or by: mountain chalets, for shepherds; little sold
Best seasons: summer, autumn; availability of goat's milk, end of curing
  period
Milk: goat's milk
Fat content: 45%
Type: pressed, uncooked
Rind: washed
Curing: humid, in cool cellars, about 2 months
Form: flattened disk
Dimensions: 8 to 10 in. in diameter, 2 in. thick
Weight: 3 lb. 5 oz. to 4 lb. 7 oz.
Packaging: unwrapped
Selection:
  Appearance: smooth and sound, pinkish ochre to gray-beige rind
  Feel: supple and velvety smooth
  Smell: light goat smell
  Taste: mild flavor with bouquet and tang (2–3)

What to watch out for: grainy texture, brittleness, sharpness (preferred
by local users)
Use: mountaineer's snack, end of meals
Appropriate wines: all fruity and lively wines of Savoy and elsewhere
Origin of name: summer pasturing region
A fairly good buy locally
Related cheeses: Tomme des Allues, Tomme de Pralognan, Tomme de
Beaufort, Tomme d'Arêche
Differences: origin, shape, size, texture, flavor

TOMME DE CREST

Province: DAUPHINE
Section; VALENTINOIS
Source: Chabeuil (Drôme); additional sources: all of Valentinois
Made in or by: farms
Best seasons: end of spring, summer, autumn; availability of goat's milk,
end of curing period
Milk: goat's milk
Fat content: 45%
Type: soft
Rind: natural
Curing: dry, in ventilated cellars, 2 weeks
Form: small round
Dimensions: 2½ in. in diameter, 1 in. thick
Weight: 3½ oz.
Packaging: unwrapped
Selection:
Appearance: delicate, bluish rind
Feel: firm with some degree of suppleness
Smell: light goat smell
Taste: nutty flavor with some bouquet (3)
What to watch for: graininess
Use: end of meals, snacks; other uses: grated in crocked *fromage fort*
Appropriate wines: light and fruity wines of Côtes-du-Rhône and Beaujo-
lais
Origin of name: largest town in producing region where the market was
held
Not a good buy

Related cheeses: goat's milk Tommes from Dauphiné, Picodons, Pélardons from the Cévennes and from Languedoc

Differences: origin, size, texture, flavor

TOMME AU FENOUIL

Province: SAVOIE
Milk: cow's milk
Fat content: 20% to 40%
Type: pressed, uncooked, flavored with fennel
Rind: natural
Flavor: 3
In other respects similar to TOMMES DE SAVOIE (see this listing)

TOMME AU MARC

Province: SAVOIE
Source: Beauges, Tarentaise, Beaufortin; additional sources: various mountain valleys
Best seasons: winter; Tommes that keep best are those of late summer
Milk: cow's milk, partly skimmed
Fat content: 20% to 40%
Type: pressed, uncooked
Rind: natural, brushed, then coated with fermented marc
Curing: 2 months in humid cellars with brushings and washings; aging with maceration in vats of fermented grape marc, 3 to 4 months in cool cellars; 1 month in warm cellars
Form: rather thick disk
Dimensions: 8 in. in diameter, 2½ in. thick
Weight: 3 lb. 5 oz. to 4 lb.
Packaging: unwrapped, coated with marc
Selection:
  Appearance: very sound cheeses, despite intense surface fermentation
  Feel: rather firm, not hard
  Smell: strong smell of alcoholic fermentation
  Taste: very full sharp flavor (5–7)

What to watch out for: putrefaction, internal deliquescence, blackish
color, excessive flavor (sometimes preferred)
Use: end of meals, snacks
Appropriate wines: Mondeuse, red wines of the Jura: Pupillin, Buvilly,
Les Arsures
Origin of name: character of cheese and material in which it ferments
Brief history: a cheese which is usually prepared near wine-producing
region for the domestic needs of the farms of chalets
Not a good buy. Very seldom on the market
Related cheeses: Chèvres Lyonnais au Gènes de Marc
Differences: type of milk, origin, shape, size, flavor

TOMME DE PAYERNE

Also known as: TOMME VAUDOISE (*see* this listing)
Country: SWITZERLAND
Canton: VAUD
Milk: cow's milk
Fat content: 50%
Flavor: 2

TOMME DU PELVOUX

Province: DAUPHINE
Milk: cow's milk or mixed cow's and goat's milk
Fat content: 40%to 45%
Flavor: 3
In other respects similar to the countless other Tommes produced in the
Alps

TOMME DU REVARD

Province: SAVOIE
Source: Mont Revard

Best seasons: end of spring, summer, autumn; availability of milk, end
    of curing period
Milk: cow's milk
Fat content: 30% to 40%
Type: pressed, uncooked
Rind: natural
Curing: dry, 1 month in cool and humid cellars; 1 month in warm cellars
Form: more or less flatttened cylinder
Dimensions: 8 in. in diameter, 2½ to 3 in. thick
Weight: 3 lb. 5 oz. to 4 lb. 6 oz.
Packaging: unwrapped
Flavor: 3
In other respects similar to **TOMME DE SAVOIE**

TOMME DE ROMANS

Province: **DAUPHINE**
Source: Romans-sur-Isère (Drôme); former best source: Saint-Romans
    (Isère)
Made in or by: commercial plants
Best seasons: summer, autumn; cow's milk superior in summer and
    autumn
Milk: cow's milk
Fat content: 50%
Type: soft
Rind: natural
Curing: in dry ventilated cellars, 3 weeks
Form: flat disk
Dimensions: 4½ in. in diameter, 1 in. thick
Weight: about 9 oz.
Packaging: not wrapped, on straw
Selection:
    Appearance: delicate, bluish-gray rind
    Feel: supple without any soft spots
    Smell: light lactic smell
    Taste: slightly sour, mild to nutty (3)
What to watch out for: lack of homogeneity, oversalting, graininess
Use: end of meals

Appropriate wines: light and fruity Beaujolais, supple and fruity Côtes-du-Rhône

Origin of name: most important market

Brief history: this cheese was formerly made from goat's milk

A good buy

Related cheeses: half goat's-milk Tommes from any part of Dauphiné or Languedoc

   Differences: origin, size, texture, flavor

TOMME DE SAINT-MARCELLIN

Province: DAUPHINE

(*See* SAINT-MARCELLIN)

TOMME DE SAVOIE

Province: SAVOIE

Source: Les Beauges (Haute-Savoie), Les Belleville (Savoie); additional sources: low-lying valleys of Tarantaise and Maurienne ranges (Savoie)

Made in or by: farms, fruiteries, factories

Best seasons: end of spring, summer, autumn; availability of milk, end of curing period

Milk: cow's milk

Fat content: 20% to 40%

Type: pressed, uncooked

Rind: natural

Curing: dry, 1 month in humid and cold cellars, 1 month in warm cellars

Form: more or less flat cylinder

Dimensions: 8 in. in diameter, 2½ to 5 in. high

Weight: 4 lb. to 6 lb. 11 oz.

Packaging: unwrapped

Selection:
> *Appearance:* regular, gray rind, dotted with bright red and yellow pigments; when cut, homogeneous appearance
> *Feel:* supple
> *Smell:* pronounced mold smell
> *Taste:* not very pronounced nutty flavor (3)

What to watch out for: cracked rind, grainy texture, mixed pink and brown color, bitter taste
Use: end of meals, snacks; additional uses: baked or toasted toppings
Appropriate wines: all light and fruity Savoy wines; also lively wines: Mondeuse, Les Abymes
Related cheeses: low-fat Tommes, full-fat Tommes, Vachard, Saint-Nectaire
> *Differences:* origin, size, texture, flavor

TOMME DE SOSPEL

Province: COMTE DE NICE
Milk: sheep's milk or goat's milk
Fat content: 45%
Type: pressed, uncooked
Rind: natural
Flavor: 2–4
Cheese similar to VALDEBLORE *(see* this listing)

TOMME DE VALBERG

Province: COMTE DE NICE
Milk: sheep's milk
Fat content: 45%
Type: pressed, uncooked
Rind: natural
Flavor: 2–3
(See VALBERG)

TOMME DE VALDEBLORE

Province: COMTE DE NICE
Milk: sheep's milk
Fat content: 45%
Type: pressed, uncooked
Rind: natural
Flavor: 2–3
(See VALDEBLORE)

TOMME VAUDOISE

Also known as: TOMME DE PAYERNE
Country: SWITZERLAND
Canton: VAUD
Source: vicinity of Payerne; additional sources: Canton of Vaud to the
    southeast
Made in or by: small dairies
Best seasons: all year; cheese is shipped out almost fresh
Milk: cow's milk
Fat content: 50%
Type: soft
Rind: almost nonexistent
Curing: very short, 1 week
Form: small flat disk
Dimensions: 4 in. in diameter, 1 in. thick
Weight: about 7 oz.
Packaging: paper
Selection:
  Appearance: practically rindless surface; white interior
  Feel: very tender
  Smell: light lactic smell
  Taste: creamy, slight anise flavoring (2)
What to watch out for: grainy texture, insufficient curing
Use: end of meals
Appropriate wines: all light and fruity white wines: Dorin from the Vaud
    region, Neufchâtel Perlant

Origin of name: shape of cheese and its place of origin
Related cheeses: Vacherin, Reblochon
  Differences: origin, shape, size, texture, flavor

TOMME VAUDOISE AU CUMIN

Country: SWITZERLAND
Canton: VAUD
Source: Payerne and vicinity; additional sources: Broye Valley
Made in or by: small traditional dairies
Best seasons: end of spring, summer, autumn; best milk
Milk: cow's milk
Fat content: 45%
Type: soft, flavored with cumin
Rind: very thin
Curing: in humid cellars, 2 weeks after draining (maximum)
Form: small rectangular loaf
Dimensions: 5 in. long, 2½ in. wide, 1 in. thick
Weight: 6 oz. or 7 oz.
Packaging: paper, with brand name
Selection:
  Appearance: white surface and interior
  Feel: very tender
  Smell: light lactic smell
  Taste: creamy, slight anise flavor (2)
What to watch out for: lack of homogeneity in texture
Use: end of meals
Appropriate wines: all light and fruity wines: Dorin from the Vaud region, Neufchâtel Perlant, Fendant from Valais
Origin of name: shape of cheese and place of origin
Related cheeses: apart from the flavoring, Vacherin and Reblochon
  Differences: origin, shape, size, texture, flavor

TOMME DU VERCORS

Province: DAUPHINE
Section: VERCORS, ROYANS

Source: areas of medium elevation in the mountain range; additional
    source: low-lying valley of the Isère, right bank
Made in or by: farms; production dying out
Best seasons: end of spring, summer, autumn; availability of goat's milk
Milk: goat's milk
Fat content: 45%
Type: soft
Rind: natural
Curing: dry, in dry and cool cellars
Form: small disk
Dimensions: 3½ in. in diameter, 1 in. thick
Weight: 3½ oz.
Packaging: unwrapped
Selection:
  Appearance: delicate bluish skin
  Feel: firm
  Smell: light goat smell
  Taste: not very spicy, nutty flavor (3)
What to watch out for: excessive desiccation, saponification
Use: end of meals, snacks; additional uses: in *pétafine*
Appropriate wines: somewhat light, fruity Côtes-du-Rhône
Origin of name: producing region
Related cheeses: all goat's-milk Tommes of Valentinois, Crest, Chabeuil,
    etc.
  Differences: origin, texture, flavor

TOUPIN

Province: SAVOIE (CHABLAIS)
Source: Abondance Valley
Made in or by: small mountain dairies; production dying out
Best seasons: autumn, winter; milk from mountain pastures, end of cur-
    ing period
Milk: cow's milk
Fat content: about 45%
Type: pressed, cooked
Rind: washed
Curing: in cold and humid cellars; 4 to 8 months
Form: tallish cylinder
Dimensions: 8 in. in diameter, 6 to 8 in. high

Weight: average 13 lb. 3 oz.

Packaging: unwrapped

Selection:

  Appearance: delicate, fairly smooth rind, light gray to light brown in
      color

  Feel: firm, homogeneous, supple

  Smell: no special smell

  Taste: fruity flavor with some bouquet, not very spicy (3)

What to watch out for: toughness, cracked rind

Use: end of meals; additional uses: cheese toppings

Appropriate wines: all light, fruity, and durable reds, whites and rosés:
      Crépy, Gamay de Chautagne

Origin of name: resemblance to a cooking pot, called a *toupin* in patois

A fairly good buy

Related cheeses: mountain Gruyères, Comté, Beaufort

  Differences: origin, shape, size, texture, flavor

TOURNON-SAINT-PIERRE

Province: TOURAINE

Source: Tournon and the immediate vicinity; additional source: La
      Brenne

Made in or by: farms

Best seasons: end of spring, summer, autumn; availability of goat's milk

Milk: goat's milk

Fat content: 45%

Type: soft

Rind: natural

Curing: dry, 3 weeks

Form: tallish truncated cone

Dimensions: 3 to 4 in. at the base, 3½ in. high

Weight: 7 oz. to 11 oz.

Packaging: unwrapped

Selection:

  Appearance: delicate bluish skin

  Feel: firm

  Smell: light goat smell

  Taste: mild and nutty (3)

What to watch out for: excessive dryness, grainy texture, excessive salti-
      ness

Use: end of meals
Appropriate wines: all fruity and lively reds, whites and rosés of Touraine: Amboise, Azay-le-Rideau, Cour-Cheverny
Origin of name: central town of the milk-producing region
A fairly good buy
Related cheeses: Sainte-Maure, Pouligny-Saint-Pierre
  Differences: origin, shape, size, texture, flavor

TRANG'NAT

Province: LORRAINE
Source: village of Failly
Made in or by: homes, for domestic use; not sold
Milk: cow's milk
Fat content: about 45%
Type: soft, salted, peppered, lightly crusted over
Curing: in cellars, 3 weeks
Use: snacks, end of meals; basic ingredient in the preparation of GUE-YIN
Flavor: 1–2

> *Recipe:* Fill a stone crock with the cheese (it will take several cheeses), cover it and set in a warm part of the house. Within a month the cheeses will "go bad" and become *gueyin,* a *fromage fort* or strong cheese.
> Auricoste de Lazarque: *La cuisine messine*

TROO

Province: ORLEANAIS (VENDOMOIS)
Flavor: 3
Variety of Loir Valley goat's-milk cheese
(See MONTOIRE)

TROUVILLE

Province: NORMANDY (PAYS D'AUGE)
Flavor: 4
Trade name of an old and very famous farm-produced PONT-L'EVEQUE

CENDRE DE TROYES

(See other CENDRES)

URT

Province: BEARN
Milk: cow's milk
Fat content: 40% to 50%
Flavor: 2
Manufacturing site of a brand of SAINT-PAULIN

VACHARD

Province: AUVERGNE
Source: Dore mountains
Made in or by: farms, exclusively
Best seasons: summer, autumn; superior quality of milk from pastured
      cows
Milk: cow's milk
Fat content: 45%
Type: pressed, uncooked
Rind: natural
Curing: dry, in humid cellars, 2 months
Form: flat disk
Dimensions: 8 in. in diameter, 1½ in. thick
Weight: 3 lb. 5 oz.
Packaging: unwrapped
Selection:
   Appearance: unblemished rind without mold
   Feel: supple to firm consistency
   Smell: strong smell of mold
   Taste: pronounced spicy tang (4)
What to watch out for: vermiculated rind, grainy and brittle texture
Use: end of meals
Appropriate wines: light and fruity Côtes-d'Auvergne, Côtes-Roannaises,
      Beaujolais

Origin of name: type of milk
Brief history: perhaps the ancestor of Saint-Nectaire
A good buy locally
Related cheeses: Saint-Nectaire, Murol
   Differences: origin, coarseness, flavor, appearance

VACHERIN D'ABONDANCE

Province: SAVOIE (CHABLAIS)
Source: Abondance Valley
Made in or by: farms
Best seasons: end of autumn, winter; rich milk from stall-fed cows
Milk: cow's milk
Fat content: 45%
Type: soft
Rind: washed
Curing: in cold cellars under humid conditions, 3 months
Form: thick pancake
Dimensions: 10 in. in diameter, 1½ in. thick
Weight: 3 lb. 5 oz.
Packaging: encircled by a band of spruce bark, set in a box; cheese
   adheres to bottom of box
Selection:
  Appearance: smooth pink to light brick-red rind
  Feel: supple, tender to runny
  Smell: light smell of fermentation and resin
  Taste: mild, slightly balsamy flavor (2)
What to watch out for: rough, wrinkled or moldy rind (cheese tough and
   bitter)
Use: end of meals
Appropriate wines: fruity white wines from Savoy: Crépy, Roussette,
   Montmélian; light and fruity red wines of Savoy: Gamay de Chau-
   tagne, Mondeuse
Origin of name: type of milk used
Related cheeses: other Vacherins of Beauges, French and Swiss Vacher-
   ins of the Joux valleys
  Differences: origin, size, texture, flavor

VACHERIN DES AILLONS

Also known as: VACHERIN DES BAUGES
Province: SAVOIE
Milk: cow's milk
Fat content: 45%
Type: soft
Rind: washed
Flavor: 2
Similar to VACHERIN DES BAUGES *(see* this listing)

VACHERIN DES BAUGES

Also known as: VACHERIN DES AILLONS
Province: SAVOIE (LES BAUGES)
Source: Aillons Valley; additional sources: Canton of Châtelard (Haute-Savoie)
Made in or by: farms
Best seasons: end of autumn, winter; very rich milk during winter stall feeding
Milk: cow's milk
Fat content: 45%
Type: soft
Rind: washed
Curing: in cool cellars, 3 months
Form: thick pancake
Dimensions: 10 in. in diameter, 1 in. or more thick
Weight: average 4 lb. 7 oz.
Packaging: ringed by a strip of bark, set in a box; cheese adheres to bottom of box
Selection:
  Appearance: smooth, light-pink rind
  Feel: very tender and supple
  Smell: light smell of mold and of resin
  Taste: mild, creamy, balsamy (2)
What to watch out for: rough, wrinkled rind; tough and bitter cheese; moldiness
Use: end of meals

Appropriate wines: all delicate, fruity white wines of Savoy: Crépy, Ripaille, Roussette, Montmélian; light and fruity reds of Chautagne; Mondeux from Arbin

Origin of name: type of milk used

Brief history: undoubtedly goes back to the distant past, to the time when the mountain dwellers had not come together to form fruiteries or cooperatives. At that time they did not make large cheeses and did not know how to prepare the cooked type. In the 12th century these cheeses were called Vachelins

Related cheeses: French and Swiss Vacherins of high Jura Mountains, Vacherin from Dranses Valley

    Differences: origin, size, texture, flavor

VACHERIN FRIBOURGEOIS

Country: SWITZERLAND

Canton: FRIBOURG

Source: Le Moléson; additional sources: La Gruyère

Made in or by: small dairies, fruiteries

Best seasons: spring, summer; produced in the low mountains, end of curing period

Milk: cow's milk

Fat content: 45%

Type: soft, lightly pressed, uncooked

Rind: washed, brushed

Curing: humid, in cool and humid cellars, 3 to 4 months, according to thickness

Form: small wheel

Dimensions: 16 in. in diameter, 3 in. thick

Weight: 19 lb. 13 oz. to 22 lb.

Packaging: unwrapped, encircled by a band of resinous bark

Selection:

    Appearance: smooth, very thin rind, yellowish gray to pinkish gray in color

    Feel: supple on the surface

    Smell: light smell of mold and of resin

    Taste: slightly sourish, balsamy taste (2)

What to watch out for: bitterness, grainy texture

Use: preparation of Fribourg fondue; additional uses: if perfect, end of
   meals

Appropriate wines: all light and fruity wines from Cantons of Vaud,
   Neufchâtel and Valais

Origin of name: type of milk used and place of origin

Brief history: The most likely hypothesis is that the cheese is a survival
   from the time when the milk was not yet heated to make Vachelins,
   the predecessors of then unknown Gruyère cheeses. It is reasonable
   to suppose that the small quantities of very rich milk that the cows
   produced when kept in stalls did not lend themselves readily to
   other methods of preparation for use in the home. Then as now
   cheese was the mainstay of the mountaineers' diet.

A fairly good buy locally

Related cheeses: Tomme d'Abondance
   Differences: origin, flavor, packaging

VACHERIN MONT-D'OR

Province: FRANCHE-COMTE

Source: Joux valleys; Les Hôpitaux-Neufs; additional sources: Champag-
   nole, Les Planches

Made in or by: farms, chalets

Best seasons: end of autumn, winter; made in the autumn in chalets, end
   of curing period

Milk: cow's milk

Fat content: 45%

Type: soft

Rind: washed

Curing: humid, in cool cellars, 2 to 4 months, depending upon size and
   thickness

Form: flat cylinder

Dimensions: widely variable: from 8 to 12 in. in diameter, 1 to 2 in. thick

Weight: 3 lb. 5 oz. to 8 lb. 1 oz.

Packaging: circled by a band of resinous sapwood, set in a box; cheese
   adheres to bottom

Selection:
   Appearance: light, smooth, pink rind
   Feel: firm but supple

Smell: light smell of fermentation and resin

Taste: mild, creamy, slightly balsamy taste (2)

What to watch out for: wrinkled, rough rind; moldiness; toughness; hardness; bitterness

Use: end of meals

Appropriate wines: all fine and light fruity wines of Savoy: Crépy, Roussette, Montmélian; light and fruity red wines of Chautagne, Jura, Beaujolais

Origin of name: type of milk used

Related cheeses: Vacherin de Beauges, Vacherin d'Abondance, Vacherins from the high Swiss Jura

VACHERIN MONT-D'OR

Also known as: MONT-D'OR DE JOUX

Country: SWITZERLAND

Canton: VAUD

Source: Les Charbonnières; additional sources: valleys of Joux

Made in or by: chalets in the low mountains or on plateaus

Best season: end of autumn, winter, spring; cheese made when herds are not being moved to pastures

Milk: cow's milk

Fat content: 45%

Type: soft

Rind: washed

Curing: humid, in humid cellars, 2 to 3 months, according to thickness

Form: flat cylinder

Dimensions: 5¾ to 11½ in. in diameter, 1¼ to 1½ in. thick

Weight: 1 lb. 2 oz. to 6 lb. 8 oz.

Packaging: box; encircled by a band of spruce wood

Selection:

Appearance: smooth, moist, pink rind

Feel: soft, almost liquid

Smell: light smell of mold and of resin

Taste: mild, slightly balsamy flavor (2)

What to watch out for: wrinkled rind, insufficient fluidity, insufficient curing, bitterness (when overcured)

Use: end of meals

Appropriate wines: all light and fruity white wines from the Cantons of Vaud and Neufchâtel

Origin of name: type of milk used and place of origin

Note: For maximum enjoyment runny Vacherin is not cut into slices; the entire rind is removed and the cheese is served with a spoon

Related cheeses: Vacherin de Bauges, Vacherin d'Abondance

Differences: origin, quality, savor

How to select one and how to store it.

In selecting a Vacherin there is no need to waste any time poking it. A quick glance at the color and the general appearance of the surface is sufficient for the connoisseur. The retailer is well informed and can give helpful advice to the buyer. One should remember that big cheeses are usually better made than small ones. On the other hand, one should take care not to pick a cheese larger than the household can eat, for once it is cut, the cheese cannot be kept very long without losing some of its precious qualities.

The following rules should be observed in storing a Vacherin: Never put it in the refrigerator; if possible set it in a cool, humid place. In any case place a flat stick or piece of glass against the cut surface to prevent the cheese from "running." Dampen the outside of the box, sprinkle it with salt and wrap it in a damp cloth. If it is to be kept several days, rinse the surface once or twice with salt water.

Now you know, dear reader, the secret of how to keep this noble delicacy at hand, in readiness for gastronomic pleasure at any hour of the day . . . perhaps when you come home late one evening from choir practice or some other friendly gathering!

C.A.G.

VALBERG

Province: COMTE DE NICE
Flavor: 2
Another version of VALDEBLORE or TOMME DE VALBERG

VALDEBLORE or TOMME DE VALDEBLORE

Province: COMTE DE NICE
Source: Upper Tinée Valley
Made in or by: mountaineer; gradually disappearing, very little on the market
Best seasons: end of autumn, winter, beginning of spring; availability of milk, end of curing period
Milk: sheep's milk
Fat content: 45%
Type: pressed, uncooked
Rind: natural
Curing: dry, with touches of humidity and brushing, from 3 to 6 months, according to the intended use
Form: wide flat cylinder
Dimensions: 12 to 14 in. in diameter, 2 to 3 in. thick
Weight: 19 lb. 13 oz. to 26 lb. 4 oz.
Packaging: unwrapped
Selection:
  Young cheeses:
    Appearance: pinkish-gray rind
    Feel: tender but not soft
    Smell: very little smell
    Taste: lactic flavor, mild and creamy (2–3)
  Old cheeses:
    Appearance: gray-brown rind
    Feel: hard but nonetheless with a bit of elasticity
    Smell: somewhat strong sheep smell
    Taste: pronounced sharpness (4–6)
What to watch out for: too thick or cracked rind, hard and brittle texture, sharpness (locally considered a good quality)
Use: end of meals; additional uses: grated as a condiment in local dishes
Appropriate wines: fruity, well-balanced red wines from Villars, Saint-Jammet, Belley
Origin of name: place of origin
Related cheeses: Tomme d'Annot, Tommes des Allues, Tomme de Courchevel
  Differences: origin, shape, size, texture, flavor

VALENÇAY FERMIER

Province: BERRY

Source: northern Indre Department; additional sources: Touraine, Charentes, Poitou *(see VALENÇAY LAITIER)*

Made in or by: farms

Best seasons: end of spring, summer, autumn; availability of goat's milk

Milk: goat's milk

Fat content: 45%

Type: Soft

Rind: natural, dusted with powdered charcoal

Curing: in ventilated drying rooms, 5 weeks

Form: low truncated pyramid

Dimensions: 3 by 3 in. at base, 3 in. high

Weight: 9 oz. to 11 oz.

Packaging: unwrapped

Selection:

  Appearance: deep blue skin; very regular shape

  Feel: firm without being tough

  Smell: light goat smell, light mold smell

  Taste: mild and slightly nutty (3)

What to watch out for: desiccation or excessive fermentation, softening just beneath the skin, excessive saltiness, granular texture

Use: end of meals; additional uses: macerated in crocks for use at the end of the year

Appropriate wines: all fruity, dry and lively white wines of Berry and Touraine

Origin of name: invented name referring to the largest town in the producing region

Related cheeses: Levroux, Pouligny, Selles-sur-Cher

  Differences: origin, shape, size, texture, flavor

VALENÇAY LAITIER

Also known as: PYRAMIDE

Source: Touraine, Anjou, Charentes, Poitou

Made in or by: commercial plants

Best seasons: all year, frozen goat's-milk curds and powdered milk used

Milk: goat's milk

Fat content: 45%
Type: soft
Rind: bloomy
Curing: dried in ventilated drying rooms, 3 to 4 weeks
Form: low truncated pyramid
Dimensions: 3 by 3 in. at base, 2½ in. high
Weight: approximately 9 oz. to 11 oz.
Packaging: wrapper
Selection:
  Appearance: white rind without gray pigmentation
  Feel: firm with some degree of suppleness
  Smell: strong smell of mold and goat smell
  Taste: slightly saponified (3)
What to watch out for: graininess, saponification, excessive saltiness
Use: end of meals
Appropriate wines: all dry white wines, all light and fruity red wines:
    Reuilly, Chinon, Bourgeuil
Origin of name: shape of cheese and commercial manufacture *(laitier*
    means dairy)
A fairly good buy
Related cheeses: other commercial goat's-milk cheeses
  Differences: origin, shape, size, texture, flavor

VENACO

Province: CORSICA
Source: vicinity of Venaco, Corte; additional sources: Niolo plateau
Made in or by: mountain cabins, exclusively
Best seasons: end of spring, summer, during summer pasturing; availabil-
    ity of sheep's or goat's milk (sheep's milk cheeses begin in the
    winter, in the sheepfold)
Milk: goat's or sheep's milk
Type: soft
Rind: natural, scraped
Curing: humid, in rock caves, 3 to 4 months
Form: square with rounded edges, with marks from the basket in which
    it was molded
Dimensions: 5 to 5½ in. square, 2 in. thick
Weight: 1 lb. 2 oz. to 1 lb. 9 oz.

Packaging: unwrapped
Selection:
  Appearance: surface of pared cheese is grayish white
  Feel: firm and oily
  Smell: strong smell of confined fermentatation
  Taste: powerful sheep flavor, sharp (4–5)
What to watch out for: excessive hardness, excessive sharpness, graininess, internal larvae
Use: dessert, local snack; additional uses: mashed and soaked in wine and marc, yielding an extremely strong and sharp cheese
Appropriate wines: all the harsh, solid wines of the Corsican cape and of Patrimonio; very tannic and alcoholic Madiran, Cahors, etc.
Origin of name: nearest large market town
Related cheeses: all cheeses from the Niolo plateau; very strong, very sharp Roquefort
  Differences: origin, texture, shape, size, flavor

VENDOME BLEU

Province: ORLEANAIS
Source: Villiers-sur-Loir; additional sources: Loir Valley
Made in or by: farms, exclusively; production dying out
Best seasons: summer, autumn; best milk, end of curing period
Milk: cow's milk
Fat content: 50%
Type: soft
Rind: natural
Curing: dry, in humid tufa caves, 1 month
Form: small thick disk
Dimensions: 4½ in. in diameter, 1½ in. thick
Weight: 7 oz. to 8 oz.
Packaging: unwrapped
Selection:
  Appearance: delicate pale-blue rind
  Feel: firm
  Smell: light smell of mold
  Taste: fruity flavor with some bouquet (3)
What to watch out for: graininess, excessive saltiness
Use: end of meals

Appropriate wines: all light red wines of the Loir Valley, of Touraine, Beaujolais, etc.
Origin of name: chief market
Related cheeses: Olivet, Pannes, Patay, Villebarou
  Differences: origin, shape, size, texture, flavor

VENDOME CENDRE

Province: ORLEANAIS
Source: Villiers-sur-Loir; additional sources: Loir Valley
Made in or by: farms, exclusively; production dying out; little sold
Best seasons: summer, autumn, winter; availability of milk, end of curing period and storage life
Milk: cow's milk
Fat content: 50%
Type: soft
Rind: natural, coated with ashes
Form: small irregular disk
Dimensions: 4½ in. in diameter, 1½ in. thick
Weight: about 8 oz.
Packaging: unwrapped
Selection:
  Appearance: somewhat thick shape
  Feel: firm but not tough
  Smell: faint smell of mold
  Taste: very fruity flavor, slightly saponified (3–4)
What to watch out for: excessive saltiness, excessive saponification
Use: farmer's snack
Appropriate wines: all fruity and full-bodied red wines of Loire Valley: Bourgeuil, Chinon, Champigny
Origin of name: principal marketplace
Related cheeses: Olivet Cendré, Champenois Cendré, Argonne Cendré
  Differences: origin, shape, size, texture, flavor

VERMENTON

Province: BURGUNDY (AUXERROIS)
Source: Val du Puits
Made in or by: farms; production almost ended
Best seasons: end of spring, summer, autumn; availability of goat's milk, ease of curing
Milk: goat's milk
Fat content: 45%
Type: soft
Rind: natural
Curing: dry, in dry cellars, 2 weeks
Form: small cone
Dimensions: 2 in. in diameter at base, 2 in. high
Weight: about 2 oz.
Packaging: unwrapped
Selection:
  Appearance: clean shape, delicate bluish skin
  Feel: firm
  Smell: light goat smell
  Taste: not very spicy, nutty flavor (3)
What to watch out for: desiccation, saponification
Use: end of meals, snacks
Appropriate wines: white wines of Saint-Bris, Irancy, Chablis; all light and fruity local reds and rosés
Origin of name: place of origin
Related cheeses: all goat's-milk cheeses of Mâconnais and Charolais
  Differences: origin, shape, size, texture, flavor

VERNEUIL

Province: TOURAINE
Flavor: 3
Source and trade name of commercially manufactured goat's-milk cheeses of various shapes and sizes, especially SAINTE-MAURE

VEZELAY

Province: BURGUNDY
Flavor: 3
Farm-produced goat's-milk cheese similar to cheese produced in Dornecy and Lormes (Nièvre)

VIEUX LILLE

Also known as: BOULE DE LILLE and MIMOLETTE *(see* these listings)
Province: FLANDERS
Flavor: 3

VILLEBAROU

Province: ORLEANAIS
Source: Villebarou and vicinity; additional sources: Maroilles and Saint-Denis-sur-Loire
Made in or by: farms; production dying out
Best seasons: summer, autumn; availability of milk, end of curing period
Milk: cow's milk
Fat content: 45%
Type: soft
Rind: natural
Curing: dry, 3 weeks
Form: very flat disk
Dimensions: 7 in. in diameter, 1 in. thick
Weight: 1 lb.
Packaging: unwrapped, on plane-tree leaves
Selection:
  Appearance: delicate bluish rind
  Feel: firm without soft spots
  Smell: light smell of mold
  Taste: pronounced flavor with some bouquet (3)
What to watch out for: graininess, runniness
Use: end of meals

Appropriate wines: pale reds (Vin Gris) from Orléanais; reds or rosés of Touraine-Amboise or Cour-Cheverny
Origin of name: place of origin
A fairly good buy locally
Related cheeses: Olivet, Vendôme Bleu
   Differences: origin, shape, size, texture

VILLE-SAINT-JACQUES

Also known as: BRIE DE MONTEREAU (legal name)
Province: ILE-DE-FRANCE
Milk: cow's milk
Fat content: 45%
Type: soft
Rind: natural
Flavor: 4
(See BRIE DE MONTEREAU)

VILLIERS-SUR-LOIR

Province: ORLEANAIS
Region: VENDOMOIS
Flavor: 3
Farm-produced goat's-milk cheese originally from the region of Montoire (Loir-et-Char)

VOID

Province: LORRAINE
Source: vicinity of Void (Meuse); additional sources: Commercy, Vaucouleurs
Made in or by: farms; production dying out
Best seasons: summer, autumn; availability of milk, end of curing period
Milk: cow's milk
Fat content: 40% to 45%
Type: soft

Rind: washed
Curing: humid, in humid cellars, with washings, 2 months
Form: rectangular loaf of square cross-section
Dimensions: 6 to 8 in. long, 2½ in. wide and high
Weight: 1 lb. 9 oz. to 1 lb. 14 oz.
Packaging: unwrapped
Selection:
  Appearance: smooth light-brown rind
  Feel: supple
  Smell: strong tangy smell
  Taste: very spicy with some bouquet (4)
What to watch out for: overskimmed milk, toughness, crumbling
Use: end of meals, snacks
Appropriate wines: all lively full-bodied wines of Burgundy or Bordeaux: Irancy, Fleurie, Saint-Emilion
Origin of name: central market in the producing region
A good buy
Related cheeses: Limburger, Hervé, Maroilles
  Differences: origin, shape, size, texture, flavor

VOVES CENDRE

Province: ILE-DE-FRANCE
Source: Voves and vicinity; additional sources: Beauce, Dreux region
Made in or by: farms; production dying out (old, overcured Dreux cheeses are often substituted for the real thing)
Best seasons: summer, autumn; availability of milk, end of curing period and storage life
Milk: cow's milk
Fat content: 40%
Type: soft
Rind: natural, coated with ashes
Curing: dry, 1 month in humid cellars, then 2 to 3 months in cases filled with wood ashes
Form: flat disk
Dimensions: 5 to 5½ in. in diameter, 1 in. thick
Weight: about 1 lb. 2 oz.

Selection:
  Appearance: unblemished rind
  Feel: still supple
  Smell: light smell of mold
  Taste: very fruity, spicy flavor (4)
What to watch out for: desiccation, blackish color, ammonia smell, saponified taste
Use: end of meals, harvesters' snacks
Appropriate wines: all full-bodied spiritous red wines (Chinon, Côteau de Touraine, Beaujolais)
Origin of name: largest market
A fairly good buy
Related cheeses: Olivet, Pannes, Patay, Vendôme, Dreux
  Differences: origin, shape, size, texture, flavor

Cheese produced partially or entirely on farms

Beaufort.

Brebis des Pyrénées.

Brie.

Camembert.

Cantal.

Chaource.

Chevrotin.

Colombière.

Comté.

Coulommiers.

Époisses.

Ervy.

Esbareich.

Fourme d'Ambert.

Fourme de Laguiole.

Fourme de Montbrison.

Fourme de Roquefort.

Gex.

Langres.

Laruns.

Livarot.

Maroilles.

Morbier.

Munster.

Niolo.

Pavé or Carré d'Auge.

Pont-l'Évêque.

Reblochon.

Septmoncel.

Tomme Boudane.

Tomme Grise.

Vacherin.

Vendôme.

Special Cheeses and Non-French Cheeses

SPECIAL CHEESES

Cheeses differ in the milk used, in methods of manufacture and in shape and size, depending on the customs and resources of the regions in which they originate.

Economics, custom, and the season determine whether they will be fat or lean, soft or hard, fresh or fermented. They are not always eaten the way they emerge from molds or from the drying room or the cellar. Cheeses produced when milk is plentiful and prices are low are set aside and treated to prolong their storage life.

In regions where dairying is not the main agricultural industry, milk is scarcer. There the farmers' wives usually keep a few cows or other livestock as a source of extra income. When they make cheeses to feed farm workers during the summer, they try to economize by using skimmed milk. Such are the cheeses that we find in the ash boxes of Orléanais, Beauce Brie, Champagne and the Ardennes. Dry and stable, although slightly saponified, they are the main dessert at harvest time. Examples are cendré d'O-livet, cendré de Vendôme, cendré de Voves, cendré des Riceys, cendré de Rocroi. . . .

In the regions where herds of goats predominate, the best summer cheeses are wrapped in grape leaves, plane-tree leaves or chestnut leaves, placed in stone crocks and doused with white wine or brandy. Treated in this way they become powerful, aromatic desserts for Christmas and New Year's. The same treatment is given to the many Chabis of Berry, Poitou and Touraine. The Cabécous of Quercy become Picadous, and the Picodons of Tricastin, Valentinois, Vivarais or Velay slowly turn savory and oily over the course of months of storage.

Goats are nearly always most at home in wine-growing regions where the soil is poor and cows cannot find sufficient pasture. At the end of the summer dry cheeses are specially prepared for the grape harvesters: Crottins de Chavignol du Sancerrois or Boutons-de-Culotte du Mâconnais. Dry, brown with age, they have nothing in common with commercial cheeses incorrectly called Crottins or Boutons.

These old cheeses usually end their careers by being grated into Fromages Forts; that is, by being blended with other white or hard cheeses and moistened with leek stock, white wine, brandy, oil or other liquids. In some regions the crocks are covered with a thick layer of freshly pressed marc to produce a confined alcoholic fermentation and a powerful aroma that is most pleasing to an enlightened palate. Popularly these cheeses are eaten to whet one's thirst for wine. As examples we may cite Fromage en Pot and Trang'nat from Lorraine, twin brothers of Belgian Pottekees; Fromage Fort from Burgundy, Lyonnais and Mount Ventoux; Foudjou from Vivarais, and Pétafine from Dauphine. All these are sharp and spicy.

Various other practices have given rise to special cheeses. In the regions where large cheeses such as Gruyère are made, the farmers utilize boiled-down whey or *metton,* a casein byproduct that constitutes the basic ingredient of the famous Cancoillotte of Franche-Comté. In Lorraine and in Luxembourg, *mattons* or *stinkende kees* plays the same role in the preparation of Fromage Cuit. Cancoillotte is melted down in salt water or in white wine seasoned with pepper or garlic. It is then served as is or laced with butter to add the oiliness it normally lacks. It is spread on buttered toast for breakfast and is served at various other meals and snacks throughout the day, at the farmhouse or in the fields.

In poorer regions, when they skimmed off the cream from the milk to churn butter, they used to cook down the buttermilk (the liquid that drains from the butter before it is washed) to obtain the makings of low-fat cheeses (10% to 15% fat content), which are economical foods rather than desserts. This is how the Gaprons d'Auvergne and the various Boulettes of the North of France originated. Intended for home use, these rustic cheeses satisfied the needs and tastes of local consumers and were not for general sale. Nowadays, promoted to the role of *specialité,* they have undergone a transformation as a result of the changed economic situation. Gone is the thrift of the past. The excessive amount of cream now used in making soft fermented cheeses does not improve their flavor and, in fact, often leads to imperfect ripening and undesirable odors. This is one of the reasons why older connoisseurs of cheese find the taste of many familiar cheeses changed.

Among the special cheeses there are also unground, macerated cheeses which are kept immersed in various liquids. Gris Puant de Lille, Fromage Fort de Bethune, and Fromage de Bergues stand for several weeks in brine and are then sometimes washed with beer to change their microorganisms and to develop a different taste and smell. The Normans used to soak their Livarots in cider to increase (as if there were any need to) the virile bouquet of this "colonel" of cheeses.

Many other specialities owe their original tastes and aromas to spices and seasonings that are incorporated into the cheese. Examples are Munster with cumin, Gérômé Anisé, Dauphin with tarragon and pepper, Boulette d'Avesnes with parsley and pepper, Gapron with garlic, Leyden cheese with cloves, Morbier with resinous soot, Sapsago with fenugreek.

Some other cheeses are wrapped in aromatic leaves and piled on top of one another so that secondary fermentation processes will accelerate development of the perfume and flavor. Examples are Pebre d'Ai (Poivre-d'Âne) or Banon à la Sarriette (Banon with summer savory), real Fromage au Foin (hay cheeses) of Orléannais fermented in hermetically sealed cases, and Arômes de Lyons. Tommes de Savoie are stacked in casks and covered with marc and then with earth to keep out insects and other vermin. Vacherin owes its balsamy flavor to a strip of spruce or other resinous sapwood that is wrapped around the cheese before it is boxed.

In warm regions cheeses, like salt pickles, are plunged in olive oil. This is an effective method of preservation and protects the cheese from insects. Such cheeses are to be found in Algarve (Portugal), Andalusia (Spain), Sicily, Sardinia, Greece and almost all the countries of the Near East.

In our day many of these customs are disappearing in France. Chemists and technicians working for the dairy industry strive to approximate the taste and appearance of the vanishing archetypes without respecting the original recipes. This is why we see Fondus au Marc (processed cheeses) that attempt to supplant Tommes fermented in marc and why we find certain Cendrés with bloomy rinds that could never have developed if the cheeses were coated with ashes when they began to dry. Fromage au Foin (hay cheese) and Fromage à la Fougère (fern cheese) are also imitations. Pleasant enough in themselves, they bear little resemblance to the original products.

New varieties of processed or emulsified cheeses flavored with Kirsch and decorated with walnuts tend to fall into the dessert category. They are of course just new versions of the classic processed cheeses that have been around for decades, the cheeses with ham, sausage, tomato, pickles, pimento, cumin, caraway and various other vegetable ingredients.

The big food stores offer their customers many cheeses that are more interesting in their novelty—a new cheese comes out almost every month—than in their intrinsic merit. Besides the traditional Carrés de l'Est such as Recollet, Lutin and Petit Pâtre with their 45% to 50% butterfat content, we find richer cheeses such as Geram or Geramont. More or less successful concoctions based on cream cheese or processed cheese and coated with pepper, savory or some other aromatic flavorings (Samos, Tartare, Crottes, and Délices are the brands most freqently encountered) form the basis of the assortment. These "specialties" have added little to our basic stock of cheeses.

Flavored cheeses

1. Flavoring added to outside of cheese

Triple-Cream cheeses (Boursin type)
     -au Cumin (cumin)
     -au Paprika
     -au Poivre (pepper)
     -à la Sarriette (summer savory)
     -au Romarin (rosemary)
     -à l'Ail (garlic)
     -aux Fines Herbes

Goat's-milk cheeses
     Banon au Pebre d'Ai, savory and rosemary   Provence

Sheep's-milk cheeses
     Tomme de Camargue, bayleaf and thyme   Provence

II. Flavored internally

Fresh cheeses

Aettekees, chives and onion	Belgium
Bibbelskäse, chives and onion	Alsace
Boulette de Cambrai, tarragon and parsley	Flanders
Gérômé Anisé, cumin	Lorraine
Munster, cumin	Alsace
Boulette d'Avesnes, pepper, parsley, tarragon	Flanders
Dauphin, tarragon, pepper	Flanders
Tomme au Cumin, cumin	Switzerland, Vaud
Leyden with cumin	Netherlands
Leyden with cloves	Netherlands
Present with cumin	Netherlands
Tomme au Fenouil, fennel	Savoy

Processed cheeses

Crème de Gruyère aux Herbes (fenugreek)	Switzerland
Crème de Gruyère au Cumin	Switzerland
Fondu au Jambon	Switzerland
Fondu au Kirsch	Germany
Fondu aux Noix	France
Fondu aux Raisins	France

Foreign cheeses available in France

APPENZELL	Switzerland	hard cheese
ASIAGO	Italy	uncooked pressed cheese
BEL PAESE	Italy	uncooked
BURRINO	Italy	
CACIOCAVALLO	Italy	
CHEDDAR	Great Britain	uncooked pressed cheese
CHESHIRE	Great Britain	uncooked pressed cheese
EDAM	Netherlands	uncooked pressed cheese
EMMENTAL	Switzerland	hard cheese
FIORE SARDO	Italy	lightly pressed soft cheese
FONTAL	Italy	uncooked pressed cheese
FONTINA	Italy	uncooked pressed cheese
GORGONZOLA	Italy	soft cheese with internal mold
GOUDA	Netherlands	uncooked pressed cheese
GRUYÈRE	Switzerland	hard cheese
HERVÉ	Belgium	soft washed-rind cheese
LEYDEN	Netherlands	uncooked pressed cheese
LIMBURGER	Belgium	soft, washed-rind cheese
MIMOLETTE	Netherlands	uncooked
MONTASIO	Italy	
MOZZARELLA (cooking)	Italy	fresh
PARMESAN	Italy	hard cheese
PECORINO ROMANO	Italy	cooked pressed cheese
PECORINO SARDO	Italy	

PECORINO SICILIANO	Italy	uncooked pressed cheese
PRESENT	Netherlands	uncooked pressed cheese
PROVOLONE	Italy	
QUARTIROLO	Italy	uncooked pressed cheese
REMOUDOU	Belgium	soft washed-rind cheese
SBRINZ (grating cheese)	Switzerland	hard
SCAMORZE	Italy	
SCHABZIEGER (SAPSAGO)	Switzerland	hard
STILTON	Great Britain	soft cheese with internal mold
STRACCHINO	Italy	uncooked pressed cheese
TALEGGIO	Italy	uncooked pressed cheese
TILSIT	Switzerland	uncooked pressed cheese
TOMME AU CUMIN	Switzerland	soft cheese
TOMME VAUDOISE	Switzerland	
VACHERIN FRIBOURGEOIS	Switzerland	soft washed-rind cheese
VACHERIN MONT-D'OR (also a French version)	Switzerland	soft washed-rind cheese

Cheese Tours of France

If you go to the Alps

**ask for one of these
local cheeses**

Banon
Chevrotin
Picodon de Dieulefit
Poivre-d'Âne
Tomme des Aillons
Tomme de Chèvre de Corps
Tomme de Montagne
Tomme du Vercors

**with one of these
local wines**

Chatillon-en-Diois
Crozes-Hermitage (white)
Marignan
Sainte-Marie-d'Alloix (white)
Saint-Ismier
Seyssel
Vin Rouge de Mondeuse d'Arbin

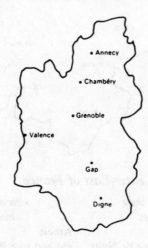

If you go to the Center of France

**ask for one of these
local cheeses**

Bessay
Bleu de Loudes
Briquettes du Forez
Chevrotin de Conne
Cabécou d'Entraygues
Cabécou du Fel
Creusois
Fourme de Salers

**with one of these
local wines**

Chanturgue
Costières-du-gard
Fel
Saint-Pourçain-sur-Sioule
Vin des Côtes Roannaises (Ambierle)
Vins de Pays

Pelardon des Cévennes
Picodon de Saint-Agrève
Rigotte
Souvigny
Tomme de Brach

If you go to the Center-East of France

ask for one of these *local cheeses*	*with one of these* *local wines*
Cancailotte	Arbois
Chèvre de la Montagne de Nuits	red and rosé Bourgogne d'Irancy
Chèvre de Beaune	Mâcon
Chevret	Pouilly-sur-Loire (white)
Chèvreton de Mâcon	Rosé d'Orches
Cîteaux	Vin Blanc de Tannay
Dornécy	Vins de pays (Doubs)
Emmental	
Lormes	
Pierre-Qui-Vire	
Vacherin Mont-d'Or	
Vermenton	

If you go to the Center-West of France

ask for one of these *local cheeses*	*with one of these* *local wines*
Brebis d'Oléron	Anjou
Chabichou	Anjou-Saumur
Chabis	Coteaux-de-la-Loire
Couhé-Vérac	Cru de Bouille-Loret
Mothe-Saint-Héray	Marigny-Brizay
Sainte-Maure	Vins de pays (Rosnay, Mareuil,
Troise-Cornes	Talmont)

If you go to the East of France

ask for one of these *local cheeses*	with one of these *local wines*
Cendré de l'Argonne	Bouzy Rouge
Chaource	Bruley
Gérômé	Côtes-de-Toul
Langres	Pagny (Vin Gris)
Riceys	Pinot Gris
	Vin Rouge de Saint-Hippolyte

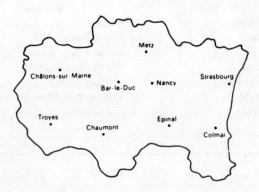

CHEESE TOURS OF FRANCE

If you go to South of France

ask for one of these *local cheeses*	*with one of these* *local wines*
Brousse de la Vesubie	Costières-du-Gard
Pélardon d'Anduze	Côtes-du-Ventoux
Petit Chèvre de montagne	Lirac (Rosé)
Picodon de Valréas	Picpoul
Tomme de Chèvre de montagne	Pinet (white)
Tommes Arlésiennes	Palette
Tommes de Sospel	Saint-Jeannet
	Villars-sur-var
	Vins de la Gaude

If you go to the North of France

ask for one of these *local cheeses*	*with one of these* *local wines*
Boulette d'Avesnes	Eau-de-Vie de Cidre (apple brandy)
Cendré de Rocroi	
Dauphin	Eau-de-Vie de Genièvre (gin)
Fromage Fort de Bethune	Vin Nature de la Champagne
Rollot	Wumbrechier (brandy)

If you go to Normandy

*ask for one of these
local cheeses*

Boursin
Camembert Fermier
Pavé de Moyaux
Pont-l'Évêque Fermier
Trappiste de Bricquebec
Triple Bondard

*with one of these
local wines*

Calvados du Pays d'Auge
Cider

If you go to the West of France

ask for one of these local cheeses	*with one of these local wines*
Caillebotte	Coteaux-d'Ancenis
Campénéac	Coteaux-de-la-Loire
Chabis	Gros Plant (white)
Fromage du Curé	Jasnières (white)
Meilleraye	
Trappiste d'Entrammes	

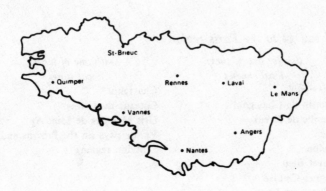

If you go to the Pyrenees

ask for one of these local cheeses	*with one of these local wines*
Arnéguy	Corbières
Brebis Frais	Côtes-du-Haut-Roussillon
Chèvre Frais	Irouléguy
Esbareich	Fitou
Orrys	Madiran

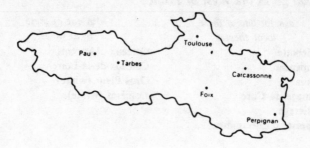

If you go to the Paris region

ask for one of these local cheeses	*with one of these local wines*
Chavignol	Chavignol
Crottin de Chavignol	Coteaux-du-Loire
Geuille de Dreux	Gris Meunier de Saint-Ay
Gien	Vin de pays (in the Provins and
Melun	Melun region)
Olivet Bleu	
Pannes Cendré	
Villiers-sur-Loire	

If you go to the Southwest

ask for one of these *local cheeses*	*with one of these* *local wines*
Amou	Blayais
Chèvre	Buzet
Cabécou de Gramat	Cahors
Edam (Bordeaux)	Cocumont (white)
Fromage Frais aux Fines Herbes	Fronsac
Rocamadour	Pacherenc du Vic-Bilh (white)
	Pécharmant
	Vins de Lavilledieu
	Vins du pays (Aire-sur-l'Adour)

How to Serve, How to Store, How to Enjoy

How should cheeses be served at table?

Even if you have only two cheeses (or perhaps just one) they should always be served on a tray with, if possible, a few slices of whole-grain bread and some butter. They should never be served on a plate. Cheese deserves special treatment.

What sort of tray should one have?

Opinions on this subject vary. Curnonsky, for example, advocated a glass tray, and in many restaurants cheese is served on a marble tray.

I personally recommend a wicker, or preferably, a wooden or ceramic tray with, if possible, leaves, napkins or paper doilies spread between the cheeses and the tray. I have a weakness for the blue pottery of Rouen: the discreet tint sets the cheese off nicely. I am not opposed to decorating the tray with fresh leaves, provided that this is not overdone.

As for the napkin between the surface of the tray and the cheeses, that is a matter of personal taste.

How should the tray be arranged?

Cheeses should be eaten in order of increasing flavor. I suggest arranging them in a circle, from the strongest to the most fermented. If you wish, you may stick in a little label of origin, or even a number to indicate relative strength of the flavor.

Very strong cheeses may be served separately (on a second tray) to avoid using the same knife. (Caution! Try to find out ahead of time if any of your guests are allergic to goat's-milk or sheep's-milk cheeses.)

So-called dietetic cheeses (which contain little or no fat) may be served on a small separate tray.

Butter, which some people like to add to Roquefort and other cheeses (it is not a crime), may be served at the same time. Preferably the butter should be unsalted because all cheeses are salted anyway. Note that in Roquefort people say: No butter with our cheese. Of course, the Roquefort there is seldom sharp.

If some cheeses have a tendency to run (soft cheeses in particular), slivers of wood or marble wedges may be used to contain them. Until the tray is served it should be covered with a damp cloth.

If you serve the cheeses a second time (at another meal) be sure that the tray looks neat, with each cheese evenly trimmed.

When do you eat the rind of the cheese?

Never. Turn a deaf ear to those who greedily tell you "That's the best part!" Or to those who assert with a scientific air that the rind is an antibiotic. There is no circumventing the rule: You must remove the rind, the site of the formation and development of molds and yeasts on most cheeses.

Avoid the use of breadcrumbs, once very much in fashion: people used to scrape off the surface of Camemberts and other thin-rinded cheeses and sprinkle breadcrumbs over them so that they would not have to be stripped in public.

How should cheese be cut?

With a knife dipped in hot water, and then wiped dry, the same way you slice fois gras. It is better to have two knives for each tray (one for mild-flavored cheeses, the other for strong-flavored cheeses). If you are serving Roquefort there should be a special, very thin knife, which is heated at the table. Do not forget that a fork is essential, too.

EXAMPLES OF FAT CONTENT OF CHEESES

Low-fat (0% to 20% fat): Cancoillotte
Part-fat (20% to 40% fat): Feuille de Dreux
Full-fat (40% to 45% fat): Dutch cheese
Extra-fat (45% to 60% fat): Camembert
Double-cream (over 60% fat): Monsieur-Fromage
Triple-cream (over 75% fat): Brillat-Savarin
Above 77% butterfat cheese cannot be made.

HOW TO SERVE

One ounce of Camembert, a little less than an ounce of Gruyère or ½ ounce of goat's-milk cheese replaces a glass of milk.

What sort of bread should be served with cheeses?
It depends on your preference. I like rustic breads, but I have nothing against other types. Crackers, for example, go very well with pressed cheeses such as Cantal, Chester or Gruyère.

Should condiments be passed around with the cheese tray?
Yes. Just as some people like to tone down flavors with butter, others like to heighten them. This explains the use of mustard with hard cheeses (Gruyère, Comté, Emmental), of cumin or caraway with Munster, brandies with Roquefort, etc. Some people use pickles, gherkins, Worcestershire sauce, even catsup.

I am not in favor of such additions. "You spoil your palate with pickles," Léon-Paul Fargue used to say. But let's try to be tolerant. After all, today's tastes are not the same as yesterday's.

On occasion you may add to your tray various condiments such as:
—chives, shallots and garlic (for fresh goat's-milk cheeses)
—young white onions (for Roquefort and Camembert)
—celery, ground walnuts (for Cheshire or Leicester). (In Rouergue, walnuts often accompany Roquefort.)
—parsley, chervil, tarragon, radishes (for white cheese)
Do me one favor, though: don't overdo condiments.

When should cheese be served?
This question may seem superfluous; yet it is worthy of our attention.

Some people recommend that salad and cheese should be served at the same time (this practice is current in Italy). This is a mistake. In England, cheese is served after dessert. Cheese should be served *between* the salad and the dessert. Cheeses neutralize the astringent vinegar or lemon juice in salad dressings and prepare the taste buds for the suaver sensations of dessert.

Does cheese always call for wine?

There is a very close connection between wine and cheese, but not all cheese-producing regions are necessarily wine-drinking ones. Cider may accompany Norman cheeses, and beer may accompany cheeses from the North of France or from Alsace. Livarot tastes very good with cider from the Auge region or even with a drop of old Calvados. Beer (as long as it has some body) is a good accompaniment to fresh and sharp goat's-milk cheeses flavored with wild or garden herbs. With partly aged Munster, however, I recommend (as do the Alsatians) Gewürztraminer. The dockers of Dunkirk drink black coffee with their Maroilles.

These exceptions aside, I maintain that cheese does call for wine.

As to which flavor goes with which, I am very tolerant. White wines are often quite good with unaged or slightly aged cheeses and with fresh goat's-milk cheeses. Thinking up new and original combinations can be fun. The great gastronomic chronicler R. Courtine did not hesitate to recommend Château-Yquem with Roquefort.

How should cheese be stored?

I have already stated that you must never buy too much cheese in advance. That does not mean, of course, that you have to throw out cheeses that you have started. You can store them in the refrigerator under certain conditions.

This is what you should know:

To stay perfect, a cheese must be kept in a cool, humid atmosphere between 50° and 42° Fahrenheit, according to the type of cheese (below that temperature cheese gets tough). Where can you find the right temperature and the right humidity? In the vegetable drawer of your refrigerator. Note that the storage temperature varies with the cheese:

• Fresh cheeses, double- and triple-cream cheeses, Gruyères, Emmental, Comté (and hard cheeses in general) are kept at 42°. Put them in plastic bags.

- Semi-soft cheeses (Saint-Nectaire, Port-Salut, Tommes, etc.) are kept at temperatures of 46° to 50°. Wrap them tightly to avoid contact with air.

- Goat's-milk cheeses require the same precautions and a temperature of 50°. If you wish, you may omit the wrapping and allow them to dry out.

- Cheeses with internal molds (Roquefort, Bleus, etc.) are kept at 46° to 50°. Wrap them in a damp cloth and put them in a plastic box.

- For soft bloomy-rind cheeses (Camembert, Brie, Neufchâtel, Carré, etc.) and washed-rind cheeses (Pont-l'Évêque, Munster, Livarot, Maroilles, etc.) the ideal temperature is 50°. For Camembert, Brie and other cheeses of the same family in boxes. I recommend a special treatment: Do not refrigerate; leave them in the original packaging and wrap them in a damp cloth (but for no more than three days).

- Never use a cheese bell, which is, at best, a sorry anachronism.

- Always be sure to take cheeses out of the refrigerator (or the cellar) one hour before they are to be eaten so that they will be at room temperature when they are served.

Last, remember that there are very dry cheeses which keep almost indefinitely. Parmesans and Sbrinzes hundreds of years old have retained all their flavor (even though they may be a bit hard) and all their nutritional value!

Does cheese make you fat?

Cheese is high in calories and in energy value; on the average, three ounces of cheese is equivalent to half a pound of meat. However, there is little risk of weight gain if you consume moderate amounts of cheese in the framework of a well-balanced diet.

It is very important to understand that the fat content of a cheese, as indicated on the label, does not refer to the cheese as a whole but rather to a dry extract of the cheese; in other words, in the case of a Camembert weighing eight ounces in its hydrated state, the "50% fat" refers only to the four ounces of dry extract, so that the 50% is really only 25% when the cheese is eaten in its normal, moist condition. Simple arithmetic then tells us that the ordinary eighth portion of camembert (one ounce) contains in fact no more than one-fourth ounce of fat—far too little to ruin a diet! In general, the fat content of hard cheeses is greater than that of soft cheeses. They are, of course, proportionately richer in minerals, calcium and phosphorus. They are rich in the B vitamins as well.

Isn't cheese hard to digest?

No. This allegation is directed most often at fermented cheeses, but it really is meaningless because all cheeses, with the exception of the fresh cheeses, are to a greater or lesser extent fermented.

Ferments, whether present in larger or smaller amounts, are basic to cheese and may be considered a form of predigestion.

Without getting bogged down in medical arguments, I would limit the so-called "heavy" cheeses to the soft, washed-rind cheeses whose greater density tends to slow down their assimilation by the body. Not all doctors, however, are of this opinion.

CALORIES AND CHEESE

- *Vitamins:* Soft cheeses and especially cheeses with internal mold are good sources of B vitamins.
- *Calories:* vary according to the butterfat content:
    Fresh cheese: 100 calories for 4 ounces
    Soft cheese: 283 calories for 4 ounces
    Hard cheese: 368 calories for 4 ounces

Children may be given cheese at a very early age: ages 2 to 5, ½ ounce; ages 6 to 9, 1 ounce; older children, the same quantities as for an adult. From a nutritional standpoint it is a very good idea to give cheese as a snack to children who will not drink milk.

Adolescents will benefit greatly from a liberal intake of cheese

(2 to 3 ounces) as a source of calcium (indispensable during this period of growth) and of phosphorus (good for the brain).

Last of all, cheese is highly recommended for pregnant women and for nursing mothers (1 to 2 ounces a day) as a source of calcium.

Is it possible to finish aging a cheese at home?

One can set up a cheese cellar in the home, just as one can set up a wine cellar or a humidor for cigars.

However, it takes patience and regular attention. You cannot stock up on cheeses as if they were wines and expect them to improve as the years go by.

● First, it is vital to keep a close watch on conditions in your cellar. The temperature should be between 45° to 50° and the humidity (a must) between 85% and 95%.

● The next step is to secure the advice of a cheesemonger about which products to keep in your cellar and how to set up an aging program.

Do not forget that:

Roquefort should be aged at a temperature of 45°.

Soft cheeses (Camembert, Brie, etc.) ripen fairly quickly above 60 degrees. They should be eaten within 48 hours.

Semi-soft cheeses (Saint-Paulin, Saint-Nectaire, etc.) and Bleu cheeses remain in good condition for about a week.

Hard cheeses keep longer.

Mountain cheeses—Parmesan and the like—keep indefinitely.

How should cheeses be placed in the aging cellar?

On open slatting. Bloomy-rind cheeses should be turned over every 24 hours to prevent excessive fermentation.

Washed-rind cheeses should be washed every 48 hours and wrapped in a cloth wrung out in salt water.

How about cheese in restaurants?

I prefer a restaurant that offers me two or three carefully selected cheeses in perfect condition to a restaurant that offers me scraps of 20 different cheeses that do not interest me.

If it is a good one, a single cheese can make me happy.

If I do not drink wine, may I drink water with cheese?

Never. Not even with mild cheeses. Water and cheese together can cause a stomach ache. Better take no cheese at all if you do not take a drink that is slightly alcoholic. Another possibility is to take the cheese and drink nothing.

Man has yet to find a better companion to cheese than wine.

Recommended combinations

FRESH CHEESES
(Suisse, Demi-sel, Double-Crème)

light white wines or dry and lively rosés

BLOOMY-RIND SOFT CHEESES
(Camembert, Coulommiers, Brie)

racy, fruity, full-bouqueted, elegant, fine red wine

WASHED-RIND SOFT CHEESES
(Livarot, Munster, Mariolles

solid and virile sappy wines with a generous bouquet

GOAT'S-MILK CHEESES
(Leuroux, Sainte-Maure, Chavignol

local wines of the same region, especially very dry and fruity white wines

BLEU CHEESES
(local Bleus and Roquefort)

spiritous, full-bodied, bracing red wines

SEMI-SOFT CHEESES
(Saint-Paulin, Tomme)

soft, light fruity white wines or rosés

HARD, DRY CHEESES
(Comté, French Emmental)

dry local white wines or full-bouqueted red wines

PROCESSED CHEESES
(cheese spreads)

Table wines

Which wine did you serve with your main dish?	Which are the cheeses that are especially good with this wine?

Reds

Light

Beaujolais Bourgogne Passe-Tout-Grain Bordeaux Côtes-de-Bourg	Chèvre du Mâconnais, Saint-Marcellin Saint-Nectaire, Reblochon, Tomme de Savoie, Chevrotin

Fruity

Beaujolais-Villages Côtes-du-Rhône Bordeaux-Listrac Bordeaux Côtes-de-Fronsac Chinon Bourgueil Champigny, Mondeuse Coteaux-de-Touraine	Neufchâtel: Bondon, Bondard, Coeur, Bleu de Bresse, Sain-Gorlon, Gorgonzola, Chester, Cheddar, Cantal, Laguiole, smoked Edam, smoked Gouda, Mimolette, Sainte-Maure, Valençay, Chabichou, Mothe-Saint-Héray, Chaource, Saint-Florentin, Olivet cendré, Vendôme Cendré

Solid

Brouilly Hautes Côtes-de-Beaune Côtes-du-Rhône-Villages Bordeaux Saint-Émilion Bordeaux Haut-Médoc Bordeaux Graves Côtes-de-Provence Corbieres du Rousillon Patrimonio, Fitou, Cahors	Camembert, Coulommiers, Brie de Meaux, Brie de Melun, Rollot, Époisses, Monsieur-Fromage, Brie de Montereau, Olivet Bleu, Vendôme Bleu, Langres, Munster, Fourme d'Ambert, Bleu de Gex, Maroilles, Gris de Lille, Roquefort, Boulette d'Avesnes, Niolo, Venaco; very strong cheeses

Rosés

Soft
Pinot d'Alsace
Pinot du Sancerrois
Gros Plant du Muscadet

Boursin, Délice de Saint-Cyr, Explorateur, Chavignol and other tender goat's-milk cheeses, Saint-Paulin, Fromage du Curé

Fruity
Arbois Rosé
Bordeaux Clairet

Morbier, young Comté, Edam, young Gouda

Full-bodied
Tavel
Côtes-de-Provence

Picodon de Valréas, various Trappist cheeses, Banon à la Sarriette, Triple-Crème aux Herbes

Whites

Light
Pinot d'Alsace
Pinot du Sancerrois
Gros Plant du Muscadet

Boursin, Délice de Saint-Cyr, Explorateur, Chavignol and other tender goat's-milk cheeses, Saint-Paulin, Fromage du Curé

Fruity
Anjou Cateaux-de-la-Loire
Bourgogne-Mâcon

Caillebotte, Jonchée, Chèvre Frais, Gruyère, Comté, Emmental

Note: The preceding wines were chosen because of their representative nature and in general because of their more or less reasonable prices.

INDIVIDUAL PREFERENCES
of some highly qualified experts

COURTINE (La Reynière)
1. Fourme d'Ambert with Chanturgue (a very rustic wine)
2. Brie with Bouzy
3. Reblochon with Vin de La Mondeuse (a red wine from Savoy)

TOURNEBROCHE (Roland Tremblay)
1. Camembert with a Savigny-lès-Beaune
2. Pont-l'Èvêque with a Côtes-de-Brouilly or a Morgon
3. Cabécou de Rocamadour with Condrieu or a fairly young Chablis

AMUNATEGUY
1. Fourme d'Ambert with a Gigondas or a Marcillac (a red wine from Rouergue)
2. Camembert with Beaujolais
3. Mountain Comté with a Volnay

PHILIPPE COUDERC
1. Roquefort with a great Burgundy or Bordeaux and even a Sauterne, but no butter
2. Brie de Meaux or Brie de Melun with a Moulin-à-Vent
3. All goat's-milk cheeses, from fresh to completely dry, from the mildest to the strongest, with a red Rully

Note that Fourme d'Ambert is one of the most popular cheeses with the experts. It is, in fact, an excellent cheese. Nevertheless, I personally prefer other cheeses.

Here are my choices:
1. Brie de Meaux with a Savigny-lès-Beaune
2. Époisses with a Corton
3. Roquefort with a Madiran or a Cahors

What cheeses may be used in cooking?

Fondue: Use fruity and oily Comté or Swiss Gruyère.

Raclette: Use fruity and dry Conches or Bagnes.

Welsh rarebit: Use Cheshire or Cheddar.

Onion soup: Use very fruity and oily Comté.

Gratin dishes: Parmesan (Stravecchio) or very fruity Comté.

Cheese doughs and pastry: Use Parmesan and Gruyère, half and half. Parmesan because it does not make strings. Add a little Comté to make it richer.

Béchamel sauce: Very fruity and somewhat dry Comté to keep the sauce from becoming too sticky.

AUSTRIA

The following words on the labels of Austrian cheeses indicate their fat content:

Doppelfett: double cream	65% butterfat
Dreiviertelfett: slightly skimmed	35% butterfat
Halbfett: half-cream	25% butterfat
Mager: skimmed	less than 15% butterfat
Ueberfett: extra cream	55% butterfat
Viertelfett: quarter-cream	15% butterfat
Vollfett: creamy	45% butterfat

PRINCIPAL CHEESES

There are many imported cheeses, but there are good Austrian cheeses too: Bergkäse (mountain cheese, available throughout Austria), Alpkäse (Alps).

These two cheeses are light in color, firm, and range from mild to strong in taste, depending upon how long they have been aged.

There is also Mischlinskäse, somewhat strong; Trappistenkäse, comparable to French monastery cheeses; Tilsiter (Tilsit—see the Dictionary) and Bier or Stangenkäse, of softer consistency.

In northern and in southern Austria one finds some soft cheeses: Limburger, Romadur, Schlosskäse—all very creamy.

The most popular cheese in Austria, however, is Edelpilzkäse, which is fairly strong with a slightly overripe taste.

Let us note, too, Mondseerkäse, comparable to Limburger, and Butter or Salami, a cheese in the shape of a sausage, soft in texture and mild in flavor, despite its occasionally penetrating smell.

BELGIUM

PRINCIPAL CHEESES

Limburger, Hervé, Remoudou are imported into France.
See the Dictionary.

OTHER CHEESES

Fromage de Bruxelles, Fromage Mou de Marquée, Boulette de Namur.

CANADA

See UNITED STATES.

In Canada one finds most of the cheeses of the United States and at least four indigenous ones: Canadian Colby, more tender than American Colby; Eremite, a cow's-milk Bleu; Oka (Quebec region), similar to French Port-Salut; washed-curd or Canadian Cheddar, milder than American cheddar.

GREAT BRITAIN

PRINCIPAL CHEESES

Caerphilly, Cheddar, Cheshire, Derby, Dunlop, Lancashire, Stilton, Wensleydale.

GOOD LOCAL CHEESES

Cottenham (Cambridgeshire), Blue Dorset (Dorset), Glouces- ter (Gloucestershire), Leicestershire, Suffolk cheeses, York (Yorkshire).

Name of cheese	Region of origin	Characteristics
Caerphilly	Wales. Originated in the small village of Caer- philly. Nowadays pro- ducing area extends from Somerset to Wiltshire	Supple consistency, mild flavor, no coloring
Cheddar	Somerset (mainly around town of Cheddar)	Semi-hard texture but "porous," sometimes colored with carrot juice, sometimes with an extract from mari- golds
Cheshire	Cheshire and Lancashire	Mild, whole-milk cheese,

		45% butterfat, firm consistency. Most are white. Some are colored red with carrot juice. The Bleus are comparable to French Bleus in the distribution of *penicillium glaucum* throughout the cheese
Derby	Derbyshire	Midway between a Cheddar and a Cheshire; sometimes has a tendency to turn sour
Dunlop	The best source is Scotland. Named after the little town of Dunlop in the north of Ayrshire	Smooth creamy white cheese, mild creamy flavor, sometimes slightly sourish
Lancashire	Lancashire (mainly along the shore of the Irish Sea)	Mild cheese, becomes slightly acid when it has been aged for three months. Excellent on toast
Stilton	Huntingdonshire	See Dictionary. The best of the English cheeses, to my taste
Wensleydale	Yorkshire	The only great English Bleu that can compare with Stilton. Smaller in size. Sometimes available unaged and then called Wensleydale White

GERMANY

There are many good cheeses in Germany but few great ones. Here is a list of the principal sorts:

Frischkäse	throughout the country
Fruhstuckskäse	different regions
Hartkäse	throughout the country
Limburgerkäse	see the Dictionary
Mainzerkäse	different regions
Nieheimer hoffenkäse	Westphalia
Quark	throughout the country
Romadurkäse	Bavaria

Sauermilchkäse	throughout the country
Schnittkäse	throughout the country
Spitzkäse	different regions
Tilsiterkäse	Tilsit, see the Dictionary
Weichkäse	throughout the country
Weisslackerkäse	Bavaria
Wilstermarskäse	Schleswig-Holstein

GREECE

PRINCIPAL CHEESES

Agrafa, Feta, Gruyère, Kasseri, Kofalotyri, Kopanisti, Mitzithra, Pindos, Skyros.

Name of cheese	Place of origin	Characteristics
Agrafa	Different regions	High-quality hard cheese comparable to Greek Gruyère
Feta	Different regions	Soft sheep's-milk cheese beloved by the Greeks. Pasteurized. To be eaten fresh (as soon as it leaves the mold)
Gruyère	Different regions	High-quality hard sheep's-milk cheese
Kasseri		Goat's-milk or sheep's-milk cheese, softer but of the same type as Kefalotyri
Kefalotyri	Different regions	Hard, very salty goat's-milk or sheep's-milk cheeses
Kopanisti	Different regions	Blue cheese with a rather strong, peppery flavor
Mitzithra	Vicinity of Athens	Somewhat coarse sheep's-milk cheese
Pindos	Different regions	Same cheese, but possibly of higher quality than Kefalotyri
Skyros	Island of Skyros	Hard cheese of fairly high quality

IRELAND

PRINCIPAL LOCAL CHEESES

Gruth, Millsen, Tanag, Tath

For the most part, however, the Irish like imported Cheddar.

ITALY

PRINCIPAL CHEESES

Asiago, Bel Paese, Caciocavallo, Cacio Fiore, Crescenza, Fiore Sardo, Fontina, Gorgonzola, Grana, Mascarpone, Montasio, Mozzarella, Pannerone, Parmesan, Pecorino Romano, Provolone, Quartirolo, Robiola, Scamorza, Scanno, Stracchino, Taleggio.

GOOD LOCAL CHEESES

Bagozzo (Brescia), Battelnatt (Piedmont), Bitto (Lombardy), Bra (Piedmont), Canestrato (Sicily), Casigiola (Sardinia), Groviera (Piedmont and Lombardy), Lodigiano (Lodi region), Mantede (Naples), Moliterno (Calabria and Lucania), Pagliarini (Piedmont), Pepoto or Pecorino Siciliano (Sicily), Pietracatella (Sannio), Provatura (Southern Italy), Provola (Southern Italy), Ragusano (Sicily), Veneto (Venetia).

Name of cheese	Region of origin	Characteristics
Asiago	Vicenza, Verona, Padua, Venice	See Dictionary
Bel Paese	Upper Lombardy	See Dictionary
Caciocavallo	Sorrento, Abruzzi, Northern Italy	See Dictionary
Cace Fiore or Caciotta	Different regions	See Dictionary
Crescenza	Lombardy, Piedmont and Venetia	Variety of Stracchino. Creamy and somewhat mild, interior is straw yellow
Fiore Sardo	Sardinia	See Dictionary
Fontina	Val d'Aoste	See Dictionary
Gorgonzola	Milan region	See Dictionary
Grana	Different regions	See Dictionary

Mascarpone	All Italy	Soft and delicate cow's-milk cheese of creamy consistency. Best seasons: autumn and winter. Often served as a dessert when mixed with sugar, cognac, coffee or Chartreuse
Montasio	Venetia	See Dictionary
Mozzarella	All Italy	Formerly made from water-buffalo's milk, nowadays from cow's milk. See Dictionary
Pannerone	Northern Italy	Variety of Stracchino. Flat rectangular cow's-milk cheese
Parmesan	Modena, Parma, Reggio nell'Emilia, Mantua, Bologna	See Dictionary
Pecorino		
Romano	Rome region, Sardinia	See Dictionary
Provolone	Naples region, Calabria, Palermo, etc.	See Dictionary
Quartirolo	Lombardy	See Dictionary
Robiola	Alps	Variety of Stracchino. Soft, rich, sometimes mild, sometimes sharp flavor. The sharp cheese is considered the better one by the Italians
Scamorza	Different regions	See Dictionary. Much like Mozzarella
Scanno	Scanno (Abruzzi)	Variety of Pecorino. One of the best
Stracchino	Different regions	See Dictionary
Taleggio	Lombardy (mainly around Bergamo)	See Dictionary

NETHERLANDS

PRINCIPAL CHEESES
Edam, Gouda, Leyden, Present, etc.
OTHER CHEESES
Commissiée, Frisian cheese with cumin, Kanter, Middelbare.

PORTUGAL

PRINCIPAL COW'S-MILK CHEESES
Bola, Ilha (Queijo da)
Bola resembles Edam; Ilha resembles Cheddar.
PRINCIPAL GOAT'S-MILK AND SHEEP'S-MILK CHEESES
Cabreiro, Ovelheira, Rabacal, Saloio, Serra (mountain cheeses which exist in numerous varieties).

RUMANIA

There are several good cheeses. The one most often imported into France is Brinza, an immaculately white, mild flavored, sheep's-milk cheese which is cut into cubes and preserved in salt water. It comes from the foot of the Carpathian Mountains.

Others are Kaskaval (sheep's milk), Katshkawalj (sheep's milk), Monostorer, Peneteleu.

In general, the Rumanians follow Italian methods in the production of their cheeses.

SCANDINAVIA

DENMARK

PRINCIPAL CHEESES
Danish Bleu, Danbo, Elbo, Fynbo, Molbo, Samsoë.

SWEDEN

PRINCIPAL CHEESES

Mysost, sweetened cheese (a curiosity); Herrgärdsost, the most popular Swedish cheese (hard cow's-milk cheese); Presost; Västerbottensost; Väasgotaost.

NORWAY

Gammelost and Pultost, the best Norwegian cheeses; Norwegian Mysost (there is also a Mysost made from goat's-milk whey); Nokkelost, a spiced cheese; Pultost (other names: Kndost, Ramost).

SPAIN

PRINCIPAL CHEESES

Manchego, Roncal, Villalon.

LOCAL CHEESES

Cabrales (Asturies, Santander), Cebrero, Piedrafita del Cebreno (various regions), San Simon (Lugo, Galicia), Ulloa (Galicia).

Name of cheese	Region of origin	Characteristics
Manchego	La Mancha	White or yellow, hard, cylindrical, sheep's-milk cheese with many small holes or none at all. Very buttery (57% butterfat). Very pleasant taste. The best cheeses are to be found around Ciudad Real
Roncal	Navarre, Aragon, Basque provinces, and northern Spain	Smoked, hard, cow's-milk cheese, yellow in color with small holes, occasionally fairly strong smelling
Villalon	Leon, Zamona, Valladolid, Palencia	Sheep's-milk cheese also called Patte-de-Mule, soft cheese eaten fresh

SWITZERLAND

PRINCIPAL CHEESES

Appenzell, Emmentaler, Gruyère, Vacherin Mont-d'Or.

OTHER CHEESES

Piora (Ticino), Saanen (see Dictionary), Sbrinz (see Dictionary), Sapsago (see Dictionary), Toggenburger (Alps, Saint Gall region), Vacherin de Fribourg (Fribourg canton, see Dictionary).

Name of cheese	Region of origin	Characteristics
Appenzell	Saint Gall Canton, Turgovie, Zurich	See Dictionary
Emmentaler or Swiss Emmental	Bern Canton	See Dictionary
Swiss Gruyère	Fribourg Canton, Vaud, Neufchâtel, Bern Jura	Slightly less fat than Emmentaler, smaller holes ranging in size from that of a pea to that of a hazelnut. The oldest hard Swiss cheese—mention of it goes back to the 12th century
Vacherin Mont-d'Or	Joux Valley (Vaud Canton)	See Dictionary

UNITED STATES

PRINCIPAL CHEESES

American bleu (blue, blue mold) made the same way as French Bleus; Brick (Wisconsin), a soft, mild cheese; Burmeister (Wisconsin); Camosun (semi-soft, like Gouda); Chantelle (semi-soft from Illinois); American Cheddar; Colby, similar to Cheddar; cold-pack cheese (often flavored); Coon (variety of Cheddar); Cornhusker (Cheddar from Nebraska); Creole (from Louisiana); Hand (rather strong cheese from Pennsylvania, New York, Wisconsin, Illionois); Herkimer (New York State Cheddar); Liederkranz (Ohio), comparable to Limburger; Monterey (or Monterey Jack; California), semi-soft pasteurized cheese; Mysost (Illinois, Michigan, New York); Old Heidelberg (Illinois), comparable to Liederkranz and Limburger; Pineapple (Connecticut), shaped like a pineapple; Poona (New York), soft cheese tasting like a mild Limburger; Sage (various states), a spiced Cheddar; Swiss (Wisconsin, Illinois, Idaho, Minnesota, Ohio, Utah, Wyoming), hard cheese, second only to Cheddar in popularity in the United States.

The principal French cheeses exported and sold abroad are: Camembert, Pont-l'Évêque, Reblochon, Saint-Paulin, Roquefort, Carré de l'Est, Brie in sections and boxed, Bondon, Neufchâtel, Murol (the last three mainly in Belgium) and a few goat's-milk cheeses.

I wish to thank my good friend André Simon, president or the Food and Wine Society and a great connoisseur, for the invaluable help that he has given me in the preparation of this chapter.

CHEESES OUTSIDE FRANCE

GLOSSARY

A

ACID: characteristic of milk which has turned sour as a result of the action of microorganisms and which is no longer suitable for additional processing.

ACIDITY: (a) a factor in the coagulation of milk, together with temperature and rennet enzymes

(b) the cause of the flavor of curds or of fresh cheeses at the onset of lactic fermentation.

ACIDULOUS: sourish, having a slightly acid flavor.

AEROBE: a microorganism which lives only in the presence of oxygen; for example, *penicillium album* or *penicillium candidum, penicillium glaucum.*

Penicillium album, the bloom of bloomy-rind cheeses, develops naturally. *Penicillium glaucum,* the veining in cheeses with internal molds, develops only when the interior of the Bleu cheese has been aerated by means of needles *(see* Needles).

AMMONIACAL: descriptive of a cheese that has passed optimum maturity and has begun to give off an ammonia smell.

ANAEROBE: a microorganism which does not require air or free oxygen for maintaining life.

ANNATTO: yellowish-red pulp surrounding the seeds of the annatto tree which is used to color certain cheeses. Livarot, Maroilles and Munster are colored right after *ressuage,* before undergoing the first cycle of washings. Formerly red Dutch cheeses and Chester were also colored with annatto.

APPELLATION D'ORIGINE: a specific definition of a particular cheese, recognized by law, regulating:

(1.) the breed of the cows, sheep or goats

(2.) the area where the milk is produced

(3.) manufacturing techniques

(4.) the composition of the product

(5.) its physical characteristics

(6.) its specific attributes.

The manufacturing techniques, the composition of the product and the physical characteristics are those which have come down from time immemorial or those which are sanctioned by custom.

The following cheeses have been granted the *appellation d'origine:* Beaufort, Bleu des Causses, Bleus du Haut Jura, Cantal-Salers, Chaource, Laguiole-Aubrac, Maroilles, Neufchâtel, Reblochon, Roquefort, Saint-Nectaire, Salers-Haute-Montagne.

Observance of these regulations is supervised by the Institut National des Appellations d'Origine. This same organization also supervises the *appellation d'origine* for wines.

AROMATIZED: a cheese whose flavor and smell have been altered by an admixture or coating of aromatic vegetable substances.

AROMES: name used in the Lyons region for goat's-milk, part goat's-milk and pure cow's-milk cheeses (Pélardon, Picodon, Saint-Marcellin, Rigotte) that have been steeped in marc.

ASTRINGENT: taster's term for an acid flavor. By extension applies to an acrid taste as well.

B

BECS: small oblique fissures that form beneath the rind of very oily Gruyères with very few holes.

BIROU: local name for the needles used to aerate Roquefort cheeses and foster the growth of mold within them.

BLEU: (a) generic name of cheeses with internal molds (for example, Bleu de Bresse)

(b) appearance of a cheese with a naturally bluish rind (for example, Olivet Bleu).

BLOOM: (a) to release a floral perfume. A cheese may give off the scent of the meadows

(b) the growth of *penicillium candidum* on the surface of bloomy-rind cheeses.

BLUE MOLD: name commonly given to *penicillium glaucum* when it appears as a parasite on the surface of bloomy-rind cheeses or uncooked pressed cheeses.

BONDARD: a family of cheeses from upper Normandy whose shapes suggest the bung (in French, *bonde)* of a barrel.

BONDON: a group of cheeses from upper Normandy shaped like the bung (in French, *bonde)* of a great tun.

BOUCANE: smoked. By extension, used to describe cheeses dried in the open air.

BOULETTE: group of cheeses molded by hand into a more or less spherical or conic shape.

BOUQUETE: agreeably aromatic.

BOUTON DE CULOTTE: (in English, *trouser-button)* fanciful name for small dried cheeses of the Mâcon region.

BREAKING UP CURD: the division of the curd into tiny grains either by hand or by machine. Breaking up the curd is a necessary step in the preparation of uncooked pressed cheeses which must be drained swiftly (for example, Saint-Paulin) and in the preparation of cooked or hard cheeses (for example, Comté).

For soft and washed-rind cheeses, the curd is broken into coarse particles.

BRIQUE, BRIQUETTE: a group of cheeses shaped like a brick.

BROUSSE: a group of Mediterranean cheeses made from milk which has been stirred (in Provençal, *brousser)* while it was being heated.

BRUSHED: descriptive of the rind of an uncooked or cooked pressed cheese which has been lightly brushed (in French, *brossé)* by hand or by machine during the course of its curing or ripening (for example, Gruyère).

BURON: rustic creameries where cheese is made in the mountains of Auvergne.

BUTTERMILK: liquid byproduct of churning cream to make butter.

C

CABANE: stone huts in which the shepherds of Causse mold and salt white Roquefort cheeses.

CABECOU: generic name (derived from *cabre,* the word for goat in the patois of Languedoc, with the diminutive ending *cou)* of a group of tiny goat's-milk cheeses.

CAMBALOU or **COMBALOU:** a section of the limestone plateau of Larzac including the town of Roquefort and its famous cheese cellars.

CANCOILLOTTE: generic name for processed cheeses from Franche-Comté based on *metton,* cooked-down whey.

CASEIN: an important constituent of milk, the part which solidifies during coagulation. In the course of ripening, the casein of soft cheeses becomes soluble, the casein of pressed cheeses becomes soft, and that of cooked dry cheeses becomes hard.

CASEIC FERMENT: popularly called "red mold." It affects the ripening of soft cheeses.

CASERETTE: a rush or straw basket *(cagerette* in the upper Norman dialect); also the fresh cheese which is drained in such a basket.

CELLAR: underground room or cave where cheeses are brought for curing or storage. Cellars used for curing and aging cheeses should have systems for the regulation of air temperature and humidity.

The caves of Roquefort contain basins of water. Currents of moist air encourage the growth of the *penicillium roqueforti* mold on slices of rye and wheat bread set out for this purpose.

After 3 or 4 months the tinfoil on the cheeses is removed. A taster samples one of the cheeses of the batch and decides upon the length of the final stage of curing, which may vary from 1 to 2 weeks.

The colors of Roquefort are smooth creamy white and teal blue. Not all Roqueforts have exactly the same taste even though they are all made according to the same recipe. The taste depends upon the temperature, the ventilation and the humidity of the various caves within which they ripen.

CAYOLAR: stone huts serving as shelters for the shepherds of Béarn.

CENDRE: generic name of cheeses ripened in ashes (in French, *cendrés),* generally produced in wine-growing regions.

CHABICHOU: diminutive of Chabi, the name of small goat's-milk cheeses in Poitou.

CHALET: a wooden building serving as both cheese factory and residence for the cheesemakers of the Alps and of the Jura Mountains.

CHARBONNE: descriptive of a farm-produced goat's-milk cheese which has been dusted with powdered charcoal (in French, *charbon)* to speed the drying of the surface and to encourage the spontaneous growth of blue molds.

CHARPENTE: wine-taster's term signifying that a wine is somewhat rich in alcohol and tannin.

CHAUMES or HAUTES CHAUMES: the high pasturelands of the Vosges Mountains where farmers' Munster is made.

CHEESE MITE: a minute whitish mite infesting the rind of certain hard or semi-soft cheeses.

CHEVRETON: generic name of the goat's-milk cheeses of Burgundy and the Massif Central.

CHEVROTIN: a group of hard goat's-milk Tommes from Savoy.

COAGULATION: the transformation of the casein of milk into a coherent mass of curds forming the basis of any given cheese. (Synonym: curdling.)

COMMERCIAL CHEESES: cheeses produced in a mass-production plant.

COOKED: (a) nature of hard cheeses whose curds have been heated (for example, Emmental)

(b) an accident in the fermentation of Gruyères resulting in an enormous hole.

CREAM: (a) the fatty constituent of milk

(b) name of certain processed cheeses (for example, Crème de Gruyère).

CREMET: generic name of white cheeses made with cream in the Provinces of Anjou, Maine and Brittany.

CROTTIN: somewhat dry, brownish goat's-milk cheeses from Berry.

CROUTE: French word for the rind of a cheese.

CRU: well-defined region giving rise to the characteristic qualities of a milk. Thus cheeses made from Normandy milk do not taste the same as cheeses made from Burgundy milk.

CRUMBLING: pounding by hand or by machine certain uncooked pressed cheeses (for example, Cantal or Cheshire) or certain soft cheeses with internal molds (for example, Fourme d'Ambert or Bleu d'Auvergne).

CURDLED MILK: milk that has been subjected to the coagulating action of rennet as the first step in the manufacture of cheese.

CURDLING: preliminary step in the manufacture of cheese, produced by the action of rennet. A synonym of coagulation.

CURING: the treatment of a cheese to cause it to ripen, generally in suitably arranged undergound cellars under regulated conditions of temperature and humidity.

Curing may be effected under dry or humid conditions and may require brushing, rinsing or soaking of the cheese. It may involve the use of salt water, whey, beer, cider, oil, white wine or brandy; of charcoal, powdered charcoal, marc, aromatic herbs or hay. The length of the curing period increases when temperatures are low and when the cheese is large.

Rule: When cheeses are of the same nature and structure, the length of the curing period is proportionate to the thickness of the cheese.

Why? The curing of the cheese is the result of the dissolution of the casein (the basic constituent of milk) by the action of ferments. Curing takes place in humid cellars (except for goat's-milk cheeses, which are simply set out on slatted shelves to drain and are exposed to circulating air of the storeroom). When all the casein has been dissolved, the cheese is said to be "done."

Naturally the conditions under which curing takes place vary according to the nature of the cheese that we wish to obtain. What is more, we may speed up or slow down the action of the ferments by changing the temperature of a cellar.

Nevertheless, for cheeses of the same type subjected to similar conditions of curing, it remains true in every case that the thicker

524

the cheese, the longer the curing, simply because it takes longer for the ferments to penetrate to the heart of a thick cheese.

Very wide but very thin cheeses like Brie de Meaux (1 inch thick) need only 1 month, whereas Pavé d'Auge (a much smaller cheese but 2½ inches thick) needs 4 months.

D

DESALPE: the return of the herds from summer pastures in the mountains.

DESICCATION: excessive dryness resulting from the drying effect of the atmosphere upon the surface and subsequently upon the interior of a cheese.

DOUBLE CREAM (DOUBLE-CREME): legal name for a cheese containing between 60% and 74% butterfat.

DRAINING: step following the molding of cheese. Soft cheeses are allowed to drain naturally; hard or cooked cheeses are squeezed or pressed to speed the removal of moisture.

DRAINED INSUFFICIENTLY: state of a soft cheese in which the spontaneous exudation of whey has not been complete.

DRY EXTRACT: the solid material of a cheese that remains after total desiccation. On the average, soft cheeses contain about 50% dry extract and 50% water.

DRYING: operation undertaken, if necessary, before the curing of soft cheeses. An indispensable step in the preparation of goat's-milk cheeses.

E

EMULSION: a suspension of fine particles or globules of one liquid within another. Milk is an emulsion.

ENRICHED MILK: milk to which cream has been added.

EYE: synonym for hole or opening in Gruyère.

F

FAISSELLE: cheese drainer.

FAMILY: group of cheeses having the same characteristics or based on the same manufacturing techniques. Cheeses may be divided into eight families:

(1) drained or undrained fresh cheeses (Suisses)
(2) bloomy-rind soft cheeses (Camembert)
(3) washed-rind soft cheeses (Livarot)
(4) natural-rind soft cheeses (Chèvre or goat's-milk cheese)

(5) internal-mold soft cheeses (Bleu de Bresse)

(6) uncooked pressed cheeses (Saint-Paulin)

(7) cooked pressed cheeses (Gruyère)

(8) processed or emulsified cheeses (cheese spreads).

FAT CONTENT: the fat content of a cheese is of a complex nature. Fat is one of the fundamental components of dairy products and the proportion of fat is always indicated on the label in terms of the dry extract.

FERMENTATION: development process which every cheese undergoes after its manufacture, coinciding, in the case of pressed soft cheeses, with the ripening of the cheese. There are three types of fermentation:

(1) in fresh cheeses, lactic fermentation

(2) in soft cheeses, caseic fermentation

(3) in hard cheeses, propionic fermentation.

FERMENTED: state of a cheese which has been subjected to the action of alkalizing ferments which have made the casein of soft cheeses wholly or partially soluble.

FERMENTS: various alkalizing microorganisms. The principal ones are:

(1) lactic ferments neutralizing the lactic acid of fresh cheeses

(2) caseic dissolving ferments of soft cheeses

(3) propionic ferments which break down fat in hard cheeses and release carbon dioxide, forming holes or eyes.

FERMIER: descriptive of a cheese produced on a farm by traditional methods.

FEUILLE: generic name of a group of cheeses that are wrapped in one or more plane-tree, grape or chestnut leaves.

FEUILLETE: (in English, *flaky)* descriptive of a cheese that tends to separate into several layers. It results from the use of excessively shrinking curd or from too long a wait between successive fillings of the molds.

FILM: thin rind arising spontaneously from the drying of the surface of a cheese.

FLEURINES: currents of air laden with humidity and spores of the various fungi that thrive in the caves of Roquefort.

"One sees chinks in the rock which admit cool air currents blowing from south to north; a very small number of caves receive air currents from the east; those from the south are the most desirable. It has been noted that the warmer the outside temperature, the cooler and stronger the drafts become. The temperature within the caves varies according to their exposure and the outside temperature. The south wind is especially conducive to cooler temperatures within the caves.''

This text by Chaptal, who was a professor in Montpellier, slightly contradicts what we have said about the constant temperature of the fleurines. The variable temperatures of Chaptal's day, however, have given way to an even temperature of about 45°, in part maintained by artificial means.

FONDU: a cheese which has been melted down and blended with other dairy products, usually liquid or powdered milk, cream, butter, casein, or whey. Flavoring may or may not be added.

The name Fromage Fondu is restricted to processed cheeses whose dry weight constitutes at least 50% of the total weight and whose butterfat content constitutes at least 40% of the dry weight.

The name Fromage à Tartiner or Fromage pour Tartine (English equivalent: *cheese spread)* is restricted to processed cheeses whose butterfat content is similar to the preceding, but whose dry weight constitutes between 44% or 50% of total weight.

The word *fromage* (cheese) in either of these names may be replaced by the name of the cheese used, on condition that the latter constitutes the sole basic material or at least 75% thereof, with the remaining 25% coming from a similar cheese (for example, Crème de Gruyère).

The name Crème de ... or Crème de ... pour Tartine is restricted to processed cheeses in which the cheese specified in the name is the sole basic material and contains, respectively, at least 50% or 44% of the dry weight in butterfat. Butter or cream may be added.

FORM: visible shape of a product. Cheese are grouped as

(1) large cheeses (for example, Gruyère)

(2) small cheeses, which are grouped further by their geometric shape (for example, Pont-l'Éveque is a square cheese).

Mountain regions generally produce large cheeses because handling large quantities of milk locally is practical. One member of a cooperative may process about 2,100 quarts of milk a day and be able to preserve the cheese for 4 months until the cattle are returned from the summer pastures.

FORMAGGIO: Italian word for cheese.

FOURME: generic name of a family of cheeses of Languedoc origin, produced mostly in Auvergne.

FRESH CHEESE: a cheese sold and consumed immediately after drainage with no further curing. Fresh cheeses are usually unsalted and are whipped smooth for use in Suisses and other nonfermented specialties. They do not undergo aging or any fermentation other than lactic fermentation.

FROMAGE: French word for a molded food: Fromage de Tête, and Fromage de Hure, etc. Formerly many desserts and ices were called *fromages*. Now the term designates a caseous product of the type whose manufacture is described under Manufacture.

FROMAGE FORT: generic name for cheeses that are kneaded or beaten to a paste, mixed with flavoring or aromatic substances and fermented in crocks.

G

GAPRON: a cheese made from buttermilk, which in the Auvergne dialect is called *gape* or *gap*.

GAZIMELLE: generic name of goat's-milk cheeses from the Cévennes.

GENE: dialect term for the dry marc left after the pressing of grapes for wine. It is used to flavor some goat's and cow's-milk cheeses in wine-producing regions. The characteristic aroma results from confined alcoholic fermentation.

GOULEYANT: wine-tasters' informal term for a light, fresh wine that flows freely.

GRANA: generic name of granular Italian grating cheeses made in Emilia. The principal one is Reggiano. The best known Grana outside Italy is Parmiggiano (Parmesan).

GRAS: (in English, *full-fat*) descriptive of cheeses prepared from unskimmed milk. Also describes young and tender Dutch cheeses.

GRATARON: a family of goat's-milk cheeses from the Beaufort region.

GRUYERE: name given in France to all large cheeses: Comté, Beaufort, Emmental. In Switzerland it designates a cheese from the Jura Mountains of the Fribourg Canton.

GUILD: association of merchants in the Middle Ages which regulated the quality of goods sold by members and codified relationships among members and between members and the authorities.

GUILDE DES MAITRES FROMAGERS (MASTER CHEESEMONGERS' GUILD): association founded by the author to promote better relations between quality producers and conscientious master cheesemongers.

Through the Confrérie des Compagnons de Saint-Uguzon (Fellowship of Saint Uguzon) it seeks to stimulate cheese lover's interest in cheeses that are dying out or disappearing from the market.

H

HALOIR: a cheese drying room or heated and ventilated area where soft cheeses are placed to drain and eventually to develop surface molds.

HARD: descriptive of a cooked cheese (for example, Emmental).

HIGH: taste of a cheese in which fermentation has led to development of a flavor comparable to that of ripe game (in French, *faisandé*).

HOLE: eye or opening; internal opening in hard cheeses such as Gruyère, Emmental, Comté, Beaufort. A well-formed hole that is spherical and equidistant from other holes is a sure sign of quality in cheeses of this type.

Oval, closely set holes are not a sign of a good quality. Many people erroneously believe that a multitude of large holes is desirable.

HUMID: descriptive of that part of a cheese which is not casein, not fat and not mineral salts, but rather a residual amount of whey in suspension. The percentage of fat indicated on the label is expressed in terms of the dry matter of the cheese and does not take into account any moisture present in the cheese.

HUMIDITY: moisture present in the air in a cellar or any other place; it is conducive to the growth of molds on the surface of cheeses. The atmospheric humidity of such areas should range between 85% and 95%, depending upon the type of cheese being cured.

HYDRATED: containing water. Antonym: anhydrous.

HYDROPHILOUS: water-loving. Molds which require a very humid environment for their development are hydrophilous.

HYGROMETRY: measurement of humidity in the air.

J

JASSERIE: shepherd's hut in the Livradois mountains (Auvergne) where Bleu Fourmes are produced.

JONCHEE: a rush basket in which certain fresh cheeses of Poitou are contained, and, by extension, the cheese itself.

K

KAAS: Dutch word for cheese.

KASE: German word for cheese.

KEES: Flemish word for cheese.

L

LABELING: by law all cheeses must carry a label indicating their origin, the name of the product and the name of the maker. The name of the product constitutes the brand name of a commercial product or the type of a traditionally made product.

LACAUNE: breed of sheep whose milk is used to make Roquefort.

LACTATION: period during which animals produce milk. Cows have no reproducing season and therefore no fixed lactation period. Because of the seasonal nature of their reproductive cycle, goats and sheep do have set lactation periods. For sheep this extends from autumn to spring; for goats, from spring to autumn. This is true of course only in temperate climates.

LACTIC: of or pertaining to milk as

(a) the lactic fermentation of fresh cheeses

(b) lactic acid develops in the curd.

Describes the smell of fresh cheeses or of certain soft cheeses that have been shipped out too young.

LAITIER: French word meaning:

(a) dairyman

(b) product made entirely from milk

(c) product made in a commercial establishment (for example, Brie Laitier and beurre laitier or creamery butter).

LAWS: all cheeses sold in France are manufactured in accordance with the terms of the laws of Aug. 1, 1905, and July 2, 1935. Numerous decisions have clarified their applicability to labeling of cheeses according to their origin.

At the international level certain cheeses are protected by provisions of the Stresa Convention *(see* this heading).

LENURES: small horizontal fissures that develop during the ripening of very fatty Gruyères with few or no holes, such as Beaufort or mountain Comté. Connoisseurs prefer Gruyères with *lénures.*

LISSEE (SMOOTHED): descriptive of a fresh cheese that has been processed in a *lissoir,* or mashing apparatus, as a step in its manufacture (e.g., Petit-Suisse).

M

MACERATED: descriptive of a cheese which has been immersed for a prolonged period of time in a potable liquid, whether flavored or unflavored. Maceration or soaking transforms the fermentation and changes the taste of the cheese, which usually becomes strong and sharp. Puant de Lille, for example, is macerated for 3 months in brine and then in beer.

MACHE: wine-tasters' term indicating that a wine leaves a tannic after-taste.

MANUFACTURE: the transformation of milk into cheese involves six basic operations:

1. curdling by the addition of rennet to obtain curds and whey; the latter is then drawn off

2. breaking up the curd two or three times to allow further draining before the curd is put into molds

3. molding, which gives shape to the future cheese

4. salting, either by rubbing in salt or by immersion in brine

5. draining and drying to remove the remainder of the whey in a cheese

6. curing and aging in cellars under various conditions of temperature and humidity as long as necessary for the cheese to complete its fermentation and develop its qualities. If anything has gone wrong in the previous steps, the cheese will never develop normally and will deteriorate.

These six operations are common to all cheeses that have been aged or have undergone internal fermentation. Fresh cheeses are merely drained and are most often unsalted.

Additional steps are necessary in the production of uncooked pressed cheese. The curd is broken up more finely and is pressed to speed removal of the whey.

In the case of cooked cheeses there is a further step: heating the curd, after it has been broken up, in the whey to harden the curd. With these cheeses, as with the previous ones, salting is by immersion in a bath of salt water.

There are as many different ways of making cheese as there are types of cheese. When the objective is to obtain a soft cheese which retains some moisture, care is taken to fill the molds in such a way as to prevent excessive "breaking" of the curd. This is the case with Brie, Camembert, and bloomy-rind Carré de l'Est.

If the objective is a somewhat less soft cheese, some breakage is permitted so that the curd will lose more whey and be less apt to favor the growth of *penicillium candidum*. Such cheeses are softened by washings and become "washed-rind cheeses"—Maroilles, Munster and Livarot.

When a firmer cheese is desired, the curd is broken up, with or without heating.

When a cheese has defects it is usually because the first operations and, in particular, the forming and draining of the curd have been improperly carried out. Aging will not correct these defects; on the contrary, it will bring them to light and aggravate them. On the other hand, if the cheese has no defects, aging will bring out all its good qualities.

In the curing cellars, the rind of the cheese, hitherto nonexistent, will begin to form and thicken, especially in the case of soft cheeses. For the hard and semi-soft cheeses, preliminary saltings will have already produced a rind.

The rind has a very important function beyond the function of protection that it fulfills for hard cheeses. It counteracts the moisture within the cheese by permitting the growth of hydrophilic molds that "pump out" the water and create a favorable environment for the spread of ferments to the inside of the cheese.

When the rind is not well formed, it cannot fulfill its proper function. If it is defective, the cheese itself will not be correctly shaped, the development of the ferments will suffer and the end product will not be satisfactory.

All this leads us to the classification of cheeses into families. Each family comprises all cheeses that are comparable in nature and rind. Since they all have similar characteristics, they are all subject to the same defects and injuries. The criteria for judging their appearance will be more or less the same for all cheeses within a given family.

Leaving out the fresh cheeses and the processed cheeses, we may assign all cheeses to one or another of the following categories:

1. *Bloomy-rind soft cheeses*

So called by reason of their texture and the appearance of their rind, which is covered with white down or fuzz of the *penicillium candidum* mold and is dotted with reddish pigments. Chief representatives: Brie, Camembert, Carré de l'Est.

2. *Washed-rind soft cheeses*

Their texture is comparable to the preceding but is slightly more dehydrated. They are incapable of sustaining the growth of molds on their surface and consequently lack a rind which would prevent them from drying out. As a consequence they are washed periodically to maintain the degree of internal moisture needed for proper fermentation. This treatment gives them a smooth varnished appearance and a color that ranges from straw yellow to deep brick red, depending upon the duration and the number of the washings. Chief representatives: Pont-l'Évêque, Munster, Maroilles, Livarot.

Pont-l'Évêque is sometimes cured dry, which changes its appearance, giving it a grayish color.

3. *Natural-rind soft goat's-milk cheeses*

These cheeses are more or less soft, depending on the treatment of the curd, which does not undergo curing in the strict sense, but rather a more or less thorough draining and drying. The cheeses simply dry out as they age.

There are two types:

1. Farmers' goat's-milk cheeses with blue rinds that form spontaneously in the cellars where they are left to dry

2. Commercial goat's-milk cheeses with thick white rinds due to the presence of *Penicillium candidum* which is introduced into the curd and permitted to develop while the cheese is drying.

Commercial producers use this method because hydrophilic molds pump moisture out of the cheese more rapidly and enhance its keeping qualities.

4. *Cheeses with internal molds, called Bleu cheeses or Persillés*

These cheeses, like soft cheeses, are neither pressed nor cooked. Most frequently they are made from crumbled curds which have been sprinkled with *pencillium glaucum*.

They are of two types:

1. The Bleus with a natural dry rind, treated merely with dry brushings, or slightly dampened brushings if they appear to be too dry: Bleu du Haut Jura, Bleu de Gex, Bleu de Septmoncel, Bleu de Sassenage, Fourme de Livradois d'Ambert, Fourme de Pierre-sur-Haute. They are sold with a brand label and no wrapper.

2. Bleus whose rind has been pared down by scraping and is ordinarily tacky: Bleu d'Auvergne, Bleu des Causses, Bleu du Quercy. They are sold in a foil wrapper.

Roquefort must be specially classified as a Persillé because it is the only cheese in the category to be made from pure sheep's milk and it would be incorrect to put it on the same level with cow's-milk cheeses, which are quite different. The surface of the rind is trimmed and thinned by scraping and the cheese is wrapped in foil. It, too, may be classified as a soft cheese that is neither pressed nor cooked.

The most desirable of all these cheeses are the ones in which the blue veins are densest and most evenly distributed.

Unlike other cheeses, these cheeses ripen from the inside out. Consequently the outside of the cheese is the least ripe part.

The growth of the bronze-green mold is dependent upon the perforation and aeration of the cheese by special large needles during the ripening period. The humidity of the curing cellars must be very high.

5. *Semi-soft cheeses, more properly called uncooked pressed cheeses*

This name and definition indicate that the cheeses are wrapped in canvas before being placed in the molds. The movable lids of the molds are subjected to pressure to speed the draining of the cheeses. The marks of the cloth are visibly imprinted on the rind of the cheese. Curing and aging take place in cool, very humid cellars. Chief representative: Saint-Nectaire, Saint-Paulin, Cantal-Salers, Tomme de Savoie.

6. *Hard or cooked cheeses*

These cheeses which, if not hard, are at least always firm, owe their qualification of "cooked" to the fact that the curd, after it has been broken up, is heated in the whey before it is wrapped in cloth and placed in the mold. The curd is pressed down as far as possible in the mold to remove the greatest amount of moisture.

The cheese is subjected to the action of special ferments and, during the course of ripening in a warm cellar, swells and develops openings or holes of various size in various patterns of distribution, depending upon the variety of the cheese.

These are large cheeses weighing from 44 to 110 pounds. The rind is natural and is brushed and washed while the cheese is aging. Color ranges from straw yellow to brown, and the rind is tough and unyielding to the touch. Before they are shipped out, the cheeses are oiled to prevent further drying. The chief representatives are Emmental, Parmesan, Comté and Beaufort.

It is said that there are more than 700 recipes for making cheese, secret methods that are handed down from father to son.

METTON, MATTONS: dialect words in Franche-Comté and in Lorraine designating a type of *recuite* or cooked-down whey used in the manufacture of Cancoillotte.

MICROFLORA: the molds that develop on or within cheeses.

MICROORGANISMS: the microbial agents active on milk curd and curing cheeses (e.g., yeasts and ferments).

MILK: liquid secreted by the mammary glands of female mammals for the nourishment of their young. Cow's milk is the most frequently used in human nutrition. Sheep's and goat's milk are used much more rarely. In tropical lands, ass's, camel's and water-buffalo's milk are also used. In the East, mare's milk is used; in Tibet, yak's milk, and in the Andes, llama's milk.

Cream is taken from milk to make butter and milk itself is curdled to make cheese.

Milk may be used "whole"—just as it comes from the animal, partially or totally skimmed, or enriched with cream in varying proportions.

Milk may be dried in the form of a powder which may be used in baking and for special diets. Dried milk is readily preserved even in tropical climates.

Milk is composed mainly of water, casein, fat, lactose, albumin and mineral salts. It is a practically complete food.

MILLE TROUS: (in English, "thousand holes") descriptive of the appearance of a defective Gruyère riddled with small, close-set holes.

MOLD: container made of wood, ceramic, metal or plastic of varying shape which molds or shapes cheese.

MOLDS: common term for the microflora that grow on the surface of bloomy-rind cheeses or within Bleu cheeses.

There are two types of molds:

(1) the external molds or white "bloom" which results from the seeding of the curd with selected strains of *penicillium candidum;* natural, unselected strains of bluish mold that grow on the surface of goat cheeses

(2) internal molds produced by cultures of *penicillium glaucum* in blue-veined cow's-milk cheeses or mixed cow's- and goat's- or cow's- and sheep's-milk cheeses; by cultures of *penicillium roqueforti* in the case of Roquefort.

MONASTERY CHEESE: cheese produced by a religious community. Cheeses with names incorporating the phrases ". . . de Abbaye de . . ." or ". . . de Trappe de . . ." are monastery cheeses.

MOUSSE: state of a cheese whose surface is just beginning to be invaded by a white mold, *penicillium candidum.* At this stage, cheeses are taken from the drying room and put in the aging cellars.

N

NATURAL: descriptive of the rind of a cheese which has not been seeded with selected strains of mold and has not been washed during aging. Farm goat's-milk cheeses are natural-rind cheeses. In certain cases, however, drying of the surface is effected by dusting with powdered charcoal.

NEEDLES: in the curing of internal-mold cheeses indispensable tools used to aerate the interior of the cheese and to introduce *penicillium glaucum* into ordinary Bleus (e.g., Bleu d'Auvergne) and *penicillium roqueforti* into Roquefort.

NERVEUX: wine-tasters' term indicating a slight acidity that brings out certain organoleptic qualities.

NUTTY: (in French, *noiseté)* taste of cheese, especially goat's-milk cheese, which suggests the flavor of fresh hazelnuts.

O

OILED: descriptive of the rind of a hard cheese which has been rubbed with oil to prevent desiccation during long periods of aging (for example, Parmesan, Sbrinz, Emmental).

OPEN: (in French, *ouvert)* descriptive of large cheeses, mainly Emmental, in which the holes are very numerous.

ORGANOLEPTIC: affecting or making an impression upon an organ, as an impression on the sense of taste and the sense of smell.

ORIGINE: descriptive of a product made in the same place where its raw materials are produced.

A "fromage d'origine" is made where the milk comes from. A "vin d'origine" is made where the grapes are grown.

Increased demand has led to the use of milk, grapes or wine gathered from within somewhat larger districts set by law or sanctioned by custom. These arrangements are supervised by the Institut national des Appellations d'origine and by certain other regional bodies.

OST: word for cheese in the Scandinavian languages.

OVERDRAINED: a cheese that has lost more than the normal amount of moisture and is therefore unfit for curing and ripening.

OVERFERMENTED: a cheese in which excessive fermentation has led to the production of an ammonia odor and a sharp, rancid or saponified flavor.

OVERRIPE: (in French, *suraffiné)* overfermented; a cheese that has passed the stage of optimum ripeness.

OVINE: pertaining to sheep; the smell and taste of sheep's-milk cheeses.

P

PARAFFINED: waxed; as the rind of certain cheeses prepared for export to distant lands. The rind of Edam cheeses is paraffined.

PASSE: overcured or overaged. In some regions the term is synonymous with "aged."

PASTEURIZATION: partial sterilization of a milk.

A cheese may be prepared from raw milk or from pasteurized milk.

Because they contain very few bacteria, goat's and sheep's milk are never pasteurized; at least for cheeses to be sold in France. When we speak of pasteurized-milk cheeses we are speaking mainly of cow's-milk cheeses, which are by far the most numerous of all cheeses.

Pasteurization is necessary because of increased production and consumption. If no label of origin is required, regions which have no particular cheeses of their own can furnish milk for the manufacture of cheeses in other regions. For example, some Tommes de Savoie are made from milk which comes from Vendée. Vendée milk is brought to the curing cellars of Savoy and that is that. The cheese would not necessarily be any the worse for this, except for the fact that the milk must be pasteurized to avoid souring or deterioration during shipment.

From an economic standpoint, pasteurization is in step with the times. It stabilizes cheese and assures it a longer life, which suits the housewife very nicely, not to mention the storekeeper. For this reason you may be sure that all fresh cheeses are made from pasteurized milk.

Tastes change. Today people prefer products that are guaranteed to be hygienic, even if the taste suffers; this despite the fact that products lacking such guarantees are not in the least bit harmful, and are far more authentic in taste.

By eliminating certain bacteria and microorganisms in the milk, pasteurization causes it to lose much of its character. This is not too important in the case of cheeses which are naturally mild. On the other hand, a Livarot or a Munster made from pasteurized milk, even when properly cured, is not really a Livarot or a Munster. Cheese should have the taste that we have come to expect of it. That is why I stock pasteurized cheeses only in certain seasons (mainly in winter) when the taste of pasteurized cheese and the taste of the natural cheese are fairly close.

PASTEURIZED MILK: milk partially sterilized for consumption or for use in the large-scale production of cheese.

PATE: French word for the interior of a cheese as opposed to the rind.

PAVE: generic name of a tall square cheese from Normandy.

PELARDON: a family of goat's-milk cheeses from the Cévennes.

PENICILLIUM: family of molds that grow on the surface of soft bloomy-rind cheeses *(penicillium candidum)* or within Bleu cheeses *(penicillium glaucum)*. Roquefort is seeded with spores of *penicillium roqueforti.*

PERSILLE: cheeses with internal molds. To distinguish pure sheep's-milk Roquefort, it is described as a Persillé rather than as a Bleu.

PETIT-LAIT: common French word for whey, or the serum which results from the coagulation or curdling of milk.

PICODON: generic name for strong-flavored goat's-milk cheeses from the Rhône region.

PIGMENTED: descriptive of the surface of a cheese which is suffused with various colored molds.

PIQUANT: *see* Sharp.

PLEUREUR: (in English, *weeping*) descriptive of a large cheese such as Beaufort, Comté, Emmental or Gruyère in which the holes are damp with whey mixed with salt, the consequence of aging for about a year under optimum conditions. The sign of a very fine product.

PRESS: mechanical or hand-operated device used to squeeze quick-drained broken-curd or cooked broken-curd cheeses.

PRESSED: descriptive of cheeses which have been subjected to the action of mechanical or hand presses to complete the process of draining.

POURRI: (in English, *rotten*) inaccurately used to describe a Metton cheese that is ready to be melted down for Cancoillotte.

PRODUCTION: France produces about 580,000 tons of cheese annually or more than 25 pounds per capita. Camemberts and other soft cheeses represent about 200,000 tons of this total; cooked pressed cheeses of the Gruyère type, 120,000 tons; uncooked pressed cheese such as Saint-Paulin or Cantal, 100,000 tons; various specialties, 95,000 tons; fresh cheeses, 40,000 tons, and process cheeses, 25,000 tons.

PROPIONIC FERMENTATION: of hard cheeses breaks down fat and releases carbon dioxide, producing holes in the cheeses.

PUANT: (in English: *stinking*) family of cheeses of northern France characterized mainly by a strong odor resulting from fermentation.

Q

QUEIJO: Portugese word for cheese.

QUESO: Spanish word for cheese.

R

RAMQUIN: dialect term for a small goat's-milk cheese from Bugey.

RANCID: stale; rank; descriptive of a full-fat cheese in which the butterfat has undergone oxidation.

RANCIDITY: staleness; rankness. Some full-fat cheeses have a tendency to acquire a rancid taste before acquiring a saponified taste.

RAW: natural, having undergone no transformation.

REBLOCHER: Savoyard dialect term for the action of draining the cows' udders after incomplete milking to obtain the "richest" milk.

RECUITE: French term for the caseinous material obtained by reheating *(recuire)* the whey that remains from the curd used for Gruyère. It is the basic ingredient of a lean Savoyard cheese called Brise-Gout. A similar cheese called Brisago is made in Italy; Ricotta is also a *recuite* or whey cheese. It is possible that French Rigotte was originally a whey cheese, too.

RENNET: diastase that coagulates milk; usually prepared from the fourth stomach of young ruminants.

RESSUAGE: step in the manufacture of cheese which takes place immediately after salting, in a ventilated drying room. (In English, *sweating.)*

RIGOTTE: a family of small cheeses of the Lyons region and of Forez.

RIND: external protective layer of a cheese. Rinds are of various types:

(a) soft cheeses: film formed by the accumulation of generations of molds and ferments. Area where the ferments develop and from which they begin to work their way inside.

(b) cooked and uncooked pressed cheeses: film formed by the hardening of the outer caseinous layer of the cheeses. It forms as soon as the cheese is salted and thickens as the cheese ages.

Rinds may be bloomy, washed, natural, brushed, oiled or paraffined *(see* these listings).

RIPE: state of a soft cheese in which the casein has been totally dissolved and softened to the very center (for example, Camembert). Equivalent to "aged" for semi-soft and hard cheeses (for example, Emmental).

A cheese that is insufficiently ripe will not give off its full aroma and bouquet; a cheese that is overripe loses most of its qualities. Some cheeses are purposely consumed when insufficiently ripe. At this stage they are said to be *moussé* (mossy) *(see* Moussé).

RIPENING ROOM: warm cellar where fresh white Gruyère cheeses are placed to develop holes under the action of propionibacteria.

ROGERET: family of goat's-milk cheeses from the Cévennes which have undergone a reddish fermentation.

RUNNINESS: excessive fluidity of a cheese caused by insufficient draining and excessive heat.

S

SALTING: (in French, *saltage)* step in the manufacture of cheese which comes after the unmolding of fresh cheeses. It may be done in either of two ways, depending to the nature of the cheese:(1) hand sprinkling for small soft cheeses(2) immersion in brine for uncooked pressed cheeses and for cooked cheeses.

In modern multimold processes, the latter method can be used for small broken-curd bloomy-rind cheeses as well.

Salting speeds the draining of soft cheeses. In the case of uncooked and cooked pressed cheeses it hardens the outer layer of caseous material, causing a rind to form. The more often a cheese is salted, the thicker and tougher its rind becomes.

SAPONIFIED: flavor of cheeses which appear to be rancid, mainly cheeses preserved in ashes, old goat's-milk cheeses, crocked Fromage Fort.

SCHMELZKASE: German word for processed cheese.

SEC: (in English, *dry)* (a) wine-tasters' term designating a wine in which the sugar has been completely fermented(b) state of a cheese in an advanced stage of desiccation (for example, Chèvre Sec).

SECOND GROWTH: (in French, *regain)* rowen or renewed growth of grass in the meadows and pastures after summer heat and drought. Flowering plants bloom again among the grasses, lending a special flavor and aroma to the milk of the grazing animals.

SEEDING: reincorporation of yeasts, molds and ferments into pasteurized milk so that a balanced cheese may result.

SERUM: whey.

SHARP: (in French, *piquant)* descriptive of a cheese with a taste that bites the tongue.

SKIMMED MILK: milk from which part of or all the cream has been removed.

SOFT: (a) (in French, *mou)* defect of an insufficiently drained or excessively runny cheese. It is a pejorative term that has nothing to do with soft cheeses as a type.

(b) (in French, *molle)* descriptive of an uncooked, unpressed fermented cheese.

SOUDURE: French term for the period when the feed of animals is changed and various irregularities occur in the taste of cheese due to the switch from fresh forage to oil cake, silage or dry hay.

SPORE: reproductive body of a mold or fungus.

STALLING: the keeping of herds in barns.

STANDARD MILK: in France, the legal standard for milk is 34 grams or a little over an ounce of butterfat for each kilogram (2.2 pounds) of milk.

STERILIZED MILK: milk that has been subjected to prolonged heat to eliminate all living microorganisms. Sterilized products keep almost indefinitely. Sterilized milk is unsuitable for cheese making.

STRESA CONVENTION: named for the village in Italy where it was signed, it protects the use of cheese names at the international level. Signatories of the convention are: Austria, Denmark, France, Italy, the Netherlands, Norway, Sweden and Switzerland. The French cheeses which are protected are Camembert, Brie, and Saint-Paulin. Roquefort is protected by special provisions.

T

TANNIC: taste of wine which has stood for a long time in a wooden vat, allowing the alcohol in the wine to dissolve the tannin of the wood. The taste is close to being astringent.

TASTEFROMAGE: Confrérie des Chevaliers du Tastefromage de France. A cheese society founded in 1954, it has helped to make French cheeses known throughout the world. The author, founder and grand master of the society, has participated in its activities since its inception and has coordinated these activities with those of the French Wine Society.

TOMME: a family of small cheeses: the small goat's-milk cheeses of Dauphine, and small Savoyard cheeses.

TOUPIN: a cheese in the shape of a pot *(toupin* in the patois of Savoy). In Provence, this term designates an earthenware cooking pot and in the Jura Mountains of the Fribourg Canton a big tin bell hung around the neck of the "queen" or oldest cow of a herd.

TRANSHUMANCE: French term for the summer cattle drive to the high mountain pastures. *Inalpe* is another term.

TRAPPIST: generic name given to cheese made in monasteries which live under the Trappist rule.

TRIPLE CREAM (TRIPLE-CREME): legal name for cheese containing more than 75% butterfat.

TROIS CORNES: a cheese of Poitou molded in the shape of a triangle.

V

VENTILATION: special arrangements for speeding the flow of air to dry cheeses.

VENTILATED: said of an enclosed space provided with openings or fans for the circulation of air.

VERMICULATE or VERMICULATED: descriptive of a cheese displaying grooves in the rind which resemble those made by worms.

VINEUX: French wine-tasters' term indicating a wine which is particularly spiritous and well balanced.

VACHERIN: family of mountain cow's-milk cheeses that are encircled by a band of spruce.

W

WASHED: (in French, *lavée*) describes the rind of a soft or uncooked pressed cheese which has been washed periodically during aging to keep it supple and moist. The rind of a cheese may be washed with salt water, whey, beer, cider, wine, brandy or oil.

WHOLE MILK: milk as it comes from the cow.

WHITE: descriptive of a fresh cheese.

Y

YIELD: (a) ratio of the amount of milk used to the weight of the finished cheese: for soft cheeses this is about 12.5%; for pressed cheeses, about 10%, and for hard cheeses, about 8% or 9%. For example, it takes 2 quarts of milk to make approximately 8 ounces of ripe Camembert; 16 quarts of milk to make a bit less than 5 pounds of ripe Brie, and about 1,250 quarts of milk to make an Emmental weighing 220 pounds.(b) milk yield of animals: One cow can produce from 8 to 20 quarts of milk per day (16 on farms in Brie). A goat gives 1 to 1½ quarts three times a day. A sheep gives about 4/5 quart a day (about 100 quarts during the milking season).

Country: FRANCE
Province: the three Pyrenean provinces
Source: various commercial dairies or co-operatives
Milk: cow's milk, pasteurized
Fat content: 45% to 50%
Type: pressed, uncooked
Rind: tinted brown, paraffined
Curing: in humid, cool cellars, 2 months
Dimensions: 8 to 12 in. in diameter, 2½ to 3 in. thick
Weight: about 4 lb. 7 oz. to 15 lb. 7 oz.
Packaging: paper or plastic film
Selection:
  Appearance: plastic, hard rind
  Feel: very tender and elastic
  Smell: light lactic smell
  Taste: mild flavour (2-3)
What to watch out for: texture too hard, lactic fermentation
Use: all table uses, in sandwiches, may be used in vegetable gratin
  dishes
Appropriate wines: all light wines
Origin of name: trade mark
Brief history: descended from cheeses formerly originating in the
  Pyrenean Ariège area, made in the mountains
Related cheeses: all Saint-Paulins and monastery cheeses
  Differences: flavour, quality of milk, smell, texture

SAMOS 99

Country: FRANCE
Province: no particular province
Made by: BEL dairies and their subsidiaries
Best seasons: no particular best seasons, manufacture very regular
Milk: cow's milk, pasteurized
Fat content: 60% (double cream)
Type: fresh, flavoured
Rind: none
Curing: none, keep cool
Form: rectangular, 2½ in. × 4 in. × 1 in.
Weight: about 4 oz.
Packaging: foil wrapping
Selection:
  Appearance: soft
  Consistency: creamy

Smell: very slight
    Taste: mild flavour, naturally partaking of the seasonings: herbs, paprika or pepper
What to watch out for: will not keep
Appropriate wines: table wines
Related cheeses: all fresh, creamy, flavoured cheeses
    Differences: no differences in production except in the quantity of herbs and spices

TARTARE

Country: FRANCE
Province: no particular province
Made by: Establissements BONGRAIN-GERARD and their subsidiaries
Best seasons: no particular best seasons
Milk: cow's milk, pasteurized
Fat content: over 60%
Type: fresh, flavoured with herbs and garlic
Rind: none
Curing: none, keep cool
Form: small cylinder
Dimensions: 2½ in. in diameter, 1 in. thick
Alternative form: small, conical, transparent plastic container, similar in dimensions and weight (4 oz.)
Alternative packaging: square box, or outer wrapping, containing six small cheeses each weighing about 1¾ oz.
Consistency: soft
Smell: slight, seasoned with the flavourings
Taste: mild, partaking of the flavourings
What to watch out for: keep cool
Use: at meals, or in sandwiches
Appropriate wines: good table wines
Origin of name: trade mark
Brief history: a recent creation
Related cheeses: all double and triple cream flavoured cheeses

GERAMONT

Country: FRANCE
Province: LORRAINE
Made by: commercial dairies
Best seasons: all year
Milk: cow's milk, pasteurized
Fat content: 56%

Type: soft
Rind: bloomy
Curing: dry, in cool cellars, about 1 month
Form: oval
Dimensions: 5 in. × 3 in. × 1 in.; alternative dimensions 4 in. × 2½ in. × 1 in.
Weight: the larger cheese 9 oz., the smaller cheese 5¼ oz.
Packaging: in cardboard box
Selection:
  Appearance: tender and supple
  Smell: slight smell of mould
  Taste: pronounced flavour (3)
What to watch out for: chalky texture, rind too red, ammoniac flavour
Use: end of meals
Origin of name: long-established trade mark
Related cheeses: all Eastern French square cheeses with bloomy rind

CHAUMES

Country: FRANCE
Province: the Atlantic Pyrénées
Made by: commercial plant
Best seasons: all year
Milk: cow's milk, pasteurized
Fat content: 50%
Type: pressed, uncooked
Rind: washed
Curing: in humid cellars, 1 month
Form: circular
Dimensions: 7 in. in diameter, 1½ in. thick
Weight: About 4 lb. 7 oz.
Selection:
  Consistency: tender
  Rind: thin and supple
  Smell: slightly lactic
  Taste: very mild
What to watch out for: few defects, but may dry out in heat or if kept too cold
Use: end of meals, Welsh rarebit
Related cheeses: Saint-Paulin, Saint-Albray
Origin of name: trade mark
Brief history: created by the cheesemakers whose name it bears

NEW CHEESES

Country: FRANCE
Province: the Atlantic Pyrénées
Made by: the Chaumes commercial cheesemaking plant
Best seasons: all year
Milk: cow's milk, pasteurized
Fat content: 50%
Type: pressed, uncooked
Rind: bloomy
Curing: in humid cellars, 1 month
Form: circular
Dimensions: 7 in. in diameter, 1½ in. thick
Weight: about 4 lb. 7 oz.
Selection:
  Consistency: tender
  Rind: thin and supple
  Smell: slight smell of mould
  Taste: very mild
What to watch out for: few defects, but any found may be due to the
  cheese being kept in poor conditions
Use: end of meals, Welsh rarebit
Related cheeses: Chaumes, Saint-Paulin, Saint-Albray
  Differences: origin and manufacturing techniques

SAINT-ALBRAY

Country: FRANCE
Province: the Atlantic Pyrénées
Made by: commercial plant
Best seasons: all year
Milk: cow's milk, pasteurized
Fat content: 50%
Type: pressed, uncooked
Rind: washed
Curing: in a humid cellar, 1 month
Form: circular, indented
Dimensions: 7 in. in diameter, 1½ in. thick
Weight: about 4 lb. 7 oz.
Selection:
  Consistency: tender
  Smell: slightly lactic
  Taste: very mild
What to watch out for: few defects any found may be due to poor
  conditions of transport or storage: hardening of rind, bitter flavour

Use: end of meals
Appropriate wines: all table wines
Related cheeses: Chaumes, Belle des Champs, Saint-Paulin

SAINT-ANDRE

Country: FRANCE
Province: ROUERGUE
Made by: commercial production by Etablissements Soulié
Best seasons: all year
Milk: cow's milk, pasteurized
Fat content: 75%
Type: soft
Rind: bloomy
Curing: in a dry cellar, 1 week
Form: circular
Dimensions: 5½ in. in diameter, 1¼ in. thick
Weight: 1 lb.
Selection:
  Rind: thin and bloomy
  Smell: slight smell of mould
  Taste: very mild
  Consistency: buttery
Packaging: wooden box
What to watch out for: rind too thick and downy, ammoniac smell, saponified flavour
Use: end of meals, in cocktail canapés
Appropriate wines: all light, fruity red wines, also dry whites and rosés
Brief history: the name is a trade mark
Related cheeses: Brillat-Savarin, Grand-Vatel
  Differences: origins, slight differences in flavour due to origin, fineness of texture

ILE DE FRANCE

Country: FRANCE
Province: LORRAINE
Made by: commercial production by Etablissements Henri Hutin
Best seasons: all year
Milk: cow's milk, pasteurized
Fat content: 60%
Type: soft
Rind: bloomy
Curing: in a dry cellar, 1 week

NEW CHEESES

Form: oval
Packaging: cardboard box
Selection:
   Appearance: light, slightly bloomy rind
   Consistency: tender without elasticity
   Smell: slight smell of mould
   Taste: slightly nutty
What to watch out for: ammoniac smell to the rind, saponified flavour
Use: end of meals
Appropriate wines: dry, fruity whites and rosés, fruity reds
Related cheeses: all double cream cheeses with bloomy rind

GOURMANDISE

Country: FRANCE
Province: ILE DE FRANCE
Made by: commercially made by Etablissements Siclet
Best seasons: all year
Milk: processed cheeses are all commercially made from pasteurized
   milk
Fat content: 50%
Type: processed
Rind: none
Appearance: decorated with walnuts, or may be flavored with kirsch,
   with walnuts, pepper or herbs, or smoked
Curing: none
Packaging: in plastic film and carton
Dimensions and weight: in various sizes from 3½ oz. to 4 lb. 7 oz.
Form: circular and cylindrical, or semi-circular
Selection: a standardized commercial product; hard to make a parti-
   cular choice
What to watch out for: defects are rare, and due only to poor conditions
   of transport or storage
Use: end of meals, snacks
Appropriate wines: all soft, fruity white, rosé and red table wines
Related cheeses: all processed cheeses and cheese spreads, flavoured to
   plain

PIPOCREM

Country: FRANCE
Province: BRESSE, PAYS DE L'AIN
Made by: Grièges co-operative dairy
Best seasons: all year

NEW CHEESES

Milk: cow's milk, pasteurized

Fat content: 50%

Type: internal mould

Rind: natural

Curing and storage: in humid cellars, 2 to 3 weeks, according to the size of the cheeses

Form: cylindrical

Weight: 5 oz. to 4 lb. 7 oz.

Packaging: small cheeses: aluminium foil with cardboard disc. Large cheeses: foil only.

Selection:

  Appearance: blue rind

  Feel: tender and firm

  Smell: slight smell of mould

  Taste: medium to pronounced flavour (3-4 according to the amount of curing)

What to watch out for: fermented, sticky rind, pinkish interior, saponified or ammoniac flavour

Use: end of meals

Origin of name: trade mark

Brief history: Sain-Gorlons made as smaller cheeses after the end of the last war

Related cheeses: Sain-Gorlon, Gorgonzola

  Differences: origins and length of curing (larger for the bigger cheeses which thus become stronger)

Other name: Bleu de Bresse

SUPREME DES DUCS

Province: BURGUNDY

Made by: commercially produced by Etablissements J.P. Renard

Origin: La Chapelle Vieille Forêt

Best seasons: all year

Milk: cow's milk, pasteurized

Type: soft

Rind: bloomy

Fat content: 60%

Curing: dry, in a cellar, for 2 weeks

Form: oval

Dimensions: 5 in. × 3 in. × 1 in.

Packaging: paper and cardboard box

Selection:

  Appearance: pale rind

  Consistency: tender, not runny

  Smell: slight smell of mould

  Taste: mild

NEW CHEESES

What to watch out for: defects are rare and can result only from poor
   conditions of storage
Use: end of meals
Appropriate wines: light, fruity red wines
Origin of name: trade mark
Brief history: created by the makers
Related cheeses: all soft, rich cheeses with a creamy texture

VACHEROL

Province: no particular province
Made by: commercial plants
Best seasons: all year
Milk: cow's milk, pasteurized
Type: pressed, uncooked
Rind: washed
Curing: in damp cellars, with washing
Form: flat cylinder
Dimensions: 7 in. in diameter, 1¼ in. thick
Weight: 4 lb. 7 oz.
Packaging: in transparent plastic film
Selection:
   Appearance: clean
   Consistency: tender
   Smell: slight
   Taste: very mild (2)
What to watch out for: defects are very rare, and due to bad handling
   during transport or bad storage conditions
Use: end of meals, Welsh rarebit
Appropriate wines: fruity, light red wines
Origin of name: trade mark
Brief history: a relatively recent invention

RAMBOL

Country: FRANCE
Province: ILE DE FRANCE
Type: processed cheese generally made of pasteurized milk
Made by: commercially made by Etablissements Rambol
(other details as for GOURMANDISE)

Country: FRANCE
Province: POITOU
Made by: small dairies and commercial plants
Milk: goat's milk
Best seasons: summer, autumn
Fat content: minimum 45%
Type: soft
Rind: natural
Curing: in a dry cellar
Form: cylindrical
Dimensions: 14 in. long, 3 to 4 in. in diameter
Weight: average weight 4 lb. 7 oz.
Packaging: paper and wooden box
Selection:
   Appearance: fine rind
   Feel: oily
   Smell: slightly lactic
   Taste: slightly nutty
What to watch out for: granular, crumbly texture
Appropriate wines: light, fruity reds. Touraine and Poitou white wines
   highly recommended
Use: end of meals
Related cheeses: all pure goat's milk cheeses made by small dairies

PAVE DU BLESOIS or DE SOLOGNE

Country: FRANCE
Province: ORLEANAIS
Best seasons: summer, autumn
Milk: pure goat's milk
Fat content: minimum 45%
Type: soft
Rind: natural
Curing: in a dry cellar
Form: square
Dimensions: 3½ to 4 in. at the sides, 1 in. thick
Weight: 9 to 10½ oz.
Packaging: on straw in wooden boxes
Selection:
   Appearance: well shaped, regular rind
   Feel: very buttery
   Smell: slight smell of goat
   Taste: slightly nutty (2-3)

What to watch out for: too much salt, granular texture, acidity
Use: end of meals, on toast
Origin of name: from the cheese's shape and place of origin
Brief history: a very old farm-made cheese for home consumption, which had not been made for a long time
Related cheeses: similar to all other farm-made pure goat's milk cheeses

LES VIGNOTTES

Province: CHAMPAGNE, LORRAINE
Area: Perthois, Barrois
Made by: commercial dairy
Milk: cow's milk, pasteurized
Type: soft
Rind: bloomy
Fat content: 72%
Curing: dry, in a cool cellar, 1 or 2 months according to the degree of maturity desired
Best seasons: no best season, as the milk is pasteurized
Source: found only in the locality of Pansey
Form: thick disk
Dimensions: 8 in. in diameter, 3 in. thick
Weight: 4 lb. 7 oz.
Related chesses: all triple cream cheeses with this high level of fat content
Selection:
  Appearance: slightly downy white surface
  Feel: firm but not hard
  Smell: slightly lactic, slight smell of mould
What to watch out for: over-maturity, saponification
Use: end of meals or snacks on bread or toast
Appropriate wines: all good light, fruity table wines
Origin of name: trade mark chosen by the producer